SACRED VIOLENCE
IN EARLY AMERICA

EARLY AMERICAN STUDIES

Series editors:
Daniel K. Richter, Kathleen M. Brown,
Max Cavitch, and David Waldstreicher

Exploring neglected aspects of our colonial,
revolutionary, and early national history and culture,
Early American Studies reinterprets familiar themes
and events in fresh ways. Interdisciplinary in character,
and with a special emphasis on the period from about
1600 to 1850, the series is published in partnership with
the McNeil Center for Early American Studies.

A complete list of books in the series is available from the publisher.

SACRED VIOLENCE
IN EARLY AMERICA

SUSAN JUSTER

PENN

UNIVERSITY OF PENNSYLVANIA PRESS

PHILADELPHIA

Published by
University of Pennsylvania Press
Philadelphia, Pennsylvania 19104-4112
www.upenn.edu/pennpress

Printed in the United States of America
on acid-free paper

1 3 5 7 9 10 8 6 4 2

A catalogue record for this book is available from the
Library of Congress.
ISBN 978-0-8122-4813-5

To Rhys Isaac (1937–2010)

CONTENTS

Writing a book on religious violence can be a dark enterprise. The subject is dispiriting, the reading grim, and the moral stakes high—especially in this era of heightened awareness of the violent propensities of *all* the world's great religions. But it has also been a profoundly inspiring experience. This is not a topic about which people are agnostic or indifferent, and the conversations I've had over the past decade with scholars, friends, and family have been richly rewarding. I've come to understand early modern Anglo-Americans— my subjects—and the craft of history-writing from new perspectives, and to expand my mental and moral horizons in order to comprehend the terrible power of faith to destroy what humans most cherish. I am not writing a brief for or against the argument that organized religion is inherently violent, nor am I trying to understand modern episodes of religious violence through the lens of the past. The past is the past, and the present is not the past updated. A prolonged exposure to the corrosive rhetoric of sacred violence in a time and place quite distant from our own only reinforces my conviction that history never simply repeats itself, even if we can discern disquieting echoes of the past in the present.

It's hard to overstate just how omnipresent religious ideas and language were in seventeenth-century English America. The first European settlers in North America were children of the Reformation, that seismic breaking apart of Western Christendom that created new texts, doctrines, and practices, and destroyed old ones. But it can be just as hard to remember that these men and women, living on the very edges of the known world and struggling to survive, were not always preoccupied with religious matters, as historians of the early modern world have sometimes assumed. We know that their exposure to scripture and their grasp of theology were impressively deep, and we know that the vast majority of the books they read and the letters and journals they wrote concerned religious topics. But we also know that they worried about whether their children would live and their crops flourish, about whether they would survive the next Indian attack or smallpox epidemic or political eruption in London. I have tried to respect the immense power of the sacred in this period of schism, religious war, and institutional reconfiguration, and to recognize at the same time that there was more to life in the first English colonies than arguing about the "real presence" of Christ in the Eucharist or punishing heretics. For better or for worse, the textual evidence colonial historians have to work with overwhelmingly privileges the religious over (forgive the anachronism) the secular—there are far more extant sermons than account books in seventeenth-century Anglo-America. This, of course, tells us something important about the priorities of colonial readers and printers. But the world of print was not coextensive with the world of lived experience, however central literacy was to the Protestant disciplinary regime that remade individual believers and entire communities in the aftermath of the Reformation.

There will be much talk of blood shed and suffering endured in the pages to follow. This was the language of colonial encounter—a language that was often just as brutal and disorienting as the experience of settlement itself (or *un*settlement, as recent scholarship has emphasized.) Amid all the talk of just how new and raw the "New" World was to English men and women in the early seventeenth century, we can easily miss or misconstrue the patterns of belief and habits of thought that linked the first settlers umbilically to the world they had left behind. Despite the earnest pleas of some of my readers to abandon the term "New World" altogether as a holdover from an older imperial school of history-writing that often treated the Americas as a tabula rasa on which Europeans imprinted their own political and cultural forms, I have chosen to retain the phrase with the hope that readers will mentally add the scare quotes that signal the irony behind the term "new." My intention is to call into question the entire assumption of "newness" surrounding our narratives of first encounter which, as I hope will become clear, bore a disturbing resemblance to some of the worst episodes in post-Reformation Europe.

Returning to the first years of English settlement in North America has been a kind of professional refresher course for me, a chance to revisit old texts and familiar historiographies and to explore new historical terrains, in particular the fertile historical literature on late medieval and early modern European religion. I was extraordinarily fortunate to begin and end this book in two of the most privileged settings in the American academy: the Institute for the Humanities at the University of Michigan, where I held the Helmut F. Stern faculty fellowship in 2004–5, and the Huntington Library in San

Marino, California, where I was the Robert C. Ritchie Distinguished Fellow in 2014–15. I began thinking and reading about sacred violence at the Institute for the Humanities in the company of a group of remarkable scholars whose friendship and intellectual curiosity I continue to cherish. To my Institute friends—Mika Lavaque-Manty, George Hoffman, Linda Gregerson, Bruce Frier, Will Glover, Danny Herwitz—I owe the genesis of the book. Our conversations about the epiphenomenal and literary parameters of the "sacred" and of "violence" charted an intellectual path I pursued (with pauses for various administrative duties) for the next ten years. I completed the manuscript in the glorious environs of the Huntington Library, a truly paradisaical place that nurtures the soul and body as well as the mind of its resident scholars. To my Huntington friends—Roy Ritchie, Steve Hindle, David Hall, Ann Little, Matt Kadane, Chris Kyle, Dympna Callaghan, Brent Sirota, Tim Harris, Kathleen Wilson, Urvashi Chakravarty, Kevin Lambert, Julie Park, Susan Barbour, Carla Mazzio, Joe Glatthaar, Sandra Rebok, François and Carol Rigolot, Matthew Fisher, Steve Snobelen, Adria Imada, Matt Behar, Frank Guridy, Catharine Franklin—I owe the finished product. I'm not sure they will all approve of the way the book turned out, but their probing questions and unrivaled knowledge of the early modern Anglo-American world have left indelible marks on the manuscript. A special thanks to David Hall and Matt Kadane, who read chapters and pushed me to rethink the nature of Reformed religion and its relationship to the Enlightenment, and to Hannah Jones for keeping us all sane. In Pasadena, Sharon Salinger was the first person to read an entire draft of the book, and her friendship and enthusiasm for the project were unexpected gifts of my Huntington year.

Several friends and colleagues at the University of Michigan have read portions of the manuscript over the years: Valerie Kivelson, Paolo Squattriti, Hussein Fancy, Helmut Puff, Sueann Caulfield, Leslie Pincus, Jay Cook, Matt Lassiter, and Howard Brick. My deepest gratitude goes to them all for reading the very first drafts of book chapters and reassuring me that this was a book that could speak to different scholarly audiences. I have had the great good fortune to work with exceptional graduate students over the years, and I thank them here for their fresh insights, contagious curiosity, and occasional research assistance—James Dator, Susanna Linsley, Melissa Johnson, Joost Van Eynde, Kate Silbert, Amanda Hendrix-Komoto, Sara Babcox First, Andrew Rutledge, Marie Stango, Ronit Stahl, and Alyssa Penick. Kate Silbert helped put the index together, and her good sense and good humor were greatly appreciated. Val Kivelson has been a comrade-in-arms and role model, and our weekly lunches are the one unalterable event in my calendar. Whatever else is happening in our lives, we make time to share a meal and talk about our work, our families, and our challenges every week. Other Michigan friends, few of whom have actually read portions of the book but all of whom have lent an ear and an encouraging pat on the back, deserve a shout-out: Mary Kelley, Tim McKay, Don Herzog, Abby Stewart, Danielle Lavaque-Manty, Lisa Disch, Andreas Gailus, Angela Dillard, Anne Manuel, Netta Berlin, and Arnold Juster. My London friends, especially Amanda Vickery and John Styles, have for many years now made that city my home away from home, and I thank them for all the great meals and spirited conversation they supplied on my semiannual visits to the British Library and National Archives. Over the years, a series of conversations with Michael Meranze about the coercive aspects of early modern institutional practices have brought much needed clarity and focus to my own thinking on the subject, while discussions with Chris Grasso and Jon Butler helped remind me that not all early Americans were religious, or religious in the same way. Jane Kamensky and Ed Gray's invitation to contribute a chapter on evangelical religion to the *Oxford Handbook of the American Revolution* (2012), while not directly relevant to this project, gave me the opportunity to think through religion's relationship to the material and print cultures of the seventeenth and eighteenth centuries at an opportune moment.

A version of Chapter 4 originally appeared as a chapter in the book of essays I coedited with my dear friend and colleague Linda Gregerson, *Empires of God: Religious Encounters in the Early Modern Atlantic*, published by the University of Pennsylvania Press in 2011. I thank the Press for permission to use this material. My relationship with the University of Pennsylvania Press goes back three books now, and each time Peter Agree has guided the book through the process with his sharp wit and even sharper editorial eye. I owe a special thanks to the anonymous Press reviewers and Daniel Richter, Susan Amussen, and Mike Zuckerman, who all read the manuscript in its entirety and saved me from errors large and small—as well as asking me to explore further the relationship of sacred violence to other forms of violence in the early modern world. Susan Amussen invited me to present the chapter on blasphemy to the Center for the Humanities at the University of California-Merced, and Chris Grasso and Jon Butler helped organize a conference around the theme of "Religion and Violence" at Yale University in 2008 that brought together scholars from a variety of disciplines to interrogate the category and historical parameters of the phenomenon of sacred violence.

This book is dedicated to Rhys Isaac, the shaman of early American cultural history and an irrepressible spirit who was far too young when he passed away in 2010. Rhys was the most generous scholar I have known. He went out of his way to befriend junior scholars and graduate students at conferences, loved to meet new people and share stories with them, delighted in being challenged over his sources and interpretations, and exuded an utter joy in the art of history-writing that was infectious. For such a diminutive man, he was a giant among colonial historians, and I am grateful to have walked in his shadow. When I was awarded a Collegiate Chair from the University of Michigan in 2014, I chose to name it in his honor.

SACRED VIOLENCE
IN EARLY AMERICA

Introduction

See that ye destroy all places where the nations which we
conquer serve their gods. . . . Overthrow their altars and
break their pillars and burn their groves with fire and hew
down the images of their gods.

—Deuteronomy 12:2

A visitor eager to know how Christianity fared in England's American colonies in the 1600s would be struck by what was *not* there. To quote David Hall,
"no cathedrals, no liturgy, no church courts, no altars or candles, no saints
days or Christmas, no weddings, no pilgrimages nor sacred places, nor relics;
no godparents, or maypoles, no fairy tales, no carnival."[1] If the visitor was
familiar with Europe's bloody and protracted wars of religion—the violent
underbelly of the Protestant and Catholic Reformations that tore the continent apart for nearly two centuries—he would surely add: no pogroms; no
religious riots on the scale of the infamous St. Bartholomew's Day Massacre
in Paris in 1572; no "stripping of the altars," desecration of saints' images, or
other orchestrated acts of iconoclasm; no (with four notable exceptions) executions for heresy, blasphemy, or any other religious crime; no burning of
witches or infidels or *autos-da-fé*; no forced conversions or mass expulsions
of dissenters; no Inquisition. There is, of course, a direct connection between
the two lists—it's hard to be an iconoclast without icons to smash, to hunt
heretics effectively without an Inquisition. Religious violence on a mass scale
needs large groups of people willing to kill and to die for their faith, helpfully
concentrated in towns for easy access to one another—not scattered settlers
and isolated plantations.

[1] David D. Hall, *Worlds of Wonder, Days of Judgment: Popular Religious Belief in Early
New England* (Cambridge, Mass.: Harvard University Press, 1989), 4–5. Hall is riffing on
Henry James's famous description of Americans' lack of civilization in his 1879 work of liter-
ary criticism, *Hawthorne*.

It's no wonder, then, that the image of early America as a land of religious freedom has been so enduring. Our students tell us this year after year on history exams, no matter how much evidence we present to the contrary, and the publishing industry has made a small fortune on books extolling the American republic as the birthplace of religious freedom. Scholars, too, have by and large supported this origins story, though by "religious freedom" they usually mean not freedom in the modern sense enshrined in the First Amendment, which protects the right of citizens *to* the "free exercise" of their faith without government interference or constraint, but freedom *from* coercion, *from* violence, *from* persecuting prelates and harsh penal laws. For a complex variety of reasons having to do with the weakness of ecclesiastical institutions, the availability of land to which dissenters could flee, the multi-sectarian background of European settlers, the legacy of vicious religious war at home, and a pragmatic attitude toward difference born of the struggle to survive in a harsh and alien land, colonial Americans seem to have escaped the worst excesses of what historians call the "confessional age" of European Christendom, when nations and empires lined up across the fault line of the Reformation and used all the considerable powers at their disposal to repel the enemy faith and maintain orthodoxy at home. A universal church became a patchwork of confessional states, arrayed across the face of Europe and, in time, across the Americas like so many game pieces on a chessboard, where each move provoked a countermove. The colonial possessions of these Catholic and Protestant empires usually figure as pawns, providers of expendable foot soldiers in the game of imperial war, or as sanctuaries, offering respite to the persecuted and the dispossessed of the Old World. The English colonies in North America were certainly both, at times. From Puritan invocations of their "errand into the wilderness" to escape the persecuting hand of Archbishop Laud to the Catholic and Quaker havens founded by Cecilius Calvert and William Penn, the image of the colonies as religious sanctuaries has exhibited a powerful pull on the American national imaginary. The architects of England's overseas empire were more likely to see the colonies they helped create as bulwarks against the menace of a predatory global Catholicism, which had already sprouted noxious offshoots in New Spain and the West Indies. Far from being religious sanctuaries, England's North American colonies were designed in large part to be weapons of religious war—frontier outposts that would halt the spread of Catholic empires and establish a toehold for the Protestant cause in the New World.

My aim is not to settle the question of whether the first generations of

English émigrés were escaping or perpetuating Old World religious conflicts—clearly they were doing both, often at the same time—but to dig deeper in time, to recover certain hidden or, in some cases, repudiated strata of colonial Americans' famously tolerant religious climate. How does the religious landscape of the first English colonies look when we begin the story not with the founding of Jamestown in 1607 or the first Puritan colony (Plymouth) in 1620 but in 1517 (when Luther issued his ninety-five theses) or 1534 (when Henry VIII was declared the head of the Church in England)? Or, pushing farther back, in 1401, when the first English law criminalizing heresy was passed? Or, to be even more adventurous, in 1208, when the first holy war of Christian against Christian was declared? Colonial American historians were long ago forced out of our comfortable parochialism, to expand our chronological and geographical scope in order to understand the hearth cultures from which New World societies sprang and the complex webs of exchange that bound them together; indeed a new generation of Atlantic historians has pioneered a truly global history that unites the Old and New Worlds of Europe, Africa, and the Americas into a single frame. My geographic reach is far more modest, encompassing only England and its charter colonies, but I want to bring the medieval and early modern worlds together—at least along the crucial dimension of religious ideology. Brad Gregory's impassioned, if overly partisan, plea for the continued relevance of medieval structures of thought for understanding the religious world we inhabit today is but one example of how a "genealogical" approach that considers continuities in historical forms over a long time span can bring buried meanings to light.[2]

Sacred Violence in Early America is a deep cultural history of the theology of violence: the presuppositions, referential chains, and linguistic homologies that structured how early Americans narrated, rationalized, fantasized about, and occasionally apologized for violence against a variety of religious "others"—heretics, sectarians, and, especially, Indians. Unearthing the logics that sustained such paradigmatic acts as warfare, captivity, conversion, heresy-hunting, and iconoclastic attacks on sacred objects requires that we listen closely to English justifications for their own actions with an ear attuned to the rich semiotic and devotional traditions that had developed in western Christendom over some three hundred years as one faith shattered into many.

---

[2] Brad S. Gregory, *The Unintended Reformation: How a Religious Revolution Secularized Society* (Cambridge, Mass.: Belknap Press of Harvard University Press, 2012).

Through a process we might call an archaeology of discourse, each chapter takes a distinct theological paradigm—blood sacrifice, holy war, malediction, and iconoclasm—and peels away the discursive layers to reveal the medieval and early modern antecedents that gave form and meaning to seventeenth- and eighteenth-century episodes of colonial violence. Shards of language (metaphors, commonplace phrases, biblical passages, textual referents, speech caught on paper by ear-witnesses, even individual words and their etymologies) are the raw materials I'm working with to reconstruct the grammar of religious encounter in early modern Anglo-America. The recurrence of images of altars and charred flesh, for example, tells us that the burning of Indian villages evoked European debates over the continued relevance of blood sacrifice in a Reformed world; the language of dispossession by which native peoples were driven from their lands was grounded in legalistic and biblical notions of a Christian heritage deeded by God to his "New Israel"; debates over whether to kill or cure unrepentant blasphemers harkened back to the English Civil War era legislative battles to silence the zealous sectarians who were threatening to destroy the Puritan commonwealth from within; and the destruction of Indian bodies bore a disturbing resemblance to iconoclastic campaigns to alter the material shape of Christianity. My approach is to identify and then tug, sometimes vigorously, at the ideological and rhetorical threads that bind early American religious violence (or, more properly, *accounts* of colonial violence) to Europe's wars of religion. Certain threads—the theme of blood sacrifice, for example—run like a bright red line through the entire corpus of colonial texts, while others (cannibalistic metaphors or images of unruly tongues) surface here and there, subtle refrains in the larger chorus of Christian lamentation about sin and its violent consequences.

Such a *longue durée* approach has its risks. Much of the particularity that historians cherish—the who, what, when, and where of the episodes of violence I narrate—will, inevitably, be flattened, and experts in the various fields I venture into will surely wish for more nuance and less generalizing in my abbreviated treatment of their scholarly terrain. Reformation historians may quibble with my account of the theological jostling over the "real presence" of Christ in the Eucharist, just as medievalists will want a finer-grained discussion of the distinction between blasphemy and heresy or of the iconographic impulses of the Latin Church. But I hope my debts to the enormous scholarship that has inspired and challenged me over the course of this study are as clear as any differences of interpretation that may have arisen along the way: a work of synthesis like this could not exist without the veritable library of local, regional, and confessional studies that comprise the vibrant field of early modern religious history. What is "new" here is not so much the individual findings, many of which have been known to scholars for a long time, but the assembling and juxtaposing of these historical fragments to create a discursive map of the early modern Anglo-American encounter with religious others.

To begin at the beginning: What do we mean by "religious violence"?[3] What is "sacred" about the kind of violence envisioned and experienced in the New World, what differentiates it from other kinds of violence—imperial, racial, juridical, civil? When the colonial militia quoted scripture while exulting in the burning of an Indian fort, in which five hundred men, women, and children lost their lives, should we see this as a *religious* or a *racial* killing? When the framers of the Puritan commonwealths of Massachusetts and New Haven provided specific Old Testament references for the laws mandating death for blasphemers and sorcerers, were they acting as theocrats or simply like prudent lawgivers everywhere after the Reformation? When the Anglican governor of Virginia accused the Puritans in New England of inciting the region's Indians to massacre his people in 1644, was this political brinkmanship or genuine religious antagonism? The history of colonial violence abounds in such ambiguous episodes. It is almost never the case that a straightforward affirmative answer can be given to the question, "Is this an example of sacred violence?" And the range of answers to this question provided by historians is impossibly broad, from sweeping generalizations about the sacred nature of *all* violence committed since the death of Christ to more modest attempts to provide a sheet against which boxes can be ticked to identify the specific genus of religious violence. (Claiming direct inspiration from God? Check. Waging war on Jews and Muslims? Check. Engaging in savage modes of warfare? Maybe.)

Scholars from other disciplines have led the way in locating the "sacred" in the annals of historical violence imagined, enacted, and decried. Anthropologists, especially, have dissected the symbolic structures of the world's religions, almost all of which were founded on an original act of violence (the crucifixion of Christ, the persecution and forced migration of the Prophet Muhammad and his followers to Medina, Abraham's near-sacrifice of his son, Isaac, at the

---

[3] A useful introduction is John D. Carlson, "Religion and Violence: Coming to Terms with Terms," in *The Blackwell Companion to Religion and Violence*, ed. Andrew R. Murphy (Oxford: Wiley-Blackwell, 2011), 5–22. See also Bruce Lincoln, *Holy Terrors: Thinking About Religion After September 11*, 2nd ed. (Chicago: University of Chicago Press, 2006); and Charles Selengut, *Sacred Fury: Understanding Religious Violence* (Walnut Creek, Calif.: Alta Mira, 2003).

command of Jehovah, the extreme asceticism and spiritual death of Siddhartha).[4] René Girard's widely influential *Violence and the Sacred* (1977) located the origins of the Judeo-Christian tradition in the paradigm of blood sacrifice, in which a chosen victim (first animals and humans, then God himself in the form of Christ) is sacrificed to appease the deity and ensure the salvation of humanity.[5] In the past twenty years we have seen an explosion of interest in the phenomenon of sacred violence, spurred in part by recent political events but reflecting a much deeper fascination with the subjective, "irrational" side of human experience. "Violence studies" now encompass everything from semiotics to neurobiology, as well as more conventional topics such as pain, torture, war, crime, slavery, sexual abuse, and, yes, religious rituals.[6] Killing is something humans do often and well. And they often invoke a higher power or higher cause when justifying to themselves and others why they kill.

By "sacred violence," I mean violence that is motivated and justified in significant part by religious aversion and/or desire. This fairly modest definition sidesteps most of the questions other scholars have argued over—particularly how to parse the various factors that lie behind historical episodes of religious violence. The roots of most acts of violence are multilayered and tangled: we lash out at people, objects, and ideas because of strong emotion (fear, lust, disgust, envy, malice), because of powerful ideological impulses (to defend kith and kin, to avenge wrongs done to us and our loved ones, to honor or supplicate a higher power), or because we are instructed or compelled to do so by authorities who command our allegiance and our service. Some violence is purposeful and instructive, some is impulsive and

[4] *Violent Origins: Walter Burkert, René Girard, and Jonathan Z. Smith on Ritual Killing and Cultural Formation*, ed. Robert G. Hamerton-Kelly (Stanford, Calif.: Stanford University Press, 1987).

[5] René Girard, *Violence and the Sacred*, trans. Patrick Gregory (Baltimore: Johns Hopkins University Press, 1977), and *The Scapegoat*, trans. Yvonne Freccero (Baltimore: Johns Hopkins University Press, 1986). See Kathryn McClymond's recent review of the Girardian legacy in "Sacrifice and Violence," in *The Blackwell Companion to Religion and Violence*, ed. Andrew R. Murphy (Oxford: Wiley-Blackwell, 2011), 320–30.

[6] For a small and admittedly idiosyncratic sampling of this literature, see Ariel Glucklich, *Sacred Pain: Hurting the Body for the Sake of the Soul* (New York: Oxford University Press, 2001); Michael A. Bellesiles, ed., *Lethal Imagination: Violence and Brutality in American History* (New York: New York University Press, 1999); V. A. Gatrell, *The Hanging Tree: Execution and the English People, 1770–1868* (New York: Oxford University Press, 1994); John Keane, *Reflections on Violence* (London: Verso, 1996); Jody Enders, *The Medieval Theater of Violence: Rhetoric, Memory, Violence* (Ithaca, N.Y.: Cornell University Press, 1999); and *Violence and the Body: Race, Gender, and the State*, ed. Arturo J. Aldama (Bloomington: Indiana University Press, 2002).

nihilistic. The most compelling attempt to identify a genetic marker for "sa-cred" violence remains, to me, Natalie Zemon Davis's insight (made forty years ago) that such violence is a ritual of purification or calculated desecra-tion, intended either to restore the boundary between the sacred and the pro-fane or to render profane what others find sacred.[7] Those who have followed her lead tend to locate the sacred dimension of certain acts of violence more in the realm of culture (including language) than in their sociological or po-litical context, though what makes Davis's analysis so persuasive is her insis-tence that culture and society are always entangled categories.[8]

At the end of the day, I am less interested in distinguishing religious from other forms of colonial violence than in describing the combustible mixture of sacred and profane fears and desires that led English men and women to behave—at some times, in some places—in such a savage manner toward their enemies in the New World. So this is not an exercise in classification so much as an exploration of a complex and richly sedimented discursive ter-rain. And by highlighting the religious element in colonial narratives of vio-lence I do not mean to suggest that other motives and meanings were not present as well. I am not saying that religion is the "real" cause of the events I'm describing, nor am I trying to apportion blame among the various factors (ethnic prejudice, land greed, imperial politics, cultural disgust, alongside theological aversion) that lie behind these episodes of colonial violence.

The first place we often look for evidence of a religious sensibility in early modern texts is to scripture—the presence, and placement, of biblical refer-ences to confirm, explicate, or rebut. But here, the task is more difficult than it might at first seem. Of one thing we can be sure: quoting scripture is never enough to attach the label "sacred" to any given act. Early modern Christians, especially those of the literate Protestant sort, quoted scripture liberally in their daily lives; it was their lingua franca. (The availability of online, text-searchable versions of the King James and the Geneva Bibles is a godsend to scholars who suspect that the specific phrases they're seeing in colonial

---

[7] Natalie Zemon Davis, "The Rites of Violence: Religious Riot in Sixteenth-Century France," *Past & Present* 59 (May 1973): 51–91. See also Denis Crouzet, *Les Guerriers de Dieu: La violence au temps des troubles de religion (vers 1525–vers 1610)*, 2 vols. (Seyssel: Champ Vallon, 1990).

[8] See, for example, Rhys Isaac, *The Transformation of Virginia, 1740–1790* (Chapel Hill: University of North Carolina Press, 1982); David Nirenberg, *Communities of Violence: Perse-cution of Minorities in the Middle Ages* (Princeton, N.J.: Princeton University Press, 1996); and David Sabean, *Power in the Blood: Popular Culture and Village Discourse in Early Modern Germany* (New York: Cambridge University Press, 1984).

documents were taken directly from the Bible.) So deeply woven into the everyday speech and literature of early modern Anglo-Americans was scripture that it can be easy to underestimate or misunderstand the biblicism of these "children of the Word." In our day, we say that "familiarity breeds contempt." But the exact opposite was the case in the seventeenth century, when the constant exposure to the words of the Old and New Testaments (and to core devotional texts like John Foxe's 1563 *Book of Martyrs*) bred not indifference but profound identification. The words became part of the very air Protestants breathed and the spiritual food they ingested on a daily basis. Speaking biblically was thus akin to a dialect, a "living idiom," learned in childhood and practiced to the point of instinctual habit, not necessarily a mode of argumentation.[9] (Although it was sometimes that, too.) In a world of unprecedented (male) literacy rates, *not* knowing one's Bible was grounds for suspicion; accused witches were often asked to recite a prayer or read from the Bible. If they failed, they were cast out of the community of saints and consigned to the devil. (George Burroughs's flawless recitation of the Lord's Prayer on the scaffold in Salem during the infamous witch panic of 1692 stunned the crowd and nearly saved his neck.)

One kind of colonial violence is notably missing from this account, and its absence highlights the methodological difficulties of studying religious encounters in the earliest English settlements. The violence inflicted by European slave traders and slave owners on African bodies and souls was arguably the paradigmatic form of colonial exploitation in the age of sail. The full dimensions of the tragedy of African enslavement in the New World are only beginning to be told, as scholars have turned their attention in recent years from the labor regime of the antebellum plantation to the original acts of human expropriation and trafficking that constituted the slave trade from the fifteenth through the eighteenth century.[10] Atlantic slavery was an institution rooted in violence from the beginning, and the scale of the damage—to people, families, communities, institutions, and faith traditions—is almost incalculable. What Jon Butler called the "spiritual holocaust" of Atlantic slavery (a provocative phrase that sparked a lively rejoinder among historians of Afri-

---

[9] Naomi Tadmor, *The Social Universe of the English Bible: Scripture, Society, and Culture in Early Modern England* (New York: Cambridge University Press, 2010), 13; see also Jonathan Sheehan, *The Enlightenment Bible: Translation, Scholarship, Culture* (Princeton, N.J.: Princeton University Press, 2005).

[10] Stephanie E. Smallwood, *Saltwater Slavery: A Middle Passage from Africa to American Diaspora* (Cambridge, Mass.: Harvard University Press, 2007); Marcus Rediker, *The Slave Ship: A Human History* (New York: Penguin, 2007).

can America) may not have entirely destroyed African religious systems and indigenous traditions of spiritual knowledge and leadership, but it undeniably altered the terms on which English settlers first encountered Africans and their strange gods.[11] In one of the cruelest ironies in a story shot through with cruelty both ironic and intentional, Africans came to the Americas by and large as deracinated and despiritualized individuals—as men and women whose existence (in the eyes of their masters) was limited to the basic human functions of working, reproducing, and dying. They were not, except in the most superficial and historically distorted ways, members of recognizable ethnicities or nations or faith communities.

This was especially true in the first decades of settlement in English America, where the number of African slaves was small and their dispersal among numerous scattered farms and individual households obscured their collective identity—at least, so far as can be determined by reading narratives of encounter. Colonial observers and writers simply did not seem to notice, or to comment on, systematic features of African spiritual traditions and customs, nor did they devote much missionary energy to converting Africans.[12] In fact, for most of the colonial period converting slaves was considered an act of subversion rather than an act of mercy or piety. For all the ink spilled by English writers on the urgent need to save the heathen and conquer the "devil's dominion" for God and crown, the heathens in question were Indian souls, not African ones. The 1682 Fundamental Constitution of South Carolina protected

[11] Jon Butler, *Awash in a Sea of Faith: Christianizing the American People* (Cambridge, Mass.: Harvard University Press, 1990), chapter 5, "Slavery and the African Religious Holocaust." For rejoinders, see Sylvia R. Frey and Betty Wood, *Come Shouting to Zion: African American Protestantism in the American South and British Caribbean to 1830* (Chapel Hill: University of North Carolina Press, 1998); and Philip Morgan, *Black Counterpoint: Slave Culture in the Eighteenth-Century Chesapeake and Low Country* (Chapel Hill: University of North Carolina Press, 1998). One strand of this debate has focused on the role of Islam among African slaves; by some estimates, as many as 10 percent of slaves may have been Muslim. See Michael A. Gomez, *Exchanging Our Country Marks: The Transformation of African Identities in the Colonial and Antebellum South* (Chapel Hill: University of North Carolina Press, 1998), and *Black Crescent: The Experience and Legacy of African Muslims in the Americas* (New York: Cambridge University Press, 2005).

[12] This was especially true of the mainland colonies; in the British West Indies, where large numbers of African slaves were present as early as the 1640s, one can find ethnographic observations of African spirituality and religious practices. See, for example, Richard Ligon, *A True & Exact History of the Island of Barbados* (London, 1657), which noted that "most of them [Africans] acknowledge a God, as appears by their motions and gestures" (47). On the whole, however, the English literature of religious discovery is far richer for native Americans than for Africans.

the religion of Indians, such as it was ("their Idolatry, Ignorance or Mistake gives us no right to expel or use them ill"), while giving white settlers a blank check to disregard the religious status of Africans: "Every Freeman of Carolina shall have absolute power and authority over Negro slaves of what opinion or Religion whatever."[13] One important consequence of this basic indifference to the spiritual state of Africans in America was that violence against them was largely ignored. The biblical injunction to holy violence that serves as the epigraph to this introduction—"See that ye destroy all places where the nations which we conquer serve their gods"—resounded clearly in the wars of extermination against Indian peoples; the daily acts of humiliation and pain endured by enslaved Africans had no obvious scriptural warrant. We have no complex rhetorical justifications for the mutilation, dismembering, and burning of African bodies comparable to Cotton Mather's magisterial *Decennium Luctuosum*, which celebrated the late century Indian wars as a New World reenactment of the Old Testament campaign against the Amalekites. Violence against Africans was an everyday occurrence, and too often unrecorded; violence against Indians was disturbing enough to Christian colonists to generate the kinds of texts explored in this book. It may be remarkable to historians of early modern Europe that burning at the stake (the traditional penalty for heresy) was inflicted only on Africans in the English colonies, but it was utterly unremarkable to the colonists themselves. By the middle of the eighteenth century, a religious argument about slavery would emerge in the American colonies, prompted by Quaker misgivings about the infamous trade in which they were so deeply implicated, but it's hard to find even the faintest trace of religious reflection about the roots of violence by or against Africans in the first century of settlement. All this is not to say that theological preoccupations played no role in colonial accounts of violence against enslaved men and women, only that religious language and ideas are absent from these accounts in ways that are legible.

Focusing so intently on the violence of the colonial encounter runs the very real risk of conveying a false impression that the early English settlements were, to quote the title of Karen Armstrong's latest meditation on western religion, vast "fields of blood." (The Puritan divine John Cotton said it more lyrically: "When the eyes are bloud-shotten, or looke through a red glasse, all

---

[13] Quoted in Jon Sensbach, "Slaves to Intolerance: African American Christianity and Religious Freedom in Early America," in *The First Prejudice: Religious Tolerance and Intolerance in Early America*, ed. Chris Beneke and Christopher S. Grenda (Philadelphia: University of Pennsylvania Press, 2011), 195–217 (quotation on 204–5).

things about them will appear red and bloudy.")[14] There has been a vigorous, and largely salutary, effort among scholars in multiple disciplines to rescue religion from the charge of excessive bloodlust. Spurred by a deep discomfort with the atavistic response of many contemporary critics across the political spectrum to the sectarian violence unfolding in the Middle East and other parts of the world as simply one more example of religion's eternal impulse to kill its enemies, critics like Armstrong and William Cavanaugh insist that religion (by which they mean organized religion) is no more inherently violent or destructive than any other realm of human endeavor.[15] This is a timely and important reminder not to let our personal or scholarly feelings of aversion at the terrible things people have done, and continue to do, in the name of God predispose us to assume an inherent and necessary connection between religion and violence. Much—perhaps most—of the violence I explore in the chapters that follow would have taken place with or without the theological impulses that are my primary interest, even if the form and the expression of that violence were deeply indebted to Europe's complex confessional history.

But at the same time, we shouldn't let religion off the hook, especially in the era of Latin Christendom's rise to hegemonic power and the shattering of that hegemony in late medieval and early modern Europe. In our popular imaginings of the past, no era more typifies the human propensity toward violence than medieval Europe when crusades were launched against whole populations and the Inquisition tortured and killed thousands of nominal Christians at home.[16] The oft-repeated tale of the crusader who, when asked how to distinguish heretics from the godly, replied, "Kill them all; God will

[14] John Cotton, *The Bloudy Tenet Washed and Made White in the Bloud of the Lamb, or, The Bloudy Tenet discust and discharg'd of bloud-guiltinesse, by Just Defense* (London, 1647), 3.

[15] Karen Armstrong, *Fields of Blood: Religion and the History of Violence* (New York: Knopf, 2014); William Cavanaugh, *The Myth of Religious Violence: Secular Ideology and the Roots of Modern Conflict* (New York: Oxford University Press, 2009).

[16] While there are no exact figures for the number of people killed by the Spanish Inquisition, recent studies suggest the figure is between one thousand and two thousand. Henry Kamen, *The Spanish Inquisition: A Historical Revision* (New Haven, Conn.: Yale University Press, 1998), 59–60; E. William Monter, *Frontiers of Heresy: The Spanish Inquisition from the Basque Lands to Sicily* (New York: Cambridge University Press, 1990), 53. In contrast, some five thousand men and women were executed for heresy in the sixteenth and seventeenth centuries, and if we expand this figure to include those whose deaths were the indirect result of legal prosecution or popular protest (those who died in prison, for example, or who perished in religious riots), the number quickly climbs into the tens of thousands. Gregory, *Salvation at Stake*). And the casualty figures for the wars of religion are truly astonishing: between 20 and 40 percent of the entire population of Central Europe was killed during the Thirty Years' War (1618–48).

know his own" sums up the bloodthirsty mentality we associate with medieval Christendom. It was not, however, until the Reformation unleashed the
forces of dissent and schism on Europe that truly horrific levels of religious
violence scorched every corner of the continent. If the Inquisition was mostly
a phantom in the medieval period, terrifying all but punishing only the exemplary few, no one was safe from the flames of war from the 1560s through
the end of the seventeenth century.[17] From the brutal eighty-year revolt of the
Dutch provinces against Spain to the Thirty Years' War in Germany (which
came to epitomize savagery for an entire generation of Christians), the eight
wars that France fought to suppress its Huguenot minority in the second half
of the sixteenth century, and the Civil Wars in England—Europe reeled from
the hammer blows of religious war.[18] This was total war, unsparing, and accompanied by an outpouring of tracts and pamphlets that papered Europe's
urban centers in atrocity narratives. The era of European religious war is one
of the darkest in human history, and the overseas possessions of these feud-
ing Christian empires were not spared its ravages.[19] The more we explore the

[17] Armstrong, *Fields of Blood*, 225.

[18] William Cavanaugh (*Myth of Religious Violence*) makes a forceful case that the idea of an
"era of religious war" was an ideological creation of modern nation-states, for whom the wars
of the Reformation served as a foil against which to justify their own monopolization of state
violence. It's a valid point, though the extent and virulence of popular violence against religious
objects, people, and communities during the sixteenth and seventeenth centuries cannot be
determined by looking only at wars between states; while it is true that there was often no simple confessional divide separating the combatants in Europe's national wars of religion, it is
undeniable that arguments about theology and devotional disciplines lay behind the execution
of heretics, the mobilization of popular sentiment in times of war, and the destruction of sacred
objects and faith communities during riots and iconoclastic campaigns. As John Morrill said,
"No scholar thinks that the European wars of religion were only about religion. . . . [They] concerned competing visions of state formation . . . and the social distribution of power at a time
of economic and demographic change; but . . . religious poles are the ones around which most
other discontents formed, religious arguments dominated the debate on the choices people
made, and religious dynamism determined the stages through which the wars ran." Morrill,
The Nature of the English Revolution: Essays (London: Longman, 1993), 37.

[19] For a textbook overview of this era, see Mark Konnert, *Early Modern Europe: The Age of
Religious War, 1559–1715* (Toronto: Broadview Press, 2006). On specific wars, see Barbara
Diefendorf, *Beneath the Cross: Catholics and Huguenots in Sixteenth-Century Paris* (New York:
Oxford University Press, 1991); Alastair Duke, *Reformation and Revolt in the Netherlands*
(London: Hambledon Press, 1990); Geoffrey Parker, ed., *The Thirty Years' War*, 2nd ed. (Lon-
don: Routledge, 1997); Ronald G. Asch, *The Thirty Years' War: The Holy Roman Empire and
Europe, 1618–1648* (New York: St. Martin's Press, 1997); Christopher Hill, *The World Turned
Upside Down: Radical Ideas During the English Revolution* (London: Temple Smith, 1972); John
Morrill, "The Religious Context of the English Civil War," in *The English Civil War*, ed. Richard
Cust and Ann Hughes (London: Arnold and Hodder, 1997); and *England's Wars of Religion,
Revisited*, ed. Charles W. A. Prior and Glenn Burgess (Farnham: Ashgate, 2011).

prehistory of colonization, the more we have come to recognize that the conquest and settlement of the New World was in fact the final bloody chapter of the Reformation Wars.[20]

In English America, this is, emphatically, a Protestant and not just a Puritan story, though (as is always the case in studies of colonial religion) Puritan authors provide much of the textual evidence. While Puritans differed from their Anglican, Lutheran, and sectarian cousins over key points of doctrine, these were mostly differences in degree, not of kind. On almost all the important theological controversies that constituted the discursive backdrop to the rationales of violence I'll be exploring, Puritans agreed with their Protestant brethren; they simply expressed their opinions more volubly, and usually with greater heat, than others. So while the majority of my sources come from New England, it's important to recognize that similar discussions were happening elsewhere in the North American colonies wherever the English tried to extend their dominion over native peoples and lands, as well as over internal enemies. We're accustomed to hearing stories of Puritan lay men and women confronting their ministers over the finer points of theology, but on an unremarkable day in 1658 a Protestant and a Jesuit got into a spirited argument in Maryland over the latter's "doctrine." The Jesuit, boasted his Protestant antagonist, could not hold his own, "his memory being but weake in Scripture."[21] Fewer such stories have been preserved in the historical records for the southern colonies, but we have no reason to believe they did not occur on a regular basis. Puritans had no monopoly on belligerent rhetoric, nor did they ground this rhetoric in unique theological positions on such issues as the role of sacrifice in the crucifixion or the presence of Christ in the Eucharist. By the early seventeenth century, after a hundred years of doctrinal wrangling and internecine turf battles between Reformers, Europe's Protestants had reached a rough consensus around the key points of difference that separated them from their Catholic opponents. And by the late seventeenth

[20] Scholars of native America have been among the first to recognize the connections between Europe's religious wars and the brutal conquest of New World societies. Daniel Richter, *Before the Revolution: America's Ancient Pasts* (Cambridge, Mass.: Belknap Press of Harvard University Press, 2011); David E. Stannard, *American Holocaust: Columbus and the Conquest of the New World* (New York: Oxford University Press, 1992). For a transnational perspective, see the essays collected in *Empires of God: Religious Encounters in the Early Modern Atlantic*, ed. Linda Gregerson and Susan Juster (Philadelphia: University of Pennsylvania Press, 2011).

[21] *Archives of Maryland, Proceedings of the Provincial Court 1658–1662*, Volume 41, ed. Bernard Steiner (Baltimore, 1922), 146.

century, as Reformed Protestantism faced a resurgent and newly militarized Catholic offensive that threatened to destroy all the gains that had been made since Luther first broke with the Catholic Church, the imperative to maintain a unified front was more urgent than ever. Minor differences in dogma or practice could not be sustained when the very survival of the Reformation was at stake.[22]

At the heart of the Protestant Reformation was a rethinking of the relationship between the material and the spiritual world. The simplest way to imagine this change is to picture the inside of a church before and after the Reformation. If we were to venture inside a parish church in England in 1500, we would see an altar enclosed by wooden rails, protected from view by a rood screen, with images of the saints adorning the walls and a large cross erected above the altar. If we were to venture into that same church in 1600, the altar rails, rood, and saints' pictures would all be gone (perhaps the cross would remain, though in all likelihood without the figure of Christ nailed to its three corners), the walls whitewashed and the interior stripped of all ornamentation. Inside this church the ceremony of the mass would be very different as well: the liturgy would now be performed in English rather than in Latin, only baptism and communion (out of the original seven sacraments) would be celebrated, the priest would no longer wear a surplice or alb, and there would be no more bowing, crossing, incensing, genuflecting, or kissing of the crucifix or one another. Instead the congregation would sit in silence as the Word of God was read and interpreted by the priest (who was now more likely to be called a minister). From an environment rich in sounds, smells, images, and tactile encounters both divine and human to an austere space of scriptural contemplation and prayer—such was the sensory transformation of the Church under the Reformation. Behind this reconfiguration of the principal site of worship lay a theological and epistemological shift of profound significance. Put most starkly, the material world was both rejected as a source of spiritual knowledge and repressed as a site of temptation and contamination by Reformers intent on restoring the Christian church to its original, pristine state.

This shift is the central analytical concern of the book. We will explore the theological and ritual ramifications of the Protestant assault on the material, an assault that was never—could never be—completely successful. As any post-Freudian knows, what humans try to repress will always come back in one form or another. And one of the key arguments of the book is that the material came back with a vengeance in the New World, as English colonists came face-to-face with new gods and new rituals that forced them to confront the unresolved tensions between the material and the spiritual within their own religious practice. New World accounts of native cannibalism, for instance, prompted uneasy comparisons with the ongoing debate among Reformers about whether Christ was bodily present in the communion wafer. Indian war practices of ritualized torture and corpse dismemberment reminded English Protestants that they, too, approved of dismemberment as a punishment for heretics and blasphemers, and had tortured human figures in their iconoclastic campaigns against religious art. The scriptural metaphor of false prophets and idolaters as "ravening wolves" took on literalist overtones as English colonists did battle with real wolves and their human avatars in the forests of North America. Throughout the narratives and episodes examined in this book, the unsettling presence of the material—flesh and blood, human organs like the tongue and the heart, predatory animals like the wolf and the serpent, annihilating elements like fire and water—in New World religious encounters is the unifying motif.

For over a century, from 1607 to 1715 (when the last major colonial Indian war was fought in South Carolina), English America experienced recurring friction with external and internal enemies, heretical outbreaks, and epidemics of slanderous and sacrilegious speech. These were, to paraphrase the title of a recent book on the origins of English America, "barbarous years."[23] But where others locate the "barbarism" of this fraught century in the encounter with a savage land and its savage peoples, my version shares more with Joseph Conrad's dystopic novel *Heart of Darkness*. Like Conrad's African explorer Charles Marlow, the English men and women who settled North America ventured into a strange and frightening land only to discover that the darkness lay within, in the very religious passions and fears that had driven them across the Atlantic in the first place.

---

[23] Bernard Bailyn, *The Barbarous Years: The Peopling of British North America: The Conflict of Civilizations, 1600–1675* (New York: Vintage, 2012).

CHAPTER 1

Blood Sacrifice

What, feed on Human Flesh and Blood? Strange mess!
Nature exclaims. *What barbarousness is here?*
—Edward Taylor, *Sacramental Meditations* II.81

THEY SHOULD BE BREAD FOR US.
—Captain John Mason, 1637

At the end of a calamitous period in which the Puritan commonwealth of Massachusetts had endured a long war with its northern Indians and an even longer battle with Quakers and witches, Cotton Mather sat down to survey the physical and spiritual damage. That these assaults were linked was obvious to a Puritan accustomed to deciphering the providential messages God regularly sent his chosen people. Rather than reach for providentialist language, however, Mather used images drawn from the sacrificial cultures of medieval Europe and New Spain to justify the English victory over the Devil and his human and Indian minions. "The Flame of War then Raged thro' a great part of the Country, whereby many whole Towns were Laid in Ashes, and many Lives were Sacrificed," he marveled. "A Spaniard, that was a Sould-ier, would say, *That if we have a good Cause, the smell of Gunpowder in the Field is as Sweet as the Incense at the Altar*. Let the Reader judge after these things, what scent there was in the Gunpowder spent for Nine or Ten Years together in our War with the Indian Salvages."[1]

---

[1] Cotton Mather, *Decennium Luctuosum, An history of remarkable occurrences, in the long war, which New-England hath had with the Indian salvages, from the year, 1688. To the year 1698* (Boston, 1699), 11–12, 19.

Mather's jeremiad was directed not only to his fellow Puritans who, he felt, had called this hell down upon their own heads by their manifold sins but more pointedly at one particular opponent: the Quaker Thomas Maule. A few years before, Maule had published a jeremiad of his own accusing Mather and his clerical cronies of being the true enemies of Christ. Maule, too, invoked the language of sacrifice for his own rhetorical ends. The Quakers, God's pure "Lambs" who crossed the Atlantic to carry the "Lamb's War" to the stronghold of Calvinist orthodoxy in the 1650s and 1660s, were "offered up at their bloody Altar" like so many sheep to the slaughter. Hundreds had been whipped, branded, incarcerated, and exiled by order of the colony's magistrates in the forty years since their arrival, and four paid the ultimate price, hanged with great fanfare on Boston Commons when they refused to obey the order of banishment. These four unfortunates, Maule wrote, were "driven to their bloody Altar with Drums, Guns, and Swords, and cut down, even to the breaking of their skulls, and in a barbarous manner dragged their Naked Bodies in a Roap, with the gnashing of the Teeth; in which inhuman manner they threw their naked Bodies into a stinking Pit, near to their Bloody Altar."[2]

Here, at the close of the first century of English colonization of North America, we have the spectacle of dueling altars: the fragrant altar of Indian war and the "bloody altar" of sectarian violence. For a scholar of Puritanism, the imagery is jarring. Not for the viciousness of its rhetoric against despised "others"—the "persecutory" impulses of early modern Christians have long been a favorite subject of historians and literary scholars—but for its stunning invocation of altars and incense, two of the most recognizable "papist" icons in the Protestant polemical arsenal.[3] The appearance of such popish terms in the writings of hard-line Protestant sectarians unsettles some familiar truths about the theological and discursive world of the Reformed.

The two quotations I've juxtaposed as epigraphs to the chapter hint at an important connection between Protestant sacramentalism (Edward Taylor's critique of transubstantiation) and English-Indian warfare (John Mason's exhortation during the Pequot War of 1637). This chapter argues that, contrary to the conventional view that English Protestants, especially those of the Calvinist variety, embraced symbolic over literal readings of such key sacraments as

[2] Thomas Maule, *Truth held forth and maintained according to the testimony of the holy prophets . . . With some account of the judgements of the Lord lately inflicted upon New-England by witch craft* (New York, 1695), 197.

[3] John Stachniewski, *The Persecutory Imagination: English Puritanism and the Literature of Religious Despair* (New York: Oxford University Press, 1991).

baptism and the Lord's Supper, the field of English-Indian encounters in the New World offered a veritable feast of flesh and blood that proved irresistible to Protestants hungry for concrete evidence of their status as God's chosen people. The theme of *consumption*—in all its material and allegorical meanings—provides a powerful structuring metaphor in English accounts of their military and missionary endeavors in North America, linking theological debates over sacrifice, sacrament, and satisfaction to colonial themes of conquest, dispossession, and extermination. Let us, with Mather, ask "what scent there was" in these colonial chronicles of sacrifice demanded, extracted, and reputed.

"What Sacrifices Have We Now to Offer?": The Sacramental Reformation

Exploring theological justifications for violence in New World texts takes us back to some of the earliest doctrinal disputes of the Reformation era, indeed to the Christian era more generally. Nothing less than the foundational moment of Christianity itself—the incarnation, death, and resurrection of God in human form—is at the center of these debates. For the crucifixion not only ushered in a new stage of sacred history, according to Christian theologians, but signaled the advent of a new postsacrificial stage of human history, according to modern anthropologists and theorists of religion.[4] The death of Christ (or, more accurately, the Christian interpretation of the meaning of that death) was thus a paradigm-shifting event in the history of religion. At first glance, his death was yet another example of the kind of blood sacrifice that the ancient Hebrews and pagans alike had performed, using living things (animals, birds, or, rarely, humans) as burnt offerings. The gift of that which we hold most precious, blood, to the gods through ritualized killing is such a central feature of human culture in almost every age and every place that

---

[4] René Girard, *Violence and the Sacred*, trans. Patrick Gregory (Baltimore: Johns Hopkins University Press, 1977), and *The Scapegoat*, trans. Yvonne Freccero (Baltimore: Johns Hopkins University Press, 1986). For a succinct review of anthropological theories of sacrifice and Girard's challenge to the anthropological view, see Bruce Chilton, "The Hungry Knife: Towards a Sense of Sacrifice," in *Jesus in Context: Temple, Purity, and Restoration*, ed. Bruce Chilton and Craig A. Evans (Leiden: Brill, 1997), 91–108; for an extended critique, see his *The Temple of Jesus: His Sacrificial Program within a Cultural History of Sacrifice* (University Park: Pennsylvania State University Press, 1992). According to Jonathan Klawans, most scholars of sacrifice remain "under the Girardian spell." Klawans, "Pure Violence: Sacrifice and Defilement in Ancient Israel," *Harvard Theological Review* 94.2 (April 2001): 133–55 (quotation on 137).

many anthropologists consider it one of the essential elements of religion it-self.[5] For the first Christians, the biblical story of Abraham's willingness to sacrifice his only son, Isaac, at God's command was as much prophecy as parable, foreshadowing a greater act of sacrificial generosity to come.

That prophecy seemed to be fulfilled in the incarnate Christ, offered up on the cross at Calvary. But just what kind of a "sacrifice" was the death of Christ? Was it an act of propiation—a means of appeasing the gods by shed-ding blood in order to avert judgment? An act of expiation—an atonement for past sins that actually removed the stain of the offense rather than merely placating God? Did the sacrifice of Christ satisfy a prior bargain, create a new cycle of exchange, or end the sacrificial economy altogether? And what did his death mean for his apostles and followers, those who would gather to-gether in enclaves to await his return and anticipate their own eventual resur-rection? Would they, too, have to sacrifice their lives (or the lives of their enemies), or was Christ's offering sufficient to encompass the collective guilt of humanity for its past and future sins?

Medieval theologians offered various interpretations of Christ's sacrifice, dividing in particular over propiatory versus expiatory readings, but in gen-eral understood his death within a sacrificial economy that envisioned a vast "treasury of merit," a kind of cosmic storehouse, to which God and the saints both contributed and on which humans could draw to advance their quest for salvation by petitioning the residents of heaven to share some of their wealth with those still struggling on earth. The theory of satisfaction articu-lated most fully by the twelfth-century Benedictine monk Anselm of Canter-bury stipulated that man and God were bound in a reciprocal, if vastly unequal, relationship of (human) obligations and (divine) mercies on terms entirely determined by the deity but that nonetheless operated according to

[5] There has been a lively debate among scholars of religion and anthropologists since the 1980s about the usefulness of the term "sacrifice" as an analytical category and the centrality of sacrifice to the study of religion more generally. On the one hand, critics such as Marcel Deti-enne reject the concept altogether and believe it should be consigned to the trash bin of his-tory along with other nineteenth-century anachronisms such as "totem" and "taboo." On the other hand, Luc de Heusch believes it is possible to come up with a minimal definition of the term (a gift to the gods that involves some kind of violent division) that preserves its value for studying religious cultures across time and space. Marcel Detienne, "Culinary Practices and the Spirit of Sacrifice," in *The Cuisine of Sacrifice Among the Ancient Greeks*, ed. M. Detienne and Jean-Pierre Vernant, trans. Paula Wissing (Chicago: University of Chicago Press, 1989), 1–20; Luc de Heusch, *Sacrifice in Africa: A Structuralist Approach*, trans. L. O'Brien and A. Morton (Bloomington: Indiana University Press, 1985). John Milbank reviews this literature in "Stories of Sacrifice," *Modern Theology* 12.1 (January 1996): 27–56.

intelligible social rules such as commensurability (the punishment should fit the crime), proportionality (good and evil are not polar opposites but exist on a continuum), corporatism (the corporate body is held responsible for the good and bad deeds of its members), and—crucially—mutualism (both parties value and benefit from the exchange).[6] Every action on earth produced a reaction in heaven, every deed its proper reward or punishment.

By the time of Christ's incarnation, the cumulative sins of humanity had created such a vast overdraft of guilt that only God himself could satisfy the debt. His son—the flesh-and-blood Christ, tortured and killed—was the ultimate payment. Theologians sometimes disagreed whether Christ redeemed the debt of humanity through an act of penal substitution (undergoing the punishment deserved by others) or an act of incorporation (absorbing the sins of the world into his own body), but in either case his death was simultaneously satisfaction and sacrifice.[7] In this spiritual economy, the sacrifice of Christ on the cross thus occasioned a game-changing deposit of merit into the treasury, sufficient, as Christians believed, to entirely negate the collective burden of guilt incurred by mankind to that day. And hereafter, the nature of sacrifice would change to reflect the altered relationship between man and God: never again would God ask his people to sacrifice their very lives, or the lives of their children, to atone for their sins. But they would still need to perform lesser forms of ritual abnegation and penance, as long as sin—and the devil—continued to operate in the world. The cycle of action-reaction that bound God and man together was not broken, merely reconstituted under new terms of engagement.

The medieval theory of satisfaction fell victim to the Reformation's refiguring of God's relationship to man. Among the many Catholic "superstitions" rejected by Luther, Calvin, and their allies was the notion of cosmic circuits of exchange linking man, God, and spiritual intermediaries (saints, angels, the souls in purgatory) through ritual petition and acts of devotion. For Reformers, God could not be satisfied. The idea alone was nonsensical. He stood alone and above, omnipotent and omniscient, needing nothing and owing

---

[6] John Bossy, *Christianity in the West, 1400–1700* (New York: Oxford University Press, 1985).

[7] Caroline Walker Bynum surveys the complex landscape of late medieval views of Christ's sacrifice in Part IV, "Sacrifice and Soteriology," of her *Wonderful Blood: Theology and Practice in Late Medieval Northern Germany and Beyond* (Philadelphia: University of Pennsylvania Press, 2007). For a condensed version of Bynum's argument, see her "The Power in the Blood: Sacrifice, Satisfaction, and Substitution in Late Medieval Soteriology," in *The Redemption: An Interdisciplinary Symposium on Christ as Redeemer*, ed. Stephen T. Davis, Daniel Kendall, and Gerald O'Collins (Oxford: Oxford University Press, 2004), 177–204.

nothing to mankind. He could not be requited, he could not be appeased, and he most certainly could not be bargained with: he was only to be worshiped. As historians of the Reformation have shown, this radical severing of the liturgical, ritual, and emotional threads that tied man to his Creator (and to his past, in the form of ancestors who were now expelled from Purgatory, another casualty of the iconoclastic impulse of the Reformation) left Protestants in something of a spiritual void, with no one to intercede for them, no one to make satisfaction for their sins. This void was, of course, filled in time with new intermediaries and new devotional aids—consider the enduring appeal of prophets and wonders in the post-Reformation world, and the rich array of textual material produced to counsel and comfort saints on the arduous path to salvation—but the adamant rejection of the very notion of satisfaction meant that God would never again be the author or recipient of sacrifices in the Old Testament sense. Assigning the incarnate Christ to the role of sacrificial lamb "makes God to be [man's] debtor," in John Calvin's words—a notion both preposterous and monstrously arrogant.[8] Even in the remote wilds of New England, an untutored Indian convert understood that Christ's sacrifice could not be repeated. "Noah sacrificed and so worshipped. This was the manner of old time. But what sacrifices have we now to offer? My answer is, we must offer such as Abraham offered. . . . Only, God requires not us to sacrifice our *sons*, but our *sins*—our dearest sins."[9] The Puritan divine Thomas Hooker put it bluntly: Christians "have properly now no sacrifice."[10]

The Protestant critique had as much to do with disgust as with doctrine. Ancient rituals of sacrifice, whether performed by Christians or pagans, were, in a word, too bloody. Animal sacrifice was nothing but a "pious cruelty" in the

[8] Jonathan Sheehan, "Altars of the Idols: Religion, Sacrifice, and the Early Modern Polity," *Journal of the History of Ideas* 67 (October 2006): 649–74 (quotation on 652–53).

[9] A speech of an Indian minister, Nishoken, quoted in Cotton Mather, *Magnalia Christi Americana, or, The Ecclesiastical History of New-England from its first planting in the Year 1620 unto the year of our Lord 1698* (Boston, 1702), 570. Among the orthodox, it was a sign of religious lunacy to attempt to re-create the sacrifice of Isaac; see Thomas Hutchinson's account of one deluded Quaker in Massachusetts who attempted to "sacrifice his son in imitation of Abraham" but was "happily prevented" by the townspeople. Hutchinson, *The History of the Colony and Province of Massachusetts-Bay* (Cambridge, Mass.: Harvard University Press, 1936; orig. pub. 1764–67), 174. John Cotton took a much harsher view of a similar case in Ireland, in which a man "burnt his owne sonne in the fire, in the imitation of Abraham, and called in his Neighbours to rejoyce in beholding the power of his faith." The man, he wrote approvingly, was executed for "that unnaturall barbarous cruelty." Cotton, *The Bloudy Tenent, washed and made white in the bloud of the Lambe* (London, 1647), 22.

[10] Quoted in Debora K. Shuger, *The Renaissance Bible: Scholarship, Sacrifice, and Subjectivity* (Berkeley: University of California Press, 1994), 76.

words of the poet John Suckling, and he praised the Reformation for dispelling the barbaric notion that God would "be pleased with the bloud of beasts, or delighted with the steam of fat." (Only "Mahometans" were as advanced as Protestants in this regard.)[11] Blood is everywhere in medieval and Reformation-era discussions of sacrifice, including the sacrifice of Christ. For all its wonderful curative and regenerative properties, blood always signaled death as well as life, suffering as well as compassion. Caroline Walker Bynum's most recent work on blood devotions in late medieval Christendom shows us just how potent a symbol, and a substance, blood was—and how vital to the lived religion of the time as well as to the most rarefied theological debates. Drinking the blood of Christ, bathing in the blood shed by his side wound, sprinkling blood on material objects and living things to sanctify them, washing one's hands in blood before undertaking a sacred task—late medieval men and women were enormously inventive when it came to imagining and summoning up the quasi-magical powers of blood (especially the blood of Christ) in their devotions.[12] So much "blood frenzy" (in Bynum's phrase) created a backlash by the sixteenth century, and an almost visceral disgust at the excesses of lay devotions helps explain the iconoclastic fervor of a Reformation that sought to replace emotional frenzy with methodical deliberation, ecstatic and somatic forms of worship with the cooler disciplines of reading and writing.

Blood revulsion helps explain another favorite target of the Reformers: the Catholic notion of the "real presence" of the body and blood of Christ in the Lord's Supper. The eucharistic wars of the sixteenth and seventeenth centuries are a favorite subject of Reformation historians, and we have learned to parse with some precision the range of views on the Protestant side, from Luther's notion of sacramental union and Beza's idea of "substantive presence" to Zwingli's and Calvin's more radical rejection of the "real presence" altogether.[13] But we cannot comprehend these debates over the presence (or absence) of Christ in the communion wafer and wine without first under-

[11] Ibid.

[12] Caroline Walker Bynum, "The Blood of Christ in the Later Middle Ages," *Church History* 71 (December 2002): 685–714, and *Wonderful Blood*, passim.

[13] Lee Palmer Wandel, *The Eucharist in the Reformation: Incarnation and Liturgy* (New York: Cambridge University Press, 2006); Christopher Elwood, *The Body Broken: The Calvinist Doctrine of the Eucharist and the Symbolization of Power in Sixteenth-Century France* (New York: Oxford University Press, 1999); Francis Clark, *Eucharistic Sacrifice and the Reformation* (New York: Oxford University Press, 1967). For a succinct overview of these sacramental debates among Reformers, see E. Brooks Holifield, *The Covenant Sealed: The Development of Puritan Sacramental Theology in Old and New England, 1570–1720* (New Haven, Conn.: Yale University Press, 1974), chapter 1.

standing the broader sacrificial economy that linked Christ's birth and death with the sacramental culture of medieval Christianity. The sacraments of baptism and the Lord's Supper were instituted by the church fathers as palpable reminders if not actual re-creations of the incarnation of God in human form, and the medium of signification was the very body of Christ himself. When Christians were baptized into the church, they were washed in the blood of Christ; when they communed at the altar, they ate his flesh and drank his blood. Both sacraments were thus ritualized reenactments of the sacrifice of Christ ("he does on the altar what he did on the Cross").[14] And as such, the Protestant reformulation of the notion of sacrifice itself entailed a wholesale rethinking of the meaning and role of the sacraments. Thus the redesignation of the *altar* (a place where sacrifices are performed) as a *communion table* (a place where the family of God breaks bread together) in the Reformed church. Protestant treatises on the Lord's Supper referred to it most often as a "banquet"—"a spiritual banquet," a "holy banquet," a "heavenly banquet," or, in the satirical title of one early seventeenth-century play, "the Bloody Banquet."[15] Thomas Cramner spelled out the logic in 1547: "The use of an altar is to make a sacrifice upon it: the use of a table is to serve for men to eat upon. Now when we come to the Lord's board, what do we come for? To sacrifice Christ again, and to crucify him again, or to feed upon him that was only once crucified and offered up for us?"[16] The singularity and sufficiency of Christ's sacrificial death meant that it could not be repeated—even in the act of communion. Moreover, the bread consumed at the communion table should be "common bread"—"intended solely to feed the stomach" (Calvin's words)—to drive home the message that this was not expiation but commemoration. The fellows at Emmanuel College in Cambridge, the heart of the radical Reformation in England, pointedly took the sacrament while "sitting in a common way at a common eating table," wearing everyday clothes rather than vestments.[17]

[14] Alger of Liege, *De Sacramentis*, quoted in Bynum, *Wonderful Blood*, 215.

[15] Gary Taylor, "Gender, Hunger, and Horror: The History and Significance of 'The Bloody Banquet,'" *Journal of Early Modern Cultural Studies* 1.1 (Spring–Summer 2001): 1–45.

[16] Regina M. Schwartz, "Real Hunger: Milton's Version of the Eucharist," *Religion and Literature* 31 (Autumn 1999): 1–17 (quotation on 5).

[17] Ann Kibbey, *The Interpretation of Material Shapes in Puritanism: A Case Study of Rhetoric, Prejudice, and Violence* (New York: Cambridge University Press, 1986), 50. Martha Finch describes similar communion practices in colonial Plymouth, where the saints sat at or stood around a table covered with a plain white linen cloth rather than kneel at an altar. Finch, *Dissenting Bodies: Corporealities in Early New England* (New York: Columbia University Press, 2010), 159–60.

Reconfiguring the communion altar as a table solved one theological problem (the role of sacrifice after the death of Christ) but left unresolved another: what, exactly, did it mean to "feed upon" the body of Christ? What kind of a "meal" were Christians supposed to make of the wafer and wine consumed at the Lord's Supper? After all, a favorite rhetorical move among Reformers was to compare the Catholic notion of transubstantiation to ritual cannibalism ("papal anthropophagy," in John Milton's phrase).[18] Reformers made a meal, so to speak, of the polemical possibilities offered by the grotesque prospect of eating God: for Nicholas Ridley, the doctrine of the "real presence" was akin to "that beastly kind of cruelty of the 'Anthropophagi,' that is, devourers of man's flesh." Zwingli was even more direct. "I have now refuted, I hope, this senseless notion about bodily flesh," he wrote in his *Commentary on True and False Religion*. "In doing that my own object was to prove that to teach that the bodily flesh and sensible flesh of Christ is eaten when we give thanks to God is not only impious but also foolish and monstrous, unless perhaps one is living among the Anthropophagi."[19] The Church of England declared it "repugnant" to imagine that communicants "do carnally and visibly press with their teeth" the actual "bodily presence . . . of Christ's flesh and blood in the sacrament of the Lord's Supper."[20] True believers, Calvin said, knew the difference between "eating sacramentally and eating really."[21] At its most vulgar, Protestant depictions of the absurdity of eating God reached scatological proportions. In one of his more graphic passages, Milton imagines the path of the host through the body's digestive tract: ingesting the body of Christ in communion "drags it back to earth . . . to be broken once more and crushed and

[18] Maggie Kilgour, *From Communion to Cannibalism: An Anatomy of Metaphors of Incorporation* (Princeton, N.J.: Princeton University Press, 1990); Piero Camporesi, "The Consecrated Host: A Wondrous Excess," in *Fragments for a History of the Human Body*, vol. 1, ed. Michael Feher, Ramona Naddaff, and Nadia Tazi (New York: Zone, 1989).

[19] Quoted in James C. Nohrnberg, *The Analogy of "The Faerie Queene"* (Princeton, N.J.: Princeton University Press, 1976), 712.

[20] Taylor, "Gender, Hunger, and Horror," 32. Anglicans in the English colonies faithfully followed the lead of their mother church: the opening oath recorded in the vestry minutes of Christ Church in South Carolina, 1708, declares, "We underwritten doe Sollemnly and Sincerely in the presence of God Profess, Testifie and Declare that we doe believe yt in the Sacrement of the Lords Supper there is not any Transubstantiation of ye Elements of Bread and Wine into the Bodey and Blood of Christ." Quoted in Louis P. Nelson, *The Beauty of Holiness: Anglicanism & Architecture in Colonial South Carolina* (Chapel Hill: University of North Carolina Press, 2008), 180.

[21] John Calvin, *The Institutes of Christian Religion*, trans. Henry Beveridge (Edinburgh, 1845), XVII:34, II:591, quoted in Sheehan, "Altars of the Idols," 653.

ground, even by the fangs of brutes. Then, when it has been driven through all the stomach's filthy channels, it shoots out—one shudders even to mention it—into the latrine."[22] French Protestants were especially fond of scatological metaphors. Agrippa d'Aubigné's "Against the Real Presence," an "outrageous" but by no means atypical specimen, belongs to the genre of religious satire that likened Catholics to *théochèzes*, or "God-shitters": "After he has lunched on his God on Sunday, / You should worship his turd on Monday."[23]

But the polemics of Protestant writings on the Eucharist obscure a deeper ambivalence toward the intractable problem of how to come to terms with Christ's humanity—his flesh-and-bloodness. At the end of the day, there remains the irrefutable fact of Christ's life and death. If, as Calvin wrote, "by his blood we were cleansed," how did this transaction work precisely?[24] Luther, in particular, insisted that Christ's "true natural flesh" was what connected the incarnation to communion in the first place and thus could not be discarded so easily. "Without the body and blood of Christ, the new testament would not be there," he argued. "I would like to hear exactly why Christ's flesh is of no avail when it is physically eaten, and not also when it is physically conceived and . . . [when] hanging upon the Cross."[25] The structuring metaphor of Christianity—word made into flesh—worked only when both elements, language and body, were present in at least some form. Reformers divided over the *form* that the physical presence of Christ would take in the sacraments, not the sacramental necessity of his presence. To quote Jonathan Sheehan, reformers did not *want* to—*could* not—"leave the sacrificial flesh entirely behind."[26] Even radical Reformers who recoiled at the notion of physically savoring the flesh and blood of Christ in the Lord's Supper had no trouble *imagining* the sight, taste, and smell in graphic language that often

[22] Kilgour, *Communion to Cannibalism*, 84.

[23] George Hoffman, "Anatomy of the Mass: Montaigne's 'Cannibals,'" *Proceedings of the Modern Language Association* 117 (March 2002): 207–21 (quotation on 215).

[24] Jonathan Sheehan, "Sacrifice Before the Secular," *Representations* 105 (Winter 2009): 12–36.

[25] Martin Luther, *Confession Concerning Christ's Supper*, in *Luther's Works*, vol. 37, ed. Robert H. Fischer (Philadelphia: Fortress Press, 1955), 338; Kyle Pasewark, "The Body in Ecstasy: Love, Difference, and the Social Organism in Luther's Theory of the Lord's Supper," *Journal of Religion* 77 (October 1997): 511–40 (quotation on 531).

[26] Sheehan, "Altars of the Idols," 654. For a nuanced reading of the ambivalence toward the "real presence" in the poetry of another English metaphysical poet, George Herbert, see Robert Whalen, "George Herbert's Sacramental Puritanism," *Renaissance Quarterly* 54 (Winter 2001): 1273–1307.

bordered on the grotesque. When "thou seest the Bread broken and the Wine poured forth," wrote the English divine Richard Sibbes, "this should stirre thee up to bee in the same estate . . . as if thou sawest him sweate water and bloud."[27]

Visualization was not an unintended by-product of reformed sacramentalism but in fact key to Protestant conceptions of the Lord's Supper, a way of preserving something of the corporeality of Christ in the sacrament without slipping into the error of transubstantiation. "When thou seest the Bread broken, and the Wine powred forth," William Premble advised, "thinke on Christ torn and rent in his precious body."[28] Samuel Willard's *Sacramental Meditations* dwelled at some length on the concrete analogies between bread/flesh and wine/blood as he urged his parishioners to contemplate the "meal" they were about to consume: "Bread is not made without Grinding of the grain to dust, and being parched with Water and Fire; and Christ became Food for Souls to live on, by being bruised, for our Sins and scorched in the Fire of God's wrath, and so he is made fit for us to feed upon." (Willard beat a hasty retreat to a more orthodox position after spooling out this fanciful simile: "I expect [Christ] not to be here corporeally present by an impossible Transmutation," he clarified, but by a "Spiritual Taste" and "Spiritual Digestion" only.)[29] Calvin was well aware that the discipline of visualizing the crucified Christ in the bread might mistakenly lead believers to "dream" that the body of Christ is "put there to be touched by the hands, to be chewed by the teeth, and to be swallowed by the mouth."[30] By the end of the seventeenth century, some Puritans were becoming concerned that the emphasis on visioning the broken body of Christ during communion was leading to idolatry, the "worshipping of imaginations," as one preacher put it.[31] The tendency of words to literalize themselves—to become the thing they express—was understood by Protestants to be a prime danger of their commitment to a

[27] Arnold Hunt, "The Lord's Supper in Early Modern England," *Past & Present* 161 (November 1998): 39–83 (quotation on 60).

[28] Taylor, "Gender, Hunger, and Horror," 32. On Puritan theories of visualization, see Theodore Dwight Bozeman, *To Live Ancient Lives: The Primitivist Dimension in Puritanism* (Chapel Hill: University of North Carolina Press, 1988); Paul Corby Finney, ed., *Seeing Beyond the Word: Visual Arts and the Calvinist Tradition* (Grand Rapids, Mich.: Eerdmans, 1999); and David Morgan, *Visual Piety: A History and Theory of Popular Religious Images* (Berkeley: University of California Press, 1998).

[29] Samuel Willard, *Some Brief Sacramental Meditations, Preparatory for Communion at the Great Ordinance of the Supper* (Boston, 1711), 12–13, 176–177.

[30] Taylor, "Gender, Hunger, and Horror," 32.

[31] Cited in Holifield, *Covenant Sealed*, 55.

linguistic rather than material mode of communication with the divine, one that required strict vigilance and constant verbal discipline.[32]

No one was more adept at this kind of metaphorical exercise than the Puritan poet and minister Edward Taylor, whose eucharistic meditations (some two hundred in all, composed between 1682 and 1725) have long captivated literary and religious scholars for their lurid depictions of the body and blood of Christ. And no one better illustrates the theological dangers that lurk behind such a promiscuous approach to figuration. Doctrinally, there is simply "no excuse" for Taylor's almost primitive version of sacramentarianism.[33] The constant refrain of altars wreathed in "spicy" fragrance and dripping in "sweet" blood conjures up forbidden images of pagan sacrifices, with their incense and burnt offerings. More heretically, readers are invited to partake in a cannibalistic feast at Taylor's altar in language that would make a Catholic blush.

> Lord thine Altar make mee,
> Then Sanctify thine Altar with thy blood:
> I'll offer on 't my heart to thee. . . .

> Lord, make my Flesh thy Golden Quill wherethrough
> I vitall Spirits from thy blood may suck;
> Make faith my Grinders, thy Choice Flesh to chew. (Med. 82)

The polymorphism of Taylor's imagery is a striking example of the Protestant strategy of demystification through domestication. "I began to see, nay feel, God in fire, meat, [in] every providence," Taylor's fellow divine Thomas Shepard confided to his journal.[34] If God can be found anywhere, why not in the crude objects of everyday life—quills, beer, scrub brushes, dripping pans, spinning wheels? But surrounding these very ordinary objects was an extraordinary profusion of sensory associations that seems to belie the "plain style" Protestants strove to achieve in their devotional texts. There is nothing plain about Taylor's meditations, which are every bit as baroque as those of his fellow

[32] For an analysis of the problem of literalization in Puritan semiotics, see Anne Myles, "Arguments in Milk, Arguments in Blood: Roger Williams, Persecution, and the Discourse of the Witness," *Modern Philology* 91 (November 1993): 133–60.

[33] Herbert Blau, "Heaven's Sugar Cake: Theology and Imagery in the Poetry of Edward Taylor," *New England Quarterly* 26 (September 1953): 337–60 (quotation on 338).

[34] *God's Plot: Puritan Spirituality in Thomas Shepard's Cambridge*, rev. ed., ed. Michael McGiffert (Amherst: University of Massachusetts Press, 1994), 109.

metaphysical poet but confessional rival Richard Crashaw. Where Crashaw saw "Purple Rivers" of Christ's blood gushing from his wounds, Taylor saw a "Springtide Flood" of "Covenantall blood" carrying humanity down a river of sin.[35] The Puritan Taylor and the Catholic Crashaw shared a common fascination with the broken and bleeding body of Christ in their sacramental texts, and to read them side by side is to suspect (wrongly, but not unreasonably) that the Protestant assault on the "real presence" was a theological sideshow only.

Such a suspicion would only be strengthened if one were to peruse the many devotional guides for Christians preparing to receive the Lord's Supper written by utterly orthodox ministers like Boston's Cotton Mather. Since Mather's writings on New England's Indians wars will feature so prominently in the discussion to come, it is worth spending a moment with his *Monitor for Communicants*, written in 1714 and a perennial "steady seller" thereafter. As did other Protestant ministers, Mather advocated visualizing the bread and wine in material terms. "You must behold a Sacrificed Saviour; the Lamb of God!" he began. "When you see the Bread, your Thoughts must be on that Body which God prepared for your Saviour, therein to make himself a Sacrifice and an Offering. When you see the Wine, your Thoughts must be on that Blood of the Son of God, which cleanses from all Sin." So far, so good—there is nothing here to raise any theological hackles. But Mather soon veered into more sensual visions of Christ's broken and bleeding body as he invited communicants to savor the "Feast of fat Things, Full of Marrow" that was on offer at the Lord's Supper. Quoting from a sacramental meditation by his fellow divine John Williams (who, we might note, spent several months in Indian captivity during the 1690s), Mather exclaimed, "O Canst thou see Christ's Blood running & not desire to be bathed in it! Now the cleansing & healing Streams run on both Sides of the Table; . . . O let that Blood which gushed from thy Heart and Side but drop on my Soul, and it will cleanse me from all Sin." Blood is not merely a symbolic presence in the sacramental wine for Mather and Williams but—as was true of their compatriot Taylor—has a visceral force, streaming and gushing down the communion table.[36] A prayer pasted in the commonplace book of a Carolina Anglican in the 1730s shows just how far this sacramental language had penetrated the devotional lives of the laity as well as the clergy: "O Lord in a Bath of this Water warmed in the Blood flowing from a sinners Bleeding heart and Saviour's Bloody side, shall

[35] Kathleen Blake, "Edward Taylor's Protestant Poetic: Nontransubstantiating Metaphor," *American Literature* 42 (March 1971): 1–24 (quotation on 20).
[36] Cotton Mather, *A Monitor for Communicants* (Boston, 1750; orig. pub. 1714), 6, 12–13, 20.

I not be clean if I wash. Pierce my Heart," pleaded Alexander Keith, "so that I
may wash and be clean."[37]

What are we to make of this strain of sensual, even erotic, language in
Protestant imaginings of the body and blood of Christ? Clearly by the seventeenth century Protestants had developed their own "sacramental mode of
speaking" even if they did not share in the medieval church's "sacramental
principle" that dissolved the barrier between flesh and spirit entirely.[38] "Christ
crucified [must] be preached in a Crucified Phrase," as the Puritan William
Ames explained.[39] A creative and flexible use of metaphor was part of this
discursive mode; however suspicious they remained of the power of metaphor to transgress theological and ontological boundaries, Protestants knew
that metaphor was *not* metamorphosis: it could not literally turn host and
wine into flesh and blood. Taylor was on safe ground here, despite the raw-
ness of his imagery. As he wrote in another sacramental meditation, "Bread is
still bread, Wine still is wine for sure. . . . Your touch, Tast[e], Sight say true.
The Pope's a whore. / Can Bread and Wine by words be Carnifide?" (Med.
108). But what deeper emotional or spiritual longings lay behind such poetic
forays into dangerous theological terrain? Why flirt with crypto-catholic images of sucking blood and chewing flesh when safer metaphors were at hand?
Regina Schwartz identifies a "persistent nostalgia" for the material presence
of Christ in Protestant poetics that speaks, in her words, to an unresolved
"hunger" for a more real, palpable connection to God.[40] "Hunger" is an apt
word, I think, because it evokes both need and desire. We hunger for things
we desperately want, but we also experience hunger as a necessary bodily
function. The work of Sheehan and Shuger helps us see the continued *necessity* of sacrificial hermeneutics in Protestant theology while the literary analyses of Protestant poetry reveal the deep, unsatisfied emotional and spiritual

---

[37] "A Prayer before coming to the Holy Communion," Alexander Keith Commonplace
Book, in Nelson, *The Beauty of Holiness*, 181.
[38] Blake, "Edward Taylor's Protestant Poetic." Malcolm Ross first distinguished the Catholic "sacramental principle" from Protestant views in *Poetry and Dogma: The Transfiguration
of Eucharistic Symbols in Seventeenth-Century English Poetry* (New Brunswick, N.J.: Rutgers
University Press, 1954). See also Donald Stanford, "Edward Taylor and the Lord's Supper,"
American Literature 27 (May 1955): 172–78. For an inspired reading of sacrificial theology in a
quite different Protestant context, see Donald Mathews, "The Southern Rite of Human Sacrifice," which explores the blood theology of lynching in the American South; *Journal of Southern Religion* 3 (2000), http://jsr.fsu.edu/mathews.htm.
[39] Michael Clark, "'The Crucified Phrase': Sign and Desire in Puritan Semiology," *Early
American Literature* 13 (Winter 1978/79): 278–93 (quotation on 291).
[40] Schwartz, "Real Hunger."

desire for a more embodied relationship with God that expressed itself in ecstatic contemplation of the Eucharist.

This detour through the lush undergrowth of Protestant sacramental
writing underscores the fundamental ambivalence at the heart of the Reformation's assault on the notion of blood sacrifice. In the conventional telling,
the apogee of Protestant antisacrificial theorizing is Hugo Grotius's *De Satisfactione Christi*, which appeared in 1617. Grotius, the great Dutch jurist who is
credited with elaborating the first principles of international law, penned his
seminal work to refute the Socinian notion that the crucifixion was a sign of
God's benevolence only. Christ did atone for man's sins at Calvary, Grotius
argued, but not as fulfillment of any sacrificial bargain. More than the specific
argument, however (which after all affirmed the essentially sacrificial nature
of the death of Christ), the impact of *De Satisfactione Christi* lay in its legalistic treatment of the subject. By the time of his writing, Reformed Christians
had supposedly moved so far beyond the sacrificial culture of the medieval
church that the question of blood sacrifice could be considered dispassion-
ately, as an archaic remnant of a vanished world rather than a false doctrine
to be combatted or a living practice to be repulsed.

Grotius's work displayed in its very organizational structure the historical
and theoretical path Reformers believed—and wanted others to believe—
they had traveled, albeit in reverse order: from dry legalistic discussions of
the problem of the atonement in Christian doctrine, Grotius proceeded to
ever-more fantastic and terrifying descriptions of pagan human sacrifice, including some that had occurred in his own day. Near the end of this chronicle of horrors is his account of the 1574 Spanish blockade of Leiden during the
Dutch war for independence, when the Calvinist burgomaster Pieter Van der
Werff offered himself, Christ-like, as "an edible sacrifice" to end the siege: in
Grotius's words, Van der Werff pleaded with the Spanish troops, "Put your
teeth into my body ... and put an end to your hunger. I offer you ... my
throat and my limbs." Van der Werff's heroic if cannibalistic gesture "verges
on the barbaric and repulsive," as Shuger notes, and sounds a jarring note to
scholars accustomed to reading angry Protestant denunciations of "papal
anthropophagy."[41]

It is precisely in this disjuncture that we can glimpse the enduring power of
sacramental longings for real flesh and blood in the post-Reformation world. It
is clear that Grotius himself wants to put some distance between his version of

---

[41] Shuger, *The Renaissance Bible*, 87.

Protestant sacramental culture and that of Van der Werff, whose ill-timed offer of himself as an "edible sacrifice" was spurned (thus reinforcing the message that blood sacrifices ended with Christ). The point of the anecdote was not to applaud the messianic gesture of the mayor but to evoke the "immense gulf separating [Christians] from the dripping altars and cries of burning children only half drowned out by cymbals and drums" of the pagan era.[42]

But what, we may ask, would Protestants do when faced once again with sacrificial pyres and the "cries of burning children"? Because that is precisely what happened in the New World as Europeans came face-to-face with human sacrifice, real, imagined, and vicarious. And this time it was not only the pagan "other"—the heathen and barbaric "salvages" of North and South America—who practiced blood sacrifice but Protestants themselves. To quote Benjamin Tompson, the Puritan poet who wrote his New England epic while surveying (with satisfaction) the charred remains left behind by one of the deadliest Indian wars in colonial history,

> Here might be heard an hideous Indian cry,
> Of wounded ones who in the wigwams fry.
> Had we been cannibals here might we feast.[43]

"Cannibals Here": Sacrifice in the New World, or, The Return of the Repressed

The problem of blood sacrifice, which as we have seen animated debates over a wide range of pagan and Christian practices from animal sacrifice to the crucifixion to the sacraments of baptism and the Lord's Supper, became associated in the New World with one practice in particular: that of anthropophagy, or cannibalism. From the earliest days of overseas exploration and conquest of the Americas, the figure of the cannibal was central to Europeans' visioning of the New World and its native inhabitants. In every imperial language and every colonial genre, cannibals appear as mimetic figures in which Europeans confronted the worst features of themselves and their civi-

---

[42] Ibid., 85.

[43] Benjamin Tompson, *New Englands Crisis, or, A Brief Narrative of New-England's Lamentable Estate at Present* (Boston, 1676), reprinted in *So Dreadfull a Judgment: Puritan Responses to King Philip's War, 1676–1677*, ed. Richard Slotkin and James K. Folsom (Middletown, Conn.: Wesleyan University Press, 1978), 224.

lization.[44] The cannibal was a primitive other, an ethnographic curiosity, an agent of the devil, a rhetorical scapegoat—but first and foremost, a mirror. To understand the fascination and horror evoked by the cannibal, we have to understand the ongoing debates over sacrifice, sacraments, and satisfaction that were consuming Europeans at home.

The earliest accounts of New World cannibalism came from Spanish conquistadores, who encountered powerful Indian empires to rival their own when they stepped foot on American soil. From Columbus's first skirmishes with the Caribs on Hispaniola to Cortés's epic battles with the Aztecs in colonial Mexico, the violent encounter of the Old and the New Worlds was narrated in part through the metaphor and practice of blood sacrifice (Figure 1) At first, cannibalism was understood more through the trope of hunger than of vengeance, as a (debased) version of the carnivorous habits of Europeans accustomed to eating a steady diet of roasted meats. As Frank Lestringant notes, writers "projected European culinary habits onto the American Cannibal: because meat was regularly salted at home, their morbid imaginations produced lumps of salted human flesh hanging from the beams of cannibal huts; the familiar spit roast engendered the roasting of human victims over a small fire."[45] Images of human bodies roasting on spits like sheep or pigs appear as early as 1544 but became most vividly fixed in the European imagination with the publication of the Dominican Bartolomé de Las Casas's *Short Account of the Destruction of the Indies,* first published in 1552 and translated into English as early as 1583. Las Casas was horrified by the savage treatment of the natives by his fellow Spaniards and wrote a grisly account of the destruction, enslavement, and dismemberment of Indian bodies (famously illustrated by Theodore de Bry in a series of vivid copper plates that accompanied the 1598 version of the text) that became a template for Protestant depictions of Catholic cruelty in the New World. A 1656 English translation appeared as *The Tears of the Indians* and included four of the more graphic De Bry illustrations; this was the version that Anglo-American Protestants were most familiar with and used as a touchstone for their own polemical retellings of the black legend.

[44] Stephen Greenblatt finds cannibalism to be "a powerful cultural fantasy operative in virtually all early encounters." *Marvelous Possessions: The Wonder of the New World* (Chicago: University of Chicago Press, 1991), 111.

[45] Frank Lestringant, *Cannibals: The Discovery and Representation of the Cannibal from Columbus to Jules Verne,* trans. Rosemary Morris (Cambridge: Polity Press, 1997), 24; see also Marvin Harris, *Cannibals and Kings: The Origins of Culture* (New York: Random House, 1977).

Figure 1. Aztec human sacrifice depicted in the Codex Magliabechiano,
mid-sixteenth century.

Las Casas's signature move was to depict the Spanish as *more* savage, *more*
cruel, than the Indians they so inhumanly butchered. In both cases, savagery
took the form of killing and then ritually consuming (in the case of the pagan
Indians) or, worse, chopping up human bodies for no ritual purpose at all (in
the case of the Spanish).[46] The "butcher shop" that was Spanish America was a
nightmarish image, composed by layering newer fantasies of the "cannibal
barbecue" on top of older European traditions of blood-sport and flesh-eating.
Pictures of dismembered Indian bodies hanging over a fire became one of the
most widely disseminated visual totems of colonial savagery, whether of native or European origin (Figure 2).[47] "I once saw Four or Five of their most

---

[46] Andrew Warnes analyzes the illustrations of De Bry in the context of the myth of the
"cannibal barbecue" in *Savage Barbecue: Race, Culture, and the Invention of America's First
Food* (Athens: University of Georgia Press, 2008), 35–49.

[47] E. Shaskan Bumas, "The Cannibal Butcher Shop: Protestant Uses of Las Casas's *Brevisima Relación* in Europe and the American Colonies," *Early American Literature* 35 (2000):
107–36.

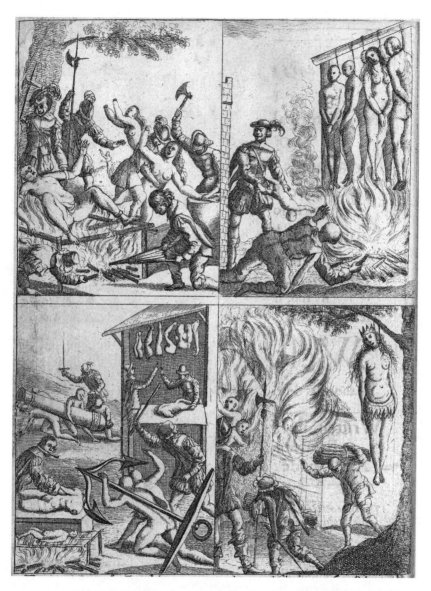

Figure 2. The New World as a human "butcher shop." Bartolomé de Las Casas, "Brevisima relación de la destrucción de las Indias" (1552).

Powerful Lords laid on these Gridirons, and thereon roasted, and not far off, Two or Three more over-spread with the same Commodity, Men's Flesh." The "Sacrilegious Merchandize" of human flesh became the primary means of transculturation in Las Casas's rendering of Spanish-Indian exchange as the ritual (if barbaric) feasts of Indian sacrifice became carnivorous free-for-alls with butchered bodies strewn across the landscape. One Spanish commander "kept a Shambles of Man's Flesh in his Army, [and] suffered Children to be kill'd and roasted before his Face." As they descended into savagery, the Spanish began to violate the most basic taboos against the desecration of the human body, even allowing their dogs ("Canibal Curs") to feast on human flesh.[48] Such vicarious cannibalism was beyond comprehension within a ritual framework. It was savagery unbound by any religious or cultural norms.

Within a generation of Columbus's "discovery" of Hispaniola, the cannibal had taken on a more specifically sacrilegious aspect. Cannibalism became increasingly associated with idolatry, with strange temples and false gods, even when encountered in ostensibly secular contexts such as warfare and the taking of captives. Images of altars dripping with blood and ringed by the smoke of charred remains (both animal and human) now accompanied the depictions of human butcher shops. Consider the following detailed account by Hernán Cortés from his *Letters from Mexico* (1520s):

> Each day before beginning any sort of work they burn incense in their temples and sometimes sacrifice their own persons, some cutting their tongues, others their ears, while there are some who stab their bodies with knives. All the blood which flows from them they offer to those idols, sprinkling it in all parts of the temple, or sometimes throwing it into the air or performing many other ceremonies, so that nothing is begun without sacrifice having first been made. They have a most horrid and abominable custom which truly ought to be punished and which until now we have seen in no other part, and that is that, whenever they wish to ask something of their idols, in order that their plan may find more acceptance, they take many girls and boys and even adults, and in the presence of the idols they open their chests while they are still alive and take out their hearts and entrails and burn them before the idols, offering the smoke as sacrifice. Some of us

---

[48] Bartolomé de Las Casas, *Popery Truly Display'd in its Bloudy Colours* (London, 1699), 7, 36, 42, 44, 79.

have seen this, and they say it is the most terrible and frightful thing they have ever witnessed.[49]

Indians were not the only ones to be sacrificed on these bloody altars. In New France, the Jesuits who were the foot soldiers of the Catholic Reformation found themselves the victim of Indian blood sacrifice—an ordeal they positively welcomed as an opportunity to experience for themselves the martyrdom of the first church fathers. The death of Father Jean de Brébeuf in 1649 became an iconic moment in narratives of Christological suffering and death in the mission field of the New World: "They told one another that the flesh of the Frenchmen must be good, and they cut great strips of it from one or the other, and ate them." Like Jesus on the cross, Brébeuf's side was pierced and "all the Barbarians came thronging to drink of it." Finally, "his heart was torn out and promptly eaten."[50]

Reading accounts like this against the discursive backdrop of Reformation-era debates over the nature of sacrifice and the assault on blood sacrifice in particular as atavistic and unchristian peels away the (self-serving) illusion that Europeans were wrestling with something truly alien and unprecedented when they tried to make sense of Indian cannibalism. Scholars have too often been misled by the tone of wonder in which these New World encounters were narrated into accepting at face value the "otherness" of human sacrifice for the first European observers. There is no question that Europeans were horrified at what they saw, but were these really practices "which until now we have seen in no other part" of the world? To Cortés, Aztec sacrifice is "horrid and abominable," "terrible and frightful," but not necessarily unintelligible for a Spanish soldier who had seen service in Europe's own bloody wars of religion as well as in Spain's New World empire. Cortés's fellow conquistador Bernal Diaz left another vivid account of human sacrifice that emphasizes the novelty more than the horror of the act: upon the walls of the Aztec temple was "a sort of Altar covered with clotted blood. On the other side of the Idols were symbols like crosses, and all were coloured. At all this we stood wondering, as they were things never seen or heard of before." Diaz was being disingenuous. Far from representing an "absolute difference

[49] Hernán Cortés, *Letters from Mexico*, trans. and ed. Anthony Pagden (New Haven, Conn.: Yale University Press, 1986), 35.

[50] Francis Parkman, *The Jesuits in North America in the Seventeenth Century* (Boston: Little, Brown, 1888), 389–91. See also Emma Anderson, *The Death and Afterlife of the North American Martyrs* (Cambridge, Mass.: Harvard University Press, 2013).

between [European] culture and the culture of the other," as Stephen Greenblatt proposed, native anthropophagy bore a profoundly uncomfortable resemblance to certain domestic practices with which Europeans were
intimately familiar: the butchering and dressing of animals, the roasting of
flesh for ceremonial feasting, and, most important for our purposes, sacramental practices surrounding baptism and the Eucharist.[51]

The cannibal's "monstrous appetite" was the defining feature of this fabu-
lous creature and, crucially, of human savagery more generally.[52] The publication of Michel de Montaigne's essay "On Cannibals" in 1580 signaled a new
phase in the European imagining of the cannibal: from a localized, exotic
figure of interest to a handful of overseas adventurers, the cannibal became a
universalized trope for all sorts of predatory practices—usury, judicial torture, slavery and the slave trade, the domination of masters over servants and
husbands over wives. New World cannibals (of whom, we should note, he
had no firsthand knowledge) were a product of nature and as such worthy of
moral consideration. Their practice of cooking and eating enemies defeated
in war was horrific, he acknowledged, but no more so than Christians' habit
of "racking" criminals or, worse, preying upon their neighbors:

> I am not sorry that we should here take notice of the barbarous horror
> of so cruel an action, but that, seeing so clearly into their faults, we
> should be so blind to our own. I conceive there is more barbarity in
> eating a man alive, than when he is dead; in tearing a body limb from
> limb by racks and torments, that is yet in perfect sense; in roasting it
> by degrees; in causing it to be bitten and worried by dogs and swine
> (as we have not only read, but lately seen, not amongst inveterate and
> mortal enemies, but among neighbors and fellow-citizens, and, which
> is worse, under color of piety and religion), than to roast and eat him
> after he is dead.[53]

The universalization of the cannibal made it a handy polemical device, a convenient shorthand for predation and bloodlust whose invocation instantly

[51] Bernal Diaz del Castillo, *The True History of the Conquest of New Spain*, quoted in
Greenblatt, *Marvelous Possessions*, 131–32.

[52] Lestringant, *Cannibals*, 24.

[53] "On Cannibals," chapter 30 in *Essays of Michel de Montaigne*, trans. Charles Cotton, ed.
William Carew Hazlitt (New York, 1877), http://www.gutenberg.org/files/3600/3600-h/3600-
h.htm (accessed June 23, 2013).

put one's opponent beyond the civilized pale. After Montaigne, Europeans saw cannibals everywhere. Even at home.

The theological subtext of these accounts of New World cannibalism and butchery is hardly a recent discovery; for readers then and now, the encounter with indigenous cannibalism following so closely on the heels of a heated polemical debate over the spiritual meaning of "eating" Christ's flesh and "drinking" his blood lent these narratives an unavoidable sacramental dimension. José de Acosta's 1590 account of Mexican human sacrifice described "idolaters" making "maize loaves mixed with the blood of the sacrifice" and eating them like Christians. Acosta even referred to these loaves as "hosts."[54] The cannibal ritual could also be compared to the sacrament of baptism, Lestringant points out; as in the "baptism of blood" that Christians celebrate as a rite of initiation into the mystical body of Christ, there is anointing with blood and the taking of new names when Indian warriors ritually consume a captive.[55] But the primary sacramental field of signification for cannibalism was the Eucharist.

One of the most important of these narratives of conquest, the Huguenot Jean de Léry's *History of a Voyage to the Land of Brazil* (1578), made the connection quite explicit—indeed made it the pivot upon which his account of how the civilized Europeans were, in the end, more savage than the pagan Indians turned.[56] Like his fellow Frenchman Montaigne, Léry understood cannibalism to be a capacious metaphor, encompassing both the literal digestion of human flesh and the figurative devouring of the poor by the rich. "One need not go beyond one's own country, nor as far as America, to see such monstrous and prodigious things," he wrote. A prime example was that of usury: "if you concede in all candor what our big usurers do, sucking blood and marrow, and eating everyone alive—widows, orphans, and other poor people, whose throat it would be better to cut once and for all, than to make them linger in misery—you will say that they are even more cruel than the savages I speak of. And that is why the prophet [Micah 3:3] says that such men flay the skin of God's people, eat their flesh, break their bones and chop them in pieces as for the pot."[57] From this analogy Léry moved swiftly, and

[54] José de Acosta, *The Natural and Moral History of the Indies*, trans. M. López-Morillas (Durham, N.C.: Duke University Press, 2002; orig. pub. Seville, 1590), 275.

[55] Lestringant, *Cannibals*, 65.

[56] Andrea Frisch, "In a Sacramental Mode: Jean de Léry's Calvinist Ethnography," *Representations* 77 (Winter 2002): 82–106.

[57] Jean de Léry, *History of a Voyage to the Land of Brazil*, trans. Janet Whatley (Berkeley: University of California Press, 1990), 132–33.

brutally, to his main point: that such figurative cannibalism was only a fore-shadowing of actual instances of anthropophagy in the context of religious war in his native land. His account is worth quoting in full.

> Furthermore, if it comes to the brutal action of *really* (as one says) chewing and devouring human flesh, have we not found people in these regions over here, even among those who bear the name of Christian, both in Italy and elsewhere, who, not content with having cruelly put to death their enemies, have been unable to slake their bloodthirst except by eating their livers and hearts? . . . And, without going further, what of France? . . . During the bloody tragedy that began in Paris on the twenty-fourth of August 1572, among other acts horrible to recount . . . the fat of human bodies (which, in ways more barbarous than those of the savages, were butchered at Lyon after being pulled out of the Saone)—was it not publicly sold to the highest bidder? The livers, hearts, and other parts of their bodies—were they not eaten by the furious murderers . . . ? Likewise, after the wretched murders of one Coeur de Roy, . . . did not those who committed this murder cut his heart to pieces, display it for sale to those who hated him, and, finally, after grilling it over coals—glutting their rage like mastifs—eat of it?[58]

Reports of cannibalism were an occasional feature of the European wars of religion (during the Duke of Alva's assault on the Netherlands, Spanish troops supposedly took to drinking the blood of their victims), and Léry was an eyewitness to two of the most infamous incidents of European anthro-pophagy, including the siege of Sancerre in 1573 and the St. Bartholomew Day's Massacre in Paris in 1572 that saw instances of cannibalism both des-perate and vengeful.[59] Moreover, his parenthetic jab at the notion of "*really* (as one says) chewing and devouring human flesh" is an unmistakable refer-ence to Protestant disavowals of the doctrine of the "real presence." Indeed, earlier in his narrative he lobbed a rhetorical grenade at his fellow missionar-ies and rivals Villegagnon and Cointe for flirting with transubstantiation de-spite their Protestant credentials (Villegagnon would later abjure and convert to Rome): they "wanted not only to eat the flesh of Jesus Christ grossly rather

[58] Ibid., 132.
[59] Robert O'Connell, *Of Arms and Men: A History of War, Weapons, and Aggression* (New York: Oxford University Press, 1989), chapter 5, "Harvest of Blood," 124–47.

than spiritually," he wrote in disgust, "but what is worse, like the savages named Ouetaca, of whom I have already spoken, they wanted to chew and swallow it raw."[60] As other scholars have noted, there are good and bad cannibals in Léry's account: good cannibals like the Tupinamba cook the flesh of their enemies; bad cannibals like the Ouetaca, and European Catholics, eat it raw.[61]

More than a century after Léry's voyage to Brazil, France was the scene once again of (Christian) human sacrifice as the revocation of the Edict of Nantes in 1695 unleashed a furious assault on the remaining Protestants who refused to abjure. The sufferings of the Huguenots preoccupied Europe's Protestant leaders and became a favorite topic of confessional polemics. To take one example—and I could provide many more—*A Faithful Account of the Renewed Persecution of the Churches of Lower Aquitaine in France* (1692) regaled the reader with horrific stories of Huguenot prisoners being sacrificed at the stake. The prisoners were first "chained to a Post, then there was a gentle Fire set under the Soles of their Feet, by which all the Callus of the Foot was shrivel'd up, till at last it fell off from the Bones; then Flambeaux were lighted and put out, and while they were hot, clapt to all the parts of their Bodies, that so they might be tortured all over." Finally, after days of such exquisite torments, "at last their Skin being quite consumed by the Fire, it reached their Vitals, and then a great Fire was kindled, into which they were thrown, and so their Bodies were burnt to Ashes, and their bones that were not wholly destroyed, were gathered and grounded to Powder, and then thrown into some River, or else into the Sea." Other victims were actually consumed. The dragoons "suck their very blood and marrow from them," and one poor girl was "found in a Cave, with her flesh sliced off from the Bones, and chopt as small as herbs to the Pot."[62]

The parallels with New World accounts of Indian blood sacrifice are startling, and in such gruesome accounts we can see how the rhetorical cycle has

[60] Léry, *Voyage*, 41.

[61] Claude Lévi-Strauss, *The Raw and the Cooked*, trans. John Weightman and Doreen Weightman (New York: Harper and Row, 1969).

[62] *A Faithful Account of the Renewed Persecution of the Churches of Lower Aquitaine in France in the Year 1692* (London, 1692), 14, 22–23. See also *The Bloudy Babylon, or, A Collection of some Particulars concerning the Persecution Raging in France against the Protestants, from the Peace of Reswick to the Martyrdom of the Reverend Monsieur Brousson, Inclusively* (London, 1698); and *The French King's Decree Against Protestants, Prohibiting them the Exercise of their Religion, &c To which is added, A Brief and True Account of the Cruel PERSECUTION and inhumane Oppressions of those of the Reformed Religion, to make them Abjure and Apostasize* (London, 1689).

come full circle. A revulsion against medieval notions of Christian sacrifice inspired Spanish and French critics of their respective empires' brutal campaigns against the Indians to draw connections between native customs and unreformed sacramental practices in the first stage of encounter. Later, and with considerable irony, the growing familiarity with Indian sacrificial customs led Europe's endangered Protestants to exploit the literature of conquest to demonize their Catholic opponents as bloodthirsty savages. No wonder scholars have been drawn to Freudian concepts like the "return of the repressed" to make sense of the European fascination with New World cannibalism. Like a "bloodthirsty doppelgänger" that "haunts" Christian Europe, the cannibal was "a recurring nightmare" from which explorers and conquistadores could not awaken.[63]

So far, all the accounts I have been analyzing come from Spanish and French sources; and indeed, the figure of the native cannibal is most fully developed in both an ethnographic and semiotic sense in these narratives. How far did the image of the cannibal penetrate the Anglo-American colonial imagination? We know that Las Casas's *Brief Account* was a perennial seller in Protestant lands after its translation into English in 1583, and a large chunk of Léry's *Voyage* was included in an English compendium of travel narratives, Samuel Purchas's 1625 collection *Hakluyt's Posthumous or Purchas His Pilgrimes*. And the reception of Montaigne's "On Cannibals" was truly international as it became one of the staples of the growing canon of Enlightenment treatises on the variety of human cultures. In the next section, I turn, finally, to the texts of Anglo-America to trace the presence of these theological debates over sacrifice, sacramental culture, and the trope of the cannibal in accounts of war and violence. While much of the violence was directed against Indians, it's crucial to note that this is not exclusively a cross-cultural or cross-ethnic story but one that encompassed other paradigmatic forms of colonial violence, including that directed against religious dissenters.

"Their Bloody Altar": Sacrifice in English America

The British were latecomers to the imperial game, and their first forays were parasitic on the technologies and knowledge developed by their European

---

[63] Lestringant, *Cannibals*, 137. See also his *Le Huguenot et Le Sauvage: L'Amérique et la controverse colonial en France, au temps des guerres de religion (1555–1589)* (Paris: Klincksieck, 1999).

competitors. Along with their Portuguese navigational tools and Dutch maps, British promoters of overseas colonization carried with them Spanish and French tales of savage peoples encountered and vanquished in the New World. Stories of human sacrifice and cannibalism were part and parcel of the intercultural baggage of all European explorers, and the English were no exception, even if real cannibals were scarce on the ground. Even in as remote and frozen a region as Arctic America, the English expected to find cannibals—and to their surprise, the native inhabitants seemed to have similar ideas about them.[64] There were no great Indian empires comparable to the Incas and the Aztec in North America when the first English adventurers set sail for what they hoped would be a quick and easy route to riches and fame, and the more powerful of the Indian chiefdoms (the Powhatan in the Southeast, the Narragansett and Abenaki in the Northeast) did not, as far as we know, practice anthropophagy on a regular basis (human sacrifice is another matter). This makes the persistence of the cannibal as a metaphor for bloodlust and predation in English narratives of discovery and conquest all the more remarkable.

So well-known were Spanish accounts of Mayan and Aztec sacrifice that they made their way into the journals and nightmares of English colonizers—often in the service of drawing a sharp contrast between the benevolent (Protestant) English and the cruel (Catholic) Spanish. Before the Puritans ever set foot in Plymouth, their leader, William Bradford, imagined in visceral detail cannibalistic tortures the "savage people" might inflict on vulnerable Christians: "flaying some alive with the shells of fishes, cutting off the members and joints of others by piecemeal and broiling on the coals, eat[ing] the collops of their flesh in their sight whilst they live, with other cruelties horrible to be related."[65] John Archdale, the Quaker who governed Carolina for a year in the turbulent initial decade of the colony's existence, included an account of human sacrifice in his *New Description of that Fertile and Pleasant Province of Carolina* (1707): "in Mexico, [there] was a Temple

---

[64] George Best's account of Martin Frobisher's journeys in the 1570s to the Arctic described the "ravennesse and bloudy disposition" of the Inuit, who relished "eating anye kinde of rawe flesh or carrion, howsoever stincking," and concluded (with no evidence) that "they had slaine and devoured oure men." The Inuit, Best was astonished to learn, "supposed us be like to be Canibales, or eaters of mans flesh." George Best, *A True Discourse of the late voyages of discouverie, for the finding of a passage to Cathay, by the Northweast, under the conduct of Martin Frobisher Generall* (London, 1578), 23–24.

[65] William Bradford, *History of Plymouth Plantation*, quoted in Alfred A. Cave, *The Pequot War* (Amherst: University of Massachusetts Press, 1996), 17.

dedicated to their chief Idol larger than Paul's [St. Paul's Cathedral], whose
Walls were two Inches thick bespread or beplasiter'd with Human Blood,
sacrificed to their Deities or Devils." As a member of a radical sect that had
experienced more than its share of barbarities as a persecuted minority,
Archdale was both accusatory and (more surprisingly) tolerant in his assess-
ment of the Spanish response. "And although I cannot excuse the Barbarity
and Cruelty of the Spaniards towards them," he continued, "yet as on God's
part it was justly brought upon them, who thereby gave them their own
Blood to drink, in lieu of what they had most barbarously shed of their
Neighbours. And indeed, Providence seemed wholly to design this Bloody
Work for the Spanish Nation, and not for the English, who in their Natures
are not so Cruel as the other." God had other plans for the natives of English
America: plague and intertribal war had providentially "thinned" the Indian
population "so that the English, in comparison to the Spaniard, have but
little Indian Blood to answer for."[66] Note the lightning-quick move from cultural aversion to theological implication to confessional complacency in this
one passage. The Indians are idolatrous, the Spanish are barbaric and cruel,
and the English are the beneficiaries of both through God's grace. And God?
God authorizes a perverted kind of sacramentalism, giving the pagan Indians "their own Blood to drink, in lieu of what they had most barbarously
shed of their Neighbours." Blood for blood—the logic of sacrifice, resurrected in the context of a Protestant polemic against Indian and Spanish
barbarism. And, moreover, sacrifice in a pre-Reformed sense: in the New
World, blood does not *atone*—it *satisfies* a prior blood debt. The explicit
quid pro quo of the transaction signals a return to older notions of sacrifice
and satisfaction, with blood as the primary medium of exchange. This narrative structure would prove incredibly durable during the first century of
English imperialism.

A distinguishing feature of Protestant colonial narratives is the ambivalent agency of Indians in inciting violence. Indians are sometimes the sole
author of the "mischief" they wreak, at other times they are merely doing the
bidding of imperial masters, at still other times they are the unwitting instruments of a supernatural power (either God or the devil). The image of Indians as the tools of the devil is one of the oldest tropes in the literature of

[66] John Archdale, *A New Description of that Fertile and Pleasant Province of Carolina* (1707), in *Narratives of Early Carolina, 1650–1708*, ed. Alexander S. Salley Jr. (New York: Barnes and Noble, 1911), 284–85.

encounter.[67] For the Spanish, Indian diabolism was just another front in the ongoing war between God and the devil for the soul of Christian Europe. English Protestants certainly did not shy away from eschatological readings of Indian "devil worship," but they tended to see the alliance between Satan and the indigenous peoples of North America as a political and economic alliance as well as a religious one: Indians were the "tenants" of North America's original landlord, the Devil; or they were part of his feudal "empire"—his vassals. As a consequence, English depictions of the diabolical relationship Indians enjoyed with their satanic overlord were quasi-legal, drawing on the language of contract as well as on the more overtly religious language of covenant or communion. We have seen how Protestant discussions of the problem of blood sacrifice assumed a more legalistic aspect in the writings of Hugo Grotius, and English narratives of their transactions with the native inhabitants are part of this larger tradition. The point is not that secular meanings of legal contract displaced older religious notions of sacrificial covenants but that the two were inextricably intertwined in the English colonial imagination.

From the first skirmishes between English soldiers and Powhatan Indians in Virginia in the 1600s through the crescendo of imperial wars that swept up the colonies north to south in the late seventeenth and early eighteenth centuries, English North America—or, at least, the literature of English North America—was awash in sacrificial blood. "And Thus was the *Vein* of *New England* first opened," Mather concluded his *Decennium Luctuosum*, "that afterwards *Bled* for Ten Years together!"[68] In reality, the vein was opened in 1609 and did not cease flowing for another one hundred years.

The story begins in Virginia. Here, the English encountered the native Powhatan (the name conferred upon a paramountcy of thirty smaller chiefdoms) who practiced human sacrifice as part of their religious and martial ceremonies, though not on the grand scale found in New Spain. George Percy, one of the first voyagers to the Chesapeake, repeated a story he had heard from his comrade John Smith (who apparently had heard it from another "adventurer," William White): "in some part of the Countrey they have

[67] Fernando Cervantes, *The Devil in the New World: The Impact of Diabolism in New Spain* (New Haven, Conn.: Yale University Press, 1997); Jorge Cañizares-Esquerra, *Puritan Conquistadors: Iberianizing the Atlantic, 1550–1700* (Stanford, Calif.: Stanford University Press, 2006); Cave, *Pequot War*, chapter 1; David Lovejoy, "Satanizing the American Indian," *New England Quarterly* 67.4 (December 1994): 603–21.

[68] Mather, *Decennium Luctuosum*, 25.

yearely a sacrifice of children." His detailed account of a Powhatan religious ceremony belongs to the transcolonial lore of Indian diabolism.

> Some of them were blacke like Divels, with hornes and loose haire, some of divers colours. They continued two dayes dancing in a circle of a quarter of a mile, in two companies, with anticke trickes.... Fourteen well favoured children, or (if you had rather heare Captain Smith) fifteen of the properest yong boyes beteene ten and fifteen yeares of age they painted white: Having brought them forth, the people (saith he) spent the forenoone in dancing and singing about them with Rattles: in the afternoon they put these children to the roote of a tree ... caused burthens of wood to be brought to the Altar, made of poles set like a steeple, where they made a great fire to sacrifice their children to the Divell (whom they call Kewase) who, as they report, suckes their bloud.[69]

The most recent anthropological study of the Powhatan concludes that human sacrifice was part of a generalized sacrificial culture among the southeastern Indians, in which things (pearls, shell beads, tobacco) as well as animals (deer) and humans were killed either as acts of retribution against criminals and prisoners of war or as acts of propiation to native gods.[70] Smith was more interested in Indian habits of war than of religion, though he was not the only adventurer to observe what he thought were pagan rituals of human sacrifice.[71] Soon enough the colonists would discover firsthand the nature of Indian warfare in English America.

After several miserable years and at least one lost colony, the small garrison at Jamestown maintained a fragile toehold on the North American continent by 1609. Dreams of amicable relations with the Powhatan and easy access to gold crumbled quickly in the malarial swamp that was the original site of the town. An unfortunate sequence of almost comical cultural miscalculations on the part of the colony's leadership (comprised mostly of hardened

[69] Samuel Purchas, *Purchas's Pilgrimage* (1614), 766–67, reprinted in *The Jamestown Voyages Under the First Charter, 1606–1609*, ed. Philip L. Barbour, vol. 1 (London: Hakluyt Society, 1969), 147–49.

[70] Margaret Holmes Williamson, *Powhatan Lords of Life and Death: Command and Consent in Seventeenth-Century Virginia* (Lincoln: University of Nebraska Press, 2003), 234–47. Williamson finds no evidence that the Powhatan practiced cannibalism (p. 240).

[71] John Smith, *The Generall Historie of Virginia, New-England & The Summer Isles* (London, 1624), 36; *Relation of Virginia by Henry Spelman 1609* (London, 1872), 27.

veterans from Europe's wars of religion) led the Powhatan to launch a series of attacks on the English colony in the spring of 1609; for the next five years, the conflict flared with neither side able to win a decisive victory. One historian has called this Anglo-Virginia's "holy war" because of the prominent role played by Indian sacred burial sites in the choreography of English assaults. The war began with a desecration; in George Percy's words, "we Beate the Salvages outt of the Island burned their howses Ransacked their Temples [and] Tooke down the Corpes of their deade kings from of their Toambes."[72] Both sides indulged in butchery, cannibalism, and blood sacrifice, with a few hints at sacramental theophagy. A servant of the Virginia Company who spent some time in captivity with the Powhatan reported that their "preests" made a "great cirkell of fier in which after many observanses in their conjurations they make offer of 2 or 3 children to be given to their god." After "ye bodies which are offered are consumed in the fier and their cerimonees performed, the men depart merily, the weamen weaping."[73] So fierce was the fighting that in the besieged fort at Jamestown the colonists took to eating one another during the infamous "Starving Time" of 1609–10, confirmed recently by archaeological evidence of knife marks on the bones of a girl buried at the site.[74] John Smith, Virginia's first historian, tells us that "so great was our famine, that a Savage we slew, and buried, the poorer sort took him up again and eat him." (Ever the curious ethnographer, Smith adds the detail that the "salvage" was "boyled and stewed with roots and herbs.")[75] As the initial siege of the fort lengthened into the bitter winter, Percy chronicled with chilling detail the descent into anthropophagical madness that gripped Jamestown. Reduced to eating cats, dogs, rats, snakes, and even the leather from their boots, the colonists in their famine began "to doe those things wch seame incredible As to digge up dead corpses out of graves and to eate them and some have Licked upp the Bloode wch hathe fallen from their weake fellowes." The "most Lamentable" act in this book of horrors occurred when "one of our Colline murdered his wife Ripped

---

[72] J. Frederick Fausz, "An 'Abundance of Blood Shed on Both Sides': England's First Indian War, 1609–1614," *Virginia Magazine of History and Biography* 98 (January 1990): 3–56; see also Erik Seeman, *Death in the New World: Cross-Cultural Encounters, 1492–1800* (Philadelphia: University of Pennsylvania Press, 2010), 87–94. Mark Nicholls, "George Percy's 'Trewe Relacyon': A Primary Source for the Jamestown Settlement," *The Virginia Magazine of History and Biography* 113 (2005): 212–75 (quotation on 244–45).

[73] *Relation of Virginia by Henry Spelman*, 26–27.

[74] "Girl's Bones Bear Signs of Cannibalism by Starving Virginia Colonists," *New York Times*, May 2, 2013, A11.

[75] Smith, *Generall Historie*, 105–6.

the Childe out of her Woambe and threw itt into the River and after chopped the Mother in pieces and salted her for his foode."[76]

This was cannibalism at its most primitive—a last resort for people literally starving to death.[77] But we can also see glimpses of a more sacramental mode of writing in English reports of the horrors they endured during this prolonged period of war and famine. In retaliation for the ransacking of Indian burial temples, one English soldier "and divers others were found also slain with their mouths stopped full of bread."[78] The primary message intended by the Powhatan was surely a secular one—"contempte and skorne thatt others might expecte the Lyke when they shold come to seeke for breade and reliefe"—but it is not too much of a stretch, I think, to imagine that another message might have been intended by the English chroniclers of these atrocities. It was simply not possible after the eucharistic wars of the Reformation to speak of licking blood and stuffing mouths with bread without some reference, however subliminal, to the body and blood of Christ. (Percy paired this anecdote with one from New Spain featuring the other eucharistic element, wine, in which a Spanish general was forced by the Indians to "drinke upp A certaine quantity of melted gowlde" as a similar rebuke; "now glut thy selfe with gowlde," his tormenters taunted the poor Spaniard, "having there sowghte for gowlde as [the English] did here for foode.")[79] William Crashaw's dedicatory to *Good newes from Virginia* imagined the very soil of the colony ("those Heathenish Earths") to have been "consecrated" by the body and blood of the Christian soldiers who had lost their lives in the war, sacrificial flesh "more worthie to bee esteemed precious reliques, then thousands that are preserved and adored in the Romish Church."[80]

When the Powhatan next attacked, within the decade, they had learned

<hr/>

[76] Nicholls, "George Percy's 'Trewe Relacyon,'" 249.

[77] As scholars have pointed out, what happened at Jamestown was a form of "constraint" cannibalism, an entirely different thing from the "ritual" cannibalism of New World peoples that fascinated European adventurers. Lestringant, *Cannibals*; Kathleen Donegan, *Seasons of Misery: Catastrophe and Colonial Settlement in Early America* (Philadelphia: University of Pennsylvania Press, 2014), 102–3. Rachel B. Herrmann evaluates the evidence for and against the reports of settler cannibalism in "The 'Tragicall Historie': Cannibalism and Abundance in Colonial Jamestown," *William and Mary Quarterly*, 3rd ser., 68 (2011): 47–74.

[78] Quoted in Seeman, *Death in the New World*, 87.

[79] Nicholls, "George Percy's 'Trewe Relacyon,'" 247.

[80] Alexander Whitaker, *Good newes from Virginia Sent to the Counsell and Company of Virginia, resident in England. From Alexander Whitaker, the minister of Henrico in Virginia. Wherein also is a narration of the present state of that countrey, and our colonies there* (London, 1613), Epistle Dedicatory.

some hard lessons. Traditional modes of fighting, which included launching small-scale skirmishes over a period of time to harry the enemy, were not sufficient: this time, the Powhatan attacked in a massive, all-out assault on March 22, 1622, which nearly succeeded in wiping the colony off the face of North America—a day that would thereafter be commemorated as a "holy-day" by the English settlers.[81] Over three hundred English men, women, and children were killed in a single day, one-fourth of the entire population of the settlement.[82] The fullest account of what came to be known as the Virginia "massacre" was published in London by Edward Waterhouse, who opens his narrative with a New World communion feast gone terribly awry: the killing began when the Indians "sat down at Breakfast with our people at their tables" and, using the colonists' tools against them, "basely and barbarously murthered, not sparying either age or sex, man, woman, or child." The "deformed Savages," no better than "wild beasts," then proceeded to hack the corpses of their victims to pieces: "and not being content with taking away life alone, they fell againe upon the dead, making as well as they could, a fresh murder, defacing, dragging, and mangling the dead carcasses into many pieces, and carrying away some parts in derision, with base and brutish triumph" (Figure 3).[83] In a pattern that would become a universal feature of Indian warfare in the English settlements, the Indians (in another account) went from house to house, "sometimes firing the houses and leaving the living children miserably to be consumed with their dead Parents in the fearfull flames."[84] At one plantation, the Indians killed Nathaniel Powell and his family, then, "butcher-like, haggled their bodies . . . to express their uttermost height of cruelty."[85] Sir Francis Wyatt, the governor at the time, saw broken bod-

---

[81] In 1623, the colonial assembly decreed that "ye 22d of March be yearely sollemnised as holy-day." Laws & Orders of the Generall Assembly, Virginia, February 16, 1623, Records of the Colonial Office, National Archives, Kew Gardens, London (hereafter CO), 1/3, no. 9.

[82] J. Frederick Fausz, "The 'Barbarous Massacre' Reconsidered: The Powhatan Uprising of 1622 and the Historians," *Explorations in Ethnic Studies* 1 (January 1978): 16–36.

[83] Edward Waterhouse, *A Declaration of the State of the Colony and Affaires in Virginia. With a relation of the barbarous massacre in the time of peace and league, treacherously executed by the native infidels upon the English* (London, 1622), 14.

[84] Edward Johnson, *Wonder-Working Providence of Sions Savior in New England* (London, 1653), 226. Johnson included a brief account of the 1622 massacre in Virginia in his chronicle of New England's Indian wars. His account is corroborated by that of Anthony Chester, who describes how "this bloodthirsty people" massacred the English "while pertaking with them of their meal." *Voyage of Anthony Chester to Virginia, Made in the Year 1620 . . . Also; A Terrible and Treacherous Massacre Perpetrated in a Cruel Manner by the Inhabitants of Virginia on the English* (Leiden, 1707), 209.

[85] *The Complete Works of Captain John Smith (1580–1631),* 3 vols., ed. Philip Barbour (Chapel Hill: University of North Carolina Press, 1986), 2:295.

Figure 3. The 1622 Indian assault on Anglo-Virginians as they sat down to
breakfast. Woodcut by Matthaeus Merian, 1628.

ies everywhere—ripped guts, burst hearts, charred flesh. "We were forced to
stand and gaze at our distressed brethren, frying in the fury of our enemies, and
could not relieve them," he lamented. Such wanton spilling of blood called for
more blood, "for the glory of God, and love toward our brethren (whose blood,
no doubt, cryeth to heaven for vengeance.)"[86] Wyatt's employer, the Virginia
Company, echoed his sentiments: "Since the innocent blood of so many Christians doth in justice cry out for revenge . . . we must advise you to root out from
being any longer a people, so cursed a nation."[87]

The lessons colonists drew from this episode are very revealing of the
blood mentality of the English. The slaughter "must needs bee for the good of

[86] Seeman, *Death in the New World*, 93–94.
[87] Council for Virginia to the Governor of Virginia, August 1, 1622, in *The Records of the
Virginia Company of London*, 4 vols., ed. Susan Myra Kingsbury (Washington, 1906–35),
3:671–72.

the Plantation," Waterhouse insisted, "and the loose of this blood to make the body more healthfull." How? "Because our hands which before were tied with gentleness and faire visage, are now set at liberty by the treacherous violence of the Savages." His words would prove a terrible prophecy, as future English conduct toward the Powhatan degenerated to a level of brutality that shocked some backers of the Virginia Company at home. "Victorie," Waterhouse counseled, "may bee gained many waies," including torching the natives' stores of grain to starve them out and sending "blood-Hounds" and "mastives" to "teare them" to pieces.[88] The final image we have from the 1622 massacre is Christopher Brooke's merciless portrait of a people whose very humanity has been stripped away:

Soules drown'd in flesh and blood;
Rotted in Evil and oppos'd in Good;
Errours of Nature, of inhumane Birth;
The very dregs, garbage, and spanne of Earth.[89]

Not surprisingly, when we turn from the southern colonies to New England, the "sacrificial mode of speaking" in accounts of colonial violence becomes more pronounced and more amenable to a theological interpretation. The first chroniclers of English colonization in Virginia were soldiers and gentlemen adventurers, not ministers, and the metaphors they instinctively reached for were martial, not scriptural. We can, I think, identify a persistent if subdued strain of sacramental allusion in these chronicles—indeed, it would be surprising if there were *no* scriptural or liturgical connotations in *any* English accounts of discovery and conquest in an age when overseas expansion was one front in the ongoing war against the imperial forces of the Catholic Reformation—but the language for the most part imports the emphasis on butchered bodies found in Spanish narratives without the accompanying theological subtext that we explored in the previous section. In the writings of New England's first historians, on the other hand, accounts of human butchery are situated within a sacramental frame of reference in ways both expected and unexpected. What unites northern and southern colonial narratives is the prominence of blood rhetoric within the master metaphor of consumption: blood, as much as if not more than flesh, is the element of cultural exchange

---

[88] Waterhouse, *Declaration of the State of the Colony and Affaires in Virginia*, 24.
[89] Christopher Brooke, *A Poem on the Late Massacre in Virginia With Particular Mention of those Men of Note That Suffered in That Disaster* (London, 1622), 22–23.

when Indians and English clashed, consumed (along with native lands, native game, and native plants) with gusto by colonists hungry for "sacrificial flesh."

Yet I would still maintain that despite the obvious differences in the sources from colonial Virginia and colonial Massachusetts, the overarching interpretive framework for understanding colonial violence was a generic Protestant ambivalence (composed of equal parts aversion and attraction) toward medieval notions of blood sacrifice, not a specifically Puritan doctrinal understanding of the "real presence" or the nature of Christ's atonement on the cross. We can see the chain of reference at work in narratives such as John Smith's *History of Virginia,* in which incidents of New World cannibalism in the Spanish Caribbean are included alongside reports of Indian butchery in Anglo-Virginia; to both will be added a more overtly theological gloss in the accounts of Anglo-Indian war in Massachusetts, Connecticut, and the northern frontier by Puritan historians like Increase and Cotton Mather. The referential chain as I'm reconstructing it thus connects Reformation-era arguments over blood sacrifice and the sacraments to New World cannibalism, the butchering and commodification of human bodies in incidents of colonial violence, and finally the return of a taste for sacrificial flesh in Puritan accounts of their controversies with Indians and heretics.

The fullest exposition of these interlinked paradigms came in the first two decades of English colonization in the region that came to be known as New England, when settlers confronted a series of deadly enemies both foreign and homegrown. From the Pequot assault on the Puritan commonwealths of Massachusetts and Connecticut in 1637 to the "free grace" controversy in the same year and the Gortonist heresy of the 1640s, the towns and meetinghouses of New England were filled with talk of blood shed and consumed.[90] We've long recognized the fateful coincidence of the Pequot War and the free grace controversy in 1637 (as Thomas Shepard noted in his diary, the Indians and the Antinomians "rose and fell together"), and scholars of rhetoric have identified a series of homologies that helped construe Indians and Antinomians as mirror images of theological threat and semiotic disorder in the Puritan imaginary.[91] Ann Kibbey's work has been fundamental to my own reading of this literature, and her suggestion more than two decades ago that the interchange-

---

[90] Following Michael Winship, I use the term "free grace controversy" rather than the more common "Antinomian controversy" to refer to the trial and expulsion of Anne Hutchinson and her followers in 1637. See Winship, *Making Heretics: Militant Protestantism and Free Grace in Massachusetts, 1636–1641* (Princeton, N.J.: Princeton University Press, 2002).

[91] *God's Plot,* 70.

ability of Pequots, Antinomians, and, eventually, witches in the sacramental "mode of signifying" that turned bread into flesh (Christ = body = bread = Pequots/heretics/witches) bears renewed scrutiny.[92] If we broaden our inquiry beyond the technical linguistic analysis that was Kibbey's focus, we can see how the widespread metaphorical linking of internal and external enemies via the sacrificial paradigm underwrote many accounts of Puritan violence.

Kibbey first directed our attention to the rhetorical parallels between sermons that called for Puritans to destroy Antichrist ("*We must burne him*," John Wheelwright thundered in a fast-day sermon) and the actual prosecution of the war, in which the Puritan militia (in)famously burned some five hundred Pequot men, women, and children alive in the attack on their stronghold of Fort Mystic just a few months later. The firsthand account written by John Mason, the militia captain who led the assault, leaves no doubt that the firing of the fort was an intentional act of sacred violence: "The Captain said, WE MUST BURN THEM, and immediately stepping into the Wigwam, brought out a Fire-brand, and putting it into the Matts with which they were covered, set the Wigwams on Fire. Thus was God seen in the Mount, crushing his enemies and the enemies of his people . . . burning them up in the Fire of his wrath and dunging the Ground with their Flesh: It was the LORDS DOINGS, and it is marvelous to our Eyes."[93] Accounts of the Fort Mystic attack provide some of the richest, and most disturbing, evidence for a sacramental mode of speaking in Puritan accounts of colonial violence. William Bradford, the governor of Plymouth colony, exulted in his history of the war in language that recalls Mason's description of the fort as "a fiery oven": "it was a fearful sight to see them thus frying in the fire and the streams of blood quenching the same, and horrible was the stink and scent thereof; but the victory seemed a sweet sacrifice."[94] Thomas Shepard called the massacre a

[92] Kibbey, *Interpretation of Material Shapes*, 103 and passim.

[93] John Wheelwright, "A Fast-Day Sermon," in *The Antinomian Controversy, 1636–1638: A Documentary History*, ed. David Hall (Durham, N.C.: Duke University Press, 1990), 165–66; John Mason, *A Brief History of the Pequot War; especially of the memorable taking of their fort at Mistick in Connecticut in 1637* (Boston, 1736), 14. The Fort Mystic massacre was long remembered, and celebrated, in New England; thirty years later, the Connecticut General Court renamed the town of Southerton "Mistick, in memory of that victory God was pleased to give this people of Connecticut over the Pequot Indians." *The Public Records of the Colony of Connecticut from 1665 to 1678*, ed. J. Hammond Trumbull (Hartford, 1852), 26.

[94] William Bradford, *Of Plymouth Plantation, 1620–1647*, ed. Samuel Eliot Morrison (New York: Knopf, 1953), 296. Increase Mather would also refer to the Pequots "frying in the Fire that was kindled upon their houses." *A Relation of the Troubles which have hapned in New-England by Reason of the Indians there: From the Year 1614 to the year 1675* (Boston, 1677), 54.

"divine slaughter," and he clearly spoke for most of his fellow ministers in praising the deaths of so many Pequots as a providential act: "the Lord hath utterly consumed the whole company," he marveled.[95]

The Indians, for their part, were horrified at what they saw. "Our Indians came to us, and much rejoyced at our victories," Captain John Underhill reported, "but cried *mach it, mach it*; that is, it is naught, it is naught, because it is too furious and slaies too many men." Underhill defended the slaughter in biblical terms: "it may bee demanded, Why should you be so furious (as some have said) should not Christians have more mercy and compassion?" Underhill retorted, "I would referre you to Davids warre, when a people is growne to such a height of bloud, and sinne against God and man . . . there hee hath no respect to persons, but harrowes them, and sawes them, and puts them to the sword, and the most terrible death that may bee: sometimes the Scripture declareth women and children must perish with their parents."[96]

More than an act of burnt sacrifice or divine retribution, the slaughter was, Kibbey argues, also a sacramental enactment—a feast of "bread" provided by the Lord, to be consumed at a joyous celebration. "I still remember a Speech of Mr. Hooker at our going abroad, THAT THEY SHOULD BE BREAD FOR US," Mason recalled.[97] A similar eucharistic echo can be found in Uriah Oakes's history of the war, which invoked Psalms 74:14 (a favorite text of New England Puritans), "Hath not the Hand of the Lord broken the head of many

---

[95] *God's Plot*, 69–70.

[96] John Underhill, *Newes from America, or, A new and experimental discoverie of New England, Containing True Relation of Their War-like Proceedings these two yeares last past* (London, 1638), 42–43. Ronald Dale Karr analyzes this exchange in " 'Why Should You Be So Furious?' The Violence of the Pequot War," *Journal of American History* 85 (December 1998): 876–909 (quotations on 877). One of the more misguided attempts to read the Fort Mystic massacre through a Freudian rather than a theological lens is Richard Drinnon's *Facing West: The Metaphysics of Indian-Hating and Empire-Building* (Minneapolis: University of Minnesota Press, 1980): "at Mystic the Saints' suppressed sexuality at last broke out and found vent in an orgy of violence. Like men in a dream they burned and shot *the flesh* they so feared and hated in themselves" (56–57, emphasis original). The source of the Puritans' untoward "fury" has long puzzled scholars; John Ferling suggested vaguely that it lay in "subliminal anxieties that could not have been understood by contemporaries on either side." Ferling, "The New England Soldier: A Study in Changing Perceptions," *American Quarterly* 33 (Spring 1981): 26–45 (quotation on 27). My own reading supports the notion of "subliminal anxieties" but places these squarely in the realm of Protestant theology and devotional practice.

[97] Mason, *Brief History*, 22. Mason's contemporary Alexander Whitaker wrote that "Bread in Scripture is usually taken for all kind of meat and drinke" in his explication of Eccl. 11.1, "Cast thy bread upon the waters: for after many daies thou shalt finde it"; *Good Newes from Virginia. Sent to the Counsell and Company of Virginia, resident in England. From Alexander Whitaker, The Minister of Henrico in Virginia* (London, 1613), 1–3.

a Leviathan in pieces, and given him to be meat to his people inhabiting the wilderness?" (Fittingly, the Pequots themselves were believed to be an especially "fleshed" and blooded people—"being fleshed with Victories over their Fellow-Indians, they began to thirst after the blood of any Forreigners, English and Dutch that accidentally came amongst them, in a way of Trade, or upon other Accounts.")[98] Cotton Mather even invoked the image of the "cannibal barbecue" in his retrospective account of the massacre: "When they came to see the ashes of their *friends* mingled with the ashes at the *fort*, and the bodies of so many of their countrymen terribly *barbikew'd*, . . . [the Pequot] howl'd, they roar'd, they stamp'd, they tore their hair."[99] Whether explicitly scriptural or more plainly figural, such descriptions of Pequot bodies being broken in pieces, baked in "fiery ovens," and turned into food for Puritan saints are disturbingly literal. They are also theologically reckless. When, several years later, English Protestants faced another "savage" opponent—the Irish who rebelled in 1641—they also turned to eucharistic metaphors but this time to condemn the barbarism of their Catholic opponents rather than to celebrate their own victory: "The Rebels took Sir Thomas Sevell, and hanged him upon a tree in his own grounds, and cut his flesh in pieces, carrying pieces thereof up and down in their hands, saying, this is the flesh of one of the Rebels against our holy Father the Pope."[100] Anglo-American Puritans may not have gone so far as to offer their pieces of human flesh to the pope, but they did consume them with unholy relish.

Indians were not the only enemies consumed by Puritans in their righteous fury against infidels and unbelievers. The flames of theological controversy claimed a few English victims as well. "The Churches are on fire," fishermen reportedly warned the ships sailing into Boston harbor at the height of the furor over Anne Hutchinson and her Antinomian faction in 1637.[101] The governor of Massachusetts at the time, John Winthrop, believed it was only "a wonder of mercy" that the Antinomians "had not set our Common-wealth

[98] William Hubbard, *A Narrative of the Troubles with the Indians of New-England from the first planting thereof in the year 1607, to this present year 1677* (Boston, 1677), 118.

[99] Cotton Mather, *Magnalia Christi Americana*, 556.

[100] *A Treacherous Plot of a Confederacie in Ireland* (London, 1641), n.p. The pamphlet literature on the 1641 rebellion recycles many of the tropes of New World warfare, including the butchering of bodies and the sacrificing of captives at the stake; see, for example, *Lamentable Newes from Ireland* (London, 1642); and *The Happiest Newes from Ireland that ever came to England* (London, 1641). See Karr, " 'Why Should You Be So Furious?' " for a detailed analysis of the parallels between Old and New World ways of warfare in the Reformation era.

[101] Quoted in Winship, *Making Heretics*, 144.

and Churches in a fire, and consumed us all therein."[102] Winthrop and the fishermen were speaking metaphorically, of course, but when news came of
Hutchinson's death at the hands of Indians in 1643 following her conviction
and banishment by the General Court, reports quickly circulated that she and
her family had been burned to death in divine retribution. "Some write that
the Indians did burne her to death with fire," Thomas Weld reported in his
preface to *A Short Story of the Rise, Reigne, and Ruine of the Antinomians*, "her
house and all the rest named that belonged to her." As it turned out, the report
was false: Hutchinson and her followers had indeed been killed by Indians, but
with hatchets, not fire. Still, in the wake of the "divine slaughter" of so many
Pequot in the flames at Mystic, a fiery end must have seemed a fitting denoue-
ment to "this American Jesabel."[103] (Weld could hardly have chosen a more apt
scriptural reference: like the burnt remains of the Pequot at Mystic, "the car-
cass of Jezebel shall be as dung upon the face of the field" [2 Kings 9:30–37].)
Thomas Shepard's autobiography reveals just how entangled were the Pequot
and the Antinomians in the Puritan mind: "The Pequot Indians were fully dis-
comfitted," he wrote, "for as the opinions arose, wars did arise, and when these
began to be crushed by the ministry of the elders . . . the enemies began to be
crushed and were perfectly subdued." The parallelism between the "crushing"
of the heretical opinions of Hutchinson and the "crushing" of the Pequot masks
the exact etiology of the threat posed by these external and internal "enemies"—
which came first?[104] It's nearly impossible to tell from this account.

Several years after the subduing of the Pequot and the Antinomians,
Thomas Shepard had a premonition that another ordeal was on the horizon.
In his journal for February 5, 1644, he noted, "At night in meditation I saw (1)
that this whole world and the churches in general were up in arms against
God. (2) Hence I saw the Lord did come forth in arms, fire, and sword and
blood against them."[105] The 1640s were a difficult time for the Puritan commonwealths for a number of reasons. The outbreak of civil war in England
called home many of the most zealous settlers to fight on the Parliamentary
side, and the sudden cessation of immigration into the colonies cut them off

[102] [John Winthrop], *A Short Story of the Rise, Reigne, and Ruine of the Antinomians, Familists, and Libertines that infected the Churches of New-England* (London, 1644), n.p. On the
actual authorship of the pamphlet, see David D. Hall, *Ways of Writing: The Practice and Politics of Text-Making in Seventeenth-Century New England* (Philadelphia: University of Pennsylvania Press, 2008), 59–66.
[103] [Winthrop], *Short Story*.
[104] *God's Plot*, 68; Kibbey, *Interpretation of Material Shapes*, 99.
[105] *God's Plot*, 133.

from much-needed infusions of currency and new blood. As important, the proliferation of radical sects in the civil war era (Baptists, Ranters, Seekers, Familists, and Quakers, among a motley assortment of smaller offshoots) spawned new heretical outcroppings in New England as well. Boston's ultraorthodox minister, John Cotton, called the 1640s the "season" when "the Spirit of Error is let loose to deceive so many thousand soules of our English Nation: So that now their hearts are become as Tinder, ready to catch and kindle at every sparke of false light." His fellow divine Peter Bulkeley lamented the rise of a "generation of the Land, that are altogether looking after new light, and new truths," a generation with "itching eares, itching minds, and itching tongues, also, itching to be fed with, and to be venting novelties."[106] Before such "novelties" the Puritans were "like Sheepe let loose to feed on fresh pasture, being stopped and startled in their own course by a Kennell of devouring Wolves."[107] Alarmed colonists like Ezekiel Rogers of Rowley pleaded with Governor Winthrop in 1639 to "cleanse our mixtures and filth" before the colony was visited by "a sore scourge."[108]

A "scourge" soon appeared in the form of Samuel Gorton, son of a London merchant who arrived in Boston in 1637 just in time to volunteer in the Pequot War. Within a year he found himself in Plymouth court for his blasphemous opinions, where he "carried himself so mutinously and seditiously" toward both magistrates and ministers that he was banished from the colony.[109] Trouble followed him from Plymouth to Providence, where his fellow exile Roger Williams complained that "Master Gorton having abused high and low at Aquidneck, is now bewitching and bemadding poor Providence." Gorton's repeated run-ins with the Puritan authorities over a ten-year stretch from 1638 to 1648 earned him a whipping, imprisonment, forced labor, exile, and—nearly—his life. They also, fortunately for us, created a paper trail that allows us to carry forward our discussion of sacrificial and sacramental "modes of speaking" in colonial accounts of violence.

Disentangling the snarl of heretical opinions imputed to Gorton and his

[106] John Cotton, *A Reply to Mr. Williams his Examination; And Answer of the Letters sent to him by John Cotton* (London, 1647), 11; Bulkeley quoted in Philip Gura, *A Glimpse of Sion's Glory: Puritan Radicalism in New England, 1620–1660* (Middletown, Conn.: Wesleyan University Press, 1984), 22. Gura's survey of heretical opinions in New England shows that the colonies experienced "an ideological fragmentation similar, though on a smaller scale, to that of its English counterpart" during the period 1630–60.
[107] Johnson, *Wonder-Working Providence*, 100.
[108] Gura, *A Glimpse of Sion's Glory*, 22.
[109] Cotton Mather, *Magnalia Christi Americana*, 504.

followers would take us pretty far afield from our main objective, but a brief overview is in order. Like the writings of so many other radical sectarians of the civil war era his publications seem almost calculatedly obscure—written in a mixture of scriptural and mystical allusions that are nearly impossible to render in logical doctrinal terms. "Whatever Mr. Gorton's religious Opinions really were," one critic sniffed, "it is now hard to tell, as 'tis to understand his most *mysterious Dialect.*"[110] Among his key ideas was a belief in the perfectibility of man through God's grace, a denial of the existence of heaven and hell except as spiritual states, and a rejection of most of the "ordinances" or "offices" instituted over the centuries by the Christian churches as "human inventions." To give a taste of his exegetical style, and in keeping with the sacramental focus of the discussion, let's look at his "monstrous" interpretation of John 6:53 ("except ye eat of the flesh of the son of man and drink of his blood, ye have no life in ye") in his 1646 tract *Simplicities Defense Against Seven-Headed Policy.* Tacking back and forth between figurative and materialist readings of the passage, Gorton provided plenty of ammunition to his critics who charged him with grossly violating the Calvinist ban on the "real presence." On the one hand, he argued for the necessity for both species (bread and wine) to be administered during communion in starkly physiological terms: "if a man should eat, or communicate in (as the meaning is) only in food for the body, and not take in moysture, or drinke, for the digestion thereof, it is the destruction of the body . . . yea, meate without moysture doth suffocate, and choak the spirits." And "againe, if wee should take in only drinke, without meat, . . . then doth the moysture presently overflow the quenching of the heat, and so breedeth either some dropsie in the body . . . or else it cumeth up into the head, and breeds madnesse, and giddiness in the brain." But despite this extended alimentary analysis of the digestive process, he insisted that "Even so, it is that mysticall body of Christ" that is received in communion, not the physical one. Such disclaimers aside, the primary analogies used to unpack scripture are material, not spiritual: "*if my child ask bread* (to supply nature in the suppressing of hunger)," he reasons, "*I cannot put a stone into his mouth (that were cruelty) but bread.*"[111]

---

[110] John Callendar, *An historical discourse on the civil and religious affairs of the Colony of Rhode-Island and Providence Plantations in New-England* (Boston, 1739); for a discussion of mystical and obscurantist styles of writing in Protestant polemics, see Susan Juster, "Demagogues or Mystagogues? Gender and the Language of Prophecy in the Age of Democratic Revolutions," *American Historical Review* 104 (December 1999): 1560–81.

[111] Samuel Gorton, *Simplicities Defense against Seven-Headed Policy, or, innocency vindicated being unjustly accused, and sorely censured by that seven-headed church-government united in New-England* (London, 1646), 103–7.

It was passages such as these that led his critics to question his sacramental orthodoxy. Governor John Winthrop recalled in his journal that Gorton had called baptism "an abomination" and the Lord's Supper "the juice of a poor silly grape turned into the blood of Christ by the skill of our magicians." Gorton, charged Edward Johnson, was "so full gorged with dreadful and damnable errors" that "he vomit[ed] up a whole paper full of beastly stuff . . . while mocking at the Sacrament of Baptisme and the Lords Supper, in an opprobrious manner, deriding the Elements Christ was pleased to institute them in."[112] Edward Winslow, the agent sent by the Massachusetts General Court to plead its case against Gorton to Parliament, called for the ultimate penalty. To label the sacrament "an abomination, madding and making drunk the world," as Gorton had done, "and all this in cool-bloud . . . Let the world judge . . . whether such men deserve to live that live thus to blaspheme."[113]

Yet as we have seen, sacramental orthodoxy was always tenuous in Protestant communities. There is nothing so shocking, so beyond the theological pale, in Gorton's writings to warrant the kind of persecution he and his followers experienced at the hands of the Puritan magistracy. His flirtation with materialist readings of the Eucharist pales in comparison with the florid rhetoric of Puritan poets like Edward Taylor. We can attribute the severity of their response—Gorton came within three votes of being executed by the General Court for heresy—to the lingering effects of the Pequot War and the free grace controversy, which created a climate of fear and panic throughout Massachusetts that mobilized latent desires for blood sacrifice to purge the land of such "uncouth, tumorous and swelling words . . . like swellings and tumours of the flesh."[114] Significantly, *both* sides saw the controversy in sacrificial terms. And both contributed to deepening the association of violence with the sacramental dismembering and ingestion of flesh and blood. Though *whose* blood, and *whose* flesh, was a point of contention.

According to William Arnold, who petitioned the authorities in Providence in 1641 to throw out this "railing and turbulent person," Gorton referred to his persecutors as "swine that held out their Nose to suck his blood."

[112] Johnson, *Wonder-Working Providence*, 186.

[113] *Winthrop's Journal, "History of New England," 1630–1649*, 2 vols., ed. James Kendall Hosmer (New York, 1908), 2:147; Johnson, *Wonder-Working Providence*, 186; Edward Winslow, *The Danger of Tolerating Levellers in a Civil State, or, An historicall narration of the dangerous pernicious practices and opinions wherewith Samuel Gorton and his leveling accomplices so much disturbed and molested the several plantations in New-England* (London, 1649), 50–51.

[114] This is a rendering of Jude 1:16; Winslow, *Danger of Tolerating Levellers*, 51.

The charge reverberated throughout the pamphlet war that followed his banishment from Massachusetts, exile in London, and defiant return to the colonies in 1648. It was Gorton (like his "coadjustors, the accursed Indians") and
not his opponents who threatened to "suck the blood of our Country-men,"
retorted Edward Winslow.[115] Gorton's letter of complaint to the Massachusetts General Court, "the great and honourable Idol Generall," drew a direct
parallel between the thirst for his blood and the thirst for the blood of Christ
in the communion wine: "[We ask] how that bloud relisheth you have sucked
formerly from us, ... having turned the juice of a poor silly Grape ... into
the bloud of our Lord Jesus by the cunning skill of your Magicians, which
doth make mad and drunke so many in the world?"[116] If their General Court
was so intent on his body and blood, he taunted the captain who led the assault on the Gortonist compound at Shawomet in 1643, "we would make him
as good a Sabbath day breakfast as ever he had in his life."[117]

Such an offer of himself as an "edible sacrifice" recalls the anecdote of the
Dutch burgomaster with which Grotius concluded his treatise on sacrifice,
and indeed Gorton harbored some messianic aspirations of his own. His followers were reported to have said after seeing Gorton whipped, "Now Christ
Jesus has suffered."[118] Whether apocryphal or not, the comparison was certainly encouraged by Gorton's own repeated references to the spilling of his
blood as a sacrificial act, designed to atone for the sins of the Puritan majority or to purge the countryside of Calvinist errors. This was a sacrificial offer
that was not redeemed: Gorton lived to fight another day. In the entire ten-
year struggle, only a few drops of real blood were shed. Far more blood was
spilled in ink than in the flesh. This, too, was a pattern that would repeat itself
throughout the colonial period as different groups of Protestants squared off
against one another over the parameters of faith. Only four Quakers (condemned by the General Court as those "Idolatrous Quakers, who set up Altars against the Lords Altar")[119] paid for their beliefs with their lives, though
many more suffered corporal punishments ranging from the lash to branding
and dismemberment. There was blood aplenty in this chapter of the Puritan
war against heresy. But for the most part, Puritans confined their fantasies of

[115] Edward Winslow, *Hypocrisie Unmasked* (London, 1646); Winslow, *Danger of Tolerating Levellers*, 30, 59.
[116] Gorton, quoted in Winslow, *Danger of Tolerating Levellers*, 34.
[117] Gorton, *Simplicities Defense*, 48.
[118] Winslow, *Danger of Tolerating Levellers*, 53.
[119] Increase Mather, *A Brief History of the Warr with the Indians in New-England* (Boston,
1676), in *So Dreadfull a Judgment*, 105.

blood and human sacrifice to the written page—at least when it came to their arguments with fellow Englishmen. When Indians were the focus of their rage, as we have seen, they did not hesitate to "consume and destroy" their enemies.[120]

The 1640s saw horrific violence against native Americans throughout North America: in Maryland, a series of bloody frontier raids by the Susquehannock in 1642 led George Calvert to order settlers to shoot all Indians on sight; in New Netherland, the newly appointed director Willem Kieft waged a slash-and-burn offensive against the local Indians with the help of none other than Captain John Underhill, who reprised his notorious raid on Fort Mystic by burning the village of Pound Ridge to the ground along with five to seven hundred of its inhabitants (an act even the Dutch West India Company denounced as "unnatural, barbarous, unnecessary, unjust, and disgraceful"); in the small but strategically located colony of New Sweden, a swaggering ex-soldier named Johan Printz arrived in 1643 and promptly declared war on the previously peaceful Lenapes, who "know nothing of God, but serve Satan."[121] Atrocities abounded on all sides, including the ritual torture of warriors, hatcheting of pregnant women, taking of body trophies, and burning alive of civilians, all of which called forth the inevitable comparisons to the bloody wars of religion abroad: "Did the Duke of Alva in the Netherlands ever do anything more cruel?" one Dutch soldier wondered after witnessing the massacre of eighty Indians by Kieft's forces at Pavonia.[122]

Protestant rage against Indians in English North America reached truly astounding levels in the last third of the seventeenth century. There is a distinctly Old Testament, even pagan, feel to the literature of Indian war in the 1670s, 1680s, and 1690s—these are stories of primitive blood feuds spiraling out of control and reaching near-genocidal levels. (Cotton Mather spoke approvingly of "exterminating the rabid animals" in his 1702 magnum opus, *Magnalia Christi Americana*).[123] "Primitive" was not an epithet in the Reformation era. Nor did it carry an evolutionary or ethnocultural connotation,

[120] Hubbard, *Narrative of the Troubles*, postscript.

[121] Bernard Bailyn chronicles the series of bloody encounters in the 1640s in *The Barbarous Years: The Peopling of British North America: The Conflict of Civilizations, 1600–1675* (New York: Vintage, 2012), 151–54 (Maryland); 218–23 (New Amsterdam); 284–87 (New Sweden). For the Indian wars in New Netherland, see Donna Merwick, *The Shame and the Sorrow: Dutch-Amerindian Encounters in New Netherland* (Philadelphia: University of Pennsylvania Press, 2006).

[122] Bailyn, *Barbarous Years*, 220.

[123] Cotton Mather, *Magnalia Christi Americana*, 575.

denoting a specific stage in human development that certain societies had
vacated sooner than others. When Protestants spoke of "primitive" Christianity they meant the kind of raw faith practiced by the apostles in the first
days after Christ's death and resurrection. Puritans, especially, hankered after
a more "primitive" faith, one that would restore the mystical body of Christ
to its most perfect incarnation before the ecclesiastical inventions of "the
church age" diminished it.[124] (Although Puritans had no monopoly on primitivist desires; the earliest settlers in Virginia were promised that they would
earn eternal fame as "the *Apostles of Virginia*" for their valiant efforts against
Satan, who "visibly and palpably reignes there.")[125] Primitive Christians enjoyed a closer, more ecstatic relationship with God, often through the exercise of such "gifts of the spirit" as the first apostles displayed. At its most
extreme, primitive Christianity meant speaking in tongues, prophesying, and
faith healing. Such was not the usage of Anglo-American Puritans. For them,
the "primitivist" impulse was an expression of their confidence in their status
as God's chosen people and, more important, their sense of living in the last
days, eagerly awaiting Christ's return in a blaze of fire and blood. My own use
of primitive marries this radical Protestant meaning to a larger Christian historical narrative about the supersession of the Old Testament by the New
Testament and the emergence of a postsacrificial paradigm in Christian
thought. Primitive here means Old Testament, the practices and beliefs of the
ancient Hebrews (including blood sacrifice and blood vengeance). In both
senses of the word, colonial narratives of violence deployed a primitive understanding of blood sacrifice, especially in the second half of the seventeenth century.

The most extensively documented Anglo-Indian war in the seventeenth
century was King Philip's (or Metacom's) War, which broke out in Massachusetts in 1675 and claimed more lives proportionally than any other war in
American history. For two years the New England countryside was aflame as
an alliance of Algonquian Indians torched everything in their path in a
seventeenth-century version of Sherman's march to the sea. More than half of
the nearly one hundred English towns that had been established from Maine
to Connecticut were attacked and some dozen entirely destroyed. One-fifth
of the colonial population was killed, and nearly half of the native population
died. The fighting began in the remote frontier regions of the English planta-

[124] Bozeman, *To Live Ancient Lives.*
[125] William Crashaw's "Epistle Dedicatory" to Alexander Whitaker's *Good newes from Virginia* (London, 1613).

tions and steadily encroached on the more densely settled coastal areas, until Indian warriors were within twenty miles of Boston itself. The war was fought as much in words as on the battlefield, as Jill Lepore has argued, and the dozens of narratives left by ministers, soldiers, and ordinary settlers (printed in large runs, to the tune of fifteen thousand copies in all between 1675 and 1682) provide a rich body of textual evidence for exploring the sacrificial paradigm of colonial violence.[126] We should never lose sight of the terrible toll exacted by fire and sword on colonial communities both native and English, however, while we delve into the linguistic representations of war. Lepore reminds us that "words and wounds are not equivalent" even if they functioned in analogous ways to shape the larger cultural meaning of the war.[127] Protestant semiotics offered considerable latitude for dissolving the distinction between words and things, as we explored earlier in the chapter, but the phenomenon of literalization had its limits. We should respect those limits, as early modern Protestants themselves did even as they were drawn to the seductive power of language to materialize their deepest fears and desires. Words are *not* wounds, even when "written in such visible and bloody Characters."[128]

The firing of Fort Mystic in 1637 became the template for war for the remainder of the century. Images of burning structures (houses, barns, meetinghouses) were pervasive in narratives of King Philip's War, often with living people inside. From the "little spark" ignited in June 1675 by the first Indian raids, a "great flame" erupted in the winter of 1675–76 "that from East to West the whole Country is involved in great trouble, and the Lord himself seemeth to be against us, to cast us off, and to put us to shame."[129] There is a numbing monotony to the litany of lives and property lost to fire in colonial accounts that does not bear exhaustive repetition here. One example may suffice, from Increase Mather's (not so) *Brief History of the Warr*: "[February 10, 1676]. Some hundreds of Indians fell upon Lancaster, burnt many of the Houses, killed and took Captive above forty persons. . . . February 21. The Indians assaulted Medfield, . . . they burnt half the Town, killed several Men, Women and Children (about eighteen in all). . . . February 25. This night the Indians fired eleven Houses and Barns in Weymouth."[130] And the Indian

---

[126] Jill Lepore, *The Name of War: King Philip's War and the Origins of American Identity* (New York: Knopf, 1998), 52.

[127] Ibid., 148.

[128] Increase Mather, *An Earnest Exhortation to the Inhabitants of New-England* (Boston, 1676), in *So Dreadfull a Judgment*, 172.

[129] Increase Mather, *Brief History*, 101.

[130] Ibid., 110–11.

"furies" kept on coming, through the bitter winter months and into the spring and summer.[131] The English retaliated in kind, torching Indian homes and fields and loosing "streams of blood, and fire, and vengeance upon the Heathen"; in one epic battle (comparable in scale to that of Fort Mystic) nearly a thousand Indian men, women, and children died in the flames inside their fort at the Great Swamp.[132] "So after much blood and many wounds dealt on both sides, the English seeing their advantage, began to fire the Wigwams where there was supposed to be many of the enemy's women and children destroyed, by the firing of at least five or six hundred of these smoaky Cells." The unexpected assault caught the Indians just as they were preparing their evening meal, so "they and their mitchin fryed together."[133] In the face of such relentless death and destruction, the English could well believe they were living in ancient biblical times, when God's enemies succumbed to fire and sword and the Israelites were tested in their own "furnace of affliction" (Isa. 48:10).

The flames of war consumed the southern colonies as well as New England in these years. There were few ministers available, or willing, to provide the sacrificial readings we have been exploring for the New England conflicts, but eyewitness accounts of Bacon's Rebellion in Virginia (1675–76) also dwelled on images of burning fields, buildings, and bodies. The misleadingly titled Bacon's Rebellion was, first and foremost, a war of revenge against the native inhabitants of Virginia who had been thwarting the colony's ambitions to expand westward ever since a peace treaty had been signed with the remnants of the Powhatan Confederacy in 1646. An ambitious newcomer, Nathaniel Bacon, rose to power among the frontiersmen and disaffected planters in the mid-1670s on his promises to ruthlessly suppress the Indian threat. Petitions from "the poore distressed subjects" in the Virginia backcountry flooded into the governor's office, pleading for military support against the Indians who "hath already most berberously and Inhumanly taken and Murdered severall of our bretheren and put them to more cruel torture by burning of them which makes our harts Ready to bleed."[134] One poor captive was even "prepared for the flames at James' towne" though he mercifully escaped.[135] When Governor

---

[131] Thomas Shepard, *The Parable of the Ten Virgins Opened & Applied* (London, 1677), 6.

[132] Increase Mather, *Earnest Exhortation*, 22.

[133] Hubbard, *Narrative of the Troubles*, 53.

[134] "Frontier Planter's Petition to Governor Berkeley," CO 1/36, fol. 139.

[135] "A Narrative of the Indian and Civil Wars in Virginia, in the Years 1675 and 1676," *Collections of the Massachusetts Historical Society*, ser. 1, vol. 1 (Boston, 1814), 7.

Berkeley was slow to act, Bacon gathered his own militia (for which he would be declared a traitor by Berkeley) and "fired and destroid" an Indian stronghold; inside were "a great number of men, woemen and children whose groans were heard but they all burnt except 3 or 4 men."[136] The English, and their houses of worship, did not escape unscathed. Desperate men and women told of neighbors "smoakingly Murder'd" in their beds by those "bloody Heathens" who set the frontier ablaze, of being made "sad Spectacles of Bloud and Ruin."[137] The culminating act of this sorry "rebellion" was the torching of Jamestown itself (a "sacralidgious action") by Bacon's forces: "Bacon sets the towne on fire," one witness wrote, then "he in the most barbarous manner converts the wholl towne into flames, cinders, and ashes, not so much as spareing the church, and the first that ever was in Verginia."[138] Bacon's untimely death from "the bloody flux" (a fitting end, as Carla Gardina Pestana has pointed out, for one who reputedly swore to the damnation of his blood) at the height of the fighting effectively ended the rebellion, and a vengeful Berkeley hanged several of the rebel leaders before being recalled to England in disgrace.[139]

A "fiery oven" indeed was English America in the 1670s. Indian and English bodies alike were turned from flesh to bread by the heat of the flames. As Benjamin Tompson put it, "Had we been cannibals here might we feast."[140] Tompson's epic poem narrated King Philip's War ("New England's hour of passion") in alimentary terms, as a "feast" of flesh and blood, both animal and human. From the killing of the cattle that devoured their cornfields to the drinking of English blood and the "roasting" of English flesh, Indians indulged their grossest appetites in the frenzy of war.

[136] Nathaniel Bacon's Victory over Indians, April 1676, CO 1/36, 77. Another account of the firing of the Powhatan fort is in T.M., *The Beginning, Progress, and Conclusion of Bacon's Rebellion in Virginia, in the Years 1675 and 1676* (repr., Washington, 1835), 11. The mass burning of Indians assembled in forts was a hallmark of war in the south as well as in the north; during the Tuscarora War (1711), Colonel James Moore's troops set fire to Neoheroka fort, killing at least two hundred; David La Vere, *The Tuscarora War: Indians, Settlers, and the Fight for the Carolina Colonies* (Chapel Hill: University of North Carolina Press, 2013), 168–69.

[137] The Virginians Plea for Opposing ye Indians without ye Governors Order, 1676, CO 1/37, no. 14 ("smoakingly Murder'd"); Petition of Inhabitants of [blank] County, July 8, 1676, CO 1/37, no. 27.I ("sad Spectacles of Bloud and Ruin").

[138] "Narrative of the Indian and Civil Wars," 26.

[139] Carla Gardina Pestana discusses the religious overtones of Bacon's Rebellion in her *Protestant Empire: Religion and the Making of the British Atlantic World* (Philadelphia: University of Pennsylvania Press, 2009), 135–39.

[140] Tompson, *New Englands Crisis*, 224.

Now [says Philip] if you fight I'll get you English coats,
And wine to drink out of their captains' throats. . . .

. . . not lacking meat or drink,
The ranging wolves find here and there a prey,
And having filled their paunch they run away. . . .

Hundreds of cattle now they sacrifice
For airy spirits up to gormandize;
And to the Moloch of their hellish guts,
Which craves the flesh in gross, their ale in butts. . . .

Tompson leaves his readers with a final grotesque image of Indians "be-smeared with Christian blood & oiled, / With fat out of white human bodies boiled."[141] How fitting that what has been called "America's first epic" is the story of a "bloody banquet," a ghoulish communion feast where ravenous Indians devour Christian blood and flesh. Such vile, stinking fare was poison even to hardened Indian stomachs accustomed to ingesting raw meat: English accounts frequently speak of their Indian tormenters "vomiting" up the unholy feast they had consumed. "Truly, Every Drop of *Blood* . . . Squeezed from the Abused People of God, proves a *Cup of Poison* to the procurers of it; It makes them at Length to Vomit their very Bowels up."[142]

As a fascinating side note, Puritan ministers were no strangers to the notion of consuming "in gross" human flesh and blood in another guise: the practice of "medicinal cannibalism," or the use of human remains ("mummy") in the preparation of medicines, was in vogue in the sixteenth and seventeenth centuries. It is striking, as Karen Gordon-Grube notes, that mummy became increasingly popular in Europe at the exact moment the eucharistic wars were heating up. The Puritan divine and poet Edward Tay-

---

[141] Ibid., 217, 218, 219, 221, 224, 226. Tompson's language here echoes Samuel Clarke's description of the atrocities of the St. Bartholomew Day's Massacre in Paris (1572), in which the "fat" of the slain Protestants was rendered into grease and sold for human consumption; *A Generall Martyrologie, Containing a Collection of all the Greatest Persecutions which have befallen the Church of Christ* (London, 1660), 2nd ed., 350.

[142] Cotton Mather, *The Present State of New-England. Considered in a discourse on the necessities and advantages of a public spirit in every man* (Boston, 1690), 31. For other references to Indians drinking English blood, see Cotton Mather: "*More English Blood, Swallowed, but Revenged. The Blood-thirsty Salvages, not content with quaffing the Blood of Two or Three persons, found at work, in a Field . . . did on Aug. 24, Kill & Take Eight persons at Kittery.*" *Decennium Luctuosum*, 124.

lor (whose graphic sacramental meditations on the flesh and blood of Christ we explored earlier) was also a physician. Among the remedies found in his "Dispensatory" could be found "mans sweate," "menstruall blood," "mans fat," "the marrow of the bones," and "the moss in the skull of dead men exposed to the aire," along with "balsalm of puppies drowned in white wine" and "the head of a black cat burned to ashes." Blood "drunk warm and new" was a remedy for the "falling sickness," while ingesting a "mans heart" would supposedly cure epilepsy. Taylor learned his craft from Johann Schroeder's influential *Pharmacopoeia* (first published in 1641; a 1644 copy was owned by Taylor), which spelled out in meticulous detail how to procure "mummy": "Take the fresh, unspotted cadaver of a redheaded man (because in them the blood is thinner and the flesh hence more excellent). . . . Cut the flesh in pieces and sprinkle it with myrrh and just a little aloe. Then soak it in spirits of wine for several days, hang it up for 6 to 10 hours, soak it again in spirits of wine, then let the pieces dry in dry air in a shady spot. Thus they will be similar to smoked meat, and will not stink."[143] Not all Puritans embraced such unorthodox methods. Cotton Mather, for one, was disgusted by the practice of using human skulls to cure disease: "I declare, I abominate it. For I take a Man's Skull to be . . . a nasty, mortified, putrified, carronish piece of our own species; and to take it Inwardly, seems an Execrable Fact that even the Anthropophagi would shiver at."[144] Having spilled so much ink decrying the cannibalistic practices of the "devil's own," Mather was in no mood to entertain other uses of human flesh and blood, however benign.

As in the image of the colonial "butcher shop" that we saw in Spanish accounts, dismemberment (scalping, chopping off hands and feet, stripping flesh from bone) played a prominent role in late seventeenth-century narratives. In English America, the colonists had extensive experience with Indian modes of war by the 1670s, including the ritual torture of prisoners at the stake. Desecration of the dead was a favorite tactic in King Philip's War, used

[143] Karen Gordon-Grube, "Evidence of Medicinal Cannibalism in Puritan New England: 'Mummy' and Related Remedies in Edward Taylor's 'Dispensatory,'" *Early American Literature* 28 (1993): 185–221; and Gordon-Grube, "Anthropophagy in Post-Renaissance Europe: The Tradition of Medicinal Cannibalism," *American Anthropologist* 90 (June 1988): 405–9. Gordon-Grube speculates that the appeal of mummy among Protestant physicians may even have been a reaction against the Catholic doctrine of transubstantiation.
[144] Cotton Mather, *The Angel of Bethesda: An Essay Upon the Common Maladies of Mankind* (Boston, 1724), 145.

by Indians and English alike to terrify and demoralize the enemy.[145] Ministers mourned the inability to bury their dead properly: "The English were not in a capacity to look after their dead," Increase Mather lamented, "but those dead bodies were left as meat for the Fowls of Heaven, and their Flesh unto the Beasts of the Earth, and there was none to bury them" (Jer. 34:20).[146] Secular chroniclers were particularly fascinated by Indian mistreatment of the dead in their accounts of the war (conveniently ignoring English complicity in the practice along the way). Nathaniel Saltonstall included several examples of what he called the Indians' efforts to "signalize their Cruelty"; the bodies of two Englishmen were found "with their Fingers and Feet cut off, and the skin of their Heads flayed off," and several Englishwomen were killed by "cutting off the head, ripping open the Belly, and skulping the head of skin and hair, and hanging them up as Trophies."[147] William Hubbard described the "subtlety and barbarous cruelty" of the Indians, which included vicarious forms of cannibalism such as feeding the butchered bodies of the English to their dogs; "they stripped the body of him whom they had slain, and then cutting off his head, fixed it upon a pole looking toward his own land. The corpse of the man slain the week before, they dug up out of his grave, cut off his head and one leg, and set them upon poles, and stripped off his winding sheet. An infant which they found dead in the house they cut in pieces, which afterwards they cast to the swine."[148]

Benjamin Church, who commanded a militia company during the war, regaled his readers with the "brutish barbarities" the Indians "exercised" on the bodies of their foes, "beheading, dismembering, and mangling them, and exposing them in a most inhumane manner." His narrative—written to "entertain" rather than to edify—teased readers with sly suggestions of anthropophagy by comparing the Indians to "blood-hounds" who "thirsted after the blood of their *English* Neighbours." He frequently interrupted his narrative to dwell on images of Indian camps where English bodies might, or might not,

[145] See Richard J. Chacon and David H. Dye, eds., *The Taking and Displaying of Human Body Parts as Trophies by Amerindians* (New York: Springer, 2007); and Hal Langfur, "Moved by Terror: Frontier Violence as Cultural Exchange in Late-Colonial Brazil," *Ethnohistory* 52 (Spring 2005): 255–89.

[146] Increase Mather, *Brief History*, 91. Erik Seeman discusses the English horror of disinterment, which they associated with Catholicism and the punishment of common criminals, in *Death in the New World*, 80–85.

[147] N. S. [Nathaniel Saltonstall], *A New and Further Narrative of the State of New England, Being a Continued Account of the Bloudy Indian-War* (London, 1676), 4, 14; N.S. [Nathaniel Saltonstall], *The Present State of New-England, with respect to the Indian War* (London, 1675), 5.

[148] Hubbard, *Narrative of the Troubles*, 75.

have been consumed. When the militia stumbled upon one abandoned Indian camp, for example, they "saw the ground where they had set their baskets bloody." Close inspection of the blood revealed that the Indians had "kindled some fires, and roasted some flesh, &c." (It was "afterwards discovered" to be "the flesh of Swine, &c. which they had killed that day.") A world of meaning is contained in those two instances of "&c."[149] The climax of Church's narrative was the capture, killing, and dismembering of King Philip's body in which the heroic captain played a bit role. Caught unawares by Church and his men, the cowardly Indians "fled at the first tydings, left their Kettles boiling & meat roasting upon their wooden Spits, & run into a swamp with no other Breakfast than what Capt. Church afterwards treated them with."[150] Like the Gortonists who taunted their would-be captors that they would be a "good Sabbath day breakfast," like the English whom Cotton Mather lamented had become a "Breakfast" to the French Indians, Philip and his men would be offered a "breakfast" of flesh and blood by vengeful English soldiers.[151]

The cannibal motif reached its rhetorical height in the ordeal of those English men, women, and children taken captive by the Indians. Captive-taking was a notable feature of these late century wars: from the handful of captivities recorded in King Philip's War (one of which produced the first English captivity narrative, soon a staple of the colonial canon), the number grew rapidly into the hundreds by the end of the century as what had been a series of regional wars between settlers and natives (King Philip's War in the North, Bacon's Rebellion in the South) broadened out into a full-scale imperial war between France and England and their respective Indian allies (King William's War, 1688–97).[152] A compendium of captivity narratives published in Boston under the title *Good Fetch'd Out of Evil* recounted the miraculous rescue of one English child taken captive by a "Crue of Indians" who "hung it before the Fire to rost it for their Supper; but that these *Canibals* might Satiate their—I want a Name for it—as well as their Hunger, they would Roast it *Alive*."[153] These stories of torture at the stake are familiar from other New World narratives

[149] Benjamin Church, *Entertaining Passages Relating to Philip's War* (Boston, 1716), in *So Dreadfull a Judgment*, 399, 401, 437, 445.

[150] Ibid., 445.

[151] Cotton Mather, *Souldiers Counselled and Comforted* (Boston, 1681), 32.

[152] Alden T. Vaughan and Daniel Richter, "Crossing the Cultural Divide: Indians and New Englanders, 1605–1763," in Vaughan, *Roots of American Racism: Essays on the Colonial Experience* (New York: Oxford University Press, 1995), 213–52.

[153] *Good Fetch'd Out of Evil* (Boston, 1706), 34–35. Throughout the text captives are described as "sacrifices" to the depravity of their Indian captors.

dating back to Columbus's day: Mather's account of the death of Robert Rod-
gers (whose unfortunate nickname was "Robin Pork" because of his "corpu-
lency") is every bit as gruesome as the narratives of Cortés. "They Danced
about him, and at every Turn, they did with their knives, cut collops of his
Flesh from his Naked Limbs & throw them with his Blood into his Face. When
he was Dead, they set his Body down upon the glowing Coals, and left him
tyed with his Back to the Stake; where the English Army soon found him. He
was left to Us, to put out the Fire with our Tears!"[154] Joshua Scottow's version
of the war traced the history of these "wicked" and "cruel Cannibals" back to
their satanic origins, drawing a direct line from the "Pequod Amalecks"
through the "Ravening Wolves of Heresy" (Hutchinson and Gorton) to the
current crop of "Cursed Cannibals" who are now "Scalping, and Fleaing of our
Bodies, burning us as Sacrifices to *Habamoch*."[155] At least a few were then subjected to additional torments, including self-cannibalism: "These horrid Cannibals . . . those Devils Incarnate have Tyed their Captives unto Trees, and first
cutting off their Ears, have made them to Eat their own Ears, and then have
broiled their whole Bodies, with slow Fires, dancing the meanwhile about
them, and cutting out Collops of their Flesh, till with lingering Tortures, they
have Martyred them to Death!"[156] Puritan ministers demanded flesh for flesh,
sacrifice for sacrifice in the face of such atrocities: "*Turn not back* till they are
consumed; . . . Let not the Expression seem Harsh, if I say to you, *Sacrifice
them to the Ghosts of the Christians whom they have Murdered*."[157]

With so many houses and bodies burned to ashes, it required no great
leap of imagination or theological insight to narrate the late century wars as a
"burnt sacrifice." They could hardly be anything else. "I doubt not it will one
day appear, that the coals which have been stolen from Gods Altar have burnt
down many of those Plantations which are now desolate," Mather concluded.
The "Temple" of God in New England had been razed by "these perfidious,
cruel, and hellish Monsters," and "*instead of a sweet smell there shall be a
Stink*"—the stink of burning flesh rather than the fragrant smell of incense.
The "stink" of this New World version of blood sacrifice told Protestants they
were in the presence of the devil's (Habamoch's) altar, not God's: "what Woes

---

[154] Cotton Mather, *Decennium Luctuosum*, 49.

[155] Joshua Scottow, "A Narrative of the Planting of the Massachusetts Colony" (1699), in
Collections of the Massachusetts Historical Society 34 (1858): 279–330 (quotations on 288, 301,
304, and 310).

[156] Cotton Mather, *Observable Things: The History of Ten Years Rolled away under the
great Calamities of War with the Indian Salvages* (Boston, 1695), 224.

[157] Cotton Mather, *Souldiers Counselled and Comforted*, 28.

indeed must we expect from such a Divel of a Moloch, as relishes Sacrifices like those of Humane Heart-Blood, and unto whom there is no musick like the bitter, dying, doleful Groans ejaculated by the Roasting Children of Men."[158] Attributing a thirst for blood to the devil's spawn rather than to God's chosen allowed the English to resurrect the medieval sacrificial paradigm without violating the Protestant taboo on human sacrifice in a Christian world. (Although, tellingly, Mather recalled this earlier world when he spoke of Christ as a "burnt offering" in one of many tracts he wrote during this time of war.)[159] It was their "Indian friends," not they, who "relished" human blood, who stole the coals from "God's Altar" to build the Devil's own in New England, who consumed the "roasted children of men" in a diabolical parody of the Lord's Supper at their stinking altar. "I have read of a people in America, that love meat best when 'tis Rotten and Stinks. The Devil is of their diet," wrote William Gurnall during King Philip's War.[160]

Anglo-American Puritans were familiar with the notion of diabolical inversion of the Christian sacraments from their long-running battle with another devilish enemy: witches. Contemporary histories of the Indian wars explicitly linked the assaults of "salvages" with the assaults of witches, as Mary Beth Norton points out in her contribution to the scholarship on the Salem trials.[161] In Scottow's narrative, for example, the language of "ravening" beasts thirsting for Christian blood links all the devil's many guises (Indians, heretics, witches) into a single trope of monstrosity. Scottow marveled that "a Damned Crew of Devils or witches at the Devils Table with Red Bread and Wine, in derision of our Lords Body and Blood, should sport and feast themselves (as some of the Confessing Witches have said, and unsaid) with that

---

[158] Cotton Mather, *The Wonders of the Invisible World: Operations as Well Historical as Theological, Upon the Nature, the Number, and the Operations of the Devils* (Boston, 1693), 16. The image of "roasting" children resurfaced in the early eighteenth-century Indian wars in the colonial South, confirming once again that Puritans had no monopoly on this quasi-sacramental rhetoric. Even before war broke out in 1715, South Carolinians were worried about "being roasted in slow fires," and their fears soon became a (rhetorical) reality as reports filtered in of Indians' "splitting open the women's young children before their eyes, whom they tormented and rosting them and making the mother eat a part of it." William L. Ramsey, *The Yamasee War: A Study of Culture, Economy, and Conflict in the Colonial South* (Lincoln: University of Nebraska Press, 2008), 160.

[159] Cotton Mather, *Observable Things*, 248.

[160] Quoted in Louise Breen, *Transgressing the Bounds: Subversive Enterprises Among the Puritan Elite in Massachusetts, 1630–1692* (New York: Oxford University Press, 2001), 165.

[161] Mary Beth Norton, *In the Devil's Snare: The Salem Witchcraft Crisis of 1692* (New York: Knopf, 2002).

which is their Torment and Torture."[162] Cotton Mather's self-serving defense of New England's witch trials, *Wonders of the Invisible World*, included several accounts of devils and witches "communicating in an Hellish Bread and Wine." Deliverance Hobbs testified at Salem that Bridget Bishop "was at a General Meeting of the Witches, in a Field at Salem-Village, and there pertook of a Diabolical Sacrament, in Bread and wine then Administered!" Another of the Salem defendants, Martha Carrier (this "Rampant Hag"), was also accused of participating in a "Diabolical Sacrament" where "they had Bread and Wine Administered unto them."[163] The "witches' Sabbath" was a recurrent motif of Anglo-American witch trials. After traveling through the air, witches assembled in the woods for a mock worship service, where they baptized one another, signed the devil's book with their blood, sang obscene hymns, sometimes copulated with the devil, and feasted on the "diabolical sacrament." As Scottow pointed out, Satan was an ingenious mimic who, enraged at the loss of his New World "Dominion," had "set up his Chappel so near to Christ's Church" in New England (now to be called "new Witchland"); "the Devil now contents not himself to imitate Jewish or Popish Modes, but he will take up the Reformed and Congregational Way." Under the withering assaults of such an "unreconcileable Adversary," America's Eden had lost its "sweet smell"—"we smell rank of Hell-bore, Henbane, and poysonful Hemlock, as if we were laid out to be the *American Anticyra*." And at the end of the day, it is God himself who cannot stomach such "smutty" New World fare: "As the Lord vomited out these Natives, to make room for us, so he now hath vomited us out, to make room for them."[164]

The explicit invocation of "Red Bread and Wine" in the witchcraft trials of the late seventeenth century marks the apex of the sacramental discourse of violence. Well before the panic in Salem claimed twenty lives, Protestant narrators of colonial conflicts had already begun to retreat from eucharistic metaphors when describing the horrors they had experienced at the hands of Indians and heretics. We can detect a subtle difference in the language of Protestant violence between the early and the late seventeenth century. The sacramental overtones of these narratives, while always present at some level, recede from view while the sacrificial paradigm came to predominate in ever more vivid language. Another way to put this is that bread—nourishment, baked in ovens, bearing a metonymic relationship to the Christian

[162] Scottow, "Narrative of the Planting," 313.
[163] Cotton Mather, *Wonders of the Invisible World*, 56, 106–7, 137–38.
[164] Scottow, "Narrative of the Planting," 312, 314, 309.

host—became burnt flesh: reduced to ashes, seared in the flames of war, bearing only a perverse resemblance to the body of Christ. This surely reflects as well the cooling of eucharistic debates in Reformation Europe, as the Protestant churches settled into established rhythms of belief and practice that operated largely below the surface of conscious attention. Calvinists and Lutherans had not resolved their differences over the "real presence" by the late seventeenth century, but they had learned to live with one another's doctrinal errors. The ebbing of doctrinal debates was accompanied by a decline in the actual observance of the sacrament of communion, which among English Protestants dipped markedly after the Restoration. Among Anglicans and Puritans, Arnold Hunt notes, the Lord's Supper "lost its hold on popular imagination" by the second half of the seventeenth century.[165]

Moreover, the contest with Rome was fought increasingly over territory and power—control of overseas dominions and the economic and political apparatus that empire created—not over hot theological issues such as transubstantiation or the efficacy of Christ's sacrifice on the cross. This is not to suggest that the wars of religion were over by 1648 or even 1700; some of the worst violence was still to come, after the revocation of the Edict of Nantes by Louis XIV in 1695 and the resultant mass expulsion and forced conversion of the Huguenot population. The war to exterminate Protestantism in France did not end until the first decade of the eighteenth century. Nonetheless, the field of battle had decisively shifted from theology to imperial politics by the time Charles II was restored to the English throne in 1660. Instead of "papal anthropophagy" Protestants now denounced papal tyranny. Anglo-American anti-Catholic hysteria probably reached its height in the period between the "popish plot" of 1678 and the conclusion of the Seven Years War in 1763, according to recent scholars, but it was expressed more through the language of racial politics than the language of theological controversy.[166]

The repercussions of this long-term shift in the Protestant International's perception of its primary religious "other" for colonial discourse were twofold. For one, the Indian menace began to shift correspondingly from the domain of the devil to the domain of imperial politics. English colonists never lost the impression of Indians as instruments of the devil, but the devil

---

[165] Hunt, "The Lord's Supper in Early Modern England," 83.

[166] Owen Stanwood, *The Empire Reformed: English America in the Age of the Glorious Revolution* (Philadelphia: University of Pennsylvania Press, 2011); Pestana, *Protestant Empire.* Peter Silver explores the racial politics of the French and Indian War in *Our Savage Neighbors: How Indian War Transformed Early America* (New York: W. W. Norton, 2009).

himself was now more likely to appear as a Frenchman or a Spaniard than a false god or idol (and, in due course of time, as the English monarch himself). The threat that loomed most menacingly over colonial heads was, in Cotton Mather's phrase, the "Half Indianized French and Half Frenchified Indians."[167] Second, the concept of blood sacrifice acquired secondary traits that shifted it significantly from the realm of religion to the realm of political economy, specifically to the domains of contract law and commodity exchange. Whether we can speak of a "commodification" of sacrifice in the late seventeenth and eighteenth centuries (since the triumph of commercial capitalism as the master metaphor in histories of the early modern era written in the 1990s, we are too quick to see commodification everywhere), we can certainly say that economic and legal understandings of blood sacrifice began to encroach on a purely theological paradigm. Of course, Shylock's infamous demand for a "pound of flesh" in Shakespeare's *Merchant of Venice* reminds us that blood sacrifice was never a "purely" theological concept, even in the sixteenth century.

In the final analysis, perhaps the most disturbing feature of Anglo-American sacrificial culture is the degree to which colonists resorted to *bargaining* with God—to slake his anger against them, to restrain his Indian avengers and turn his wrath on them instead, to retract threats of more suffering to come with promises of good behavior. The Indians attack; the English fast and offer up promises of reformation; the attacks become more furious, more lethal; the English send up anguished petitions to God begging for another chance. A town is burnt, and the Indians taunt the English with the impotency of their own prayers and rituals; the English set fire to Indian villages, hoping this burnt offering will appease God. Again and again the English invoked the blood sacrifice of Christ on the cross as both a model to emulate and a rhetorical cudgel with which to beat their enemies. With each reiteration of the sacrificial narrative, the tone becomes more wheedling, more importunate, as if English Protestants had forgotten that God could not be persuaded or bribed into bestowing his grace or withholding his judgment. Their disdain for the medieval theory of satisfaction—to quote the anthropologist Bruce Chilton, "what kind of God would take a bribe?"[168]—did not fully translate, it seems, in the spiritual wilderness that was the New World. Even such stalwart Calvinists as the New England Puritans were

---

[167] Cotton Mather, *Decennium Luctuosum*, 46.
[168] Chilton, "The Hungry Knife," 105.

reduced to bargaining their fortunes, their lives, and their children's lives to make the killing stop. There is surely a connection between the increasingly materialistic, entrepreneurial world the Puritans had created by the end of the century in their bustling seaports and their willingness to resort to bribery to appease an angry God, though just as surely this relationship was neither as simplistic nor as straightforward as Weber and his intellectual heirs believed. Still, there is no denying the emergence of a more reciprocal mode of engaging the deity by the 1670s, especially when their very lives, and the life of their commonwealth, were at stake.

In the next chapter, we will explore a different rhetorical paradigm for justifying violence against God's enemies, one that was grounded as much in legal and political traditions as in theology: that of holy war. Holy wars, or crusades, have a long and illustrious history in western Christendom, but the tradition was supposedly on the defensive by the seventeenth century as new theories of just war were articulated by mostly Reformed jurists (Hugo Grotius will figure largely in this story as well). The demise of "holy war" as a religio-legal theory in the Reformation era has, however, been greatly overstated by historians. The crusades may have ended in the thirteenth century, but Europe's Christians (including those in the New World) continued to find the concept useful as they confronted new enemies and waged new battles.

CHAPTER 2

Holy War

Cursed be he that keepeth back his sword from blood.
—Jeremiah 48:10

It is no other than God's war: God made it, God owns it,
God blesses it.
—Joseph Hall, Via Media (1626)

One spring day in 1644, a woman in Virginia noticed "globs of blood" in the wash pail that mysteriously left no stain on the clothes or on her husband's hands. This, she was sure, was a clear sign from God of "some designe of the Indians." Two weeks later the Powhatan Confederacy unleashed a deadly attack on the colony that killed some five hundred settlers.[1] Six hundred miles to the north, the Puritan governor of Massachusetts, John Winthrop, was just as quick to see God's hand in this deadly assault. "This massacre," he wrote to his fellow governor William Berkeley ("a courtier, and very malignant toward the way of our churches here," Winthrop often complained), "was the direct result of Virginia's having "driven out the godly ministers we had sent them," a reference to Berkeley's controversial decision to expel dissenting preachers from his colony.[2] To both the unnamed Virginia housewife and the Puritan magistrate, the Indian attack of 1644 was the opening skirmish in a new holy war—provoked by sin and carried out by the devil's own warriors, the savage Indians.

---

[1] Edward Bond, *Damned Souls in a Tobacco Colony: Religion in Seventeenth-Century Virginia* (Macon, Ga.: Mercer University Press, 2000), 151–52.

[2] *Winthrop's Journal, "History of New England," 1630–1649*, 2 vols., ed. James Kendall Hosmer (New York, 1908), 2:167–68.

War was, not surprisingly, something of an obsession for Europe's Christians in the Reformation era. Firsthand experience of the horrors of religious war inspired a new generation of thinkers, writers, and polemicists to anatomize the phenomenon of war—to dissect its history, biblical sanction, current guises, and theological significance for a new age. Anglo-American Protestants were active participants in this ongoing effort to understand war and violence (which were related but not the same thing), producing manuals and historical treatises at a steady rate in the fifty years preceding colonization of the New World, with titles such as *The Practice, Proceedings, and Lawes of Armes* (1593), *The Character of Warre* (1626), and *A Short Apologie for Christian Souldiers* (1588). Much of this literature was secular in origin and aim, designed to help jurists and policymakers craft an effective and defensible military strategy, but—as was always the case in the early modern period—religious and secular purposes were inextricably entwined in the project of theorizing war. In the midst of so much bloodshed (most of it Christian, spilled by other Christians), one kind of war in particular became the subject of sustained, and sometimes heated, debate: holy war.

"Holy war," or crusade, is an anachronistic term. It was so in the sixteenth and seventeenth centuries as well, even as Europe's Christians were slaughtering one another in the continent's many "wars of religion." The term itself, as we shall see, was rarely used by ministers or military strategists, and when it was, it usually carried a whiff of condescension. Crusades were, supposedly, a thing of the past—a relic of medieval fanaticism. But if the term itself was out of favor, the words and actions of early modern Anglo-American Protestants reveal just how deeply the notion of holy war against God's enemies continued to resonate.

The Strange Career of Holy War in Western Christendom

Historians once believed that European jurists had written the obituary for holy war in the sixteenth and seventeenth centuries. Renaissance humanism had, so the story goes, rescued the study of man and human society from the iron grip of the medieval church, leading to intellectual breakthroughs in a number of related fields of study. From natural philosophy to human anatomy to the psychology of violence, humanist scholars decisively reshaped the intellectual landscape of Europe, discovering laws of nature where once the inscrutable hand of God had ruled unchallenged. The study of war was one of the beneficiaries of this renewed spirit of inquiry. The biblical understanding of war saw it as the consequence of sin—God's way of punishing humanity for the transgressions they had committed (and were doomed to commit ever after) since being expelled from Eden. The depiction of war in the Old Testament, the original battlefield manual, underscored its horrific nature: war was "a plague," descending with fury on God's enemies and sometimes his own people in a paroxysm of blood and fire. The "sword of God" was ruthless, capable of dispatching entire communities in a single day. The God of the Old Testament was a "man of Warre," English preachers told their congregations repeatedly in the sixteenth and seventeenth centuries, quick to anger and slow to forgive. From the destruction of the Amalekites by the sword of Joshua at God's command ("utterly destroy all that they have, and spare them not; but slay both man and woman, infant and suckling, ox and sheep, camel and ass") to the indiscriminate slaughter of the Canaanites, Moabites, Ammonites, and all the enemies of Israel, the history of the ancient Hebrews was drenched in blood.

The superseding of the Old Testament by the New posed a serious challenge to Christian theorists of war. According to his disciples, Christ had famously declared himself a God of peace, not war. In the words of the early church father Tertullius, "The new law does not avenge itself with the avenging sword."[3] But Jesus was also recorded to have said, "I came not to send peace but a sword" (Matt. 10:34), and there was plenty of ammunition in the chronicles of the early Christians' struggles with their foes to sustain a militant defense of war in the name of religion. John Calvin addressed the question directly in *The Institutes*: "But if it is objected, that in the New Testament there is no passage or example teaching that war is lawful for Christians, I answer, first, that the reasons for carrying on war, which anciently existed, still exists in the present day" (IV:12). William Gouge's 1631 treatise on war (*God's Three Arrowes*) raised the question as well. To the objection "All these proofs are taken out of the Old Testament, which gives not sufficient warrant to Christians," he answered: "Warres waged in the Old Testament are commended in the New."[4] The English divine Richard Bernard dismissed the notion that the Christ of the New Testament was a pacifist. Yes, he was more

[3] Quoted in Grotius, *De Jure Belli ac Pacis*, http://www.lonang.com/exlibris/grotius/ (accessed July 26, 2013).

[4] William Gouge, *God's Three Arrowes: Plague, Famine, Sword, in Three Treatises* (London, 1631), 210–11.

often called a "God of Peace" than a "man of Warre," he acknowledged. But "Our Prince of peace telleth us of warrs, and is pleased to be set out as a Captain of an Host riding on horseback, and subduing his enemies, and making a slaughter of them. Hereby shewing that his Church shall have warre."[5]

Nonetheless, Christian theorists of war had to walk a fine line between the bloodthirsty precedent of the ancient world and the pacifism of the Sermon on the Mount in which Christ counseled his followers to "love thy enemies" (Matt. 5:44). Out of this tension developed one of the most influential concepts in the history of the West, that of the "just war." As with so many important theological developments, credit is usually given to St. Augustine for first articulating a theory of just war in the fifth century that distinguished it both from the vengeful wars of the Old Testament and from Christian nonviolence. For the Bishop of Hippo, just wars were defensive, limited in scope and consequence, and authorized by legitimate secular authorities. Such wars were sanctioned by God for his purposes but through the intermediary of the secular prince and could not be fought without his imprimatur. Though scholars have sometimes imposed a hard distinction between just and holy wars in the post-Augustinian tradition, the line was in fact considerably more blurred, both in theory and in practice. It's hard to imagine how it could be otherwise, considering the imbrication of secular and religious power in medieval Christendom. A prince's authority emanated from God and a true prince always did God's work in doing his own.[6] Nonetheless, we can draw some distinctions between the two concepts, considered as ideal types, in the development of Christian theories of war in the millennium between Augustine and the Reformation—a period that saw no fewer than nine crusades proclaimed by Christian kings and popes against infidels, heretics, and schismatics, as well as numerous conflicts between princes and principalities animated by religious zeal (or aversion) as well as greed and power.

For historians of religion, the classic formulation of just war and holy war begins with Roland Bainton, the church historian whose 1943 essay "From the Just War to the Crusade in the Puritan Revolution" is universally cited. Bainton broke down Christian theorizing about war into three stages: the pacifism of the early church, the just war tradition of the Roman era, and the

---

[5] Richard Bernard, *The Bible-Battels, or, The Sacred Art Military. For the rightly waging of Warre according to Holy Writ* (London, 1629), 28.

[6] Frederick H. Russell, *The Just War in the Middle Ages* (New York: Cambridge University Press, 1975); James Turner Johnson, *Ideology, Reason, and the Limitation of War: Religious and Secular Concepts, 1200–1740* (Princeton, N.J.: Princeton University Press, 1975).

crusading ideal of the Middle Ages. His definition of the "crusading ideal" has been widely adopted by scholars since: "The crusading ideal requires that the cause be holy, and no cause is more holy than religion, that the war shall be fought under God and with his help, that the crusaders shall be godly and their enemies ungodly, that the war shall be prosecuted unsparingly."[7] Unlike just wars, holy wars (or crusades) could be offensive as well as defensive, did not require the authorization of the prince, and did not need to adhere to commonly accepted norms of fair conduct. The "mood" of holy war is "righteous enthusiasm"; that of just war, "sober" calculation and, more often than not, regret.[8] Killing, in the just war tradition, was a necessary evil, the unfortunate but inevitable consequence of man's sinful nature; for crusaders, it was an opportunity for martyrdom to be devoutly pursued. The archetype of holy war in the West is the First Crusade, declared by Urban II in 1095 against infidels, which culminated in the sacking of Jerusalem in 1099 and the massacre of the Jewish and Muslim population of the city, along with the pillaging of synagogues, mosques, and other holy sites. This formula would be repeated over and over again for the next three centuries, as waves of crusaders made their way to the Holy Land with a cross embroidered on their chest and bloodlust in their hearts. Most died miserable and alone in strange lands, finding neither glory nor riches, but the crusading ideal burned brightly throughout the Middle Ages.

In the early decades of the thirteenth century, however, the script took a decisive turn. The Albigensian Crusade of 1208–29 was, in the words of Mark Pegg, "a holy war unlike any other," one that "chang[ed] forever what it meant to be a Christian."[9] For the first time, fellow Christians—heretics, yes, but still recognizably Christian—rather than Jews or Muslims were the crusaders' targets. Pegg provocatively hitches the Albigensian Crusade to the train of mass slaughter and even genocide that would take western Chris-

---

[7] Roland Bainton, "Congregationalism: From the Just War to the Crusade in the Puritan Revolution," *Andover Newton Theological School Bulletin* 35 (April 1943): 1–20 (quotation on 15). This essay was later expanded into *Christian Attitudes to War and Peace* (New York: Abingdon Press, 1960). See also David Little, "'Holy War' Appeals and Western Christianity: A Reconsideration of Bainton's Approach," in *Just War and Jihad: Historical and Theoretical Perspectives on War and Peace in Western and Islamic Traditions*, ed. John Kelsay and James Turner Johnson (New York: Greenwood Press, 1991), 121–39; LeRoy Walters, "The Just War and the Crusade: Antitheses or Analogies?" *Monist* 57 (October 1973): 584–94.

[8] Melvin Endy, "Just War, Holy War, and Millennialism in Revolutionary America," *William and Mary Quarterly*, 3rd ser., 42 (January 1985): 3–25 (quotation on 8).

[9] Mark Gregory Pegg, *A Most Holy War: The Albigensian Crusade and the Battle for Christendom* (New York: Oxford University Press, 2008), xiv, 5.

tendom from the sacking of Jerusalem to modern wars of extermination (including those in our own day); we don't need to resort to such sweeping generalizations to acknowledge that the killing of Christians by Christians was indeed something new and disturbing in the western history of religious war. We will return to the question of genocide in the context of the religious wars of the seventeenth century, but the point for now is the widening of the targets of crusade beyond the traditional enemies of the medieval church to "men, women, and children" who "looked and acted like real Christians."[10]

This more expansive model of holy war would resurface in the Reformation era, even as theologians and jurists increasingly turned away from Old Testament precedents in search of a more enlightened, and humane, theory of justifiable war. Whereas the excesses of the medieval crusades had led theologians like Thomas of Aquinas to condemn the violent persecution of heretics, the chief architects of the Reformation all endorsed the use of the (civil) sword to punish enemies of the Church.[11] Their language was unsparing. Calvin urged Christian magistrates not to be squeamish in the face of irreligion by recalling the resolve of "the meek and gentle" Moses who, "besmeared and reeking with the blood of his brethren," heeded God's command and "took vengeance on the people for sacrilege by slaying three thousand of them in one day," thus "sanctify[ing] the hands which . . . would have [been] polluted by showing mercy."[12] As he told Genevans, "You shall show yourselves rightly zealous of God's service, in that you kill your own brethren without sparing . . . to show that God is above all."[13] Luther argued that violence—even extreme violence—was justified against unbelievers because "the hand that bears the sword is as such no longer man's, but God's, and not man it is, but God who hangs, breaks on the wheel, beheads, strangles."[14] While the actual record of persecution in Calvin's Geneva has been famously

[10] Ibid., 191. See also R. I. Moore's discussion of the Albigensian Crusade in *The War on Heresy* (Cambridge, Mass.: Harvard University Press, 2012), chapter 15, "To War and Arms."

[11] Perez Zagorin outlines the Christian "theory of persecution" from the early church through the Reformation in *How the Idea of Religious Toleration Came to the West* (Princeton, N.J.: Princeton University Press, 2003), chapters 2 and 3.

[12] John Calvin, *The Institutes of Christian Religion*, trans. Henry Beveridge (Edinburgh, 1845), IV:10. See Michael Walzer, "Exodus 32 and the Theory of Holy War: The History of a Citation," *Harvard Theological Review* 61 (January 1968): 1–14, for a discussion of the prominence of the biblical example of Moses and the onslaught of the Levites in the literature on religious war.

[13] John Calvin, *Sermons on the Fifth Book of Moses* (London, 1583), 1203.

[14] Quoted in J. R. Hale, *Renaissance War Studies* (London: Hambledon Press, 1983), 487.

overstated by historians (despite the severity of his language, only one man, Michael Servetus, was actually put to death for his beliefs during Calvin's reign as magistrate),[15] the strident rhetoric of holy war espoused by the Reformers was at odds with the humanist strain of secular war theorizing that blossomed in the sixteenth and seventeenth centuries, thus setting up a potential clash of ideological positions that would mark debates about religious war throughout the Reformation era.

Hugo Grotius's seminal work *De Jure Belli et Pacis* (1623) is considered by many to be the locus classicus of Renaissance theorizing about war, the foundational text from which international conventions of military conduct would be developed. Grotius was not the first jurist to condemn holy wars— the Italian priest turned Protestant Alberico Gentili had written in the 1590s that "There is no religion so wicked as to order an attack upon men of a different belief"—nor was he the last; in the 1690s, Franciscus de Vitoria famously declared that "Difference of religion is not a cause of just war."[16] But Grotius's text laid out the argument in clear, legal language that mirrors his approach to dismantling the medieval notion of blood sacrifice that we explored in the first chapter. The prolegomena of *De Jure Belli et Pacis* offers a nightmarish vision of the religious wars of his own day: "I saw in the whole Christian world a license of fighting at which even barbarous nations might blush. Wars were begun on trifling pretexts or none at all, and carried on without any reference of law, Divine or human; it is as if . . . frenzy had been openly let loose for the committing of all crimes."[17] Premised on a firm distinction between natural law (which governed the affairs of princes and kingdoms) and divine law (which governed the relationship of man to God), Grotius proceeded systematically to lay out the rules by which war could, and could not, be waged. Wars for blood-sport, for the deliberate inflicting of pain or for revenge alone, were for "savages." Wars fought for dominion over peoples in the "unknown parts of the earth" or out of "a desire to rule others against their will on the pretext that it is for their good"

---

[15] Marilynne Robinson has written eloquently of the unfair treatment of Calvin by religious scholars and historians; see *The Death of Adam: Essays on Modern Thought* (New York: Picador, 1998), especially the introduction, 1–27, and "Puritans and Prigs," 150–73.

[16] Gentili, *De Jure Belli Libri Tres*, quoted in Jill Lepore, *The Name of War: King Philip's War and the Origins of American Identity* (New York: Knopf, 1998), 109; de Vitoria, *De Indies et de jure relectiones* (1696), quoted in Joris van Eijnatten, "'Religionis Causa': Moral Theology and the Concept of Holy War in the Dutch Republic," *Journal of Religious Ethics* 34.2 (December 2006): 609–35 (quotation on 619).

[17] Grotius, *De Jure*, prolegomena.

are likewise unjust (hence calling into question the morality of the entire conquest of the New World). Most important, wars must be fought according to clear and universally accepted *rules*: "Least of all should that be admitted which some people imagine, that in war all laws are in abeyance. On the contrary war ought not to be undertaken except for the enforcement of rights; when once undertaken it should be carried on only within the bounds of law and good faith."

Turning specifically to the case of religious war, Grotius acknowledged "there is a dispute" over "whether war may be waged on account of crimes against God." The examples he summoned up to probe further this question reveal the influence of contact with the alien religions of the New World on war theorizing at home. "Just as those are worthy to be excused, and certainly not to be punished by men, who, not having received any law revealed by God, worship the powers of the stars or of other natural objects, or spirits . . . so we must class with the impious rather than with the erring those who establish with divine honors the worship of evil spirits, whom they know to be such, or of personified vices, or of men whose lives are filled with crimes. To be classed as impious also are those who worship gods with the shedding of innocent blood."[18] The ambivalence of Reformers to the religion of American "savages" is on display here—to the extent that native peoples worship objects of nature or lesser "spirits," their faith could be considered misguided but not "impious." When they worshiped the devil or engaged in human sacrifice, however, they deserved the punishment meted out by Christian conquistadores.

The question of religious war concerned battling not only the superstitions of pagans but also the more dangerous impieties of heterodox believers at home. After posing the general question of whether war may be waged on account of "crimes against God," Grotius offered four different rules governing Christian response to irreligion: (1) "Wars cannot justly be waged against those who are unwilling to accept the Christian religion"; (2) "Wars are justly waged against those who treat Christians with cruelty for the sake of their religion alone"; (3) "Wars may not be justly waged against those who err in the interpretation of the Divine law"; and (4) "But war may justly be waged against those who show impiety toward the gods they believe in."[19] The back-and-forth nature of these rules reflects the ever-shifting terrain of just war

---

[18] Ibid., book 2, chapter 20 ("On Punishments"), XLIV.
[19] Ibid., XLVIII, XLIX, L, LI.

thinking among Reformers as they confronted a series of "others" who did
not fit easily into the traditional categories of God's enemies: New World Indians and sectarians. Though they had often proven "unwilling to accept the
Christian religion," Indians should nonetheless be spared—except when they
"treat Christians with cruelty for the sake of their religion alone." Heterodox
Christians who "err in the interpretation of the Divine law" should be tolerated, but those who "show impiety" deserve to be punished. Within these
four rules, then, one couplet argued for the waging of war against Indians
and heretics, the other for clemency. This ambiguity could not be resolved by
historical and legal analysis alone: in the heat of battle against religious enemies both old and new, Europe's Christians would put these propositions to
the test.

European theorists across the continent took up the question of when
and how to wage war against religious enemies, but the debate was perhaps
most developed in England as tensions between conformists and nonconformists heated up and the country veered closer to outright civil war in the
late sixteenth and early seventeenth centuries.[20] These decades—the exact
time when thousands of English Protestants were considering, and undertaking, the fateful decision to remove to the New World—saw a remarkable outpouring of sermons and treatises on the question of holy war. Of the roughly
half a million sermons that English churchgoers heard in the period 1580–
1630, J. R. Hale estimates that "a significant number, a *really* significant number, echoed the endorsement of military violence."[21] Across the religious and
political spectrum, Protestant theologians and jurists argued over whether
God still commanded his people to take up arms against unbelievers as he
had in the Old Testament—and if so, where the moral and political limits on
their authority to act in his name were to be drawn. The first work in English
devoted entirely to the history of the crusades was published in 1639, on the
very brink of civil war (Figure 4).[22] Thus when war did finally break out in
1642, English Protestants were well armed to engage the fight in print as well
as on the battlefield.

[20] For a critique of the overemphasis on the English case in histories of holy war thinking,
see van Eijnatten, " 'Religionis Causa.' "
[21] Hale, *Renaissance War Studies*, 490.
[22] Thomas Fuller, *The Historie of the Holy Warre* (London, 1639).

Figure 4. The futility and waste of holy war as depicted in the first
English-language book on the subject. According to the caption,
Europe's Christians "went out full but returned empty" from the
crusades. Thomas Fuller, *The Historie of the Holy Warre* (1639).

Fighting the "Brats of Babylon":
The English Civil War as Holy War

In the early 1620s, Francis Bacon—philosopher, scientist, and courtier—pondered the prospect of holy war in a series of notes scribbled for his own perusal, later published in 1629 as *An Advertisement Touching an Holy Warre*. In the mode of his fellow humanist Hugo Grotius, Bacon posed a series of questions lawmakers should ask themselves before waging war against religious enemies: whether war is lawful for a Christian state "onely and simply for the Propagation of the Faith"; whether war is lawful to recover countries that were "once Christian . . . though now they be utterly alienated"; whether war is justified to "free [Christians], and deliver them from the servitude of the Infidels"; whether war is needed "for the Purging and Recovery of Consecrate Places, being now polluted and Prophaned"; whether war should be waged "for the Revenge, or Vindication of Blasphemies, and Reproaches against the Deity . . . Or for the Effusion of Christian Bloud, and Cruelties against Christians, though ancient and long since past; Considering that Gods Visits are without limitation of Time." And finally, and most pertinently to the Anglo-American conversation about just war and holy war, whether "a Holy Warre may be pursued, either to the Expulsion of a People, or to the Enforcement of Conscience, or the like Extremities."[23] There are no definitive answers to these questions here; the *Advertisement* was not a legal brief but a collection of preliminary thoughts, constructed as a conversation among stock characters (a Catholic and a Protestant zealot, an orthodox and a moderate divine, a soldier, a statesman, and a courtier). The dialogue breaks off abruptly after a lengthy speech by one of the zealots, thus giving far more weight to the argument for rather than against holy war, despite Bacon's own reservations on the question. The view that probably came closest to his own is the one he attributed to the statesman: "I am of opinion, that . . . there is no *Possibilitie* of an *Holy Warre*. And I was ever of opinion, that the *Philosophers Stone* and an *Holy Warre*, were but the *Rendez-vous* of Crackt Braines."[24]

Bacon's scorn notwithstanding, there were plenty of "crackt braines" around to mount a robust defense of holy war in the 1620s and 1630s. The fact

---

[23] Francis Bacon, *An Advertisement Touching an Holy Warre*, in William Rawley, *Certain Miscellany Works of the Right Honourable Francis Lo. Verulam, Viscount St. Albans* (London, 1629), 77–134 (quotation on 115–16).

[24] Ibid., 109–10.

that most of them were Puritans should not distract us from noticing that orthodox churchmen also debated the merits of religious war in these decades. Surveying this literature as a whole reinforces the perception that just war and holy war were not hard-and-fast categories with separate histories and biblical etiologies but variations on a single theme. Some writers conflated the two into a single entity, others highlighted the differences between secular and religious wars, but none argued that holy war was sui generis, a special type of war reserved for those special and rare occasions when God intervened directly in the affairs of man. Even the most "crassly belligerent" advocates of holy war did not deny that in the current day God worked through lawful magistrates rather than by divine revelation in the declaring and waging of war against his enemies.[25] Nor did writers dispute the necessity of waging war against fellow Christians when the cause was righteous: as the moderate Puritan William Gouge argued, "The cause of warre is more to be respected than the persons against whom it is waged. If Protestants should give just occasion of warre, warre might justly be undertaken against them."[26] What separated the out-and-out proponents of holy war from more measured affirmations of the lawfulness of wars of religion within the just war tradition was the willingness to consider extreme measures (the killing of noncombatants and the mass slaughter of entire communities) and the insistence that God's soldiers as well as his generals be godly men. It was not enough that magistrates had the authority of God to declare wars in his name—those who did the actual fighting had to be paragons of Christian virtue as well. And, by extension, those who fought on the other side were by definition *ungodly* men, sinners who deserved to die, if not outright soldiers of the Antichrist.[27] The demonizing of the enemy went hand in hand with the removal of customary restraints on the waging of war in the writings of the most zealous holy war advocates to create the possibility of total war: wars of extermination as well as divine punishment. *This* was the theological Rubicon that was crossed in holy war theo-

[25] Barbara Donagan, "Codes and Conduct in the English Civil War," *Past & Present* 118 (February 1988): 65–95 (quotation on 76n40).

[26] Gouge, *God's Three Arrowes*, 213.

[27] Michael Walzer argues that the notion of the "Christian soldier" was expanded by radical reformers to include all saints, whether civilians or in arms: "Whoever is a professed Christian he is a professed soldier, or if no soldier no Christian." *The Revolution of the Saints: A Study in the Origins of Radical Politics* (Cambridge, Mass.: Harvard University Press, 1965), 279. See *The Christian Soldier: Religious Tracts Published for Soldiers on Both Sides During and After the English Civil Wars, 1642–1648*, ed. Robert Thomas Fallon (Tempe: Arizona Center for Medieval and Renaissance Studies, 2003), for a sampling of English Civil War–era sermons devoted to the godly soldier.

rizing in the decades before the English Civil War, with deadly consequences for English Protestants (and their foes) at home and abroad.

To illustrate the distance between moderate and radical positions on holy war in the 1620s and 1630s, let's look at the discussion of how war was to be waged in two influential texts: William Gouge's *God's Three Arrowes* (1631) and Alexander Leighton's *Speculum Belli Sacri* (1624).[28] At first read, the two do not seem that far apart on the question of whether God's wars were subject to customary moral constraints. Both agreed that while killing was necessary, it was never to be relished, however holy the cause. "*No true Christian can, or may delight in warre*," Gouge wrote. "He may on just cause wage warre: but there is a great difference betwixt the doing of a thing, and delight therein. . . . They [who delight in war] are worse then savages, yea than savage beasts."[29] Alexander Leighton seemingly agreed: Christians must "hate" God's enemies "with a *perfect hatred*," he insisted. But "they must not, like vultures, or Harpies, rejoycingly glut themselves in the sight of blud-shed, as the Dragon and the scarlet whore of Rome doth." An example of the "unquencheable bloud-thirst" of Rome was Charles IX of France, who, viewing the massacre of Protestants in Paris in 1572, "breathed out this bloudy speech: how good is the smell of the dead enemie."[30] The rhetoric is certainly more sanguinary in Leighton's call to arms than in Gouge's scholarly treatise, but the message is the same: Christians can kill in the name of God but in moderation, and without pleasure. Yet the biblical precedents Leighton supplies to support his contention that "the Lord biddeth us sanctifie War" come from the bloodiest pages of the Old Testament, stories in which the Israelites are

---

[28] Timothy George traces the shift from moderate to more radical positions on holy war in "War and Peace in the Puritan Tradition," *Church History* 53 (1984): 492–503. As he points out, the blurring of just war and holy war in Puritan thought reflects a particular "biblical hermeneutic" that tended to collapse the distance between the Old and the New covenants. See also Peter Lake, "The Moderate and Irenic Case for Religious War: Joseph Hall's *Via Media* in Context," in *Political Culture and Cultural Politics in England: Essays Presented to David Underdown*, ed. Susan Amussen and Mark Kishlansky (Manchester: University of Manchester Press, 1995), 55–84; Stephen Baskerville, *Not Peace But a Sword: The Political Theology of the English Revolution* (London: Routledge, 1993).

[29] Gouge, *God's Three Arrowes*, 350. This was a common caveat in holy war sermons; as Jeremiah Burroughs put it, "Let none think that though we thus justifie taking up Arms, that therefore we are of those that delight in War; God forbid." *A Briefe Answer to Doctor Fernes book tending to resolve conscience about the subjects taking up of arms* (London, 1643), 8.

[30] Alexander Leighton, *Speculum Belli Sacri, or, The looking-glasse of the holy warre* (London, 1624), 248. In later years, Leighton's zeal landed him in trouble: he was convicted of sedition, was degraded from orders, had his nose slit, and was imprisoned in 1630 for a period of ten years.

seen glorying in the utter destruction of their enemies. Joshua's victory over
the Amalekites makes its obligatory appearance, as does Moses' smashing of
the idols of the Canaanites: "The Lord telleth the Israelites that if they destroy
not all the idols of the *Canaanites*, that *his anger should be kindled against
them*, and he would destroy them suddenly." And, Leighton reminds his
readers, "Our case and Israel's is much alike."[31] Gouge did not ignore these
precedents, but for him the Old Testament stories of indiscriminate slaughter
were "extraordinary" not "exemplary" cases, "matters of admiration [rather]
than imitation."[32] While Gouge exhorted Christians to "Slay in love," Leighton calls for "perfect hatred."[33]

The most belligerent of the pre–English Civil War sermons was arguably
Thomas Barnes's *Vox Belli* (1626), which represents the outer limits of holy
war theorizing. From the very first pages Barnes acknowledged that "*I may
(possibly) be censured by criticall carpers, for . . . inciting so bloudy a business.*"
But since "*the call being not* mine *but the Lords*," he did not scruple to lay out
the case for sacred violence in unstinting terms.[34] Taking as his text Jeremiah
48:10, "*Cursed be he that keepeth backe his sword from blood*" ("a Text so terrible, that at the first it made me fearfull to meddle with it," he confessed),
Barnes proceed to apply the passage to the religious conflicts of his own day,
"considering that there are Canaanites to be smitted at home, Christians to
bee succoured abroad." As the scripture suggests, waging war against God's
enemies is not only just but necessary, and those who refuse the commission
will be forever cursed. *Vox Belli* is a particularly blood-drenched specimen of
the Puritan war sermon, constructed around the image of the sword that
"drinks" blood, that will not be sated until "the blood of thousands" has been
consumed. Barnes has nothing but contempt for those who would plead the
pacifism of the New Testament as a warrant against religious war, mocking
"the fantasticall conceit of the *Anabaptisticall* sect, *That it is not lawfull for
true Christians to make warre.*" "Is not the stretching out the sword to bloud
sometimes God's worke? Is it not a worke as *from* him, so *for* him? Is not his
command the ground of it?" he demanded. Barnes came dangerously close to

[31] Ibid., 239, 290.

[32] Gouge, *God's Three Arrowes*, 295.

[33] In *The Churches Conquest Over the Sword* (1631), Gouge included a marginal note,
"Slay in love," when condemning the taking of pleasure in the act of killing, quoted in Donagan, "Codes and Conduct," 76. For another exhortation to hate, see Thomas Calamy, *The
Souldiers Pocket Bible* (London, 1643): "Do not I hate them, O Lord, that hate Thee? . . . I hate
them with an unfeigned hatred as they were mine utter enemies" (19).

[34] Thomas Barnes, *Vox Belli, or, An Alarum to Warre* (London, 1626), Epistle Dedicatory.

endorsing the notion that God directly commanded certain wars, exactly the kind of special appeal to divine authority that the Reformation had supposedly repudiated. "We had need have a special care," he cautioned, "that we have a special call to put this habite upon us, lest we exercise a lawlesse cruelty." In a remarkable turn of phrase, Barnes put forward an affirmative case for excessive violence, arguing that "the stretching out of the sword to bloud, requires the putting on of a kinde of cruelty, the kind of cruelty wee see in Samuel, who hewed Agag in pieces without any shew of compassion."[35] There was "nothing cruell which God commands," agreed William Bridges.[36]

To moderates, this was the kind of sophistry more appropriate to crafty Jesuits than godly Protestants. Cruelty was cruelty, whether perpetrated in God's name or not. William Ames insisted that neither "children nor ordinarily Women or any other quiet men should be hurt."[37] (Though note the qualifier "ordinarily," which leaves the door open for killing innocents in *extra*ordinary cases.) Ames parted company with his more radical Puritan brethren in disavowing the Israelite slaughter of the tribe of Benjamin (Judg. 20:23) as an act of indiscriminate violence. This would prove to be a favorite verse of Anglo-American Protestants in their many battles against those Reformed Christians they considered enemies of the faith in the sixteenth and seventeenth centuries, and one quick litmus test to distinguish moderate from radical positions within the Puritan community is the frequency with which phrases from this passage appear in their writings: "And the children of Israel went up and wept before the LORD until even, and asked counsel of the LORD, saying, Shall I go up again to battle against the children of Benjamin my brother? And the LORD said, Go up against him."

When war finally came in 1642, many Protestants looked to God as well as Parliament for direction.[38] In the words of Thomas Taylor, the "soldiers of

[35] Ibid., 2, 19, 20, 21, 27, 29, 31.
[36] William Bridges, *Babylon's Downfall*, quoted in Edward Vallance, "Preaching to the Converted: Religious Justifications for the English Civil War," *Huntington Library Quarterly* 65 (2002): 395–419 (quotation on 416).
[37] William Ames, *Conscience, with the Power and Cases Therof* (London, 1643).
[38] In the 1990s, there was a lively historiographical debate over whether the English Civil War deserved the label "holy war." For different views on the subject, see Glenn Burgess, "Was the English Civil War a War of Religion? The Evidence of Political Propaganda," *Huntington Library Quarterly* 61 (1998): 173–201; Vallance, "Preaching to the Converted"; and Stephen Baskerville, "Puritans, Revisionists, and the English Revolution," *Huntington Library Quarterly* 61 (1998): 151–73. A conference held at the University of Hull in 2008 summarized more recent scholarship on the subject; see the resulting volume, *England's Wars of Religion, Revisited*, ed. Charles W. A. Prior and Glenn Burgess (Farnham: Ashgate, 2011).

Jesus Christ" are not "pressed into the field by a temporall Commander" but "fight the Lords battels, stand under CHRIST's colours"—even to the point of "do[ing] things which otherwise were unlawfull, To kill, sacke, and spoile."[39] John Arrowsmith told the House of Commons that "in time of warre, let us all learn to look beyond secondarie causes to his hand: which way soever the bullet flies, it is directed by God whom to hit."[40] The Great Protector himself, Oliver Cromwell, knew where the responsibility lay: "Is it an arm of flesh that doth these things, Is it the wisdom, and counsel, or strength of men? It is the Lord only. God will curse that man and his house that dares to think other-wise."[41] With God himself at the helm, there was no middle ground, no room for equivocation or doubt. "The Lord acknowledges no Neuters," Stephen Marshall preached to the House of Commons. "*The battle is not yours, but God's.*"[42] Preachers became agitators, actively promoting the cause of rebel-lion from their pulpits: "I shall make bold to goe one step further, and not onely to preach, but to presse the Saints to put on, keepe on and use manfully weapons of offence against the brats of Babylon."[43] The fact that the royalist faction were fellow Protestants did not deter the saints gathered in Crom-well's New Model Army—*The Souldiers Catechisme* counseled troops in 1644 "not now to look at our enemies as Country-men, or Kinsmen; or fellow Protestants, but as enemies of God and our Religion, and siders with Anti-christ, and so our eye is not to pitie them, nor our sword to spare them."[44] Neighbors and brethren who fought against "God's Army" would be repaid "eye for an eye, a tooth for a tooth, burning for burning, eare for eare, liberty for liberty, and blood for blood."[45] Violence was not only necessary, it was glorified: "The violent, and only the violent, and all the violent, do at length certainly obtain what they strive for," Richard Sibbes insisted. "Success is tied to violence."[46]

---

[39] Thomas Taylor, *A Treatise of Contentment leading a Christian with much patience through all afflicted conditions . . . The Holy Warre, in a Visitation Sermon* (London, 1641), 193, 216.

[40] John Arrowsmith, *The Covenant Avenging Sword Brandished in a Sermon Before the Honourable House of Commons* (London, 1643), 6.

[41] Quoted in Bainton, "Congregationalism," 16.

[42] Stephen Marshall, *Meroz Cursed, or, A Sermon Preached to the Honorable House of Commons* (London, 1641), 22, 43.

[43] Joseph Boden, *An Alarm Beat Up in Sion, to War against Babylon* (London, 1644), 15–16.

[44] *The Souldiers Catechisme* (London, 1644), 14.

[45] Quoted in Vallance, "Preaching to the Converted," 416.

[46] Quoted in Baskerville, *Not Peace But a Sword*, 205.

Preachers who supported the royalist side were more circumspect in describing the conflict as a religious war. As Henry Hammond said, "no war for Religion is to be accounted a lawfull war." Yet he proceeded to offer an elliptical defense of religious war that was typical of royalist propaganda: "It is possible for a man to fight for Religion, and yet not upon colour of Religion," he argued.[47] Edward Symmons came closer to advocating holy war in preaching to the king's troops on the text, "An evill man seeketh only Rebellion, therefore a cruell Messenger shall be sent against him (Prov. 17:11): Let God direct the bullet or arrow as it pleaseth him, . . . then 'tis God, and not man that killeth." Because God was the true author of the war, those fighting for the king were absolved of the sin of spilling Christian blood. "Whatever bloud of theirs you shed in battell is not innocent bloud," he explained, "but as guiltie bloud as ever was shed by Christians in a just warre since the beginning of Christianity."[48]

The notion of a "loving violence" captures some of the theological tension that lay at the heart of holy war theorizing. As one Parliamentarian minister put it, citing the biblical precedent of the killing of Saul's son Jonathan for his disobedience, "It was indeed a loving violence to Jonathan; so is all the violence that the Parliament offers, a loving violence to the Kingdome."[49] God kills in order to save, and his kings and soldiers must do the same. This had long been the justification for the persecution of heresy—killing the bodies of heretics in the service of saving their souls. (Thus the admonition to "slay in love.") But in the heat of battle, loving violence sometimes turned into bloodlust. The propaganda machinery of the English Civil War served up a steady diet of stories of barely containable bloodlust fed by religious fervor. One oft-repeated anecdote put Oliver Cromwell himself at the Battle of Dunbar in 1650, gloating over his victory: "Oliver was carried on with a divine impulse; he did laugh so excessively as if he had been drunk; his eyes sparked with spirits."[50] Sermons published at the height of the fighting urged the army to

[47] Henry Hammond, *Of Resisting the Lawfull Magistrate Upon the Colour of Religion* (London, 1643), 1, 23–24.

[48] Edward Symmons, *A Militarie Sermon, Wherein by the Word of God, the Nature and Disposition of a Rebell is Discovered, and the Kings True Souldier Described and Characterized* (London, 1644), 26, 28. On the spectrum of royalist views, see Glenn Burgess, "Wars of Religion and Royalist Political Thought," in *England's Wars of Religion*, 169–92.

[49] Burroughs, *A Briefe Answer*, 3. The notion of "loving violence" can be traced to Augustine, who argued that the church "persecutes in the spirit of love." *A Treatise Concerning the Correction of the Donatists*, in *A Select Library of the Nicene and Post-Nicene Fathers of the Christian Church*, ed. Philip Schaff, 4 vols. (New York, 1886–90), 4:637.

[50] David Little, "Some Justifications for Violence in the Puritan Revolution," *Harvard Theological Review* 65 (October 1972): 577–89 (quotation on 586).

be pitiless, to pursue the other camp with a "hungry" sword that "thirsted" for flesh and blood. Once God has drawn his sword, Jeremiah Burroughs declared, "he many times will not put it up again, until it bee bathed, filled, satiated, drunk with blood." Or, as Thomas Coleman put it, "God's sword hath not eaten flesh enough."[51] The "sacramental aura" surrounding this rhetoric is unmistakable: "they who oppressed [the church] shall be fed with their own flesh and made drunk with their own blood," Stephen Marshall prophesied.[52] To speak of "the covenant avenging sword" as having "been made fat with the flesh, and drunk with the blood of so many" is to evoke the kind of eucharistic language we explored in the previous chapter; like cannibalism, like sacramental anthropophagy, the bloodlust of holy war represented a "monstrous appetite" that could not be satisfied by ordinary human means.[53]

Despite repeated claims that the English Civil War was "uncommonly civil," there is plenty of evidence to suggest that atrocities were committed by both sides.[54] Some of the worst examples come from the Irish Rebellion of 1641, which pitted Catholic against Protestant, where the ferocity of the fighting was matched only by the bloodthirstiness of the propaganda produced to commemorate it. Mingling several genres of atrocity tales, from Reformation-era martyrologies to New World narratives of Indian savagery, the pamphlet literature spewed forth gruesome (and patently exaggerated) tales of Protestants who were hacked to pieces, flayed alive in order to make "a drum head of their skin so that the Hereticks may hear the sound of" Catholic victory, disemboweled (especially pregnant women, whose unborn children were ripped from their wombs), strung up on trees, and otherwise tortured (Figure 5).[55]

[51] Burroughs, *A Briefe Answer*, 12; Thomas Coleman, *The Hearts Ingagement . . . preached at St. Margarets Westminster* (London, 1643), 34.

[52] Stephen Marshall, *God's Masterpiece* (London, 1645), 28. The phrase "sacramental aura" is Baskerville's; *Not Peace But a Sword*, 208.

[53] Arrowsmith, *The Covenant Avenging Sword*, 15.

[54] Blair Worden, "Providence and Politics in Cromwellian England," *Past & Present* 109 (November 1985): 55–99 (quotation on 91). See Barbara Donagan's articles on this issue, including "Codes and Conduct"; "Atrocity, War Crime, and Treason in the English Civil War," *American Historical Review* 99 (October 1994): 1137–66; and "The Web of Honour: Soldiers, Christians, and Gentlemen in the English Civil War," *Historical Journal* 44 (June 2001): 365–98.

[55] For a sampling of this literature, see Alderman Cillard, *A Continuation of the Irish Rebels Proceedings . . .* (London, 1642); *Late and Lamentable Newes from Ireland, Wherein are truly related, the Rebellious, and cruell proceedings of the Papists there* (London, 1641); *The Latest Newes from Ireland Being a Relation of the Hostile and bloody proceedings of the Rebellious Papists there, at this present* (London, 1641); *Worse and Worse Newes from Ireland* (London, 1641).

Figure 5. Atrocities in the Irish Rebellion of 1641. Samuel Clark,
A Generall Martyrologie (London, 1651).

This was standard atrocity fare in the seventeenth century, to be endlessly recycled in narratives of future wars, including colonial ones, as we have already seen. While there is a clear ethnic prejudice evident in the literature of atrocity, with most of the worst examples being attributed to Irish or Scottish soldiers, royalists and Parliamentarians were responsible for their fair share of wartime savagery, from summary executions of prisoners to the wanton killing and sometimes torture of civilians. Some of the evidence that troops violated the rules of just conduct comes from sermons condemning such behavior: as a royalist preacher warned the king's army in 1644, "To be an houre or two in hacking, and torturing a wofull wretch . . . or to wreake ones fury upon a dead carkas, is a most barbarous, cowardly thing, odious to God." It was "plainly Diabolicall to insult over men in misery, be they never so vile, never such wretched enemies"; though, he admitted, "I confess this too, that sometimes God hath (in their heat of bloud) infused into good and holy men a certain spirit, which hath appeared as a cruell spirit."[56] As was always the case in premodern wars, far more people died of disease and hunger than of wounds inflicted by the enemy; counting all deaths, the toll was somewhere in the vicinity of 180,000 dead in England alone and a staggering 600,000 in Ireland—perhaps as much as 40 percent of the total population.[57] Without diminishing the tragedy of these numbers, the vast majority of deaths were commonplace casualties of war, not the result of deliberate brutality or uncontrolled zeal. (Ireland, again, is another story.)

The sum total of the outrages committed pales in comparison to other seventeenth-century wars of religion, most notably the Thirty Years' War in Germany. English Protestants knew that war was hell. They had been earwitnesses to some of the most savage fighting in the early modern world as reports of the atrocities being committed in the name of God in German lands were widely reprinted in England. Tracts like Philip Vincent's *The Lamentations of Germany* (1638) offered graphic illustrations to accompany the horror stories of torture, dismemberment, and sexual sadism inflicted by Christians on Christians (Figure 6). Holy war advocates did not minimize the evils of war. "Is not every siege the funeral of a Citie? Every pitched battell a massacre . . . ? If a Samuel slew Agag in pieces, a David in the heat of warre fall a cutting Ammonites with swords and axes, . . . what can be expected from an Hazael once in armes, but setting fire on strongholds, slaying young

[56] Symmons, *A Militarie Sermon*, 26–27.
[57] Charles Carlton, *Going to the Wars: The Experience of the British Civil Wars, 1638–1651* (London: Routledge, 1992), 211–14.

Figure 6. Torture and murder of innocents in the Thirty Years' War.
Philip Vincent, *Lamentations of Germany* (1638).

men with the sword, dashing out infants brains and ripping up of women with child?" John Arrowsmith demanded.[58] "Warre spares none, neither man, woman, nor child, neither young nor old: Virgins and Wives in warre are ravished and vitiated: Infants are trampled without pity or mercy under the horse feet, or tossed upon spears points: Women with child are often cut up and dissected," Richard Ward acknowledged in *The Anatomy of Warre* (1642). But, and this was the crucial point, "when it is for God's people, it is lawfull."[59] Radical Puritans were prepared to wage an all-out war for the soul of England. But in the end, the anticipated "holocaust" did not happen.[60]

If there were not enough bodies in the streets or towns razed to the ground to really sustain the parallels that ministers drew with the Old Testament wars of extermination, there was nonetheless a refrain of what we can only call holy genocide in the civil war–era sermons. This surfaced in two ways: first, in fantasies of mass slaughter voiced in figurative language, and second, in elaborated explanations of the kinds of impieties that could bring God's wrath down upon an entire people as opposed to individual sinners. Fantasies of slaughter were biblical in origin, but the process of selection and emphasis among the choice examples provided in the Bible reveals a preoccupation with metaphors of consumption as the most apt way to depict the destruction of entire peoples. God's enemies were "consumed" in the sermon literature in a blizzard of holocausts, all operating through the natural laws of physics and physiology as per Reformed dictates about the end of supernatural interventions in the Church era. There were no plagues of locusts or avenging angels slaying the firstborn in the civil war literature, just implements of war honed to a deadly sharpness. Chief among these were fire and sword. Fire was the weapon most amenable to the image of consumption, as it literally annihilated all matter in its path, but as we have seen, the sword was also imagined as hungering for flesh and blood and ingesting its victims.

Fantasies aside, consigning an entire people or nation to the ash heap of history was a move fraught with legal, ethical, and religious implications, and one that more moderate advocates of religious war shied away from. It took a certain kind of recklessness (theological as well as moral) to argue for extermination over lesser forms of punishment. Commentators pointed to two situations, in particular, in which God seemed to condone genocide: in retaliation for the attempted slaughter of God's people, and when one's opponent

---

[58] Arrowsmith, *The Covenant Avenging Sword*, 8.
[59] R. W. [Richard Ward], *The Anatomy of Warre* (London, 1642), 8, 12.
[60] Worden, "Providence and Politics," 91.

was "destined" by God for extermination. The first case is relatively straight-forward; the logic of "an eye for an eye" dictated that mass slaughter be repaid in kind. But the second case is more complex. William Gouge tackled the thorny question of why God's people are sometimes "commanded to slay men and women" with this reply: "The people who were so to be dealt withal were by God devoted to utter destruction: Some, because their land was given by the supreme possessour of heaven and earth for an inheritance to his people. . . . Others were devoted to destruction because of their implaca-ble hatred, unsatiable wrath, and intolerable wrongs against the people of God: As Amalek."[61] The relevance of this train of thought will become imme-diately apparent in the next section when we turn our attention to holy war justifications for the extermination of native peoples in British North Amer-ica. In the Old World, candidates for holy genocide were harder to identify and harder still to justify. The only real enemies who fit the criterion of "im-placable, insatiable" foes of the people of God were non-Christian, Jews and Muslims. And where in the densely settled nations of Europe, with their rich Christian heritage, was one to find a people whose "land" did not belong to them, whose territory had been granted by God as a special "inheritance" to his own?

Only the Irish fit the bill. As Edward Barkley, a lieutenant in the Earl of Essex's campaign to subdue Rathlin Island in 1574, said after the slaughter of the entire population, "how godly a dede it is to overthrowe so wicked a race the world may judge: for my part I thinke there canot be a greater sacrifyce to God."[62] The English experience of "subduing" Ireland is often cited by colo-nial historians as a dress rehearsal for the conquest of North America.[63] In Ireland we see race and religion beginning to amalgamate as justifications for colonial violence in ways that seem prophetic of the course of events in En-glish America. The Irish who so violently rejected English rule were not just Catholics or savages, however—they were rebels. And in the aftermath of the Henrician Reformation, which made the king the head of the church, those

[61] Gouge, God's Three Arrowes, 295–96.
[62] Nicholas P. Canny, "The Ideology of English Colonization: From Ireland to America," William and Mary Quarterly, 3rd. ser., 30 (October 1973): 573–98 (quotation on 581).
[63] Nicholas P. Canny, The Elizabethan Conquest of Ireland: A Pattern Established, 1565–1576 (Hassocks, Sussex: Harvester Press, 1976); Canny, Kingdom and Colony: Ireland in the Atlantic World, 1560–1800 (Baltimore: Johns Hopkins University Press, 1988). For a thought-ful review of and partial rejoinder to this tendency to compare the colonization of Ireland and North America, see Audrey Horning, Ireland in the Virginian Sea: Colonialism in the British Atlantic (Chapel Hill: University of North Carolina Press, 2013).

who rebelled against the crown were also by definition religious rebels. Under the banner "Five Wounds of Christ," a series of "risings" by disaffected Christians mourning the loss of their old customs and rituals in the 1530s and 1540s created a new template for political rebellion in post-Reformation England, one in which religious motivations were inextricably bound up with economic and political ones.[64] Thereafter rebellion crossed the categories of sacred and secular, of rebellion against the king and rebellion against God. As a participant in the 1536 Pilgrimage of Grace said, "if ye call us traitors we will call you heretics."[65] In the case of the Irish Rebellion, we see the heretical connotations of political rebellion being folded into the category of holy war in ways that enhanced its discursive power.

At the end of the day, we can only conclude that the rhetoric of holy war outpaced the actual experience of war in England in the 1640s and 1650s. Thousands of soldiers lost their lives and scores of communities were left desolate by the depredations of armies aroused by fiery sermons, but when the smoke had cleared the confessional and political communities that had waged war were still intact. Anglicans returned to power in 1660 and Puritan congregations felt the sting of vengeful churchmen, but there was no mass bloodletting in the counterrevolutionary Restoration as there had been no reign of terror in the civil war era (with the exception of Ireland in 1641). Does this mean that the rhetoric of holy war was propaganda only? That ordinary soldiers, including the holy warriors in Cromwell's New Model Army, understood the difference between sermons and military orders? We know far more about what ministers said than about what believers heard, let alone did, in response to what they heard or read.[66] What can be said is that the idea of holy war was promulgated by a significant minority of Protestant ministers, that it was commingled with appeals to wage war justly for a just cause, that it on occasion led to barbarities that were well understood to be violations of the common norms of war, and that it contributed to an environment of belligerence toward religious "others" that could be mobilized under the right circumstances to justify mass violence in the name of God. The clearest example we have of this discursive concatenation is the Irish Rebellion of

[64] Richard Hoyle, *The Pilgrimage of Grace and the Politics of the 1530s* (New York: Oxford University Press, 2001); C.S.L. Davies, "The Pilgrimage of Grace Reconsidered," *Past & Present* 41 (1968): 54–76. On theories of rebellion under the Tudors, see Andy Wood, *Riot, Rebellion and Popular Politics in Early Modern England* (Houndmills: Palgrave, 2002).

[65] Wood, *Riot, Rebellion*, 60.

[66] Arnold Hunt, *The Art of Hearing: English Preachers and Their Audiences, 1590–1640* (New York: Cambridge University Press, 2010).

1641. And in North America, England's Protestants would find another "race" so destined to be "overthrown."

"Warrs of the Lord": Holy War and Genocide in English America

The first English settlers in the New World expected war. Prospective colonists were admonished to bring "Swords, Rapiers, and all other piercing weapons" along with their Bibles, tools, and food supplies. The earliest instructions from the agents of empire were to build fortified towns and to carry arms everywhere, even to church.[67] It was good advice. Colonists may not have known exactly what kind of wars they would be waging or who their enemies would be, but they knew they would not transplant Reformed Christianity abroad without a fight.

Without rehearsing the litany of war with Indians and heretics from 1609 to 1699 that the first chapter explored through the lens of blood sacrifice, I'd like to focus in the remainder of this chapter on the distinctive ways in which the holy war tradition was modified in English America in the seventeenth century. There is significant overlap between holy war and sacrificial justifications for violence, and it is sometimes difficult and, more important, misleading to try to separate the two paradigms since they were so intertwined in the theology of Anglo-American Protestants. But for the sake of analytical clarity, the focus here will be on colonial invocations of the holy war tradition outlined in the previous section. As I've argued, English Protestants were steeped in the rhetoric and history, secular as well as biblical, of holy war before they ever set foot in North America. Holy war was a living thing, not a dry academic subject, alive not only on the pages of the Old Testament but through the compelling experiences of Protestants in Germany, Ireland, and Scotland that the English read about and sometimes experienced firsthand as soldiers and exiles. As they took up arms against a series of enemies external and internal, colonial Protestants asked themselves and their leaders a series

---

[67] John Cotton, "God's Promise to His Plantation," quoted in John Ferling, "The New England Soldier: A Study in Changing Perceptions," *American Quarterly* 33 (Spring 1981): 26–45 (quotation on 27). The Connecticut Assembly in 1643 ordered "that there shall be a gard of 40 men to compleate in their Arms to the meeting euery Sabbath and lecture day." *The Public Records of the Colony of Connecticut Prior to the Union with New Haven Colony, 1636–1666*, ed. J. Hammond Trumbull (Hartford, 1850), 73.

of questions taken directly from the pages of the English war primers: Was this a defensive or an offensive war—a response to a hostile threat or a pre-emptive strike authorized by God? Did God directly "command" the war or simply authorize it to be waged in his name? Were combatants ordinary soldiers or holy warriors? Finally, and perhaps most important, how was the war conducted? With measured violence, in adherence to international norms of fair play, or unsparingly? Not every war evoked such soul searching, and those colonial physicians of the soul (the New England clergy) were the prime diagnosticians of war as well. But these were questions of universal relevance for men and women who had come of age in an era of renewed theorizing about the nature of war and whose friends and families left behind in England were on the brink of a religious war of their own making.

The clearest example of a European-style "war of religion" in the colonies occurred in Maryland, where Protestants and Catholics came to blows in the American theater of the English Civil War.[68] First in the 1640s and again in the 1650s, Marylanders divided into armed camps according to religious affiliation. These skirmishes were as much about land and power as they were about religion, but the rhetoric of the partisans on both sides mimicked the royalist-Parliamentary divide, pitting "*Roundheaded Dogs*" against "Papists and Malignants."[69] From the colony's founding, Catholics were outnumbered though they controlled the reins of government and at Baltimore's behest went out of their way to avoid antagonizing the resident Protestant majority by worshiping quietly in the manorial style of English recusant families. Mass was more often a private family affair than a public ceremony, and the rites of passage (baptism, marriage, burial) took place on plantations where the only witnesses were other Catholics. But beginning in the early 1640s, this truce was breached as local confrontations between Protestant and Catholic settlers escalated; in 1643, Thomas Bushell was reported to have said "he hoped there would be nere a Papist left in maryland by may day," and in another case a Protestant confiscated some Catholic books he found stashed in a

---

[68] The best overall treatment of the Civil War in English America is Carla Gardina Pestana, *The English Atlantic in an Age of Revolution, 1640–1661* (Cambridge, Mass.: Harvard University Press, 2004).

[69] Leonard Strong, *Babylon's Fall in Maryland: A fair Warning to Lord Baltamore, or, A Relation of an Assault made by divers Papists, and Popish Officers of the Lord Baltamore's against the Protestants in Maryland; to whom GOD gave a great Victory against a greater force of Souldiers and armed Men, who came to destroy them* (London, 1655), 10 ("*Roundheaded Dogs*"); *Archives of Maryland, Proceedings of the Council of Maryland, 1636–1667*, vol. 3, ed. William Hand Browne (Baltimore, 1885), 165 ("wicked Papists and Malignants").

neighbor's loft, saying, "Burne them Papist Devills, or words to that effect."[70] War came in 1645 when a company of privateers who had obtained letters of marque from Parliament to prey on royalist ships invaded the colony. The privateers were led by Richard Ingle, a Protestant merchant, who sailed on a ship named the *Reformation*. In the words of the Jesuit Henry More, some "enterprising heretics thinking to gratify the Parliament, invaded the colony of the Catholics." The governor fled to Virginia, and for the next two years Protestant rebels ruled the colony during a tumultuous period that came to be known as the "Plundering Time" for its depredations against Catholic settlers.[71] A petition from "diverse Inhabitants" of Maryland (concocted by Ingle) listed the grievances against the "Tyranicall Government of that Province ever since its first setling, by Recusants; whoe have seduced & forced many of his Majestys subjects, from their Religion."[72] The evidence is clear that Catholic priests and homes were targeted by the rebels; the Jesuits' plantation of St. Inigoes was plundered (among the spoils of war were their altar vessels) and two missionaries put aboard the *Reformation* in chains for transportation back to England. (Any Jesuit arriving on English soil would face the death penalty; only months before, Father Henry Morse had been hanged at Tyburn.)[73] Despite formidable odds—Parliament was in no mood in the mid-1640s to placate one of the king's cronies and a Catholic to boot—Cecilius Calvert managed to hold onto his colony, with the help of some mercenary Virginians who valued Baltimore's money over religious loyalty to their Protestant brethren across the border.

A decade later, civil war broke out again between Catholics and Protestants in Maryland. This was a more serious affair, with real casualties—some twenty dead among the four hundred armed men who met in the "Battle of the Severn" of March 24, 1655. After Ingle's Rebellion, Baltimore had tried to appease his Protestant settlers by appointing one of their own, William Stone, as governor, introducing a new "Act Concerning Religion" that promised freedom of worship to all Christians and creating a separate county (Anne

---

[70] *Archives of Maryland, Judicial and Testamentary Business of the Provincial Court, 1637–1650*, vol. 4, ed. William Hand Browne (Baltimore, 1887), 234, 441.

[71] Timothy B. Riordan, *The Plundering Time: Maryland and the English Civil War, 1645–1646* (Baltimore: Maryland Historical Society, 2004); John D. Krugler, *English and Catholic: The Lords Baltimore in the Seventeenth Century* (Baltimore: Johns Hopkins University Press, 2004), 180–83.

[72] *Archives of Maryland*, 3:164–65. The petitions included the fanciful charge of kidnaping Catholic children with the aim of forcibly relocating them to Maryland (3:171).

[73] Riordan, *Plundering Time*, chapter 11.

Arundel) for nonconformists where they could choose their own officers and hold their own courts. An uneasy peace returned to the colony for a while, but events in England again intervened to stir the embers of confessional bigotry. Under Oliver Cromwell, Parliament dispatched a commission in 1651 to reduce royalist Virginia to obedience to the republic; on their own the commissioners decided to bring Maryland in line as well. The commissioners created trouble throughout the Chesapeake between rival religious groups, with the nonconformists achieving the upper hand. By 1654 Maryland's Catholics had lost the right to worship and Governor Stone was in retreat. On July 24 the governor "condescended to lay down his power lately assumed from Lord Baltemore" and submit to a government appointed by the commissioners. A radical Protestant, William Fuller, assumed the governorship and ruled with the backing of the commissioners. Maryland descended into outright war in 1654–55 when Baltimore urged the loyal Stone to defend his family's proprietary claims, culminating in a pitched battle between proprietary and Protestant forces at the mouth of the Severn River on March 24, 1655. The so-called Battle of Severn was a rout—Stone and the proprietary party suffered heavy casualties on the battlefield and lost the political fight as well for control of the colony.[74] Among the war booty was "all their consecrated Ware," including "Pictures, Crucifixes, and rows of Beads, with great store of Reliques and trash they trusted in." A vengeful Fuller had four of the Catholic "rebels" executed, sparing Stone at the last minute.[75]

Rival reports of the affair portray it as a classic war of religion, with both sides flinging sectarian taunts and invoking the name of God. According to a Protestant account, the Catholic settlers were the first to resort to religious invective, beating their drums and shouting "*come ye Rogues, Roundheaded Dogs*" and "*Hey for Saint Maries*" as they marched upon Fuller's men assembled on the shore of the Severn. Chanting "*In the Name of God fall on; God is our Strength*," the Anne Arundel men repelled the assault: "The Charge was fierce and sharp for the time; but through the glorious presence of the Lord of Hosts manifested in and towards his poor oppressed people, the Enemy could not endure, but gave back; and were so effectually charged home, that

[74] Krugler, *English and Catholic*, 189–212 (quotation on 202). Baltimore managed to retain his proprietorship after heavy lobbying in London, signing a peace treaty with Fuller in 1658 that restored the governorship to Calvert and ended six years of civil war.

[75] John Hammond, *Hammond versus Heamans, or, An Answer to an audacious Pamphlet, published by an impudent and ridiculous Fellow, named Roger Heamans, Calling himself Commander of the Ship Golden Lion* (London, 1655), 11.

they were all routed, turned their backs, threw down their Arms, and begged mercy." God "did appear wonderfully in the field," the narrative concluded.[76] Catholic versions dismissed the claim that the proprietary battle cry was "*Hey for Saint Maries*"—or, more provokingly, "*hey for two Wives*"—as inflammatory class-baiting. John Hammond explained that although a few "rude soldiers" may have serenaded the Protestants with the "cry of *Hey for St. Maries, hey for two Wives*," the "Governours" and men "of quality" fought with honor.[77] This undercurrent of class strife reflects the social reality in the colony, where most indentured servants were Protestant and most landowners Catholic, but it also reprised the "culture wars" of the English Revolution that linked Protestant sectaries with the rabble.[78]

The Battle of Severn was the final battle of the English Civil War. But, unlike the conflict in England, the colonial version produced no comparable sermons extolling or condemning the fray as a religious war. And while other colonial conflicts have earned the label "holy war" from historians (the Anglo-Powhatan War of 1609–14, the 1622 "massacre" in Virginia), it was the Pequot War and the free grace controversy of 1637 that generated the first significant sermon literature on the nature of war in English America.[79] The conjoined battle against pagan Indians and English heretics was inaugurated by America's first holy war jeremiad, John Wheelwright's fast-day sermon of January 19, 1637—a "bitterly uncharitable sermon," in the words of historian Michael Winship.[80] Before he stepped into the pulpit at Boston's First Church in 1637, Wheelwright was already a marked man. Brother-in-law to the leader of the free grace faction in the church, Anne Hutchinson, and junior pastor to the most formidable preacher in New England, John

[76] Strong, *Babylon's Fall in Maryland*, 10–11.

[77] Hammond, *Hammond versus Heamans*, 16. Hammond's pamphlet was a response to the account written by Captain Roger Heamans, *An Additional Brief Narrative of a late Bloody Design Against the Protestants in Ann Arundel County, and Severn, in Maryland in the Country of Virginia. As Also of the extraordinary Deliverance of those poor oppressed people* (London, 1655).

[78] Bernard Capp, *England's Culture Wars: Puritan Reformation and Its Enemies in the Interregnum, 1649–1660* (New York: Oxford University Press, 2012).

[79] Fausz, "An 'Abundance of Blood Shed on Both Sides'"; Edward Bond, "Source of Knowledge, Source of Power: The Supernatural World of English Virginia, 1607–1624," *Virginia Magazine of History and Biography* 108 (2000): 105–38 (quotation on 136). In contrast to these earlier conflicts, the Pequot War was from the beginning described as "an offensive warr"; *Public Records of the Colony of Connecticut Prior to the Union with New Haven Colony*, 9.

[80] Michael Winship, *Making Heretics: Militant Protestantism and Free Grace in Massachusetts, 1636–1641*, (Princeton, N.J.: Princeton University Press, 2002), 111.

Cotton, Wheelwright had developed a reputation as a fierce critic of the colony's ruling elite. Governor John Winthrop and the men who served on his council were of a more moderate religious temperament, derided by Wheelwright and Cotton as "legalists" who privileged the form of religion over its spirit. Wheelwright's incendiary sermon earned him a conviction for "contempt & sedition" by the Massachusetts General Court and an order of banishment.[81]

What, exactly, did Wheelwright say to bring down such severe censure? The fast-day sermon is a masterpiece of the holy war genre, masking its most radical propositions under a blizzard of scriptural allusions that purported to be exemplary only. From the first lines Wheelwright insisted that his topic was spiritual warfare only: "We must all prepare for spirituall combate, we must put on the whole armour of God." When God's chosen people are harried by enemies (as they invariably will be), "we must lay load upon them, we must kill them with the word of the Lord." This message—to wage spiritual war—became progressively buried under a series of vivid biblical examples that featured swords, not words, as the implements of God's wrath. To many in the audience he seemed to be calling for the saints to literally take up arms against "Church and commonwealth." Wheelwright acknowledged as much near the end of the sermon, though even here his language skirted the line between figurative and literal violence: "*Object*. This will cause a combustion in the Church and commonwealth, it may be objected. *Answ*: I must confess and acknowledge it will do so, but what then? Did not Christ come to send fire upon the earth, Luke 12.49 . . . ? The day shall come that shall burne like an oven, and all that do wickedly shall be stubble, and this is the terrible day of the Lord."[82]

The Massachusetts governor, John Winthrop, had no doubts about Wheelwright's ultimate intentions. Winthrop's attack on the free grace proponents was published five years later in London under the title *A Short Story of the Rise, Reign, and Ruine of the Antinomians* and placed the blame squarely on the fast-day sermon as the instigator of the violence. While the text is conventionally ascribed to Winthrop, David Hall argues convincingly that the

---

[81] The General Court lifted Wheelwright's order of banishment in May 1644. He subsequently left the colony of his own free will in 1655, returning in 1662 just "in time to assist in the persecution of the Quakers." Winship, *Making Heretics*, 240.

[82] "John Wheelwright, A Fast-Day Sermon," in *The Antinomian Controversy, 1636–1638: A Documentary History*, ed. David D. Hall (Durham, N.C.: Duke University Press, 1990), 158, 163, 165.

Short Story was a collaborative effort, an example of the kind of "social authorship" common in early modern English scribal culture.[83] As Winthrop and his ministerial allies saw it, Wheelwright's defense that he had advocated spiritual battle only was disingenuous. "But it is to be objected that he [Wheelwright] expressed his meaning to be a spirituall fight and killing &c. with the sword of the spirit onely," they wrote. "It is to be granted he did so, yet his instances of illustration, or rather enforcement, were of another nature." All the historical and scriptural heroes praised in the sermon "obtained their victories with swords and hammers," not with prayer. Indeed, *Short Story* went on to argue, all wars of religion begin with "disputations and Sermons," but inevitably "they soone set to blowes, and had always a tragicall and bloudy issue." Referring specifically to the wars in Germany and the Netherlands, the pamphlet traced the process by which the "sword of the Spirit" was "changed into a sword of steele" in Europe's wars of religion.[84] The same would happen in the New World were sectarians given free rein to "infect" their poison into the lifeblood of the Puritan commonwealths.

Throughout the colonial period, the meaning of "holy war" in the sermon literature resembled Wheelwright's notion of "spiritual battle." Louise Breen argues that the fast-day sermon became the "template" for the Puritan idea of war; for the remainder of the colonial era, sermons on war incorporated aspects of Wheelwright's "original formula," including the dialectical tension between metaphorical and literal meanings of violence.[85] As an early eighteenth-century hymn put it, the "weapons of the holy war" were "tongues with wondrous words, / Instead of shields, and spears and swords."[86]

[83] David D. Hall, *Ways of Writing: The Practice and Politics of Text-Making in Seventeenth-Century New England* (Philadelphia: University of Pennsylvania Press, 2008), 59–66.

[84] [John Winthrop], *A Short Story of the Rise, Reign, and Ruine of the Antinomians, Familists, and Libertines that infected the Church of New-England* (London, 1644), 293–94.

[85] Louise Breen, *Transgressing the Bounds: Subversive Enterprises Among the Puritan Elite in Massachusetts, 1630–1692* (New York: Oxford University Press, 2001), 94. A survey of *Early American Imprints: Evans, Series I* shows that overall, the attention given to the phenomenon of war by colonial ministers grew steadily over the seventeenth and eighteenth centuries. There were ten sermons published on the subject of war in the period 1676–1707, seven in the period 1710–39, twenty in the 1740s, and an impressive eighty-four in the 1750s and early 1760s (the period culminating in the Seven Years War of 1756–63). In total, roughly 10 percent of the sermons published between 1650 and 1763 concerned war, and without exception they all reflect the just war tradition (including the subcategory of holy war) outlined earlier. These numbers are of course skewed by the relative paucity of printing presses in the first century of English settlement, and we can be sure that many more sermons on the topic were delivered in the pulpits of English America than found their way into print.

[86] Isaac Watts, *Hymns and Spiritual Songs*, 7th ed. (Boston, 1720), 283.

Preachers spoke of "wag[ing] an holy war with Sin, with our most beloved Lusts, cutting off the right hand, and plucking out the right eye," of "never ceasing Conflicts between the Flesh and Spirit."[87] The controversialist literature produced by radical sectarians was especially fond of invoking "holy war" to depict their own inner struggles with sin as well as the violence they endured at the hands of persecuting prelates. One of the fiercest controversialists of the era, the schismatic Quaker George Keith, claimed that God himself "doth proclaim a holy War" against the Puritans who had tormented innocent Quakers even to their death in New England, using not "carnal weapons" but "a Spiritual Sword and Fire."[88]

To search the extant literature for references to "holy war" can be misleading, however. The term itself was rarely used by colonial writers, and when it was, it more often referred to the medieval crusades than to contemporary conflicts. A series of twenty sacramental discourses published in 1728 by Boston's liberal pastor Benjamin Coleman condemned the "vain and ridiculous attempts of *Christians* in a long *holy war*" to capture Jerusalem from the "infidels," a war that "tho' canonized and sanctify'd by man, yet it may be the vilest and the worst before God that ever was carried on by men."[89] Other ministers were more willing to entertain the notion that the medieval holy wars were exemplary rather than egregious, applicable to the wars of the present day. After lamenting the destruction of the "Good Albigenses" by the "Popish Armies," John Danforth proceeded by way of analogy to ask if "Protestant Countries" may be at risk of a similar "Armageddon" or "Holy War" perpetrated by the modern successors of the medieval papacy.[90] Increase Mather invoked the historical precedent of the Waldensians (a proto-Protestant sect hunted nearly to extinction in the late medieval crusades) to rally New Englanders to wage war on New World infidels.[91] But on the whole, specific references to holy war whether historical or spiritual are few and far between

[87] Joseph Sewall, *The Duty of Every Man to be Always Ready to Die* (Boston, 1727), 8; Samuel Moody, *A Sermon Preached Before His Excellency Samuel Shute Esq. His Majesty's Council and the Assembly of the Province of Massachusetts-Bay in New-England* (Boston, 1721), 35–36.

[88] George Keith, *The Presbyterian and Independent Visible Churches in New-England and Else-where, brought to the test and examined . . .* (Philadelphia, 1689), 209.

[89] Benjamin Coleman, *Some of the Glories of our Lord and Saviour Jesus Christ, Exhibited in Twenty Sacramental Discourses* (Boston, 1728), 251–52.

[90] John Danforth, *Judgment Begun at the House of God: And the Righteous Scarcely Saved* (Boston, 1716), 91–92.

[91] Increase Mather, *An Earnest Exhortation to the Inhabitants of New-England to hearken to the voice of God in his last and present dispensations* (Boston, 1676), 19.

in English America. What we do find is a recurrence of certain key elements of the holy war paradigm in the literature of colonial violence, including a disturbing delight in cruelty and appeals for the total extermination of certain peoples, alongside less incendiary aspects such as the godly soldier. More so than in the Old World, narratives of military and sectarian conflicts in English America carved out an imagined space where God commanded the saints sometimes to wage ruthless, all-out war on his enemies, and to enjoy doing so.

Colonial Protestants were well aware that God did not speak directly to them, or to any of his people, in the current dispensation. They understood the difference between ordinary and special providences, and were as adept as any Christians in the western world at deciphering the various messages God sent through textual and natural intermediaries. Still, they at times felt confident that they had been called in a "special" or "extraordinary" way to deploy the sword of God against the pagans, infidels, and heretics who infested their New World sanctuaries. Cotton Mather's history of King William's War, which he was sure was "*a War of GOD*" in which "the *Indians* have been but a small part," declared this particular war "a *Strange Work* of Heaven."[92] His fellow New England pastor William Hubbard was even more insistent that King Philip's War deserved the special title reserved for true "Warrs of the Lord": "It was of old commanded by God himself," he wrote in the preface to his wildly popular account, "that a Register should be kept of those Warrs, which in opposition to others, were in a peculiar manner to be called the Warrs of the Lord: and such are these here treated of, if any, since miraculous deliverances have ceased, may truly be said to deserve that title." His detailed narrative of the conflict revealed that "in this engagement God did appear in a more than ordinary manner to fight for the English."[93] Increase Mather agreed. "What shall I say? God led his people through manifold Difficultyes and Turnings, yet by more than an ordinary hand of Providence, *He led them in a right way*."[94]

How did colonists know they were engaged in a "strange" or "more than ordinary" war? Such wars were heralded by divine omens, foretold by proph-

---

[92] Cotton Mather, *Observable Things: The History of Ten Years Rolled Away Under the Great Calamities of War with Indian Salvages* (Boston, 1699), 225, 232.

[93] William Hubbard, *A Narrative of the Troubles with the Indians in New-England from the first planting thereof in the year 1607, to this present year 1677* (Boston, 1677), preface, 102.

[94] Increase Mather, *A Relation of the Troubles which have hapned in New-England by Reason of the Indians There* (Boston, 1677), 29.

ets, and accompanied with marvelous tokens of God's presence. King Philip's War was presaged by a lunar eclipse in which could be seen "an unusual black spot, not a little resembling the scalp of an Indian." A "man of God" (Mr. Street) supposedly "foresaw the destruction of the Narragansett Nation" in 1637, proclaiming, "*If God do not destroy that people, then say that his spirit hath not spoken by me.* Surely that holy man was a Prophet?" A "hideous cry of a kennel of Wolves" echoed ominously throughout one Massachusetts town, which "was looked upon by divers as an ominous presaging of this following Calamity," just as the "globs of blood" swirling in the wash pail of the Virginia housewife with which I began this chapter were a sign of troubles to come.[95] Even Indians had premonitions that a terrible storm was coming their way: "This Last Sachim (Mattachiest) said that *The God of the English was offended at the Indians, and would destroy them in his anger.*"[96] Cotton Mather believed that the devil himself had prophesied war through the agency of a demoniac: "The *Divels* have a great Hand in Exciting and Supporting of them; and hence the last Winter, from the mouth of a possessed Child among us They gave (I think) a very broad Notice of the slaughter which the *Summer* would produce."[97]

Omens were commonplace enough in English America that by themselves, "special providences" were insufficient grounds for labeling a conflict a holy war. More significant was the cause of the conflict and the manner of its waging. Recalling Grotius's laws for the just waging of war against religious enemies, colonial apologists for war accused their Indian foes of specific acts of impiety to justify their own actions. The Plymouth chronicler Nathaniel Morton blamed the Pequots' "*horrible Blasphemy*" for the war that broke out in 1636–37 in New England. The Indians tortured and taunted the English, "and most Blasphemously in this their cruelty, bad them call upon their God, or mocked and derided them when they so did."[98] Forty years later, Increase Mather singled out "the blasphemy of those Enemies" as one cause of King Philip's War. "For some of them said, that English mans God was one Flye. . . . Therefore did the Lord bring those bloody blasphemers in a moment down to Hell, yea, and damned them above ground, when they

[95] Hubbard, *Narrative of the Troubles*, 18, 62–63.

[96] Increase Mather, *A Relation of the Troubles*, 17, 60.

[97] Cotton Mather, *Souldiers Counselled and Comforted* (Boston, 1689), 36.

[98] Nathaniel Morton, *New Englands Memoriall: Or, A brief Relation of the most Memorable and Remarkable Passages of the Providence of God, manifested to the Planters of New-England in America* (Cambridge, Mass., 1669), 99.

lay frying in the Fire that was kindled upon their houses."[99] As Jill Lepore
has noted, both sides in King Philip's War resorted to religious taunts.[100] One
company of Indian warriors donned English clothes to mock their foes and
jeered, "come out and fight if you dare; you dare not fight, you are all one
like women, we have one amongst us that if he could kill but one of you
more, he would be equall with God, and as the *English* man's God is, so
would hee be." This "blasphemous" speech "troubled the hearts of the souldiers," Captain John Underhill reported.[101] When Simon Davis shouted, "*God
is with us, and fights for us, and will deliver us*" in the heat of battle at Qua-
baug, the Indians "*shouted and scoffed* saying: *now see how your God delivers
you, or will deliver you,* sending in many shots whilst our men were putting
out the Fire," Thomas Wheeler recounted. "And many of them went to the
Towne meeting house . . . who mocked, saying, *Come and pray, & sing
Psalms,* & in Contempt made an hideous noise somewhat resembling singing."[102] Such taunts were not only to be found in Puritan New England; in
1711, during the Tuscarora War in North Carolina, attacking Indians placed
a woman they had just killed in a prayer position, kneeling with her hands
clasped together and her coat turned up over her head, to mock the pieties
of English Christians.[103]

Meetinghouses were often the site of scripted acts of blasphemy. "One of
the first houses that the Enemy destroyed in this place [Groton] was the
House of God," Increase Mather recalled. "When they had done that, they
scoffed and blasphemed, and came to Mr. Willard (the worthy Pastor of that
Church there). . . . And tauntingly said, *What wil you do for a house to pray in
now we have burnt your Meeting-house?* Thus hath the Enemy done wickedly
in the Sanctuary, they have burnt up the Synagogues of God in the Land."[104]
Under such deliberate provocations, the sword of God would not be restrained by misplaced scruples about the obsolescence of holy war. "It is a

---

[99] Increase Mather, *A Relation of the Troubles*, 54.

[100] Lepore, *The Name of War*, chapter 4, "Where Is Your O God?"

[101] John Underhill, *Newes from America; or, A new and experimentall discoverie of New
England, Containing True Relation of Their War-like Proceedings these two yeares last past*
(London, 1638), 16.

[102] Thomas Wheeler, *A Thankfull Remembrance of God's Mercy to several Persons at Qua-
baug or Brookfield* (Cambridge, 1676), in *So Dreadfull a Judgment: Puritan Responses to King
Philip's War, 1676–1677*, ed. Richard Slotkin and James K. Folsom (Middletown, Conn.: Wesleyan University Press, 1978), 247, 249.

[103] David La Vere, *The Tuscarora War: Indians, Settlers, and the Fight for the Carolina
Colonies* (Chapel Hill: University of North Carolina Press, 2013), 71.

[104] Increase Mather, *A Relation of the Troubles*, 112–13.

strange piece of dotage befallen this crazy-headed age, that man should not use the sword," Samuel Nowell scoffed in his call-to-arms. "Religion and Arms may well be joyned together; they agree so well together, that the Lord assumes the name to himself, *The Lord is a man of War.*"[105]

While the impieties of the Indians clearly marked them for lawful destruction, most colonists (especially those in New England) knew full well that it was their own sins, not those of their savage neighbors, that had ultimately provoked God's vengeance. The king's agent in Massachusetts, Edward Randolph, reported that magistrates in Massachusetts believed the "great and provoking evils" of the laity were responsible for the bloodshed, including "men wearing long hair, and perriwigs made of women's hair," as well as prophaning the Sabbath and "suffering the Quakers to dwell among them, and to sett up their threshold by Gods threshold."[106] In the colonial South, where the Anglican church had languished for much of the century, religious apathy was the provoking sin that brought down God's wrath. A pamphlet entitled *Virginia's Cure* warned of "the great danger that many of the Christians are in, of being destroyed by the Heathen, as formerly hundreds of them have been," if Virginians persisted in the "Sacriledge" of "neglecting to build Churches, Houses of God amongst them." Citing Malachi 3:9, "Ye are cursed with a Curse because ye have robbed me," the author drew a threatening parallel between the colonists and the ancient Jews: "By which Scriptures (comparing their Sins of Sacriledge together) it appears, that the Curse of God was executed upon the Jews for the same Sacriledge Virginia's Planters are guilty of, the same Sin of robbing God of his publick Worship and Service in his House of Prayer."[107] The tradition of the colonial jeremiad that flourished in the last third of the seventeenth century as English America was reeling under the hammer of Indian attacks from Maine to Maryland owed its moral power to the conviction that sin—English sin, Christian sin—was the underlying cause of the colonies' troubles. "Christians, We are all sensible, That the *Scourges* of Heaven have long been Employ'd Upon us, for our Crimes against the *Holy and Just and Good laws of the Lord our God*: Alas, our *Plagues* have been wonderful! We have been sorely Lashed, with

[105] Samuel Nowell, *Abraham in Arms, or, The first Religious General with his Army Engaging in a War* (Boston, 1678), in *So Dreadfull a Judgment*, 274, 278.

[106] Edward Randolph to Council, October 12, 1676, Records of the Colonial Office, National Archives, Kew Gardens, London (hereafter CO), 1/37, no. 70.

[107] R. G., *Virginia's Cure, or, An Advising Narrative Concerning Virginia, Discovering the true Ground of that Churches Unhappiness, and the only true Remedy* (London, 1622), 3.

one Blow after another."[108] In sermon after sermon, ministers like the indomitable Mathers leveled a relentless barrage of accusations against their sinning countrymen. "'Tis *You*, that bring whole Armyes of *Indians* and *Gallic* Blood Hounds in upon us," Cotton Mather thundered in another jeremiad. "You are perhaps the most Querimonious and Outragious of all People, in your *Discontents*."[109] The list of infractions was long, ranging from the seemingly trivial (dancing, drinking, and card playing) to the venal (whoring, idolatry, and "Sabbath breaking"). Colonial legislatures proclaimed fast days to appease an angry God, enumerating the "provoakeing evils" that had led to war: "prophanation of the Sabboth; neglect of cattechiseing of children and servants, and family prayer; young persons shakeing of the government of parents or masters; boarders and inmates neglecting the worship of God in the famalyes where they resided; tipleing and drincking; uncleaness; oppression, in workemen and traders."[110]

Most damning, the settlers had failed in the quintessential task of colonization: properly defending their cultural and religious boundaries against the savages. Rather than labor to convert the Indians, the English had become *like* them. The temptation to "go native" was strong in the early days of settlement when life was hard and authority weak, and Englishmen who chose to live among the natives became, in the words of Virginian Ralph Hamor, "both in complexion and habit like a salvage."[111] It was entirely fitting, and consistent with a typological understanding of sacred history, that God would use heathen Indians to chastise heathenized English. "It hath been commonly seen, That when the people of God have sinfully come to *imitate* the *Evil manners of other Nations*, God hath made *those* very Nations to be a sore scourge unto them...."

[108] Cotton Mather, *Humiliations followed with Deliverances* (Boston, 1697), 4. The classic work on the jeremiad sermon form remains Sacvan Bercovitch, *The American Jeremiad* (Madison: University of Wisconsin Press, 1978).

[109] Cotton Mather, *The present state of New-England: Considered in a discourse on the necessities and advantages of a public spirit in every man ... Upon the news of an invasion by bloody Indians and French-men, begun upon us* (Boston, 1690), 28.

[110] *The Public Records of the Colony of Connecticut, May 1678–June 1689*, ed. J. Hammond Trumbull (Hartford, 1859), 147–48.

[111] Ralph Hamor, *A true discourse of the present estate of Virginia and the successe of the affaires there till the 18 of Iune 1614* (London, 1615), 44. Some of the harshest punishments on record were reserved for Virginians who fled the confines of Christendom to live among the heathen. Under the notorious *Laws Divine, Morall, and Martiall* (1612), Governor Dale showed no mercy toward runaways: "Some he appointed to be hanged. Some burned Some to be broken upon wheles, others to be staked and some shott to death." Quoted in Bond, *Damned Souls*, 87.

Now since the INDIANS have been made by our God, The *Rod of His Anger*, 'tis proper for us to *Enquire*, whether we have not in some Instances, too far Imitated the *evil manners* of the *Indians?*" Mather demanded. *"This is the Vengeance of God upon you, because you did no more, for the Conversion of these Miserable Heathen."*[112] Crimes against God, English and Indian, had brought God's wrath upon the American Israel. In these narratives the Indians themselves almost disappear as actors, pawns of a vengeful God rather than historical subjects with their own political and religious agendas. Even the colonial soldier, heralded in numerous sermons as the paragon of Christian virtue, played only a bit part in these cosmic conflicts. Increase Mather was unapologetic about consigning his fellow New Englanders to the sidelines in his account of the Pequot War: "Some have thought that in these Narratives there is not due notice taken of what was done by the Massachusetts Forces. The Truth is, the Conquest obtained over the pequots was wonderfully the Lords doing."[113]

Locating blame in the colonial Indian wars was, of course, a political as well as a religious game, and as the script expanded to include "friendly" and hostile tribes, French officials, Jesuit missionaries, and Spanish commanders over the course of the seventeenth and early eighteenth centuries, isolating the specifically religious thread in the tangled web of causality is a fraught exercise. When a colonial governor like William Harris of Rhode Island writes to Whitehall blaming King Philip's War on the "blasphemous" conduct of the Bay Colony residents, we should read decades' worth of real and perceived slights suffered by the "Rogue Colony" at the hands of Puritan magistrates into this statement.[114] Colonial authorities to the South soon joined the chorus, adding their voices to those who blamed Puritan hypocrisy for the plague of Indian attacks that were desolating English America. It was surely satisfying to turn the saints' much-despised righteousness against them, especially for Anglicans still smarting from the humiliations they had endured during the Commonwealth era. As news of King Philip's War filtered into Virginia, Governor Berkeley was quick to point the finger of blame squarely at the regicides to the north. "The New-England men are ingaged in a warr with their Indians which in al reasonable conjectures will end in their utter ruine," he wrote with grim satisfaction, "and let al men feare and tremble at the justice of God on the Kings and his most blessed fathers Ennemies and

---

[112] Cotton Mather, *Observable Things: The History of Ten Years Rolled away under the great Calamities of War, with Indian Salvages* (Boston, 1699), 211, 215.

[113] Increase Mather, *A Relation of the Troubles*, 51.

[114] William Harris to Sir Joseph Williamson, August 12, 1676, CO 1/37, no. 47.

learne from them that God can make or find every where Instruments enoughe to destroy the Kings Ennimies." Comparing the Indians to powerful pagan nations of the past, the "Persian" and "Mogul" empires that had tried to destroy God's people, Berkeley traced the cause of this deadly invasion back to the "late Blessed Kings murther," of which the "New England men" were "as guilty" as those who "acted in it."[115] Berkeley was only dishing out what he had been served: recall John Winthrop's taunt thirty years earlier that the "massacre" of 1644 was the direct result of Berkeley's high-handed treatment of Puritan ministers within his own colony. Edward Johnson's more embellished account of the "great massacre" of 1644 also directly linked the attack to Virginia's inhospitable treatment of the Puritan interlopers. "Oh poor Virginia, dost thou send away the Ministers of Christ with threatning speeches? No sooner is this done, but the barbarous, inhumane, insolent, and bloody Indians are let loose upon them . . . assuredly the Lord hath more scourges in store, for such as force the people to such sufferings."[116]

Persecuting Puritans and spiteful Anglicans were not the only culprits accused of inciting Indian vengeance in the last third of the century. Many in New England believed the French, and their Jesuit allies, were behind the devastating attacks of 1675–77. Representatives of the "Pagan Nations" themselves reputedly told the deputy governor of Massachusetts that "they are Incouraged & Animated by the french at Canada."[117] Frustrated by the welter of "reports and conjuctures" flying across the Atlantic about the "causes of the late Indian warr," the crown dispatched Edward Randolph to the colony to sort out the truth. Randolph's lengthy report found plenty of blame to go around, including "vagrant and Jesuitical priests" who were rumored to be trolling the countryside, going "from Sachem to Sachem" to "exasperate the Indians against the English."[118] Anti-Catholic hysteria reached a peak at the turn of the century, and the figure of the treacherous Jesuit became a stock character in the colonists' war narratives. Sebastian Rale, a French missionary who worked among the eastern Abenaki, was credited by the English with whipping up sectarian hatred in the 1720s as the simmering conflict be-

[115] Quoted in Wilcomb Washburn, "Governor Berkeley and King Philip's War," *New England Quarterly* 30 (September 1957): 363–77 (quotation on 373).

[116] Edward Johnson, *The Wonder-Working Providence of Sion's Saviour in New England*, in *Original Narratives of Early American History*, ed. J. Franklin Jameson (New York, 1910), 3:265–67.

[117] Samuel Symonds, Deputy Governor of Massachusetts, to Secretary Joseph Williamson, Boston, April 6, 1676, CO 1/36, no. 43.

[118] Edward Randolph to Council, October 12, 1676, CO 1/37, no. 70.

tween France and England for control of North America reached a low boil on the northern frontier. The "great Incendiary" Rale was the reputed mastermind behind a threatening message tacked on the church door at Norridgewock, in which an Indian warrior promised to burn the meetinghouse to the ground in retaliation for the English firing of a French mission church. Other meetinghouses would share the same fate: "I shall not be satisfied with Burning only one or two of thine, but many; I know where they are." The note ("in the hand Writing of Father Ralle the Jesuit") concluded with an apocalyptic flourish: "And if thou wouldest know when it will have an End, I tell thee it will not have an end but with the World. If thou canst not be driven out before I Dye, our Children and Nephews will continue it til that time."[119] Less fanciful reports also made their way back to England, warning that the "just Indignation" of the crown's native subjects against the land-hungry settlers "has been improv'd by the pious Frauds of French Priests, who have taught them that the Virgin Mary was a French Woman, our Saviour born in France, and the English the Jewes that crucify'd him."[120]

However embellished with the rhetoric of anti-popery, such reports gave credence to colonial fears that their Indian enemies both heathen and Catholic had joined the global battle between Rome and the Protestant International for control of the New World. The fact that Rale, a Jesuit, was scalped by his English attackers (a fate that befell his Protestant counterpart, the Reverend Willard of Rutland, captured by French Indians in 1724) is a particularly graphic example of the collapsing of Old and New World categories of religious "others" in the crucible of holy war. (And in fact, to "make a Jesuit" of a colonial enemy came to mean "to scalp him.")[121] This was a crusade wor-

---

[119] This transcription was enclosed in a packet of letters from Governor Samuel Shute to Governor Vaudreuil of Canada complaining of French duplicity in encouraging their Indian allies to violate the neutrality treaty of 1701, dated March 14, April 23, and July 21, 1721. CO 5/10, ff. 281–300. For a discussion of Rale and his role in the simmering tensions on the northern New England frontier, see Laura Chmielewski, *The Spice of Popery: Converging Christianities on an Early American Frontier* (South Bend, Ind.: University of Notre Dame, 2012), 165–73.

[120] Thomas Bannister to the Council of Trade and Plantations, July 15, 1715, CO 5/866, no. 53.

[121] "Abstract of a letter from James Lloyd, merchant, of Boston," January 8, 1691, CO 5/856, no. 131. Willard's fate is described in a letter from Lieutenant Governor Dummer to the French governor M. de Vaudreuil, January 19, 1724/5, "List of following papers, produced by Mr. Dummer in proof of the right of Great Britain to the lands between England and Nova Scotia, and of several depredations committed by the French and Indians between 1720 and 1725," CO 5/869, Enclosure 24.

thy of the name, one that spanned continents and would determine the fate of Christendom in the Americas.

As in crusades past, success depended on the Christian virtue of the men doing the fighting. The English colonies relied on civilian militias rather than standing armies to fight their battles, and this gave them a distinct advantage in the project of turning common soldiers—a notoriously irreligious lot in the early modern world—into holy warriors. Nonetheless, the Massachusetts General Court found it necessary to issue special rules and regulations after King Philip's War broke out in 1675 to "prevent Profaneness." First, they ordered, "Let no man presume to blaspheme the holy and blessed Trinity, *God the Father, God the Son,* or *God the Holy-Ghost,* upon Pain of having his Tongue bored with a red hot Iron." Second, all "Unlawfull Oathes, or Execrations, and scandalous acts in derogation of Gods Honour shall be punished with loss of Pay, and other Punishment at discretion." (The act went on to specify what kind of punishments militia commanders had at their disposal to punish acts of sacrilege: "*By grievous Punishment is meant Disgracing by Cashiering, by the Strappado, or by riding the Wooden Horse to fetch Bloud.*")[122] Ministers added their moral weight to the civil arm by preaching sermons with titles like *Souldiery Spiritualized* and *Good Soldiers Described and Animated.*[123] Perhaps the best-known example is John Williams's *God in the Camp* (1707), which was one part jeremiad, one part camp sermon. Williams, who had survived the hazards of Indian captivity himself only to see his wife killed and his daughter Eunice lost forever to the mission Indians of Kahnawake, castigated his fellow colonists, God's "Covenant People," for not heeding the warnings of scripture, especially Jeremiah 15:13–14 ("for a fire is kindled in mine anger, which shall burn upon you"). "One would think that Frontiers & Soldiers should be engaged with all seriousness and thorowness to be holy" since "they are so often as it were in the jaws of Death, and at the mouth of the Grave," he scolded. Instead, the saints' "unsatiable Tiplings" and

---

[122] "Several Lawes and Ordinances of War past and made the 26th October 1675. By the General Court of the Massachusetts For the better regulating their Forces, and keeping their Souldiers to their duty, and to prevent Profaneness that Iniquity be kept out of the Camp," CO 1/35, no. 37.

[123] Joshua Moodey, *Souldiery Spiritualized, or, The Christian souldier orderly, and strenuously engaged in the spiritual warre, and so fighting the good fight* (Cambridge, 1674); Thomas Symmes, *Good Soldiers Described, and Animated: A sermon preached before the Honourable Artillery Company, in Boston* (Boston, 1720). See also Miles Christianus, *On Christians treated in the quality of souldiers* (Boston, 1703); and Joseph Parsons, *Religion recommended to the soldier* (Boston, 1744).

"delightful Debauching" had created "Borders of Wickedness" around their New World sanctuary, and the result was the current Indian war. "Our *Armies* should be HOLY to the Lord," he insisted, or victory would slip from their hands.[124]

The colonial Indian wars produced their own martyrs, like the English minister Shubeal Dummer, whose "martyrdom" in 1691 at the hands of "Blood-Hounds" instigated by "some Romish Misionaries who had long been wishing to Embrue their Hands in the Blood of some New-English Ministers" was part of the lengthy recounting of death and destruction compiled by Cotton Mather. His fellow New Englander Samuel Penhallow, in an unmistakable reference to the disemboweling of pregnant women by Catholic inquisitors depicted in Foxe's *Book of Martyrs*, charged that "Teeming Women, in cold Blood, have been ript open" by merciless savages. "You are Fighting, that the *Churches* of God may not be Extinguisht, and the *Wigwams* of Heathen swarming in their room: You are Fighting that the *Children* of God may not be made *Meals*, or *Slaves* to the veriest *Tygers* upon Earth. To Dy Fighting in such a Service, may pass for a sort of *Martyrdome*."[125] As William Gouge had argued, the death of a Christian soldier was paradigmatically an act of martyrdom: "There is much comfort in breathing out our last breath in Gods work. It is a kind of Martyrdome."[126] (Puritan chroniclers were, of course, silent on the hundreds of Indian "martyrs" produced by the war, with the notable exception of missionary Daniel Gookin's sympathetic account of the *Doings and Sufferings of the Christian Indians in New England*.)[127]

Over the century the accumulation of evidence—the blasphemy of the Indians, the sacrileges perpetrated by these savage "infidels," the martyrs left

[124] John Williams, *God in the Camp, or, The Only Way for a People to Engage the Presence of God with their Armies* (Boston, 1707), 2, 13, 16–18.

[125] Cotton Mather, *Souldiers Counselled and Comforted*, 32–33. The image of the pregnant woman "ript open" by Indian savages was a recurrent motif of colonial warfare; for another example, see the "Remonstrance of the Inhabitants of the Island of Antigua," April 1676, CO 1/36, no. 53, against "the Indians inhabiting in the Island of Dominco" who were "Ripping up Women with Child" and burning houses.

[126] Gouge, *God's Three Arrowes*, 217.

[127] Daniel Gookin, *An Historical Account of the Doings and Sufferings of the Christian Indians in New England in the Years 1675, 1676, and 1677* (New York: Arno, 1972). As Louise Breen shows, Gookin's history—which could not find a publisher until 175 years after the war had ended—reverses the typical providential narrative of the conflict by labeling the English "pawns of Satan" and honoring the Christian Indians who died at their hands as martyrs; *Transgressing the Bounds*, 192. See also J. Patrick Cesarini, "What Has Become of Your Praying to God? Daniel Gookin's Troubled History of King Philip's War," *Early American Literature* 44 (2009): 498–515.

dead on the field of battle—pointed to the inescapable conclusion that the
Indian wars were, at bottom, a war between God and the Devil. The Indian
King Philip himself was referred to as the "Grand Rebel" (Satan) in accounts
of the war, an epithet that was also applied to Nathaniel Bacon, the instigator
of the bloodiest Indian war in colonial Virginia.[128] The "Controversy between
Us and *Them*" was reduced by colonial ministers to stark terms: "Who is for
Jesus, against Satan, and *who is for the true Christian, Protestant Religion,
against Popery and Paganism?* You must now venture for one of those. Take
your choice, my dear Countrymen; but there is no room to be *Indifferent*."[129]
Indian America may have resembled a New World bestiary full of wolves, ti-
gers, and other "ravenous" animals to English eyes, but it was their identity as
"serpents" that bespoke their true origins. The Puritans' *"Garden of the East"*
was "infested" by "Serpents," or the devil's spawn.[130] For William Hubbard,
the killing of some fifty Indian women and children at Medfield was "a *signall
victory*, and pledge of *Divine favour*" since they were "all *young Serpents* of
the same brood."[131]

The phenomenon of demonization is, of course, not unique to wars waged
over religion. It is a truism, and a banal one at that, to say that war is a polariz-
ing experience, that it erects hard-and-fast ontological barriers around the
enemy to justify killing them. But there was something disturbingly literal
about the colonial recourse to Indian diabolism in explaining the extreme
measures taken to exterminate these "pests" from the English Eden. As we saw
in the first chapter, the English were aware—sometimes uncomfortably so—
that the Indian wars provoked the kind of savagery increasingly condemned
by humanist scholars such as Hugo Grotius as unworthy of a civilized age. As
they descended into primitive reenactments of blood sacrifice on an Old Testament scale, the constraints imposed by holy war theorists in the Old World
against "delighting in cruelty" seemed to dissolve as well. The extent to which
psychological and cultural barriers against excessive love of cruelty were truly
breached in the colonial Indian wars is difficult for the historian to discern,
since at their most psychologically vulnerable English Protestants were also
most biblically lyrical. The language of scripture stepped in to provide cultural

[128] Governor Josiah Winslow to King, June 26, 1677, CO 1/40, no. 116 ("Philip the Grand
Rebell"); Petition of Sarah Drummond, Virginia, October 10, 1677, CO 1/41, no. 75 ("that
grand rebel Nathaniel Bacon").
[129] Cotton Mather, *The Present State of New England*, 38.
[130] Cotton Mather, *Decennium Luctuosum*, 25.
[131] Hubbard, *Narrative of the Troubles*, 94.

cover when the English strayed into dangerous emotional and psychological territory. Literary scholars of Puritanism have helped us see the power of typological thinking in masking or legitimating the erotic impulses of Puritan spirituality; invoking the Song of Solomon, for example, allowed men and women to celebrate sexual desire in the guise of spiritual union with the divine.[132] The fluidity with which Puritans in particular, and English Protestants more generally, moved from figurative to literal readings of scripture in their public and private devotions makes the task of interpreting the emotion behind their bloody war rhetoric all the more tricky.[133]

How, for instance, should we read the following passage, one of the most widely quoted celebrations of the infamous assault of the colonial militia on the Pequot stronghold, Fort Mystic, in 1637 in which five hundred Indian men, women, and children were burned to death: "And thus when the Lord turned the Captivity of his People, and turned the wheel upon their Enemies; we were like Men in a Dream; then was our Mouth filled with Laughter, and our Tongue with Singing; thus we may say the Lord hath done great things for us among the Heathen, whereof we are glad. Praise ye the Lord!"[134] This particular phrase from Psalms 126 ("Then was our mouth filled with laughter, and our tongue with singing") would prove a favorite verse in the literature of war. William Hubbard deployed it to describe the joy of English prisoners of war liberated from their Indian captors in King Philip's War a half century later: "the very day before were most of our *English Captives* brought back from the Indians, and many more soon after, to the number of sixteen, whose mouths might then well be filled with *Laughter*, and their *Tongues* with *singing*, both of themselves, and all that were any wayes concerned in their welfare."[135] It might be tempting to dismiss these passages as formulaic and hence empty of genuine emotion, but to do so would be a serious misreading of

[132] Janice Knight, *Orthodoxies in Massachusetts: Rereading American Puritanism* (Cambridge, Mass.: Harvard University Press, 1994); Richard Godbeer, "'Love Raptures': Marital, Romantic, and Erotic Images of Jesus Christ in Puritan New England, 1670–1730," *New England Quarterly* 68 (1995): 355–84.

[133] On Puritan models of exegesis, see Lisa M. Gordis, *Opening Scripture: Bible Reading and Interpretive Authority in Puritan New England* (Chicago: University of Chicago Press, 2003); Teresa Toulouse, *The Art of Prophesying: New England Sermons and the Shaping of Belief* (Athens: University of Georgia Press, 1987); and Hall, *Worlds of Wonder.* On the general topic of Protestant bibliocentricity, see Alexandra Walsham, "Unclasping the Book? Post-Reformation English Catholicism and the Vernacular Bible," *Journal of British Studies* 42 (2003): 141–66.

[134] Mason, *Brief History*, 22.

[135] Hubbard, *Narrative of the Troubles*, 95.

Protestant literary practices. As David Hall and other scholars of early modern print culture have argued, it was the very routineness of scriptural allusions that made them such powerful repositories of spiritual desires and anxieties.[136] Familiarity through constant repetition bred not contempt or indifference but profound identification. Puritans saw themselves in the biblical narratives they loved to recite, and they believed that God spoke *of them* as well as *to them* in these stories of divine retribution. When the Israelites rejoiced at the destruction of their heathen enemies, so did they. Increase Mather used Psalm 21 to voice his own delight at the destruction of Fort Mystic: "God was above them, who laughed his enemyes and the enemyes of his people to scorn, making them as a fiery oven."[137]

In a classic case of cultural projection, the English sometimes attributed such unholy delight in killing to their Indian allies. William Hubbard recorded a strange exchange between a "young Sprightly Fellow" and the "English Commanders" during King Philip's War in which Indian accusations of Christian sacrificial desires were turned back against them: the young Indian asked his English captors "that he might be delivered into their hands, that they might *put him to death, more majurum*, sacrifice him to their *Cruel Genius of Revenge*, in which *brutish* and *devilish* passion they are most of all delighted. The English though not delighted in blood, yet at this time were not unwilling to *gratifie their humour*, lest by a denyal they might *dislodge* their *Indian friends*." Rather than execute the prisoner themselves, the English turned him over to their Indian allies for ritual torture and dismemberment. The defiance of this *"unsensible and hard hearted* Monster" to his ordeal at the stake, which he "found . . . as sweet, as English men did their sugar," carried a double irony surely not lost on either party: mocking both the cowardice of the English who feigned to "not delight in blood" and their lust for New World crops such as sugar, a fateful addiction that led them to lay claim to Indian territories in the first place.[138]

The Old Testament wars of religion not only authorized a delight in blood. They also provided specific historical precedent for the extermina-

---

[136] Hall, *Worlds of Wonder*.

[137] Increase Mather, *A Relation of the Troubles*, 33. Mather even attempted a joke (a poor one) over the tragedy: "whereas the Pequots observed, that the English, being willing to shew as much mercy as would stand with justice, did only captivate and not kill the Squaws, some great Indian Boyes would cry, *I Squaw, I Squaw*, thereby thinking to escape with their lives. But to be serious" (53–54).

[138] Hubbard, *Narrative of the Troubles*, postscript, 9–10. This scene is brilliantly analyzed by Jill Lepore in the prologue of *The Name of War*, 3–18.

tion of entire peoples and nations at the behest of God. Genocidal impulses can be glimpsed in a variety of English texts, however hesitant historians are to apply this term to premodern wars.[139] Official prouncements of war often granted permission to *any* colonist to kill *any* Indian, not just warriors in the field. The governor of Maryland, Charles Calvert, declared in 1664 that it is "lawful for any person Inhabiting in this province to kill slay or take prisoner any of the aforesaid Cinego or Jonada Indians that shall enter this province."[140] On a broader level, the rhetoric of extermination is everywhere in the colonial records. When the governor of Virginia called for "the extirpation of the perfidious Salvages" in the aftermath of the 1622 massacre, when a council of householders advised the Dutch director of New Amsterdam to "exterminate the savages" in 1641, when his counterpart in South Carolina boasted of the success of the English in "utterly Extirpating some little Tribes" in the 1715 Yamasee War, and when William Hubbard lauded the Narragansetts' "utter destruction, and extirpation from off the face of the earth, peradventure to make room for others . . . to come in their room" in his chronicle of King Philip's War, it's hard not to think of more modern calls for racial or ethnic cleansing.[141] (And aversion born of religious prejudice was every bit as deep and deforming in the early modern world as racial prejudice is in ours.) But "race" did not mean the same thing in the seventeenth century as it does today, and the ideological calculus behind New World campaigns of extermination was based on a very different set of premises than are modern genocidal programs. New World peoples were marked for destruction in the eyes of English colonists in large part because of their typological status as modern exemplars of Old Testament heathen nations.[142] If the English were the New Israelites, the Indians who stood in their way were the New Amalekites. The biblical allusion to the Amalekites

[139] In the case of the Pequot War, historians have disagreed over the appropriateness of the term "genocide" to describe the English offensive; see Steven T. Katz, "The Pequot War Reconsidered," *New England Quarterly* 64 (June 1991): 206–24; and Michael Freeman, "Puritans and Pequots: The Question of Genocide," *New England Quarterly* 68 (June 1995): 278–93. The argument presented here supports the claim that this was, indeed, a genocidal war.

[140] *Archives of Maryland*, 3:502–3.

[141] Petition of Governor Sir Francis Wyatt the Council and Assembly of Virginia to the King, July 1624, CO 1/3, no. 21; Bailyn, *The Barbarous Years*, 220; Governor Johnson to the Council of Trade and Plantations, January 12, 1720, CO 5/1265, no. 144; Hubbard, *Narrative of the Troubles*, 109.

[142] Jon Corrigan, "Amalek and the Rhetoric of Extermination," in *The First Prejudice: Religious Tolerance and Intolerance in Early America*, ed. Chris Beneke and Christopher S. Grenda (Philadelphia: University of Pennsylvania Press, 2011), 53–72.

is both precise and prophetic: God commanded the Israelites not only to annihilate the Amalekites but to "blot out the remembrance" of them as a people for all future generations. To kill and to forget—this was the legacy of the Amalekites for English settlers.

Thus when the Virginia Company called for "a sharp revenge upon the bloody miscreants, even the measure that they intended against us, the rooting them out for being longer a people uppon the face of the Earth" in response to the 1622 massacre, the reference would have been immediately apparent.[143] The narratives of the Pequot War made the connection explicit, even to the extent of amalgamating the name of these old and new enemies of God: "This Pequod Amalecks Name (according to Gods Oath) hath been ever since blotted out from under our Heaven," Joshua Scottow declared.[144] As had the Virginia Company, the Massachusetts General Assembly demanded that the Pequot lose their very identity as a people as well as their lives and property in the aftermath of the war. John Mason told his readers that "the Pequots were then bound by Covenant, *That none should inhabit their native Country, nor should any of them be called Pequots any more, but Moreags and Narragansetts for ever.*"[145] Cotton Mather issued a chilling prophecy at the beginning of King William's War about the fate of Indians in the New Israel: "There is a *Voice* coming from almost every side of us, there is a *Voice* from the *North*, a *Voice* from the *East*, a *Voice* from the *West*; a *Voice*, as Loud as that in the Heavens, which gave Terrour to all this Land a few Months ago. What says this *Voice*, but this, *They are going to be Cut down for ever.*" Ten years later, the prophecy seemed to have been fulfilled: the "Hand of Heaven" had "Extinguished whole Nations of the Salvages at such a rate,

---

[143] *Records of the Virginia Company, 1609–1624*, ed. Susan Kingsbury (Washington, D.C., 1906), 3:683. Edward Bond argues that this "was not the language of a crusade. . . . Rather, it was a plea for annihilation." Yet, as Mark Pegg has argued, crusades had become wars of extermination by the early modern era. Bond, "Source of Knowledge, Source of Power," 105–38 (quotation on 136); Pegg, *A Most Holy War.*

[144] Scottow, "Narrative of the Planting," 301.

[145] Mason, *Brief History*, 17. Rebranding of the enemy was not an English privilege alone; according to the iconoclast Thomas Morton, the Massachusetts conferred a new name upon the English settlers of Plymouth to signal detestation of their "savage" practices: "The Salvages of the Massachusetts that could not imagine, from whence these men should come, or to what end, seeing them perform such unexpected actions, neither could tell by what name, properly to distinguish them, did from that time afterwards, call the English Planters Wotawquenange, which in their language signifieth stabbers or Cutthroates, and this name was received by those that came there after for good." Thomas Morton, *New English Canaan, or, New Canaan: Containing an Abstract of New England* (Amsterdam, 1637), 112.

that there can hardly any of them, now be found under any Distinction upon the face of the Earth," he exulted.[146]

In defense of their policy of tribal extermination, the English resorted to another argument in the literature of colonial conquest: the notion that God had given the land of North America to his people and dispossessed its former landlord, the Devil. The English were, in John Rolfe's phrase, a "*peculiar people* marked and chosen by the *finger* of God to *possess*" the continent.[147] Mason's boastful account of the Pequot War concluded, "Thus the Lord was pleased to smite our Enemies in the hinder Parts, and give us their land for an Inheritance."[148] Quoting Deuteronomy 20:16–17 ("In the cities . . . that the Lord your God gives you for an inheritance, you shall save alive nothing that breathes, but you shall utterly destroy them"), colonial ministers told their congregations that English America was their Christian inheritance. The Anglican governor of New Hampshire was disgusted by an "insolent speech made by Mr. Mather" in the 1680s "telling the people that their Inheritance that God had given them was like to be taken away as Naboth's Vineyard was, and excited them to take armes to defend it."[149] The biblical reference is to 1 Kings 21, in which God threatens to destroy the Samarians for the murder of the Jezreelite king Naboth ("This is what the LORD says: In the place where dogs licked up Naboth's blood, dogs will lick up your blood—yes, yours!"), who had refused to give them his vineyard, declaring, "The LORD forbid that I should give you the inheritance of my fathers."

The belief that the New World was God's gift to his people thus neatly bound up two powerful ideologies of dispossession: the legal concept of ownership through proper usage, and the biblical idea of Christian inheritance. One of the more perceptive crown officials told the Council of Trade bluntly in 1715 that the colonists' ideology of possession was to blame for their Indian troubles. The settlers "frequently asserted in their Courts, that the Native Indians had no better Title to the Soil than a Bear or Deer. No wonder then that they have conceiv'd an Opinion that our Design is wholly to exterminate & Destroy them."[150] Because the natives used the land like animals rather than civilized men (roaming over it in "herds,"

---

[146] Cotton Mather, *The Present State of New-England*, 34; Cotton Mather, *Decennium Luctuosum*, 12.

[147] John Rolfe, *True Relation of the State of Virginia*, 41, quoted in Bond, *Damned Souls*, 58.

[148] Mason, *Brief History*, 44.

[149] Governor Cranfield to Lords of Trade and Plantations, May 14, 1684, CO 1/54, no. 98.

[150] Bannister to Council, July 15, 1715, CO 5/866, no. 53.

failing to erect boundaries around fields or create permanent towns, forag-
ing for sustenance rather than planting crops, wearing nothing but skin
and fur to cover their bodies), they had forfeited any claim to ownership.
As John Cotton said, "hee that taketh possession of the [land] and be-
stoweth culture and husbandry upon it, his Right it is."[151] An early sermon
promoting the Virginia Company's exploits in North America mocked
those who scrupled English land policy. If "these obiecters had any braines
in their head," they would understand the "difference betweene a bloudy
invasion, and the planting of a peaceable Colony, in a waste country, where
the people doe live but like Deere in heards, . . . where they know no God
but the divell, nor sacrifice, but to offer their men and children unto *Moloch*."[152] We have to remember that English settlers were chronically anx-
ious about their legal right to the land they occupied in North America in
the first century of colonization, as the boundaries separating plantation
from plantation, colony from colony, and empire from empire were in a
state of near constant flux and contestation. Border wars broke out with
depressing frequency along the edges of empire, and English colonists were
as likely to find themselves contending with their coreligionists and countrymen as with enemies old (French and Spanish) and new (Indian). The
one constant in this ever-shifting terrain of legal, moral, and political
claims was the Bible: and the Bible told English Christians that God was
the original and sole proprietor of the New World, no matter what crown
officials, land companies, militia bands, private speculators, or their savage
neighbors said.

I've tried in this chapter to walk a fine line between overgeneralization—
the notion that the entire conquest of the New World was one vast holy war,
or that *all* wars in early modern Anglo-America were holy wars because religion was the foundation of social and political life—and a too-literal reading
of holy war ideology that applies a checklist of attributes to determine

---

[151] John Cotton, *God's Promise to His Plantations* (London, 1630), 3. On English notions
of landownership in a comparative colonial context, see Anthony Pagden, *Lords of All the
World: Ideologies of Empire in Spain, Britain, and France, c. 1500–c. 1800* (New Haven, Conn.:
Yale University Press, 1995), chapter 3.

[152] William Symonds, *Virginia: A sermon preached at White-Chappel, in the presence of
many, honourable and worshipfull, the adventurers and planters for Virginia* (London, 1609),
15. Symonds took as his central text Genesis 12:1: "For the Lord had said unto Abram, Get
thee out of thy Countrey, and from thy kindred, and from thy fathers house, unto the land
that I will shew thee."

whether a particular conflict deserves the label.[153] Every conflict I've examined would fail the latter test; some crucial element of the original scriptural or scholarly formulation of holy war would be missing. No "pure" form of holy war existed in early modern England or America—if, indeed, it ever did in medieval Europe. But a deep familiarity with the Old Testament and a renewed interest in war as a human institution made English Protestants in the seventeenth century susceptible to the crusading ideal, even if only to assert their distance from its more primitive impulses. Anglo-American Protestants were serious readers of the Bible, and God had, after all, promised Moses to be "at war against the Amalekites from generation to generation" (Exod. 17:16). That prophecy seemed fulfilled in English America.

---

[153] As Glenn Burgess has argued, to say that war in the seventeenth century was religious because everything was religious is a "lazy argument"; "Was the English Civil War a War of Religion?" 201. For an argument that the conquest of the Americas was at root a holy war, see David Stannard, *American Holocaust: Columbus and the Conquest of the New World* (New York: Oxford University Press, 1992).

CHAPTER 3

———

Malediction

And the tongue *is* a fire, a world of iniquity.

—James 3:6

Those who would spare heretics and blasphemers are
themselves blasphemers.

—John Calvin

Charles Arabella could not help himself. Having accidentally spilled "some
scalding pitch upon one of his feet," he swore "by God." Though his "blasphemous words" were clearly "spoken in a great passion," Arabella nonetheless
found himself convicted of the crime of blasphemy, a capital offense in most
English colonies. The court mercifully ordered him to be "bored through the
tongue and fined 20£ sterling" instead of sentencing him to death; one report
claims his tongue was bored "three times." Unable to come up with the fine,
Arabella remained in prison for six months before successfully petitioning
the Council of Trade and Plantations for his release.[1]

Arabella was a resident of the colony of Maryland and his unfortunate
verbal lapse occurred in 1701, long after the Act of Toleration of 1689 had
presumably ushered in a new era of moderation in England and its overseas
possessions. Yet rather than moving to decriminalize religious offenses such
as blasphemy in the wake of that landmark legislation, the colony of Maryland revised its "Act Against Blasphemy" in 1715 to toughen its provisions. As

---

[1] Council of Trade and Plantations to Lord Dartmouth, Whitehall, December 19, 1710, Records of the Colonial Office, National Archives, Kew Gardens, London (hereafter CO), 5/721,
no. 10; see also "Petition of Ann Pauley to the Queen," November 14, 1710, CO 5/717, no. 19.

the governor of Maryland explained, "The Act for punishment of Blasphemy, prophane swearing, cursing and drunkenness ... not being thought sufficiently to provide against those enormous offenses, was reenacted, more severe penaltys inflicted and the execution of them more severely enjoyned."[2]

This chapter seeks to explain why blasphemy mattered so much to Anglo-Americans in the seventeenth century. According to the most influential account of the history of blasphemy in western Europe, we can thank the Reformation for inventing the crime—or rather, for rediscovering it by disarticulating blasphemous speech from the sin of heresy and launching the Protestant world on a quixotic crusade to tame the power of words that would leave a trail of mutilated tongues and charred texts in its wake. The Word—incarnate, literalized in scripture, sacralized from the pulpit, and profaned in ordinary speech—was arguably the most potent concept in western Christendom after the Reformation, capable of bringing whole worlds into existence and damning them to hell in the next breath. Expressed in spoken form, words took on the physical properties of their bodily hosts: the lips and tongue. Often described as the most "unruly" part of the human body, the tongue ("the wilde member") in particular spawned a large didactic literature in the sixteenth and seventeenth centuries devoted to anatomizing its disturbingly protean nature.[3]

This chapter traces another kind of "holy war" waged by seventeenth-century Anglo-American polities, that against "sins of the tongue"—a capacious category of human transgression that included (at the upper end) blasphemy, slander, and sedition, and (at the lower end) swearing, cursing, profanity, lying, frivolous or vain speech, obscenity, mockery, invective, and "billingsgate" or sailor's slang. As was the case with religious war against external enemies, the internal war within Anglo-American Protestantism over malediction was waged under special circumstances in the English colonies where talk was loose and godliness dear.[4] The story of the invention and

[2] Governor Hart to Lord Townshend, July 30, 1715, CO 5/720, no. 21.
[3] Thomas Adams, *The Taming of the Tongue* (1619), in *The Workes of Tho: Adams: Being the Summe of His Sermons* (London, 1629). A typical specimen of this literature is William Gearing, *A Bridle for the Tongue, or, A Treatise of ten Sins of the Tongue, Cursing, Swearing, Slandering, Scoffing, Filthy Speaking, Flattering, Censuring, Murmuring, Lying and Boasting, Shewing* (London, 1663).
[4] Throughout this chapter I use "malediction" in the generic sense of "bad speaking" rather than in the specific sense of "word magic." For medieval and early modern Christians, malediction was an ancient form of cursing, with roots in both the formal practices of liturgical cursing within the church and secular folk beliefs in the magical powers of words and ritual.

criminalization of blasphemy is a tale rooted in law and politics as much as in religion, and we'll have occasion in this chapter to survey the legal history of religious crimes in the New World as a species of sacred violence. We shall explore the connections between blasphemy, heresy, and sacrilege (the un-holy trinity of early modern religious crime) and trace the theological impli-cations of malediction in a religious culture that simultaneously feared and craved the "word made flesh." After a brief overview of the history of blas-phemy prosecutions in medieval and early modern Christendom, the story turns to the American colonies—the only place in the Anglophone world where blasphemy was a capital crime in the first offense.

"God's Wounds!": Blasphemy in the Christian Tradition

The most important thing to know about blasphemy in the Judeo-Christian tradition is that it is, first and foremost, a sin of the tongue. What constituted blasphemy ("reviling God" in the classic biblical sense), who was likely to blaspheme and under what circumstances, and how it was punished varied over time, but the essence of the offense as linguistic profanation remained as true in the Reformation era as it had been in the ancient world. But within that broad narrative arc of continuity lies a history of contraction and expan-sion, times when blasphemy was "the worst sin imaginable" and times when it was largely overshadowed by doctrinal errancy, a kind of distant cousin in the family of sin. If we were to chart the history of blasphemy from Jesus to Calvin, we would see a flurry of concern in the first centuries of the Christian era, followed by a trough between the fourth and fourteenth centuries, and then a steady rise thereafter, spiking in the sixteenth and seventeenth centuries.[5]

In the ancient world, the notion of impiety was triangular, encompassing

[5] This section draws on and summarizes the historiography on the definition and prose-cution of blasphemy in medieval and early modern Europe; see in particular Leonard W. Levy, *Treason Against God: A History of the Offense of Blasphemy* (New York: Schocken Books, 1981); Leonard W. Levy, *Blasphemy: Verbal Offense Against the Sacred, from Moses to Salman Rushdie* (New York: Knopf, 1993); David Lawton, *Blasphemy* (New York: Harvester, 1993); Milner S. Ball, "Cross and Sword, Victim and Law: A Tentative Response to Leonard Levy's 'Treason Against God,'" *Stanford Law Review* 35 (May 1983): 1007–31; David Nash, "Analyzing the History of Religious Crime: Models of 'Passive' and 'Active' Blasphemy Since the Medieval Period," *Journal of Social History* 41 (Fall 2007): 5–29; and Alain Cabantous, *Blasphemy: Impious Speech in the West from the Seventeenth to the Nineteenth Century*, trans. Eric Rauth (New York: Columbia University Press, 2002).

thought, speech, and action, but in the Christian era the triad began to be differentiated into heresy (doctrinal error), blasphemy (profane speech), and sacrilege (temple desecration). The *Catholic Encyclopedia*—the church's official guide to ecclesiastical history and doctrine—defines blasphemy as primarily a "sin of the tongue."[6] The linguistic nature of blasphemy was thus instrumental to its definition and shaped the nature of its prosecution: the penalties inflicted by the medieval church included mutilation or branding of the lips, boring of the tongue, muzzling, ritualized "unsaying" of the offending words, and the burning of blasphemous texts. As David Lawton points out, the Judeo-Christian tradition is "uniquely logocentric" in proscribing linguistic profanation over all other forms: "Where God is Word, the Devil is anti-Word—not merely, pace Augustine, the absence of Word, but its perversion."[7] Those who spoke profanely were said to have "the devil in one's mouth."[8]

I want to linger over the implications of this truism, that malediction is bad speaking. Blasphemy is "a conversation gone wrong," in Lawton's words, one in which the power of language to form and deform relationships (between man and God, man and man) is laid bare. Speaking properly was so important because language was what set humans apart from animals—alone among God's creatures, man uses words to communicate, to express rational thoughts, and to comprehend the divine will. Those who abused this privilege were thus no better than beasts (Figure 7 depicts the blasphemer as a black dog scampering among the swine). In proper Christian conversation, words are used to bless, to supplicate, to praise, but the blasphemer curses instead of blesses, reviles rather than supplicates, and damns instead of praises. ("Out of the same mouth proceedeth blessing and cursing" [John 3:10].) The purpose of language is inverted but its power remains intact, perhaps even enhanced. The element of inversion has led scholars to see blasphemy as a form of "play," or "carnevalised" piety, even as "an escape into fantasy" that relieved the feelings of impotence and anger that laypeople

[6] *Catholic Encyclopedia*, http://www.catholic.org/encyclopedia/view.php?id=1935 (accessed June 25, 2014).

[7] Lawton, *Blasphemy*, 6.

[8] As Goodwife Brabruck said about John Baer, "he was a cursing, swearing fellow and used to have the devil very frequent in his mouth" (1668); in another case, Samuel Graves testified that he had heard John Pinder Jr. "use the devil in his mouth often times" (1660). George F. Dow, ed., *Records and Files of the Quarterly Courts of Essex County, Massachusetts* (hereafter *Essex County Quarterly Courts*), 9 vols. (Salem, Mass.: Essex Institute, 1911–78), 4:67, 2:249.

Figure 7. A blasphemer depicted as a dog. R.B., *Wonderful Prodigies of Judgement and Mercy* (London, 1685).

often felt toward the institutional church in a confessional age.[9] The case of
Susanna Fowles (1698) turned on precisely this subversive slippage between
benediction and malediction: "at other times, on repeating the Lords Prayer,
she inverted the Expressions; and instead of the words Lead us not into temptation, she said, Lead us into temptation; and at the words, Deliver us from
evil, she said, bring evil unto us. . . . And always at the Naming the Name of
Jesus, she would say Curse him, curse him."[10] Two young sailors in Sweden
were beheaded and their remains burned in 1699 for substituting the words
"I have the devil in my heart" for "I have Jesus in my heart" while singing
hymns.[11] Holy Scripture itself could be twisted to yield a profane rather than
a pious meaning: "even Blasphemy may be pick'd out of the Bible by leaving
out a part of a Sentence," an early eighteenth-century Christian noted.[12]

In the premodern world, where the spoken word carried the power to
harm as well as heal, word magic took many forms—oath taking, charms and
curses, swearing on a sacred object like the Bible or the consecrated host,
"talking cures," petitionary prayer.[13] Words were never just words—they *did*
things as well as *meant* things. Swearing an oath (the paradigmatic form of
word veneration in the medieval world) was thus far more than a symbolic
act, signifying one's consent to a judicial or political transaction; it was an act
that carried real material consequences (for both sides) if done falsely or with
malice. *The Swearer Silenc'd* (1614) offered English Protestants several caution-
ary tales about the dire effects of false oaths. A servant in Lincolnshire who
swore "*Gods Wounds!*" was afflicted immediately with blood pouring out "in
the most fearful manner from all the joynts of his body, from Mouth, Nose,

---

[9] Aron Gurevich, *Medieval Popular Culture: Problems of Belief and Perception*, trans. G. L.
Campbell (Cambridge: Cambridge University Press, 1988), 197 ("carnevalised" piety); Lawton, *Blasphemy*, 74 ("carnavalesque"); Richard Trexler, "Reverence and Profanity in the Study
of Early Modern Religion," in *Religion and Society in Early Modern Europe, 1500–1800*, ed.
Kaspar von Greyerz (Boston: Allen & Unwin, 1984), 252; Maureen Flynn, "Blasphemy and
the Play of Anger in Sixteenth-Century Spain," *Past & Present* 149 (November 1995): 29–56
(quotation on 54–55) ("play," "escape into fantasy").

[10] *The Trial of Susanna Fowles of Hammersmith: That was Try'd at London for Blaspheming JESUS CHRIST. And Cursing the LORDS PRAYER. And who also pretended to be possest with
the Devil* (London, 1698), 18.

[11] Nash, "Analyzing the History of Religious Crime," 11.

[12] *New-England Courant*, February 17–February 24, 1724.

[13] John Spurr, "A Profane History of Early Modern Oaths," *Transactions of the Royal Historical Society*, 6th ser., 11 (2001): 37–63; Ernst Cassirer, *Language and Myth*, trans. Susanne K.
Langer (New York: Dover, 1953); Stephen Greenblatt, *Learning to Curse: Essays in Early Modern Culture* (New York: Routledge, 1990); Peter Burke and Roy Porter, eds., *The Social History
of Language* (Cambridge: Cambridge University Press, 1987).

Wrists, Knees, Heels, and Toes, and other parts of his Body, and so he died." Another unfortunate Englishman scorned a sermon on perjury, scoffing, "'I have often forsworn myself and yet my right hand is not a whit shorter than my left.' Which words he had scarce uttered when such an Inflammation arose in that hand, that he was Constrained to go to the chyrurgeon and cut it off, lest it should infect his whole Body."[14] Apocryphal stories, to be sure, fables even; but the court records of early modern Anglo-America reveal a profound belief in the power of malicious speech to inflict real bodily harm, if in less spectacular form.[15] A sordid case of domestic violence between Danell and Elizabeth Ela in colonial Massachusetts in 1681 turned on the "wrong" Elizabeth had "done" her husband "both in person and estate by her tongue. She was nothing to him but a devil in women's apparel, and if he ever had her come home without an humble acknowledgment, he hoped his hands might rot off or his legs never carry his body more."[16] One way to chart the change in the power of malediction from the medieval to the modern era is to trace the meaning of the word "curse": from its original Old English meaning of "to damn" or "consign" to God's wrath, the verb to curse was gradually demoted over the years to the narrower, more specialized Middle English verb "to excommunicate or anathematize," then to the pedestrian modern usage we are most familiar with, "to swear profanely in anger or irritation."[17]

We can get some sense of the terrible power of words to wound by listening closely to the figurative language premodern Christians used to describe bad speaking: it "pierces," "rends," "shatters," "poisons," and "burns" the bodies and souls of those at whom it is aimed. As a common English proverb put it, "a soft tongue breaketh the bone."[18] Blasphemers are "ravening Wolves in

---

[14] Thomas Doolittle, *The Swearer Silenc'd, or, The Evil and Danger of Prophane Swearing and Perjury* (London, 1614).

[15] Robert St. George, "'Heated Speech' and Literacy in Seventeenth-Century New England," in *Seventeenth-Century New England: A Conference Held by the Colonial Society of Massachusetts*, ed. David D. Hall and David Grayson Allen (Boston: Colonial Society of Massachusetts, 1984), 275–322.

[16] *Essex County Quarterly Courts*, 8:272.

[17] *Oxford English Dictionary*, http://www.oed.com.proxy.lib.umich.edu/view/Entry/46133?rskey=Rbv6oZ&result=2#eid (accessed July 2, 2014); Geoffrey Hughes, *Swearing: A Social History of Foul Language, Oaths, and Profanity in English* (Cambridge, Mass.: Blackwell, 1991), 7.

[18] William Hubbard, *The Benefit of a Well-Ordered Conversation* (Boston, 1684), quoted in Jane Kamensky, *Governing the Tongue: The Politics of Speech in Early New England* (New York: Oxford University Press, 1997), 15. See also Bartlett Jere Whiting, *Early American Proverbs and Proverbial Phrases* (Cambridge, Mass.: Harvard University Press, 1977).

Sheeps Clothing" who, "like the ungratefull Serpent, power [pour] forth thy poyson into [the Church's] bowels to her destruction."[19] At its most graphic, the bodily harm done by blasphemers and swearers was imagined as a reenactment of the crucifixion—a fresh assault on the body and blood of Christ himself. Most medieval and early modern oaths were derivatives of sacrilegious phrases that invoked the injured and rent body of Christ: "God's wounds," "by the blood of God," "by God's arms," "by God's bones," "by his nayles." Swearing in the Christian tradition is thus "tantamount to a ritual re-crucifixion," a verbal mockery of the miracle of incarnation. Spanish Inquisitors even compiled a handy guide to Christ's body parts in order to help its investigators identify blasphemous swearing.[20] Spectacular literary and iconographic depictions of the "Bloody Child" dotted devotional tracts and churches throughout medieval England—visions of Mary with her torn and bleeding child seated on her lap, bemoaning the cutting words that have crucified him afresh. A fourteenth-century Canterbury priest declared swearers to be "worse than the Jews, who crucified Christ, but did not break any one of his bones," because blasphemers "mince him smaller than men do swine in a butchery." Or, as another medieval sermon put it, "The Jews gave up Christ's body unmaimed, but the Christians cut it up in pieces, limb by limb, with the devil's sword, i.e. their tongue." The great English masterpiece of impiety, Chaucer's *Canterbury Tales*, reveled in the transgressive power of crucifying oaths: "And many a grisly ooth thanne han they sworn, / And Cristes blessed body they all torente."[21] To say, then, that blasphemy is a victimless crime, as some have suggested—a crime against an abstract idea rather than against a person or thing—is deeply misleading for the premodern world. The primary victim was the body of Christ himself.[22]

For the New England minister Samuel Willard, the ability of words to "pierce" flesh and bone was an extension of the power of the tongue as a "sharp" instrument: "The word which is used by the Hebrews for *Blasphemy*,

[19] John Meredith, *The Sinne of Blasphemie Against the Holy Ghost* (London, 1622), 57, 59.

[20] Lawton, *Blasphemy*, 10. See also Rosemary Woolf, *The English Religious Lyric in the Middle Ages* (New York: Oxford University Press, 1968), appendix G, "Complaints Against Swearers," 395–400.

[21] "The Pardoner's Tale," quoted in Hughes, *Swearing*, 61, 64; Woolf, *English Religious Lyric*, 395.

[22] David Nash, *Blasphemy in the Christian World: A History* (New York: Oxford University Press, 2007); James A. Herrick, "Blasphemy in the Eighteenth Century: Contours of a Rhetorical Crime," in *Atheism and Deism Revalued: Heterodox Religious Identities in Britain, 1650–1800*, ed. Wayne Hudson, Diego Lucci, and Jeffrey R. Wigelsworth (Farnham: Ashgate, 2014), 101–18.

signifieth to *Pierce* or bore through a thing, and the evill tongue is compared to *a sharpe and two-edged sword*."[23] In the prolix early modern English discourse on malediction, the tongue was a feral and voracious organ—"toxic, petulant, and all-consuming," in Carla Mazzio's summation.[24] George Webb's 1619 *Arraignment of an Unruly Tongue* offered a profusion of metaphors to describe the "unruly" member: "It is a *Fountaine*, whence *waters flow both sweet and bitter*, It is a *Forge* both of *Blessing* and *Cursing*, It is a *Shop* both of *precious Balme* and *deadly Poyson . . . Fire* and *Water* are enclosed in it, *Life* and *Death* are in the power of it: It is a necessarie good, but an *Unruly* evill, very profitable, but exceedingly hurtfull."[25] The theme of "unresolved opposition" is, Robert St. George argues, the leitmotif of early modern treatises on speech. Like language itself, the tongue is "both passive, and active: it is inflamed, and inflameth others. It is both *in itselfe* poysoned, and a poysoner of others."[26] "So unboundedly mischievous is that petulant member," warned Richard Allestree in 1674, "that heaven and earth are not wide enough for its range, but it will find work at home too."[27] The tongue's venom can spread more quickly and further than other kinds of harm, precisely because the spoken word—like breath, like the wind—breaches material barriers of space and form. "The hand reaches but a small compasse; the tongue goes through the world."[28]

The aggressive power and mobility of the tongue led inevitably to the coupling of verbal with social and political disorder in early modern didactic literature—especially sexual disorder. The parallels between the tongue and the penis, "that other bodily member with an apparent will of its own," led to some creative rhetorical couplings. The famed eighteenth-century evangelist Jonathan Edwards wrote cryptically in his private journal that "there is the tongue and another member of the body, that have a natural bridle, which is to signify to us the peculiar need we have to bridle and restrain these two

---

[23] Samuel Willard, *The Danger of Taking God's Name in Vain. As it was delivered in a sermon* (Boston, 1691), 7. Willard was invoking a standard biblical image of the tongue as a sharp instrument: in scripture, the tongue is a "sharp razor" (Ps. 52:2); "a sharp sword" (Ps. 57:4); "sharp" like a serpent, with "adder's poison" (Ps. 104:3); a "devouring fire" (Isa. 30:27); an "arrow" (Jer. 9:8); "an unruly evil, full of deadly poison" (James 3:8).

[24] Carla Mazzio, "Sins of the Tongue in Early Modern England," *Modern Language Studies* 28 (Autumn 1998): 93–124 (quotation on 99).

[25] George Webb, *The Arraignment of an Unruly Tongue* (London, 1619), 2–3.

[26] St. George, "Heated Speech," 279; John Abernathy, *The Poysonous Tongue* (London, 1622).

[27] Richard Allestree, *The Government of the Tongue* (London, 1674).

[28] Adams, *Taming of the Tongue*.

members."[29] The Dutch humanist Erasmus dispensed with euphemism and declared that "the tongue and the genitals [are] the two most rebellious organs," the former even more dangerous than the latter; "the tongue ha[s] to be curbed with more care than the genitals." The isomorphism of the tongue and the penis as "unruly members" worked on so many levels (physiological, metaphorical, religio-cultural) that it had become commonplace by the seventeenth century to speak of verbal and sexual disorder in the same breath, as originating in the same nexus of unchecked desire and gross materiality.

Even more than sex, though, language evoked another bodily process: eating. As Mazzio points out, "early etymologies of the word *lingua* traced the word to its root in the activities of both eating and speaking."[30] As godly words were "sweet" to the tongue ("I love to sweeten my mouth with a piece of Calvin before I go to sleep," the New England divine John Cotton confided), impious ones nauseated.[31] While Galenic theory located the source of "overheated" speech in the head and scripture pointed to the heart, vernacular texts more often described offensive speech as originating deep in the stomach, "belched" out of the mouth of the sinner. As one French priest put it, cursing was "spitting in heaven's direction."[32] Sacrilegious words were like bile, burning a passage through the esophagus and roiling the guts of blasphemers. John Meredith's sermon on the "Sinne of Blasphemie" provided an extended analysis of the difference between proper and improper ways to "eat" (symbolically, of course) the "flesh of Christ," that "most perfect Sacrifice." "The wicked tast him, but relish not the sweetness, because of their distempered pallat, or foule stomacke," he explained, "which maketh them belch up the sweetnesse againe." Those who "belch forth blasphemies" are "worse than an Infidell" because they "crucifie againe to themselves the Sonne of God."[33] At the height of the "Ranter" scare in England in the 1650s,

[29] Mazzio, "Sins of the Tongue," 100; Jonathan Edwards, quoted in Philip Greven, *The Protestant Temperament: Patterns of Child-Rearing, Religious Experience, and the Self in Early America* (New York: Knopf, 1977), 129. Roger Williams referred to "the uncircumcised lip" in his riposte to John Cotton; *Mr. Cotton's Letter Lately Printed; Examined and Answered* (London, 1644), 2.

[30] Mazzio, "Sins of the Tongue," 98. See Maggie Kilgour's discussion of the isomorphism between eating and speaking in Christian theology from Augustine to Milton in *From Communion to Cannibalism: An Anatomy of Metaphors of Incorporation* (Princeton, N.J.: Princeton University Press, 1990).

[31] Quoted in Kamensky, *Governing the Tongue*, 31.

[32] Cabantous, *Blasphemy*, 13. St. George reviews the competing Galenic and scriptural theories of the origins of impassioned speech in "Heated Speech," 282–83.

[33] Meredith, *The Sinne of Blasphemie Against the Holy Ghost*, 12, 16, 29, 35, 41–42.

one Attingworth "stood up belching forth . . . blasphemous and detestable words."[34] The most notorious of the English Ranters, Abiezer Coppe, ingeniously turned this trope on its head in his antinomian manifesto, *A Fiery Flying Roll*; in a vision he saw a "roll" or "book" on which was inscribed a chilling prophecy: "*Vengeance, vengeance, vengeance, Plagues, plagues, plagues, upon the Inhabitants of the earth; Fire, fire, fire, Sword, sword, etc.*" The scroll was then "snatcht out of my hand, & the Roll thrust into my mouth, and I eat it up, and filled my bowels with it . . . where it was bitter as worm-wood, and it lay broiling, and burning in my stomack, till I brought it forth in this forme."[35]

We'll revisit the Ranters and their carnivalesque blasphemies in the next section, but the ubiquity of the image of "belching" up blasphemies links ingestion and verbal sacrilege in a wide variety of texts drawn from the medieval and early modern eras, highlighting the sacramental dimension of the sin of malediction. Vomiting up the impious Word was a perversion of ingesting the incarnate Word in the sacrament of communion—yet another way in which the Eucharist functioned as a kind of metalanguage for Europe's Christians in the Reformation era. (There are even faint echoes of the trope of cannibalism here; the foul material that is regurgitated by blasphemers is, metaphorically, Christ's body and blood. No wonder that Dante placed blasphemers next to usurers, the cannibals of mercantile capitalism à la Michel Montaigne, in the inner ring of the seventh circle of hell.) And like the stories of Catholics excreting the Eucharist we heard in Chapter 1, false swearers came in for their fair share of scatological treatment at the hands of moralists: one tract described a London woman who "foreswore herself for a little money" and immediately "*fel down speechlesse forthwith*, and cast up at her mouth in great aboundance, and with horrible stinke, that matter, which by natures course should have been void downewards, and so died, to the terrour of all perjured and foresworne wretches."[36] In a memorable turn of phrase, Daniel Defoe called swearing "Lewdness of the Tongue, that Scum and Excrement of the Mouth."[37]

The verbal nature of blasphemy thus conjured up associations with sex,

---

[34] *The Ranters Recantation* (London, 1650), 2.

[35] Abiezer Coppe, *A Fiery Flying Roll* (London, 1650), preface.

[36] Thomas Beard, *The Theatre of Gods Judgments* (London, 1631), 178, quoted in St. George, "Heated Speech," 286.

[37] Defoe, *An Essay Upon Projects* (1697), reprinted in Ashley Montagu, *The Anatomy of Swearing* (New York: Macmillan, 1967), 184.

eating, excrement, and sacramentalism that evoked deep cultural and theological anxieties in early modern Christendom. But as a *crime*, blasphemy
was punished by church and crown because it constituted, in Leonard Levy's
words, "treason against God." Levy traces the moment when blasphemy assumed a political aspect to the trial of Jesus himself, when the Jewish elders
conspired with their Roman overlords to convict Jesus of not only reviling
God but also "claiming his kinship, powers, attributes, or honors."[38] Ultimately Jesus was put to death because he claimed to be a new king, come to
usher in a rival kingdom. The pairing of blasphemy with sedition was thus
implicit from the founding moment of Christianity itself, and over the next
two millennia church and state would work together to crush the power of
rebellious tongues, passing jurisdiction back and forth as ecclesiastical and
criminal courts worked out a complicated system of accommodation over
who had the authority to police impiety in the medieval period. The fate of
Europe's Jews hinged in no small part on this marriage of blasphemy with
sedition: neither crime alone could justify the brutal persecution and symbolic degradation suffered by Jewish communities, but together, they rendered the Jew the figure nonpareil of religious and political odium. Tragically,
the punishment meted out to the Jews for their "execrable blasphemies" included the burning of their sacred texts; Gregory IX ordered the Talmud to
be burned throughout Christendom for its blasphemies against Jesus and
Mary, leading to the infamous *autos-da-fé* throughout France that consumed
tens of thousands of manuscript copies of the Talmud and other rabbinic
writings in the late medieval period. After the invention of the printing press,
rabbinic texts by the hundreds of thousands were put to the flames.[39] On this
point, Protestants and Catholics agreed: Luther's infamous pamphlet *Against
the Jews and Their Lies* suggested "setting fire to the synagogues" to punish
Jewish blasphemy.[40]

The figure of the blasphemous Jew points to a crucial truth about the history of religious prosecution: unlike heresy (an insider's crime), blasphemy is
no respecter of persons. The scriptural justification for prosecuting blasphemy is Leviticus 24:16: "He who blasphemes the name of the Lord shall be
put to death; all the congregation shall stone him; the sojourner as well as the
native, when he blasphemes the Name, shall be put to death." The last clause

[38] Levy, *Treason Against God*, 331.
[39] Levy, *Blasphemy*, 53–54.
[40] Quoted in David Stannard, *American Holocaust: Columbus and the Conquest of the
New World* (New York: Oxford University Press, 1992), 248.

points to the essential difference between heresy and blasphemy: *all* men were liable for blasphemy, infidels and heathens ("sojourners") as well as Christians ("natives"). Only those who had been exposed to the saving truth of Christianity and had rejected it could be labeled heretics, but anyone— Jew, Muslim, pagan, even the savage Indian of the New World—who reviled the name of God could be punished for blasphemy.

In the multicultural, multilingual world of the early church fathers, before a single language assumed the privileged status that Latin would come to occupy by the fourth century, blasphemy was rampant—or, to put it differently, no one was sure where to draw the line between pious and sacrilegious speech and therefore *all* God-speak was suspect. Once the official Latin version of the Bible was produced (the Vulgate) in the 1380s, however, the linguistic free-for-all settled into predictable liturgical patterns and the din of blasphemous words receded. From Constantine to Thomas Aquinas, theologians were more interested in heresy than blasphemy, though in truth the two were so intertwined that it was difficult to determine where one left off and the other began. Heresy proved a more effective charge to wield against dissent because its noxious products (tracts, "false prophets" and the sects they spawned) were more visible than the ephemera of blasphemous words, and so anti-heresy laws remained the weapon of choice for church authorities in their efforts to build a universal and omnipotent Christendom out of the linguistic and sectarian fragments of late antiquity. The result was a startling increase in the persecution of heretics, schismatics, Jews, and lepers between the eleventh and the thirteenth centuries that transformed western Christendom into a "persecuting society," in R. I. Moore's phrase.[41]

Along the way, blasphemy as a discrete crime supposedly disappeared. "I know of no case in which a person was convicted and executed for the crime of blasphemy during the Middle Ages," Levy concludes.[42] While this may be literally true, it is a misleading statement on two levels. First, if not a capital crime, blasphemy was nonetheless among the most severely punished religious transgressions in late medieval Europe. The first significant royal statute concerning blasphemy was issued in 1263 by Louis IX upon his return from the Holy Land: "The king had so deep a love for our Lord and His sweet Mother that he punished most severely all those who had been convicted of speaking of them irreverently or of using their names in some

---

[41] R. I. Moore, *The Formation of a Persecuting Society: Power and Deviance in Western Europe, 950–1250* (Oxford: Blackwell, 1987).

[42] Levy, *Blasphemy*, xiv.

wicked oath." The punishment fit the crime, with malefactors visibly wearing the fruits of their foul words on their bodies or etched on their faces: "I saw him order a goldsmith of Caesarea to be bound to a ladder, with a pig's gut and other viscera around his neck, in such a quantity that they reached up to his nose. I have also heard that, since I came back from overseas, he had the lips and nose of a citizen of Paris seared for a similar offense." The thirteenth-century Spanish code, the *Siete Partidas*, prescribed branding on the lips with the letter "B" for second offenders and cutting out the tongue for chronic recidivists; the Spanish Inquisition favored muzzling blasphemers' mouths.[43] So blasphemy was treated as a distinct crime with its own graduated scale of corporal punishments. And second, in vernacular usage, heresy and blasphemy were blended together, and medieval jurists themselves spoke of "heretical blasphemy" and "blasphemous heresy." I'm not sure the Parisian Free Spirit burned at the stake in the thirteenth century for exuberantly proclaiming "I have become God" (a "perverse dogma" that Innocent III deemed "not so much heretical as insane") would appreciate the technical distinction that he had been burned for heresy, not blasphemy. Nonetheless, Leonard Levy is right that the default charge for religious rebels was heresy; a papal bull of 1418 declared Peter Waldo, John Huss, and John Wyclif (all founders of proto-Protestant sects in northern Europe) to be "archheretics," not blasphemers, even though their main crime was "blasphem[ing] the Lord God."[44]

The prosecution of the Lollards in England illustrates the entangled nature of blasphemy and heresy in law and popular belief. Before 1400, England was largely isolated from the heresy panics that had consumed much of the continent in the previous two centuries. (It was one of only two nations in Christian Europe, along with Castille, to be spared the Inquisition.) A solitary Albigensian was reportedly burned in London in 1210 but, if true, this was an isolated case. All this changed with the passage of *De Haeretico Comburendo* (On the Burning of Heretics) in 1401, the first English law to mandate the death penalty for a religious offense. Burning was reserved for "obstinate" or relapsed heretics, though the term "heresy" itself was left undefined and hence entirely up to the discretion of the ecclesiastical magistrates.

[43] Cabantous, *Blasphemy*, 50–51; Flynn, "Blasphemy and the Play of Anger in Sixteenth-Century Spain."

[44] Levy, *Blasphemy*, 118. Milner Ball criticizes Levy's widely accepted account of the history of blasphemy prosecutions for overemphasizing the distinction between the two crimes; "Cross and Sword."

The first victim was the Norfolk priest William Sawtry, who was burned on March 2, 1401. Nine years later the tailor John Bandy went to the flames for his beliefs, too. Sawtry and Bandy were Lollards, members of the proto-Protestant sect inspired by the Oxford don John Wyclif, who was dismissed from his post in 1381 for sacramental heterodoxy. The Lollards anticipated almost all of the theological and liturgical positions taken by the Reformers a century later: they loved plain speaking and reading the holy scripture in their own tongue and hated "popish superstitions" like transubstantiation, purgatory, the veneration of images, and the cult of saints. As Luther would so famously do, they attacked ecclesiastical abuses such as the selling of in-dulgences and clerical offices and decried the moral bankruptcy of priests.[45] The movement quickly outgrew its Wycliffite origins to become the first seri-ous heretical challenge to the English church. So frightened was crown and miter of this upstart sect that the body of Wyclif was dug up forty-four years after his death and burned.

While "Lollard" was a term of abuse and would come to be nearly synon-ymous with "heretic," the word, and the sect itself, actually has a much stronger association with verbal profanation. The etymology of "Lollard" lies in the Middle Dutch word *lollaerd*, which means "mumbler" or "mutter-er."[46] And to those who encountered them in person, the Lollards were first and foremost blasphemers, verbal iconoclasts who dismantled the rhetorical and liturgical edifice of the medieval church with their sermons and tracts.[47] Heresy courts singled out the Lollards' distinctive language as the signature of the movement. Their "plain" way of speaking and writing threatened not only the status of Latin as a sacred language but an entire hermeneutics that surrounded the Word of God with layers of institutional and rhetorical pro-tection. The Lollards stripped away these layers to reveal the Word in its es-sence and invited "christen men and wymmen, olde and yonge" to taste it on their own.[48]

The fate of the Lollards presaged a war over words that would soon tear Western Christianity apart. The Reformation marked a watershed in the his-

[45] Anne Hudson, *The Premature Reformation: Wycliffite Texts and Lollard History* (New York: Cambridge University Press, 1988); Margaret Aston, *Lollards and Reformers: Images and Literacy in Late Medieval Religion* (London: Hambledon Press, 1984).

[46] *Oxford English Dictionary*, http://www.oed.com.proxy.lib.umich.edu/view/Entry/109905?redirectedFrom=lollard& (accessed September 6, 2014).

[47] Rebecca W. Lundin, "Rhetorical Iconoclasm: The Heresy of Lollard Plain Style," *Rhetoric Review* 27 (2008): 131–46.

[48] The phrase is from the prologue to the Wycliffite Bible; quoted in ibid., 135.

tory of the church's relationship to malediction. Protestantism's enshrine-
ment of the "Word" at the very center of faith and praxis rejuvenated a whole
range of linguistic and cultural practices that had been important but secondary aspects of medieval Christendom (private prayer, biblical exegesis,
sermons, devotional practices centered on godly texts) and introduced some
new ones (most crucially, the vernacular Bible and "plain speaking").[49] We
can think of this as the return of the vernacular, in which the linguistic po-
lyphony of the early church once again resounded across western Christendom. As the power and importance of the Word in both its spoken and
written forms expanded with the spread of Protestantism throughout northern Europe, concern over profane words grew in proportion. If Luther and
his allies did not invent blasphemy—the one "unpardonable sin," according
to Calvin—they certainly reanimated it, vastly expanding its political and ex-
pressive capacities in the process.[50] While Levy sees this as primarily a pragmatic response to the uncomfortable fact that heresy was a label the medieval
church had slapped on the Reformers and therefore one they wished desperately to distance themselves from, there is a deeper theological explanation
that is rooted in the intense logocentrism (or iconophobia) of Reformed
Christianity and the unstable nature of language itself.

For Reformers, the Word was preeminently the *spoken* word: in Calvin's
hands, the gospel phrase "In the beginning was the Word, and the Word was
with God, and the Word was God" (John 1:1) became "In the beginning was
Speech, and *Speech* was with God; and *Speech* was God."[51] Scholars have paid
more attention to the much-vaunted textualism of the Reformation—its ele-
vation of reading and writing to core devotional disciplines—but ordinary
Christians encountered God most immediately, and most intensely, through
spoken language: the sermons they heard, the prayers they uttered, the devotional texts they read aloud to one another and debated in conventicles

---

[49] Lisa Gordis, *Opening Scripture: Bible Reading and Interpretive Authority in Puritan
New England* (Chicago: University of Chicago Press, 2003).

[50] While Patrick Collinson has argued that in the decades before the Reformation, "England lacked absolutely . . . any sense of what might be thought to constitute blasphemy,"
there is abundant evidence of a robust vernacular understanding of blasphemy in the kinds
of verbal skirmishes described in this chapter. Collinson, *The Birthpangs of Protestant England: Religious and Cultural Change in the Sixteenth and Seventeenth Centuries* (New York:
St. Martin's Press, 1988), 99. For a good example of the Protestant expansion of the concept of
blasphemy, see John Knox, *An Answer to a Great Number of Blasphemous Cavillations Written by an Anabaptist* (London, 1560), in which Knox rehearses the long history of the true
faith's battle with blasphemers from the Old Testament to the present.

[51] Quoted in Kamensky, *Governing the Tongue*, 30, emphasis added.

and other lay societies, the prophesying of "mechanick" preachers and the visions of radical spiritists. Even the Bible itself was considered a living, breathing thing, the very speech of God himself captured on the page. Reading the Word of God meant more than contemplating the meaning of the letters on the page; it meant *incorporating* the Word into one's very flesh. For Luther, God's word "must be in us like a . . . brand mark, burned in, not touching the heart lightly, as foam on water, or spittle on the tongue which we wont to spit out, but pressed onto the heart to remain there as a distinguishing sign which no one can remove from us."[52] Rather than draw a sharp distinction between writing and speech, then, it's more accurate to think of Protestant logocentrism as a continuum along which saints traveled back and forth between various modes of encountering the "Word." Reading was, in fact, a form of oral consumption not dissimilar to speaking, or even ingesting; recalling to their congregations the advice of the eleventh-century Benedictine St. Anselm to "Taste the goodness of your redeemer . . . chew the honeycomb of his words, suck their flavor," Protestant preachers likened the act of reading the Bible to eating the Word of God, with all the sacramental aura that metaphor implied.[53] Language was thus not a stable thing in the Reformers' world, despite the strenuous efforts of polemicists and theologians to anchor the Word in new technologies of print and textual practices.

It was precisely because language was so fissiparous that Reformers went to such lengths to nurture and protect the Word of God. In England, reform was a painfully slow affair, proceeding in fits and starts as one regime succeeded another and the death of a monarch meant an abrupt shift in religious loyalties. Because the process was so protracted and was directed largely by the state (which is not the same thing as saying reform had no popular roots), the English Reformation offers an unparalleled window into the political and

[52] Quoted in James Simpson, *Burning to Read: English Fundamentalism and Its Reformation Opponents* (Cambridge, Mass.: Belknap Press of Harvard University Press, 2007), 114.

[53] David D. Hall, *Worlds of Wonder, Days of Judgment: Popular Religious Belief in Early New England* (Cambridge, Mass.: Harvard University Press, 1989), 28–29. On Protestant attitudes toward words and texts, see John N. King, *Foxe's "Book of Martyrs" and Early Modern Print Culture* (New York: Cambridge University Press, 2006); Kevin Sharpe, *Reading Revolutions: The Politics of Reading in Early Modern England* (New Haven, Conn.: Yale University Press, 2000); Tessa Watt, *Cheap Print and Popular Piety, 1550–1640* (New York: Cambridge University Press, 1991); David Cressy, *Literacy and the Social Order: Reading and Writing in Tudor and Stuart England* (New York: Cambridge University Press, 1980); and Margaret Spufford, *Small Books and Pleasant Histories: Popular Fiction and Its Readership in Seventeenth-Century England* (New York: Cambridge University Press, 1981).

legal maneuvering over heresy and blasphemy that enshrined a word-centered disciplinary regime in Protestant Europe.[54]

Between 1401 and 1485 (when Henry VII seized the throne), fifteen Lollard "martyrs" were burned for heresy according to John Foxe's *Book of Martyrs.* Foxe included an account of another thirty-five anonymous souls at St. Giles who were "hung on gibbets, and fagots being placed under them, as soon as they were suspended, fire was set to them, so that they were burnt while hanging." A horrific death, but not one that many Lollards faced. We know that clusters of suspected heretics were hauled before ecclesiastical courts throughout the fifteenth century, where they were flogged, imprisoned, ordered to perform public rituals of abjuration—but rarely killed. Some were sentenced to wear a cloth badge with the emblem of a faggot on it; as Susan Brigden notes, "For every Lollard who died at the stake there were fifty who recanted, but recantation itself left a fearsome stigma, for ostracism awaited those who bore the badge of the abjured heretic, the mark of the faggot."[55]

The ascension of Henry's son, the remarkable Henry VIII, in 1509 marked a definite shift in the pace of heresy-hunting in England; before he dissolved the Catholic Church with a stroke of the pen in 1534, Henry sent an additional forty "obstinate heretics" to the stake—mostly Lollards, like Thomas Denys, whose disciples were forced to watch his burning in 1513 while throwing his books in the fire as fuel.[56] After the royal supremacy was declared in 1534, Henry pursued a deliberately ambiguous policy of reform and retreat, with each step toward Lutheranism followed by at least one step backward toward traditionalism. (In Christopher Haigh's memorable description, "the English ate their Reformation as a recalcitrant child is fed its supper, little by

[54] On the relationship of top-down and bottom-up versions of reform, see Christopher Haigh, *English Reformations: Religion, Politics, and Society Under the Tudors* (New York: Oxford University Press, 1993).

[55] Susan Brigden, *New Worlds, Lost Worlds: The Rule of the Tudors, 1485–1603* (New York: Penguin, 2000), 88.

[56] John Foxe, *Acts and Monuments*, 187; he counts another eight who went to their death under Henry VII. http://www.gutenberg.org/files/22400/22400-h/22400-h.htm#Page_186 (accessed September 11, 2014); Brigden, *New Worlds, Lost Worlds*, 87 (Denys). Henry VIII was an "ambidextrous" persecutor; on one notable day in July 1540 he ordered the burning of three Protestant Reformers alongside a gibbet on which hung the bodies of three Catholic priests. William Monter, "Heresy Executions in Reformation Europe, 1520–1565," in *Tolerance and Intolerance in the European Reformation*, ed. Ole Peter Grell and Bob Scribner (New York: Cambridge University Press, 1996), 48–64 ("ambidextrous" on 54). Ethan Shagan explores the sixfold execution as a "founding moment of the Anglican *via media*" in chapter 2 of *The Rule of Moderation: Violence, Religion and the Politics of Restraint in Early Modern England* (London: Cambridge University Press, 2011).

little, in well-timed spoonfulls, . . . until the plate had been emptied and the Reformation had happened.")[57] Henry's position on the vernacular Bible exemplifies this pattern. The "Bible wars" of the 1530s and 1540s pitted Reformers against traditionalists, with the king occupying the ever-shifting middle ground.[58] Henry was appalled at the idea of peasants and commoners reading the sacred scripture on their own and in 1536 ordered the execution of William Tyndale, the author of the first printed English Bible and a folk hero to the radical Reformers who surrounded the king. Tyndale was burned at the stake; his translation of the New Testament had already met the same fate. To drive the point home, a 1543 law forbade apprentices, servants, artisans, husbandmen, and women not of genteel birth to read the Bible in English. Nonetheless, English Bibles continued to be printed and read; in Shakespeare's day alone (1564–1616) over two hundred editions of the Bible appeared, with some four hundred thousand copies sold (to say nothing of the thousands of new catechisms and devotional best sellers like John Foxe's *Book of Martyrs*, which went through five printings during Foxe's own lifetime).[59]

But it was the Catholic notion of transubstantiation that became the final line of defense for the traditionalists beyond which Henry was unwilling to go. The principal heresy for which evangelicals went to the stake under Henry was denying the "real presence." The Act of Six Articles of 1539 made denial of Christ's body and blood in the Eucharist a burning offense in the first instance, an unprecedented step for English heresy laws. The most notorious

---

[57] Christopher Haigh, *The English Reformation Revised* (New York: Cambridge University Press, 1987), 15. In contrast to the view presented here, Haigh stresses the relative ease with which the reforms were accepted in England; "the piecemeal Reformation was a peaceful Reformation" (17).

[58] Naomi Tadmor, *The Social Universe of the English Bible: Scripture, Society, and Culture in Early Modern England* (New York: Cambridge University Press, 2010); David Daniell, *The Bible in English: Its History and Influence* (New Haven, Conn.: Yale University Press, 2003); Harry S. Stout, "Word and Order in Colonial New England," in *The Bible in America: Essays in Cultural History*, ed. Nathan Hatch and Mark Noll (New York: Oxford University Press, 1982), 19–38.

[59] The perennial favorite was the Geneva Bible, which a handful of English expatriates had helped translate in 1560 in Calvin's Geneva. Even after the adoption of a new authorized version in 1611, the King James Bible, most English men and women preferred the heavily annotated Geneva Bible. The Geneva Bible was the muse of the great English poets—Shakespeare, Donne, Bunyan, Milton—and was carried across the Atlantic by Puritan émigrés in the seventeenth century. The rivalry between the two versions became politically charged in the 1630s and 1640s as the nation careened toward civil war; Archbishop Laud outlawed the Geneva Bible in 1637, but Cromwell defiantly reintroduced it in 1643 when he ordered a special edition (the "Soldier's Bible") to be distributed to his New Model Army.

execution under this extraordinarily unforgiving law was the burning of the Lady Anne Askew in 1546. (When Joan Bocher of Kent was staked in 1550 for denying the humanity of Christ, she boldly taunted the bishops for burning her friend Anne "for a piece of bread, and yet you came yourselves soon after to believe and profess the same doctrine for which you burned her. And now forsooth you wil needs burn me for a piece of flesh.")[60] The fires of Smithfield were kept stoked thereafter, and while the reign of "Bloody Mary" Tudor (1553–58) was reviled throughout Protestant Europe for sending some 300 Reformers to the stake, some 200 Catholics were executed for heresy or died in prison under the "good" Elizabeth I.[61]

The very public deaths of Protestant and Catholic "martyrs" under the Tudor monarchs have come to symbolize the excesses of the English Reformation in its most repressive phase. But even under the more aggressive heresy-hunting of Henry and his children, executions were still relatively rare. In fact, despite frequent and bewildering regime changes, England's ecclesiastical laws had been steadily reformed in the direction of leniency since the 1530s under both Catholic and Protestant monarchs. Lesser penalties were preferred to execution: a 1538 proclamation ordered all Anabaptists (the bogeymen of the Reformation) and sacramentarians to depart England on pain of death, and Jesuits and seminary priests faced the same injunction in the 1570s. This is not to say that dissenters were treated gently—whipping, imprisonment, branding, and other forms of bodily mutilation were distressingly frequent in the topsy-turvy years of the sixteenth century as England ricocheted from one confessional regime to another. A Southwark woman had the letter "H" burned into her left cheek for heresy in the early 1500s; William Geoffrey was lashed in the streets of London in 1561 for blasphemously proclaiming John More, one of the many lay prophets who roamed the kingdom in these years, to be Christ himself; John Traske was flogged from one corner of London to another in 1618 and then nailed to the pillory at Cheapside through each ear while the letter "J" was burned into his forehead "in token that hee broached Jewish opynions."[62] Despite the palpable brutality of these punishments, relatively few heretics or blasphemers died for their sins, especially if we exclude

[60] Quoted in Levy, *Blasphemy*, 85.

[61] Alexandra Walsham, *Charitable Hatred: Tolerance and Intolerance in England, 1500–1700* (Manchester: Manchester University Press, 2006), 52. Walsham counts 189 executions of Catholics for treason between 1570 and 1603, with another 75 in the following seven decades.

[62] Walsham, *Charitable Hatred*, 80–81. Walsham details the range of penalties inflicted upon religious dissenters, 56–92.

the Marian executions. The last person burned for heresy in England was the Anabaptist Edward Wightman, who was staked in 1612 for "wicked heresies" and "other cursed opinions belched by the instinct of Satan."[63]

Wightman's death marked the end of an era. But it did nothing to quell the rising tide of blasphemous words and heretical doctrines that seemed to have been unleashed by the logocentrism of the Reformation. The fact that the Bible became a partisan weapon in Europe's wars of religion only underscores the radical potential of language to unsettle all hierarchies of power. There was a profound paradox at the very heart of scripture itself—the direct, unmediated Word of God that most English Protestants preferred to read in annotated form. Champions of expanded literacy, including modern historians of the book, believe that, to quote Jonathan Sheehan, "more books, more readers, and more reading bred more skepticism toward king and God alike."[64] When this skepticism was directed at "popish superstitions" and the prelate of Rome, Reformers rejoiced; when it was directed at their own magistrates and church institutions, they turned to the state to punish the offender for slander or sedition. And when God himself was the object of popular irreverence or skepticism, they called it blasphemy. In Protestant eyes, blasphemers were worse than "the Jew, the Turk, the pagan, and the heretic."[65]

If so, then England in the fifty years before the first ships left Plymouth for the New World was the worst nation in western Christendom.

A "Swarme of Sectaries":
Blasphemy in the English Revolution

The English were prolific and creative swearers. A "plague of curses" swept the country in the sixteenth and seventeenth centuries, with an explosion in slander litigation accompanying a sharp rise in sermons decrying sacrile-

[63] Ian Atherton and David Como, "The Burning of Edward Wightman: Puritanism, Prelacy, and the Politics of Heresy in Early Modern England," *English Historical Review* 120 (December 2005): 1215–50.

[64] Jonathan Sheehan, *The Enlightenment Bible: Translation, Scholarship, Culture* (Princeton, N.J.: Princeton University Press, 2005), xi. For an alternative view of the impact of expanded access to the printed word that sees the Reformation as imposing a "typographical tyranny" on the lived experience of religion, see John Bossy, *Christianity in the West 1400–1700* (New York: Oxford University Press, 1985). James Simpson likewise emphasizes the dark side of Protestant bibliocentrism in his account of the "biblical violence" unleashed by the Reformation in *Burning to Read*.

[65] Quoted in Cabantous, *Blasphemy*, 12.

gious speech as the national sin.[66] So commonplace were profane oaths in the streets and byways of the nation's towns that one preacher thought English children "must have sucked them out of their mother's breasts." (His proposed remedy: "a lawe . . . that every swearer and blasphemer should holde his hand a quarter of an houre in boyling lead.")[67]

Predictably, the Puritan commonwealth established in the 1640s and 1650s took a hard stance against heresy and malediction, though the story is more complicated than one might think. The legal machinery for prosecuting heresy was effectively dismantled by the Civil Wars: the abolition of the High Commission, prerogative, and ecclesiastical courts (which had become "an extreme grievance and vexation to the common people of England") left heresy-hunters in juridical limbo.[68] The desire to punish had certainly not disappeared—strict Presbyterians like Ephraim Pagitt demanded that blasphemers be put to death. "If such as poyson waters and fountaines at which men and beasts drinke, deserve Capitall punishment," he reasoned, how much more so do those who "poyson mens soules"?[69] The Puritan Thomas Cartwright was unapologetic about his desire to see the teachers of heresy executed: "If this be bloody and extreme, I am content to be so counted with the Holy Ghost."[70] Yet there were powerful ideological currents militating against the vigorous prosecution of heresy and blasphemy. The Revolution had, after all, been a triumph of the Protestant vernacular: the dramatic expansion of public speaking, tracts, and radical sects in the decades of war in no small measure created and sustained the republic. Words—prophetic, polyphonic, and profane—brought the republic into existence and would be responsible for its downfall. As all historians of the Civil Wars have pointed out, England was afflicted with a "swarme of sectaries" in the 1640s and 1650s—"hot" Protestants with wonderful names like Praisegod Barebones, men (and some women) who saw the demise of the king as an opportunity to push for a far more radical version of the Reformation than England had settled for under Elizabeth's temporizing

[66] James A. Sharpe, *Defamation and Sexual Slander in Early Modern England: The Church Courts at York* (York: Borthwick Institute, 1980).

[67] Arthur Dent, *The plaine mans path-way to heaven* (London, 1601), 151, 161.

[68] *An Act for the better regulating of Archbishops, Bishops, Deans, Deans and Chapters, Canons and Prebends, and the better ordering of their revenues, and for the better governing of the Courts Ecclesiastical and the Ministers thereof, and the proceeding therein*, 1641, http://www.constitution.org/eng/conpur033.htm (accessed September 15, 2014).

[69] Ephraim Pagitt, *Heresiography, or, A Discription of the Hereticks and Sectaries of These Latter Times* (London, 1645), dedicatory.

[70] Quoted in Shagan, *Rule of Moderation*, 288.

hand. Their programs for spiritual and political reform have been ably described elsewhere;[71] my focus here is on the war of words that erupted in the English press over the sectarians and their iconoclastic ways. Thanks to the verbal pyrogenics of the Seekers, Ranters, Levellers, Diggers, Baptists, Familists, Quakers, and other radical spiritists, Parliament reexamined the realm's laws against heresy and blasphemy and found them wanting. Thus began a new chapter in the history of malediction in Anglo-America, one that would have important consequences for England's overseas possessions.

The story of one beleaguered preacher from Kent can help set the scene. Richard Culmer was the kind of man the Civil War was fought for, and by—a Puritan minister who had labored long and fruitlessly in the fields to bring godliness to his patch of England. His battles over profanity, blasphemy, and sacrilege had begun even before the Presbyterian Party seized control of Parliament, when he tangled with his parishioners in the 1630s over their love of sport on the Sabbath. By 1645, a full-blown "culture war" (in Bernard Capp's words) had broken out in the Kent parish of Minster.[72] Culmer's opponents were men and women who loved strong drink, festivals, and the comfortable rituals of Anglicanism, and for whom the "reformation of manners" pursued by stern Puritans like Culmer was an affront to their customary way of life. One of his tormenters was so proficient a swearer that he was known as "*Will Wounds, because of his usual oaths, by Wounds,* &c." They pulled out all the stops in their campaign to drive the minister from his post—jeering and cat-calling from the pews when Culmer attempted to preach, cursing him as he passed in the streets ("calling him *devillish roundheadid Priest; and Ha Blew Dick, the devil break your neck:* and roaring out of the Alehouse window, as he went by; *You sirra Jack Priest,* &c"), and publishing "libels" about his misdeeds in the public prints. His "Grande Persecutor," John White, was the author of several scurrilous papers that circulated like "bile," written with "gall" instead of ink. One such specimen charged "*That he was a fantastic narrow brain'd*

---

[71] Most notably, of course, by Christopher Hill, *The World Turned Upside Down* (New York: Viking Press, 1972); but see also Peter Lake, *The Boxmaker's Revenge: "Orthodoxy," "Heterodoxy," and the Politics of the Parish in Early Stuart London* (Stanford, Calif.: Stanford University Press, 2001); David Como and Peter Lake, "Puritans, Antinomians and Laudians in Caroline London: The Strange Case of Peter Shaw and Its Contexts," *Journal of Ecclesiastical History* 50 (1999): 684–715; and David Como, *Blown by the Spirit: Puritanism and the Emergence of an Antinomian Underground in pre–Civil-War England* (Stanford, Calif.: Stanford University Press, 2004).

[72] Bernard Capp, *England's Culture Wars: Puritan Reformation and Its Enemies in the Interregnum, 1649–1660* (New York: Oxford University Press, 2012). Capp narrates Culmer's story in the introduction, 1–3.

*man. . . . That he is an impudent man, and did pisse in the Cathedral in Canter-
bury."* They threatened to hang him from the maypole he had tried to prevent
from being built and to bury him alive when he refused to officiate at the grave
(*"he would not be Chaplain to the wormes, to say grace to them before they go to
dinner and feed on the dead corps"*). Much of this was scripted blasphemy—a
creative marriage of profane speech and ritual parody that blurred the boundary between words and acts. On another occasion when Culmer refused to
conduct a burial according to Anglican rites, "one J. D. (a common swearer)
fell flat on his belly, and thrust his arm into the grave, and said aloud, *We shall
have him here, here, here shortly."* And they attacked the church itself, in a parody of the official iconoclasm authorized by the Puritan Parliament against
the material "relics" of popery.[73] In the end Culmer prevailed, but not before
his person, dignity, and faith in godly reform were sorely tested.

There were many Richard Culmers and John Whites in the 1630s, 1640s,
and 1650s. In Middlesex and the south bank of London, more than 130 men
and women were brought before the court for voicing "offensive political or
religious opinions" in the 1640s. Some denounced the Book of Common
Prayer as popish, idolatrous, "the scraps and scum of hell." A spinster declared "that she would rather go to hear a Cart wheel creak and a dog bark"
than hear the curate of Stepney preach.[74] These parish skirmishes appear to
have been localized affairs, the culmination of decades of popular anticleri-
calism and ministerial frustration. But as civil war broke out in the early
1640s, a new breed of religious preachers emerged who aligned themselves
culturally with the "rabble" and challenged the ruling Presbyterian Party
openly on theological and ecclesial grounds. The meteoric rise of these "tub-
preachers" sparked apocalyptic metaphors to describe what was happening.
Where heretics used to "peep up by one and one," John Taylor despaired in
1651 that "now they sprout by huddles and clusters (like locusts out of the
bottomless pit) They now come thronging upon us in swarms, as the Cat-
erpillers of Aegypt."[75]

[73] Richard Culmer, *A parish looking-glasse for persecutors of ministers . . . , or, The persecuted ministers apologie published by Richard Culmer . . . in defence of his father, Richard Culmer* (London, 1657), 7, 12, 17, 18–19, 21, 26–27.
[74] Keith Lindley, "London and Popular Freedom in the 1640s," in *Freedom and the English
Revolution: Essays in History and Literature*, ed. R. C. Richardson and G. M. Ridden (Manchester: Manchester University Press, 1986), 111–50 (quotations on 133, 134).
[75] John Taylor, *Ranters of both sexes, male and female: being thirteen or more, taken and
imprisoned in the gate-house at Westminster, and in the new-prison at Clerken Well* (London,
1651), 4.

The reaction among the more respectable elements of the Puritan coalition was just as forceful. New heresiographies (compendia of heterodox errors) began to appear that used exaggeration and satire to further inflame public opinion against the "swarme of sectaries" infecting the nation, and by the mid-1640s there was considerable pressure on Parliament to act by resurrecting or revising the outmoded heresy laws.[76] Some of the more ardent millenarians wanted to replace the entire English legal system with the Law of Moses (precedent had, after all, been set in the reign of Henry VIII when Bishop Latimer tried to make adultery punishable by death by stoning), but there doesn't seem to have been much stomach for returning to the brutal punishments of the Old Testament. (The English colonies were a different story, as we'll see.)[77] An early effort in 1645 ordered all copies of John Archer's *Comfort for Believers*, which Parliament deemed "blasphemous Heresy," to be burned by the common hangman at various sites throughout London. Archer himself was already dead, so beyond Parliament's reach. A test case came before the Commons that same year that exposed the weakness of the English legal system. The Westminster Assembly of Divines appeared en masse before the House to press for the "condign punishment" of one Paul Best, whose "horrid blasphemies" had landed him in jail. Best was notorious within the antinomian community in London, and even his commander in the New Model Army disowned his heterodox views. After a seven-month investigation, the House reluctantly concluded that it had, in fact, no legal way to punish Best since it had abolished the ecclesiastical courts. A bill of attainder was introduced demanding Best's death by hanging for his "execrable Blasphemies, not fit to be named," but still the House demurred. As the incorrigible Best continued to publish from jail, somehow smuggling the pages out of his cell, Parliament was, finally, spurred to act.[78]

---

[76] Pagitt, *Heresiography*; Robert Baillie, *Anabaptism, The true Fountain of Independency, Antinomy, Brownisme, Familisme* (London, 1647); *A Discoverie of 29 Sects here in London* (London, 1641); Thomas Edwards, *Gangraena, or, A Catalogue and Discovery of many of the Errours, Heresies, Blasphemies and Pernicious Practices of the Sectaries of This Time* (London, 1646); J[ohn] G[rant], *Truth Victory against Heresie: all sorts comprehended under these ten mentioned: Papists, Familists, Arrians, Arminians, Anabaptists, Separatists, Antinomists, Monarchists, Millenarists, Independents* (London, 1645).

[77] G. E. Aylmer, *Rebellion or Revolution? England, 1640–1660* (New York: Oxford University Press, 1986), 126; on Latimer's proposal, see Brigden, *New Worlds, Lost Worlds*, 181.

[78] Levy narrates the Best case in *Blasphemy*, 112–17. Best was quietly released from jail in 1647 to his Yorkshire estate, where he cheerfully resumed his mercurial career as literary provocateur.

The result was the "Draconic" Act of 1648, which rectified the vagueness of the 1401 heresy law (specific heretical doctrines were mentioned for the first time, including denying the Trinity, the resurrection, the divinity or manhood of Christ, and the sacrality of scripture) while retaining the death penalty for "obstinate" heretics and blasphemers.[79] The inaugural case tried under the new act was that of John Biddle, like Best an antitrinitarian who had been a thorn in the side of the Presbyterian establishment for many years. Fearing a sectarian backlash that might imperil his credibility with the radicals in the New Model Army, Oliver Cromwell took the case out of the hands of Parliament and decided it himself by banishing Biddle for life. (When pressed for clemency by one of Biddle's friends, Cromwell allegedly retorted, "You curl-pate boy you, do you think I'll show any favor to a man who denies his Saviour, and disturbs the government?")[80] Cromwell's sidestepping of the law proved prophetic, as it remained dormant on the books.

Two years later, however, a new Blasphemy Act was enacted that was broader and (marginally) more effective. Declaring to "their great grief and astonishment" that, despite the strictures of the 1648 act, "there are divers men and women who have lately discovered themselves to be most monstrous in their Opinions, and loose in all wicked and abominable Practices," Parliament tackled the problem again. The long list of "Atheistical, Blasphemous and Execrable Opinions" identified reads like a sectarian primer: the act singled out all persons "not distempered with sickness, or distracted in brain" who "maintain him or her self, or any other meer Creature, to be very God," who claim that "acts of Uncleanness, Prophane Swearing, Drunkenness, and the like Filthiness and Brutishness, are not unholy and forbidden in the Word of God," who profess that "Denying and Blaspheming God, or the Holiness or Righteousness of God; or the acts of cursing God, or of Swearing prophanely or falsly by the Name of God, or the acts of Lying, Stealing, Cousening and Defrauding others; or the acts of Murther, Adultery, Incest, Fornication, Uncleanness, Sodomy, Drunkenness, filthy and lascivious Speaking, are not things in themselves shameful, wicked, sinful, impious, abominable

---

[79] "An Ordinance for the punishing of Blasphemies and Heresies, with the several penalties therein expressed," May 1648, in *Acts and Ordinances of the Interregnum, 1642–1660*, 2 vols., ed. C. H. Firth and R. S. Rait (London, 1911), 1:1133–36; *The Spirit of persecution again broken loose, by an attempt to put in execution against Mr. John Biddle master of arts, an abrogated ordinance of the Lords and Commons for punishing blasphemies and heresies* (London, 1655).

[80] Levy, *Blasphemy*, 133.

and detestable."[81] This remarkable act of ventriloquism essentially allowed the authorities to "unsay" the offending words of blasphemers by repeating them nearly verbatim, a not uncommon antidote to malediction in the early modern world.[82] But even more important, blasphemy was no longer a capital offense in the second instance; the initial penalty was now six months of imprisonment, with second offenders banished upon pain of death should they return. And scarcely a month later, Parliament passed what came to be known as the Toleration Act, repealing all previous laws requiring uniformity in religious belief and practice or establishing any form of religion in England. Nonconformists were now free to attend whatever church they wished or to absent themselves altogether as long as they "be present at some other place in the practice of some Religious Duty, either of Prayer, Preaching, Reading or Expounding the Scriptures." As long as they avoided the specific heresies denominated in the 1648 and 1650 acts, the heterodox were free to say and believe anything.[83]

Within the space of two short years, then, the Puritan commonwealth had endorsed *both* religious persecution and religious toleration. Within a decade, of course, the entire commonwealth experiment was dead, along with the king and Oliver Cromwell. The abortive legislative effort to resurrect the spirit of Mosaic law against heretics and blasphemers while protecting the godly's right to free expression at the boundaries of Protestant orthodoxy would leave a lasting mark on the legal cultures of England's overseas colonies.

Historians credit one particular group of sectarians with inspiring the legislative offense against religious disorder that culminated in the Blasphemy Act of 1650: the Ranters. Perhaps as many as one hundred Ranters were charged with blasphemy under the two acts.[84] To their critics, the Ranters embodied everything that was obnoxious about the sectarians: they were flamboyant, confrontational, heterodox, and joyously profane. Historians even doubted for a while whether they really existed, so hyperbolic was the rhetoric

---

[81] *Acts and Ordinances of the Interregnum*, 2:409–12.

[82] See Kamensky, *Governing the Tongue*, for a discussion of the gendered connotations of "unsaying" as a verbal policing strategy in early New England.

[83] "Act for the Repeal of several Clauses in Statutes imposing Penalties for not coming to Church," in *Acts and Ordinances of the Interregnum*, 2:423–25; Levy, *Blasphemy*, 156–57.

[84] These prosecutions were mostly for show, though a few Ranters did receive exemplary punishments; one was sentenced to be "hung up by his Thumbs for a good space of time, and after . . . cut down to be openly whipt." *The Arraignment and Tryall, with a Declaration of the Ranters* (London, 1650), 5.

surrounding their presence in London in the late 1640s.[85] For my purposes, the heated scholarly debate over whether the Ranters constituted a coherent sectarian movement or a loose swirl of heterodox ideas, rhetorical tropes, and cultural fantasies is less important than what the controversial figure of the "Ranter" tells us about the evolving nature of blasphemy during the English Revolution. For, like their radical forebears the Lollards, the Ranters were the public face of blasphemy for an entire generation of English Christians.

The Ranters, and their opponents, excelled at producing small, cheap pamphlets with catchy titles and primitive woodcuts that were distributed by the thousands in London and other provincial cities in the 1640s and 1650s, along with the country's first newspapers and more traditional broadsides. Reading habits were transformed during these decades, as a "reading revolution" accompanied (indeed, made possible) the political and religious revolutions of the seventeenth century.[86] The Ranter pamphlets are crude affairs indeed, in all senses of the word, replete with numerous typographical errors, blatant plagiarism (although the lifting of passages verbatim from one text into another was commonplace in the seventeenth century), and pornographic images. They depict a "world turned upside down," in Christopher Hill's famous phrase, where faith became irreverence and the sacred was rendered profane. One told the tale of a journeyman shoemaker who "when he heard any mention of God, he used to laugh, and in a disdainful manner say that he believed money, good clothes, good meat and drink, tobacco and merry company to be Gods." In a "Ranting mood" the shoemaker declared "that the Devil was nothing but the backside of God."[87] The most widely reprinted illustration from the anti-Ranter tracts shows a circle of men and women dancing, eating, and sporting sexually with one another (Figure 8). The scene was meant to be a rude approximation of the Ranters' religious assemblies, where, according to one account, they spent "many days in Riotting and Revelling, Drinking, Swearing & Blaspheming; saying, There was no

---

[85] The debate was ignited by J. C. Davis, *Fear, Myth, and History: The Ranters and The Historians* (New York: Cambridge University Press, 1986). *Past & Present* devoted part of an issue to the reception of Davis's thesis: "Fear, Myth, and Furore: Reappraising the 'Ranters,'" 140 (1993): 155–210. Earlier works on the Ranters include A. L. Morton, *The World of the Ranters: Religious Radicalism in the English Revolution* (London: Lawrence & Wishart, 1970); and Jerome Friedman, *Blasphemy, Immorality, and Anarchy: The Ranters and the English Revolution* (Athens: Ohio University Press, 1987).

[86] Sharpe, *Reading Revolutions*; Ian Green, *Print and Protestantism in Early Modern England* (New York: Oxford University Press, 2000).

[87] *Arraignment and Tryall*, 2.

The Ranters Ranting:

WITH

The apprehending, examinations, and confession of *Iohn Collins*, I. *Shakespear*, *Tho. Wiberton*, and five more which are to answer the next Sessions. And severall songs or catches, which were sung at their meetings. Also their several kinds of mirth, and dancing. Their blasphemous opinions. Their belief concerning heaven and hell. And the reason why one of the same opinion cut off the heads of his own mother and brother. Set forth for the further discovery of this ungodly crew.

Behold our joy to our Fellow-Creature.

Welcome Fellow-Creature.

Let us eat while they dance.

Decemb: 2
LONDON
Printed by B. Alsop, 1650.

Figure 8. The blasphemous antics of the Ranters, the most notorious of the English Civil War–era sectarians. *The Ranters Ranting* (1650).

God, no Devil, no Heaven, no Hell, but that the Soul was mortall, and the Scripture a Fiction." (Right on cue, as they were "belching out these Blasphemies," the Devil appeared and carried away "a Hundred and Thirty of their Children in a great smoak and Fiery Flame.")[88] Ranter "ceremonies" included burlesque sermons and mock enactments of the sacraments, especially baptism and communion. At one assembly a group of Ranters parodied the Lord's Supper; while "sitting at table, eating of a piece of Beef, one of them took it in his hand, tearing it asunder, said to the others, *This is the flesh of Christ*, take and eat. The other took a cup of Ale and threw it into the chimney corner, saying, *This is the bloud of Christ*." A third chimed in and boasted that he could "make a God every morning, by easing of his body."[89] All gross exaggerations, of course, if not outright fabrications, designed to shock and disgust a respectable readership. (Though, as we saw in Chapter 1, such scatological treatment of the Eucharist had long been a staple of Protestant polemics.) But the Ranters provided plenty of fuel for the fire in their own apologetics. Abiezer Coppe, the "leader" of the movement if such a person could be said to exist, embraced a form of godly swearing, saying he would rather "heare a mighty Angell (in man) swearing a full-mouthed oath . . . cursing and making others fall a swearing, than heare a zealous Presbyterian, Independent or spiritual Notionist pray, preach, or exercise. Well! One hint more; there's *swearing ignorantly, i'th darke, vainely, and there's swearing i'th light, gloriously.*" He ridiculed the sacrament of the Eucharist, arguing that "the true communion amongst men is to have all things common."[90]

I want to pick up one thread of this polemical exchange and follow it through the broader literature of the civil war era: the mockery of the sacraments. My goal is to connect this discussion to the theological debates over the sacraments explored in Chapter 1 but also to probe the generic boundaries of blasphemy as a form of profanation.[91] The carnivalesque aspect of blasphemy, which, as we have seen, was implicit in the category itself from the

[88] J. M., *The Ranters Last Sermon: With the manner of their Meetings, Ceremonies, and Actions; also their Damnable, Blasphemous and Diabollical Tennents* (London, 1654), 6–7.

[89] *Strange Newes from Newgate and the Old Bailey* (London, 1651), 2–3.

[90] Coppe, *A Flying Fiery Rolle*, part 1, chapter 2; Abiezer Coppe, *A Second Fiery Flying Roule* (London, 1649).

[91] The anti-sacramentalism of the Ranters and other civil war sects has its roots in Lollardy, too; Wyclif's greatest heresy, the one that earned him ejection from Oxford, was his denunciation of the concept of transubstantiation in *De Eucharista* in 1379. Anticipating the position of Calvin a century later, Wyclif was horrified most by the "carnality" of the doctrine of the "real presence." Maurice Keen, "Wyclif, the Bible, and Transubstantiation," in *Wyclif in His Times*, ed. Anthony Kennedy (Oxford: Clarendon Press, 1986), 1–16.

very beginnings of Christian discourse, took center stage in the English press in the 1640s and 1650s. And in the process, the concept of blasphemy began to expand beyond the verbal to encompass sacrilegious acts as well. I don't want to overstate the distinction between speech and action, or to argue for some kind of epistemic shift from the Word to the gesture in the post-Reformation era. But I do think there was something distinctly new about the blurring of the genres of blasphemy and sacrilege in the seventeenth century that made profane speech both more dangerous and easier to *see* (as well as *hear*). Certainly the ungodly had engaged in all manner of blasphemous acts in the medieval and early modern eras, and the ecclesiastical courts are full of cases of individual acts of irreverence (pissing in the baptismal font, turning one's backside to the altar, singing bawdy songs on holy days, insulting the priest and jeering during divine services, dressing animals up in clerical vestments, and much, much more). Most of this was juvenile, fueled by alcohol and testosterone.[92] But at least some of it was purposeful and heterodox, a form of social protest at a time when the laity had little recourse to the formal channels of ecclesiastical power. When these acts began to appear in the public prints and the newspapers, however, they assumed a rhetorical and political life of their own. And blasphemy begat blasphemy: the wide circulation of stories of sectarian sacrilege led to creative appropriations and retellings, and, invariably, to imitation. The striking intertextuality of the civil war pamphlets has been remarked upon by all scholars who have read them closely, and we can trace in some cases quite precisely the line of transmission of episodes from one text to another.[93] Blasphemy, in other words, became big news in the 1640s and 1650s.

As David Cressy has shown, mock sacraments involving animals were a recurrent feature of English parish life in the reigns of every Tudor and Stuart monarch. In April 1554, a cat was hung "gibbet style" on the gallows next to Cheapside Cross. The cat was "habited in a garment like to that the priest wore that said mass; she had a shaven crown, and in her fore feet held a piece of paper made round, representing the wafer." Cats seem to have been a

[92] David Cressy has culled marvelous examples from court records and the popular press in his *Travesties and Transgressions in Tudor and Stuart England: Tales of Discord and Dissension* (New York: Oxford University Press, 2000); see chapter 11, "Baptized Beasts and Other Travesties: Affronts to the Rites of Passage."

[93] Ann Hughes brilliantly re-creates this intertextualism with reference to the most influential pamphlet of the era, Thomas Edwards's sprawling three-volume heresiography, *Gangraena*; Hughes, *Gangraena and the Struggle for the English Revolution* (New York: Oxford University Press, 2004).

particular favorite of early modern English blasphemers: Peter Simons and Joan Golding were both cited by the archdeaconry court in Sussex on separate occasions for "baptising a cat" in 1603, and Nehemiah Wallington recalled in his diary that an Anabaptist "did deride and mock of the ordinance of baptism in the baptising of a cat."[94] Some "profane atheists" used an entire menagerie to insult not just one but three Christian sacraments in Exeter in 1600; the bishop complained that they performed "a ridiculous and profane marriage of a goose and a gander; a cat having an apron, and a partlet, brought to the church to be baptised; a horse head at Launceston lately lapped in a mantle and brought to the church to baptism, and afterwards the bell tolled and rung out for the death of his head: a dead horse brought to the communion table with his feet spread upon it, as being prepared to receive the sacrament."[95] On a far more serious note, John Foxe recorded the tragic case of "one Collins a madman" who "suffered death with his dog in Smithfield" in 1538. As Foxe told the story in his *Book of Martyrs*, "Collins happened to be in church when the priest elevated the host; and Collins, in derision of the sacrifice of the Mass, lifted up his dog above his head. For this crime Collins, who ought to have been sent to a madhouse, or whipped at the cart's tail, was brought before the bishop of London; and although he was really mad, yet such was the force of popish power, such the corruption in church and state, that the poor madman, and his dog, were both carried to the stake in Smithfield, where they were burned to ashes, amidst a vast crowd of spectators."[96]

From the ridiculous to the deadly serious: the tradition of mocking the sacraments ran the gamut in early modern England. It is not surprising, then, to find modern versions of such stories making the rounds in the pamphlet wars of the 1640s and 1650s. A London heel-maker and his wife derided the sacraments of baptism and the Eucharist, declaring "that a Cat or a Dog may be as well baptised as any Child or Children in their Infancy."[97] Among the "errors" catalogued by Thomas Edwards (the "true hammer of heretics," according to one admirer) in his "huge and abusive" book *Gangraena* were "many strange things in reference to baptisme of children, dressing up a Cat like a child for to

[94] Cressy, *Travesties*, 174–76. For other examples of animal baptisms, see Mary Stoyle, *Loyalty and Locality: Popular Allegiance in Devon During the English Civil War* (Exeter: Exeter University Press, 1994), 195.

[95] Cressy, *Travesties*, 175–76.

[96] Foxe, *Acts and Monuments*, http://www.gutenberg.org/files/22400/22400-h/22400-h.htm#Page_186 (accessed September 11, 2014).

[97] Lindley, "London and Popular Freedom in the 1640s," 135.

be baptized."[98] One notorious incident that quickly found its way into his competitors' tracts was the alleged baptism of a horse at Yaxley by soldiers of the New Model Army after they urinated in the font. The irony of Cromwell's warriors desecrating rather than destroying the relics of popery would not have been lost on English readers. "If Cromwellian soldiers were not smashing fonts with hammers," David Cressy wryly notes, "they would appear to have been filling them with urine to baptize their beasts."[99] The parliamentary paper *Mercurius Aulicus* reported a similar story a few weeks later, in which soldiers in Essex's army baptized a horse with the sign of the cross, which the royalist paper *Mercurius Britanicus* ridiculed as "the highest, boldest, most impudent, ridiculous story that ever was yet vomited out by *Aulicus*."[100]

Mock baptisms were just one example of the kind of sacred (or profane) theater that thrived in the heterodox atmosphere of the English Revolution. The true masters of sacred theater were not the Ranters, however much attention they received in the yellow press, but their far more numerous and consequential sectarian cousins, the Quakers. From their beginnings in the market towns of the North in the late 1640s, the Quakers quickly emerged as the most significant of the civil war sects, with a membership that swelled into the tens of thousands and a formidable publishing arm that pumped out a constant stream of narratives, memoirs, and controversial literature. The arrest and imprisonment of George Fox, their charismatic founder, on charges of blasphemy in 1650 was the opening shot in what became a war of attrition between the Quakers and their Puritan foes. One colonial governor grimly joked that the Quakers' countermeasures were so well organized they resembled a "Joint Stock" formed expressly "to prosecute the Quarrels of all that sect."[101] This was a war that claimed real casualties, as thousands of Quakers were imprisoned, whipped, branded, and dismembered for their faith.

[98] Edwards, *Gangraena*, 1:67; Hughes, *Gangraena*, 2 ("hammer of heretics"); Levy, *Blasphemy*, 115 ("huge and abusive").

[99] Cressy, *Travesties*, 174.

[100] *Mercurius Aulicus*, week ending October 26, 1644; *Mercurius Britanicus*, November 11–November 18, 1644. The story was repeated in *Tub-preachers overturn'd, or, Independency to be abandon'd and abhor'd as destructive to the majestracy and ministery, of the church and common-wealth of England* (England, 1647), 11, and the broadside *These trades men are preachers in and about the City of London, or, A Discovery of the Most Dangerous and Damnable Tenets that have been spread within this few years* (London, 1647).

[101] Alexander Spotswood to the Council of Trade, October 19, 1711, Virginia, Huntington Library, San Marino, California, mss HM 59962. Spotswood wrote that he was "mightily embarrassed by a set of Quakers, who broach Doctrines so Monstrous as their Brethren in England have never owned, nor indeed can be suffered in any Government."

If the Ranter was the emblem of the sacrilegious blasphemer, the Quaker was the emblem of the "suffering saint"—an honorific they used to bludgeon their sectarian enemies throughout the seventeenth century. In their own eyes, they were engaged in "the Lamb's War," a fight to the death for the soul of English Christendom. Their weapons were the printed word and the theatrical gesture. Early Quakers were provocateurs, "professional skilled hecklers" who waged "guerilla war" against the standing clergy.[102] They stormed chapels and interrupted services by crying and singing aloud, refusing to doff their hats in deference to the godly authority of the minister. They went "naked for a sign," clad in only a shift or loincloth with ashes smeared on their heads and blood dripping down their faces. They poured pigs' blood on the altar, burned silks and ribbons in shops, dug up corpses and commanded them "to arise and walk." Solomon Eccles, a musician, burned his instruments and proceeded to walk through Smithfield naked, with a pan of burning coals upon his head.[103] Thomas Ibbott made himself into "an iconic sign" by simulating the distractions of a sinning world: as described by Fox, he was "moved" to "scatter his money up and down the streets, and to turn his horse loose in the streets and to untie his breeches' knees, and let his stockings fall, and to unbutton his doublet."[104] For these calculated acts of blasphemy, they received some of the harshest punishments on record for religious nonconformity in early modern England. The popular response was biblical: crowds tried to stone the Quakers, the Old Testament punishment for blasphemers. On occasion the mob prevailed—a Quaker was beaten to death in 1662 by a crowd enraged by the sight of two female Friends pouring blood on the high altar of St. Paul's Cathedral.[105]

One man, in particular, came to symbolize the brutality of the Puritan regime toward sectarians: James Nayler, the former soldier turned preacher, who entered Bristol in 1656 on a donkey in imitation of Jesus' triumphant

[102] Hill, *The World Turned Upside Down*, 106.

[103] Edward Burrough, *A Brief Relation of the persecutions and cruelties that have been acted upon the people called Quakers in and about the city of London* (London, 1662), 5; Barry Reay, *The Quakers and the English Revolution* (London: Temple Smith, 1985), 35–37; on "going naked for a sign," see Richard Bauman, *Let Your Words Be Few: Symbolism of Speaking and Silence Among Seventeenth-Century Quakers* (New York: Cambridge University Press, 1983), chapter 6. As John Miller notes, "the sheer *range* of modes of disruption is striking," with dirt and excrement featuring prominently in these demonstrations. Miller, "'A Suffering People': English Quakers and Their Neighbors, c. 1650–c. 1700," *Past & Present* 188 (August 2005): 71–103 (quotation on 80).

[104] Quoted in Bauman, *Let Your Words Be Few*, 85.

[105] Walsham, *Charitable Hatred*, 117.

entry into Jerusalem on the eve of his execution. A chorus of women accompanied him, singing, "Holy, holy, holy, Lord God of Israel." Nayler was promptly arrested and an intense debate over what to do with him ensued. For ten days, Parliament deliberated his fate, with many MPs convinced that Nayler deserved the death penalty. Richard Cromwell told Thomas Burton that Nayler "must die," and Major General Boteler reminded the House that "by the Mosaic law, blasphemers were to be stoned to death." His fellow judge Colonel Thomas Cooper argued for life in prison instead: "I think, next to life, you cannot pass a greater punishment than perpetual imprisonment, where he may not spread his leprosy. If you cut out his tongue, he may write, for he writes all their bookes. If you cut off his right hand, he may write with his left." In the end, Nayler narrowly escaped death (the vote was 96 to 82), but he was broken in body and spirit; he received three hundred lashes and was branded on the forehead with the letter B, bored through the tongue with a hot iron, pilloried, and, in a final act of humiliation, paraded through Bristol facing backward on a horse (Figures 9 and 10). The savagery of the punishment shocked the moderate Presbyterian establishment, though the more bloodthirsty members of Parliament were unappeased. Major Lewis Audley dismissed boring of the tongue as "an ordinary punishment for swearing. I have known twenty bored through the tongue." Edward Whalley thought Nayler should have had his lips "slitted" as well. But to those who complained the punishment was too mild, Colonel Richard Holland retorted, "A merchant's wife told me that there was no skin left between his shoulders and his hips. It was no mock punishment."[106]

Thanks to the "Great Book of Suffering" that Quaker chroniclers maintained and the monthly "meetings for sufferings" in which men and women told of the ordeals they had endured for the faith, the persecution of the Quakers entered into popular lore throughout the Anglophone world. Their narratives of suffering circulated as a new form of martyrology, quite self-consciously modeled on Foxe's *Book of Martyrs*, a publishing tactic that other sects would soon adopt.[107] The element of violence—graphic, corporeal—in the Quaker

[106] Robert Rich and William Tomlinson, *A True Narrative of the Examination, Tryall and Sufferings of James Nayler* (London, 1657); Leo Damrosch, *The Sorrows of the Quaker Jesus: James Nayler and the Puritan Crackdown on the Free Spirit* (Cambridge, Mass.: Harvard University Press, 1996), 211–14, 222.

[107] "Great Book of Sufferings, 1650–1856," 44 vols., Friends House, London; John Knott, *Discourses of Martyrdom in English Literature, 1563–1694* (New York: Cambridge University Press, 1993); Adrian Chastain Weimer, *Martyrs' Mirror: Persecution and Holiness in Early New England* (New York: Oxford University Press, 2011).

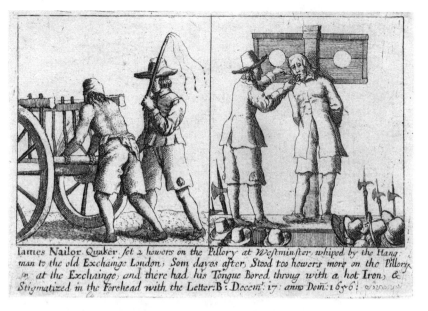

Iames Nailor Quaker ſet 2 howers on the Pillory at Weſtminſter whiped by the Hangman to the old Exchainge London, Som dayes after, Stood too howers more on the Pillory, at the Exchainge, and there had his Tongue Bored throug with a hot Iron, & Stigmatized in the Forehead with the Letter:B: Decem.ʳ 17: anno Doin: 1656:

Figure 9. James Naylor [Nayler] having his tongue bored with hot iron.
Engraving by Wenceslas Hollar, 1656. National Portrait Gallery, London.

narratives gave them a gravitas that the Ranter burlesques lacked.[108] There was
nothing amusing or risqué about the scarred and dismembered bodies on display in the Quaker accounts of sufferings. In the image of James Nayler's mutilated face, English readers could see the human cost of the "spirit of
persecution" that seemed to have been unleashed by the Revolution.

In 1671 a satire appeared that lampooned Quaker narratives of suffering
with deadly acuity. Seemingly recounting the shocking story of Mr. Baxter, an
orthodox minister in Boston who was murdered and "flayed" alive by rogue
Anabaptists, the pamphlet promised a "fall Sad account" of religious zeal narrated in Quaker style. After first tying up Mrs. Baxter and her three daughters,
the gang of Anabaptists "rudely tore the cloths from [Baxter's] back; when he

---

[108] The titles of the Quaker tracts did much of the polemical work: see, for example, the
1663 broadside *For the King and Both Houses of Parliament, Being a brief, plain, and true Relation of some of the late sad Sufferings of the People of God called Quakers, For worshipping
God, and exercising a good Conscience towards God and Man. By reason whereof 89 have suffered till death, 32 of which dyed before the King came into England, and 57 since; of which 57, by
hard imprisonment and cruel usage. 43 have dyed in this City of London and Southwark, since
the Act made against Meetings.*

IAMES NAYLOR

Of all the Sects that Night, and Errors own
And with false Lights possesse the world, ther's none
More strongly blind, or who more madly place
The light of Nature for the light of Grace.

The Shaker or Quaker.

THe Quaker is an upstart branch of the Anabaptists, lately sprung up, but thickest set in the North
parts ; the body of this Heresie is composed and
made up out of the dregs of the common people,
whom pride, conceitednesse, and ignorance , ever
most active causes in such productions here, thrust or

Figure 10. James Naylor [Nayler] with letter "B" branded on his forehead for blasphemy. Ephraim Pagett, *Heresiography* (1662).

was stript they most cruelly whipt him." Falling upon the poor man ("this innocent Lamb") "like so many Hell-hounds, they most barbarously . . . cut open his belly, and violently tore off his skin from his body. And when this holy Martyr by reason of his torments cryed out in a most dreadful manner, they said, 'twas excellent Musick." Mocking the Quakers' campaign of self-immolation, the "Lamb's War" of the 1650s, Laurance Saville turned the rhetorical excess that Anglo-American readers had come to expect from Protestant martyrologies into satire: "Oh! What a sad house is here! The Good man is stead alive, bleeding and crying out in the midst of his anguish and pain, the house swimming in bloud, the wife and children bound, and roaring out to see this poor Martyr wallowing in his bloud, and they not able to afford him any assistance." This sensationalized account ends with the death of the youngest daughter, who was "so consternated with horror, that she fell into Convulsion-fits, and dyed the next day."[109] We are halfway to the literary gothic here, with its exaggerated emotional appeal and focus on the sensational.

Tales of religious persecution thus saturated the print culture of seventeenth-century England from the Civil Wars through the Restoration, even to the point of caricature. And meanwhile the legal machinery of prosecution hummed along.[110] A landmark case in 1676 declared blasphemy to be a crime against the state as much as a crime against God and brought it under

---

[109] Laurance Saville, *Mr. Baxter Baptiz'd in Bloud, or, A sad History of the Unparallel'd Cruelty of the Anabaptists in New-England. Faithfully Relating the Cruel, Barbarous, and Bloudy Murder of Mr. Baxter, an Orthodox Minister, who was kill'd by the Anabaptists, and his Skin most cruelly flead off from his Body* (London, 1671), 5–6.

[110] The 1662 Act of Uniformity restored the privileged status and liturgical practices of the Anglican church, immediately casting thousands of Puritan ministers into legal purgatory. Some two thousand who refused to take the Oath of Supremacy were ejected from their clerical livings, becoming in effect the next wave of "martyrs" (with their own martyrologies), and a series of penal laws criminalizing nonconformity were passed in quick succession, known collectively as the Clarendon Code. Under these acts nonconforming clergy were barred from public office, and gatherings of more than five people for purposes of religious worship were barred. By the end of the seventeenth century, Puritans and Anglicans were vigorously trying to outdo one another in the victim game, competing in print for the honor of being the most persecuted party in Protestant England. The pamphlet feud between Edmund Calamy and John Walker in the early 1700s was the culminating act of this rhetorical thrust and parry; see Edmund Calamy, *An Abridgment of Mr. Baxter's History of His Life and Times: With an Account of the Ministers, &c. who Were Ejected at the Restauration of King Charles II* (London, 1702); John Walker, *An Attempt towards recovering an Account of the Numbers and Sufferings of the Clergy of the Church of England, Heads of Colleges, Fellows, Scholars, &c., who were Sequester'd, Harrass'd, &c. in the late Times of the Grand Rebellion* (London, 1714); and Edmund Calamy, *The Church and the Dissenters Compar'd as to Persecution* (London, 1719).

the jurisdiction of common law for the first time. John Taylor's confused but clearly sacrilegious pronouncements that "Christ is a whoremaster" and "I am a younger brother to Christ, an angel of God," so scandalized the House of Lords that they ordered Taylor confined to Bedlam and referred the case to the highest court in the land. Lord Chief Justice Matthew Hale sentenced Taylor to stand in the pillory in three different places, wearing a paper saying "for blasphemous words, tending to the subversion of all government," and—crucially for the history of English jurisprudence—stated that "injuries to God" are punishable in the criminal courts because "the Christian religion is part of the law itself."[111] Despite the sweeping implications of Hale's opinion, very few executions followed. And in fact, Parliament passed a new blasphemy act in 1676 that removed the death penalty entirely for all offenders.[112]

The last person executed for blasphemy in greater Britain was an eighteen-year-old Scottish lad, Thomas Aikenhead, who was hanged in 1695 for his antitrinitarian views at the insistence of Edinburgh's ministers. By 1695, the Ranters were gone, the Quakers had begun the process of transforming themselves from firebrands into quiet citizens, the Puritan Commonwealth was dead, and the swell of sacrilegious words that had rolled over the country like a tidal wave had receded. But not before ripples had reached the shores of the New World.

"Bloudy Lawes": Blasphemy in the New World

With the newly appointed governor of Virginia sitting prominently in the audience, the Anglican minister William Crashaw delivered a blistering sermon in 1610 against the specter of impiety in the infant colony. "Suffer no Papists; let them not nestle there; nay let the name of the Pope for Poperie be never heard of in Virginea," he counseled. "And (if I may be so bold as to advise) make Atheisme and other blasphemie capitall, and let that bee the first law made in Virginia." Reminding his listeners that "vaine swearing by Gods name be the common and *crying sinne of England*," he urged the governor to "let your laws be strict, especially against swearing and other prophaneness." "You know that it is a sinne *under which the earth mournes*," he concluded,

[111] Levy, *Treason Against God*, 313.

[112] James Herrick describes the shifting definition of blasphemy in "Blasphemy in the Eighteenth-Century." Three well-publicized cases occurred between 1729 and 1761.

"and your land will flourish if this be repressed."[113] From the very beginning, then, the English braced themselves for an outbreak of blasphemy when they left the settled parishes of home for the wilds of North America. Before the first ship bearing Puritans, the *Mayflower*, had even landed, one passenger had been stocked and whipped for slander and two servants had been tied up neck and heels for quarreling—not an auspicious start.[114] What they discovered was a New World Babel, a bewildering and often frightening soundscape of unintelligible native languages and loose English tongues.[115]

The leaders of the Virginia Company wasted little time in complying with Crashaw's admonition to outlaw atheism and blasphemy. The *Laws Divine, Morall, and Martiall* (known even in its own day as those "bloudy Laws") was the first comprehensive legal code in British America, indeed anywhere in the English-speaking world, and its peculiar blend of biblical warrant and harsh penalties would serve as a guiding principle for the colonial codes to follow. The authors were not jurists or ministers but military men who had seen hard service in the Netherlands and brought a crusading mentality to the task at hand. The first article would have delighted Crashaw. Article 1.2 declared that any who "speake impiously or maliciously, against the holy and blessed Trinitie, or any of the three persons, that is to say, against God the Father, God the Son, and God the holy Ghost," risked death. And the next provision, addressed specifically to those who "blaspheme Gods holy name," proscribed "severe punishment" for the first offense and "for the second, to have a bodkin thrust through [the] tongue." Third-time offenders would be put to death.[116] From there the code went on to enumerate a number of capital offenses—among them, uttering treasonous words or words critical of the company, murder, sodomy, robbery, swearing false oaths, bearing false witness, trading with Indians without permission, stealing from Indians, cheating the company, trading with sailors without permission, and sending goods out of the colony without leave. While these penalties were rarely enforced to the full extent of the law (Sir Thomas Smith later acknowledged that the laws were framed "in some cases *ad terrorem*, and in some to be truly executed"), they represent an extraordinary

[113] William Crashaw, *A Sermon Preached in London before the right honourable the Lord Lawarre* (London, 1610), 44.

[114] Bernard Bailyn, *The Barbarous Years: The Peopling of British North America: The Conflict of Civilizations, 1600–1675* (New York: Knopf, 2012), 330–31.

[115] Edward Gray, *New World Babel: Languages and Nations in Early America* (Princeton, N.J.: Princeton University Press, 1999).

[116] *For the Colony in Virginea Britannia: Lawes Divine, Morall, and Martiall, &c.* (London, 1612), 10.

attempt to create a "holy commonwealth" modeled on Mosaic law a decade before the first ships bearing Puritans would leave England for North America.[117]

The experiment in Mosaic law reached its culmination in the Puritan colonies of Massachusetts, Connecticut, and New Haven. Puritan émigrés believed they had the opportunity to do what even the regicides in England had not accomplished: replace the secular law with the law of God. As Henry Whitfield, who believed the conversion of America's Indians would usher in the millennium, enthused, "Oh the blessed day in England when the Word of God shall be their Magna Carta and chief Law Book; and when all the Lawyers must be Divines to study the Scriptures!"[118] Declaring that "the worde of God shall be the onely rule to be attended unto in ordering the affayres of gouernment in this plantation," the New Haven magistrates explicitly modeled their law code on the Old Testament. "Itt was ordered that the juridical lawes of God, as they were delivered to Moses . . . shall be accounted of morrall equity, and gen'rlly binde all offenders, and be a rule to all the courts in this jurisdiction."[119] The General Court of Connecticut cited Leviticus 24:15–16 in declaring that "If any person shall blaspheme the name of God, the Father, Son or Holy Goste, with direct, expres, presumptuous, or highhanded blasphemy, or shall Curse God in the like manner, he shall be put to death."[120] This was a significant departure from English jurisprudence, as we have seen, where death was never a first penalty but was always reserved for the obstinate.

In Massachusetts, the General Court entrusted the task of drafting a new code in 1636 to a committee headed by the formidable divine John Cotton, the leading light of a group of Protestant lawyers and clergy styled the "Mosaic legalists."[121] (Cotton's zeal for Old Testament rectitude was eclipsed only by

[117] Perry Miller, "Religion and Society in the Early Literature: The Religious Impulse in the Founding of Virginia," *William and Mary Quarterly*, 3rd ser., 6 (January 1949): 24–41 (quotation on 32). It was George Sandys who would condemn John Smith for implementing those "bloudy Lawes." See also Bond, "Source of Knowledge, Source of Power."

[118] Henry Whitfield, *The light appearing more and more towards the perfect day, or, a farther discovery of the present state of the Indians in New-England, concerning the progresse of the Gospel amongst them* (London, 1651), 29.

[119] *Records of the Colony and Plantation of New Haven, from 1638 to 1649*, ed. Charles J. Hoadley (Hartford, 1847), 21, 130.

[120] "General Courte, August 26, 1642," in *The Public Records of the Colony of Connecticut Prior to the Union with New Haven Colony, 1636–1666*, 77.

[121] The term "Mosaic legalist" is Richard Ross's, coined to describe the coterie of Protestant natural lawyers and Presbyterian theologians who worked actively from the late sixteenth to the mid-seventeenth century to reform the law codes of England and other Protestant polities. Ross, "Distinguishing Eternal from Transient Law: Natural Law and the Judicial Laws of Moses," *Past & Present* 217 (November 2012): 79–115.

that of Roger Williams, who pushed through a law requiring women to wear veils in public in 1634; Cotton ultimately got the law repealed.)[122] Cotton's draft code, known colloquially as "Moses his Judicials," is a remarkable document. Under the heading of capital crimes (or those "that deserve capitall punishment, or cutting off from a mans people, whether by death or banishment"), Cotton enumerated twenty-four distinct offenses. Heading the list was blasphemy, followed by idolatry, witchcraft, heresy, worshiping "molten or graven images," "reviling" religion or the Church, perjury, and "profaning" the Lord's Day in "a careless and scornful" manner. Secular crimes make their first appearance halfway down the list, at number 12 (treason).[123] Cotton was fearless in his pursuit of Mosaic law, even to the point of blood. As he put it in his riposte to the same Roger Williams, banished by the General Court in 1634 with the blessing of Cotton, "He that shed his own bloud to plant his Church, did never abolish that Law which enacted that his bloud should be upon him who should supplant his Church. If Christs bloud goe to plant it, let the false Christs bloud goe for suplanting it." It was far better that "a dead soule be dead in body, as well as in Spirit, than to live, and be lively in the flesh, to murder many precious soules by the Magistrates Indulgence."[124]

When the General Court finalized the new code in 1641 as "The Body of Liberties," it trimmed Cotton's twenty-four capital crimes down to twelve, keeping blasphemy at the very top of the list.[125] Though heresy was not identified by name in the 1641 code, as it had been in the Cotton version, the framers clearly intended the provisions against idolatry and blasphemy to include all forms of heterodoxy. Despite the best efforts of the colony's leaders to prevent dissenters from invading ("infesting" or "infecting," they would have said)

[122] *Winthrop's Journal, "History of New England,"* vol. 1, *1630–1649,* ed. James Kendall Hosmer (New York, 1908), 120.

[123] John Cotton, *An Abstract of the Lawes of New England, As they are now established* (London 1641), 10–11. In the section on lesser crimes, malediction again received top billing: the first crime listed was "rash and prophane swearing and cursing," which in the fourth instance would result in "branding him with a hot iron, or boring through the tongue, who hath bored and pierced Gods name" (12).

[124] John Cotton, *The Bloudy Tenet Washed and Made White in the Bloud of the Lamb, or, The Bloudy Tenet discust and discharg'd of bloud-guiltinesse, by Just Defense* (London, 1647), 83.

[125] Body of Liberties, 1641, http://www.winthropsociety.com/liberties.php (accessed September 26, 2014). Cotton wanted a more theocratic polity than the colony's magistrates could endorse; see his *Discourse About Civil Government in a New Plantation Whose Design is Religion,* published in 1663 but written in 1637 to guide the drafting of a legal code in New Haven. See also Isabel M. Calder, "John Cotton and the New Haven Colony," *New England Quarterly* 3 (1930): 82–94.

their new Eden, heretical "weeds" had cropped up almost as soon as the first towns were planted. The garden metaphor was a favorite trope of Cotton and other defenders of orthodoxy. To those who argued that "a false Religion will not hurt, if it be out of the Church, no more than weeds in the wilderness will hurt the inclosed Garden," they answered: "But what if the Garden be inclosed in the midst of a wildernesse? what if the weeds grow so neere the inclosure (or hedge) round about the Garden, that they easily creep into the Garden? what if every blast of wind blow the seeds of the weeds into the Garden, which are ready to overspread the Garden, and to choak the good herbes?" In North America, Puritans inhabited (in their view) a literal wilderness—not the spiritual wilderness of which English churchmen spoke so blithely. And this wilderness was inhabited by "ravening wolves"—here Cotton meant heretics, not Indians—who needed to be restrained; God "doth not forbid to drive ravenous wolves from the sheepfold, and to restrain them devouring the sheep of Christ," he wrote. Real weapons ("a materiall Sword of Steele"), not just spiritual weapons, were required to beat the wilderness and its feral denizens back.[126] The unprecedented harshness of the Massachusetts laws drew a sharp rebuke from the crown's solicitor general in 1677, who singled out "putting to death for matters of religion and otherwise" as one of his main objections to the charter, along with fining and whipping people for not attending church and "[having] forbid, under a penalty, the observation of Christmas Day, and other festivals of the Church."[127] The New England colonies' first law codes did not survive the demise of their original charters after the Restoration in 1660 when the crown moved swiftly to curb the troublesome autonomy of its overseas possessions. With the issuing of a new charter for Massachusetts in 1691, the Puritan commonwealth's bold experiment in Mosaic law came to an end.[128]

---

[126] Cotton, *Bloudy Tenet Washed*, 151, 158; John Cotton, *The Controversie Concerning Liberty of Conscience in Matters of Religion, Truly Stated, and distinctly and plainly handled, by Mr. John Cotton of Boston in New-England* (London, 1646), 9.

[127] Objections against the Massachusetts Charter, July 20, 1677, CO 1/41, no. 35.

[128] Though this did not mean that blasphemy and heresy were demoted as criminal offenses; in 1697, the law against heretics was revised to give magistrates a choice of penalties to impose: imprisonment, pillorying, whipping, boring the tongue "with a red hot iron," or mock execution—"provided that not more than two of the afore-mentioned punishments shall be inflicted for one and the same fact." "An Act Against Atheisme and Blasphemie," in *Acts and Resolves, Public and Private, of the Province of Massachusetts Bay* (Boston, 1869), 1:297. As late as 1782, blasphemy in Massachusetts could still be punished by "Imprisonment not exceeding Twelve Months, by sitting in the Pillory by Whipping, or Sitting on the Gallows with a Rope about the Neck, or binding to the good Behaviour, at the discretion of the Supreme Judicial Court." Quoted in Leonard Levy, "Satan's Last Apostle in Massachusetts," *American Quarterly* 5 (Spring 1953): 16–30 (quotation on 17).

Two colonies that are frequently cited in history textbooks for their pre-
cocious endorsement of liberty of conscience—Rhode Island and Pennsylvania—
allow us to explore the legal and conceptual limits of religious toleration in
the English settlements. Founded by refugees from religious persecution in
Massachusetts, Rhode Island was infamous on both sides of the Atlantic for
its defiant refusal to establish any church or impose civil or political disabili-
ties on religious dissenters. Boldly declaring itself "a DEMOCRACIE, or Popular Government," "Rogue-Island" attracted its share of malcontents and exiles
who had fled or been banished from neighboring Puritan colonies.[129] The
court records of the colony show a preoccupation with sins of the tongue in
the first decades—slander, defamation, perjury, and, above all, "improbrious
and uncvill Speeches" against leading figures, including the governor. Roger
Williams himself was in court repeatedly in the 1650s to complain about the
"open Defieance" he encountered, usually to no avail as the court refused to
prosecute.[130] In a colony where corporal punishment was rare, perjury
brought the harshest response: dismemberment by the cropping of ears (one
part of the body being made to suffer for the sins of another).[131] Liberty of
conscience was thus tied intimately to the experience of sectarian violence
experienced firsthand and the dangers of loose tongues in the absence of an
established religious authority. Roger Williams reminded Rhode Islanders in
1654 that "we have long drunck of ye cup of great liberties as any people yt we
can heare of under the whole Heaven. We have not only been long free

[129] "The Generall Court of Election began and held at Portsmouth, from the 16th of
March, to the 19th of the same month, 1641," http://avalon.law.yale.edu/17th_century/ri02.asp
(accessed February 27, 2015).

[130] For cases of slander and defamation, see the *Records of the Court of Trials of the Colony
of Providence Plantations, 1647–1662*, 2 vols. (Providence, 1920, 1922), 1:6, 18, 20, 76; 2:6, 33, 49.
Williams charged twelve men and women as "Comon Aposers of All Authority" in 1656–57;
ibid., 1:25, 26, 27, 34. For examples of "contemptuous Speeches" against the governor and
other magistrates, see ibid., 1:43, 51; 2:6, 8, 22, 28, 40, 58. Throughout these disorderly years,
only a handful of malcontents (usually fornicators who could not afford to pay their fines)
and—notably—perjurers suffered corporal punishment.

[131] One John Willis was sentenced "to have his Eares cutt in some publicke place" for
"perjury" in 1667; Ibid., 2:56. In Maryland, too, perjurers were punished more severely than
other malefactors. In June 1648, John Goneere was sentenced to "bee nayled by both the eares
to the pillory, with 3 nayles in each eare; & the nailes to bee slitt out, & afterwards to be
whipped 20 good lashes." The court insisted that the sentence be carried out "immediately,
before any other business of Court be proceed uppon." Women were not spared: Blanche
Howell lost both her ears in the same year, and Elizabeth Greene one of hers in 1663. William
Hand Browne, et al., eds., *Archives of Maryland: Proceedings and Acts of the General Assembly
of Maryland,* 72 vols. (Baltimore, 1883–1972), 4:393, 4:445, 49:87 (hereafter *Archives of
Maryland*).

(together with all English), from ye iron yoaks of wolfish Bishopes and their Popish ceremonies . . . but we have sitted quiet and drie from ye streams of blood spilt by ye warr in our native country. We have not felt ye new chains of ye Presbyterian tyrants; nor (in this colonie) have we been consumed with ye over-zealous fire of ye (so called) Godly and Christian magistrates."[132] Yet the colony paid a high price for its lax governance; by 1664, thirty years after he had been banished from Massachusetts for his heterodoxy, Williams had come to see his cherished sanctuary as a "barbarous desert."[133] The serpent in the garden was the toxic tongue.

The Quaker colony of Pennsylvania chose a different path. As in Rhode Island, the proprietor William Penn promised that all residents who "confess and acknowledge the one Almighty and eternal God, to be the Creator, Upholder and Ruler of the world" and who behave "peaceably" shall "in no ways, be molested or prejudiced for their religious persuasion, or practice, in matters of faith and worship, nor shall they be compelled, at any time, to frequent or maintain any religious worship, place or ministry whatever." The preamble to this remarkable refusal to establish *any* religion, however, makes it clear that Penn had no intention of unshackling religion from the fetters of the state. Law itself, he believed, is the result of original sin, called into existence by the inability of men to restrain their natural impulses. The main function of government is to "terrify evil doers," and to this end all Christians must obey the secular powers as they did God himself.[134] "You will find that God . . . hath empowered you to punish these impieties," he had earlier advised Charles II; "there can be no pretence of conscience to be drunk, to whore, to be voluptuous, to game, to swear, curse, blaspheme, and profane." (Among the sins on this list, he considered blasphemy "the most *Provoking Sin*.")[135] And so the Pennsylvania code went on to enumerate and proscribe all the "evil doing" men could get up to in Penn's "holy experiment": "all such offences against God, as swearing, cursing, lying, prophane talking, drunkenness, drinking of healths, obscene words, incest, sodomy, rapes, whoredom, fornication, and other uncleanness (not to be repeated) all treasons, misprisions, murders, duels, felony, seditions, maims, forcible entries, and other

[132] John Russell Bartlett, ed., *Records of the Colony of Rhode Island and Providence Plantations, in New England, 1636 to 1663*, vol. 1 (Providence, 1856), 287–89.

[133] *Records of Colony of Rhode Island*, 2:34.

[134] *Frame of Government of Pennsylvania*, May 1682, http://avalon.law.yale.edu/17th_century/pa04.asp (accessed February 27, 2015).

[135] William Penn, *An address to Protestants of all perswasions more especially the magistracy and clergy, for the promotion of virtue and charity* (London, 1679), 25, 33.

violences, to the persons and estates of the inhabitants within this province; all prizes, stage-plays, cards, dice, May-games, gamesters, masques, revels, bull-baitings, cock-fightings, bear-baitings, and the like, which excite the people to rudeness, cruelty, looseness, and irreligion, shall be respectively discouraged, and severely punished." Penn's vision of the "divine right" of government ("government seems to me a part of religion itself, a filing sacred in its institution and end") is a stark reminder that liberty of conscience did not mean the same thing in the seventeenth century that it does to us, or even to the historical generation that drafted the first amendment to the federal constitution.[136]

For the Quaker William Penn, then, a hardheaded realism (rooted in personal experience) about the prevalence of evil in the world lay behind his colony's embrace of practical toleration, not a principled objection to the exercise of secular authority over the bodies of sinning men and women. Roger Williams—whose theological justifications of liberty of conscience have earned him a well-deserved reputation as a modern visionary—came to rue the corrosion of public discourse that religious freedom had spawned and beseeched the colony's court to punish uncivil tongues.[137] Both men, in other words, were very much of their own time, not ours. Other colonies would follow their lead of coupling a general liberty of conscience with strictures on ungodly behavior.[138] Nowhere is this more starkly evident than in Maryland. Founded by George Calvert, the first Lord Baltimore, as a sanctuary for

[136] *Frame of Government of Pennsylvania.* For an example of a blasphemy prosecution, see the case of Gabriel Jones, 1705, in *Court Records of Kent County, Delaware, 1680–1705*, ed. Leon DeValinger Jr. (Washington, D.C.: American Historical Association, 1959), 328–29. Jones was accused of saying "with a lowd voice . . . Cursed be My God for Suffering me to live to be so old to be abused by Dennis Dyer." As in Rhode Island, cases of sins of the tongue (slander, defamation, swearing, abusive language) are littered throughout the early court records of Pennsylvania; in one county alone (Chester), forty-eight cases of verbal offenses were heard between 1681 and 1697, ranging from sedition and treason to "giving out evell words" (217); *Records of the Court of Chester County, Pennsylvania, 1681–1697* (Philadelphia, 1910).

[137] For a classic and still valuable account of Williams's ideas on religious liberty, see Edmund Morgan, *Roger Williams: The Church and the State* (New York: Harcourt, Brace & World, 1967), 115–42. A more modern treatment is Timothy Hall, *Separating Church and State: Roger Williams and Religious Liberty* (Urbana: University of Illinois Press, 1998).

[138] South Carolina, for example, in 1665 declared that no resident "shall be molested punished disquieted or called in question for any differences in opinion or practice in matters of religious concernment whoe doe not actually disturbe the civill peace of the said Province." *Concessions and Agreements of the Lords Proprietors of the Province of Carolina*, 1665, http:// avalon.law.yale.edu/17th_century/nc03.asp (accessed February 27, 2015).

England's beleaguered Catholic minority in 1634, Maryland's earliest codes reflect an uneasy mix of repression and liberality. On the one hand, no other colony prescribed the exact form of execution in capital crimes. Those convicted of treason were to be "punished by drawing hanging and quartering of a man [or] by drawing and burning of a Woman"; those guilty of lesser felonies such as homicide, polygamy, sodomy, and rape were to be hanged; and the worst offenders—those who committed sorcery, blasphemy, or idolatry— were to be burned alive. These were the standard punishments in England, and as in England, social rank determined the manner of death: noblemen who committed treason were to be accorded the privilege of beheading instead of drawing and hanging, while any felon who "can read Clerk like in the judgment of the Court" was to "lose his hand or be burned in the hand or forehead with a hot iron" rather than face death.[139]

On the other hand, Roman Catholics were accorded an unprecedented liberty to practice their faith: "the Holy Church within this Province shall have and enjoy all her Rights, liberties, and Franchises wholly and without Blemish" (1640).[140] Following the execution of Charles I and the establishment of the English Republic, the colony issued the famous 1649 Act Concerning Religion, one of the earliest affirmations of the right of free exercise of religion in American history. Concluding that "noe person or persons . . . shall from henceforth bee any waies troubled, Molested, or discountenanced for in respect of his or her religion nor in the free exercise thereof," the 1649 act nonetheless preceded this ringing declaration with a series of harsh penalties for certain crimes against God. Any Christian who blasphemed God, "that is Curse him, or deny our Saviour Jesus Christ to bee the sonne of God," was to be put to death, and those who "shall use or utter any reproachfull Speeches concerning the blessed Virgin Mary" were to be "publickly whipt and bee imprisoned." Ever sensitive to the potential for unruly speech to turn against the colony's leaders, the magistrates showed special vindictiveness in dealing with "mutinous or seditious speeches" against Lord Baltimore, ordering a graduated series of punishments ranging from fines to "boaring of the Tongue, slitting the nose, cutting of[f] one or both Eares, whipping, branding with a red hot Iron in the hand or forehead, [or] any one or more of these as

---

[139] *Archives of Maryland*, 1:71–72.

[140] Ibid., 96. This clause was revised under the Protectorate of Oliver Cromwell to strip Catholic residents of this protection: "none who profess and Exercise the Popish Religion Commonly called by the Name of the Roman Catholick Religion can be protected in this Province by the Lawes of England" (1654); *Archives of Maryland*, 1:341.

the Provinciall Court shall think fitt."[141] In light of these provisions, the declaration of liberty of conscience at the very end of the 1649 act reads like an afterthought. Maryland's defense of liberty of conscience was not an assertion of principle but a calculated response to the realities of sectarian factionalism that the English Civil War had unleashed, which had led to civil war in the colony itself in 1645 and again in 1655 (as we saw in the last chapter). The preamble to the clause explained that "the inforceing of the conscience in Matters of Religion hath frequently fallen out to be of dangerous Consequence in those commonwealths where it hath been practised." Most dangerous of all was the spirit of disputation, which in England had led to uncivil war, and the colony's leaders made sure such name-calling would not be tolerated in their province: all who lobbed the epithets "heretick, Schismatick, Idolator, puritan, Independent, Presbiterian, popish priest, Jesuited papist, Lutheran, Calvenist, Anabaptist, Brownist, Antinomian, Barrowist, Roundhead, Separatist, or any other name or terms in a reproachfull manner relating to matter of Religion" at a fellow (Christian) colonist forfeited ten shillings or faced a public whipping. And when the Quakers made their inevitable appearance in the colony in the 1650s, they were ordered to be "whipped from constable to constable until they be sent out of the Province."[142]

So much for the letter of the law. What about the *doings* of the law? What can we learn about the nature and history of blasphemy and heresy prosecutions from colonial court records? English colonists in the first century of settlement were prosecuted for "sw[earing] before God" (Goody Gregory, stocked for three hours in 1641), "scoffing at Religion in a Turbulent Spirit" (Henry Sherlot, a French dancing master, 1681), "sw[earing] by the bloud of god" (Robert Shorthose, "tongue put into a cleft stick," 1636), calling "the Church of Boston a whoare, a strumpet" (Francis Hutchinson, banished upon pain of death, 1641), "Diabolically Cursing" (Beleiffe Gridley, 1664), and using "passionate and unadvised words" (Arthur Mason, 1671).[143] And this

---

[141] *Archives of Maryland*, 1:244–49. As late as 1706, Maryland retained brutal corporal punishments for the crime of blasphemy; all residents who "Blasphem God" were to be "bored through the Tongue" for the first offense, "stigmatized in the Forehead with the Letter B" for the second, and executed for the third. *Archives of Maryland*, 26:321–22.

[142] "Order Against Quakers," July 23, 1659, *Archives of Maryland*, 3:362.

[143] *Colonial Justice in Western Massachusetts (1639–1702): The Pynchon Court Record*, ed. Joseph H. Smith (Cambridge, Mass.: Harvard University Press, 1961), 209–10 (Goody Gregory); *Records of the Court of Assistants of the Colony of Massachusetts Bay, 1630–1692*, ed. John Noble (Boston, 1901), 2:63 (Robert Shorthose), 2:109 (Francis Hutchinson), 3:144–45 (Beleiffe Gridly), 3:187–88 (Arthur Mason), 1:197 (Henry Sherlot).

was in Massachusetts alone. Altogether, hundreds of men and women found themselves before the bar for using words in a way that was deemed an affront to God or the church in the English colonies.[144]

Colonial statues clearly differentiated the lesser forms of malediction such as profanity and swearing from more serious ones like blasphemy. Massachusetts did not pass a general law against swearing until 1646, which exacted ten shillings for each "profane swear" uttered within its jurisdiction. Similarly, in Maryland each oath brought a separate fine of one hundred (later reduced to ten) pounds of tobacco, with half the fine going to the "publick use" and the other half to the "informer." (One notorious recidivist "swore at least one hundred oathes," earning himself a hefty fine.)[145] But in practice, magistrates found it difficult to distinguish garden-variety swearing from more deliberate mockery of God. Richard Smoolt, a servant, was charged by his mistress with "sundry grosse miscarriadges," including "scoffing at the word of God which was preached by Mr. Cheevers" and "other rebellious carriadges in the famylye." Denied the use of a cooking pot, Smoolt "bid the Divell goe with it" and turned abusive. "When his Mrs. Came to correct him for a lye, he turned againe and did wringe her by the arme. . . . He asked her daughter Rebecca if she were not with child and therein slaundered her."[146] In this one brief record are at least five different offenses: blasphemy ("the Divell goe with it"), slander, lying, disobedience, and physical assault. Not surprisingly, the court ordered the unrepentant Smoolt to be "severely whipped." Arthur Smith's (unrecorded) blasphemous words threatened to "overthrow the order & government God hath established in church & commonwealth," the New Haven court

[144] This section is based on a survey of the published court records for Connecticut, New Haven, Massachusetts, Plymouth, New Hampshire, Maryland, Virginia, Pennsylvania, New York, and New Jersey. Studies of speech crimes in particular localities within these colonies have yielded hundreds of individual cases. In one Massachusetts county alone (Essex), there were nearly 400 cases of slander in the half century before 1686 (Kamensky, *Governing the Tongue*, 7, 204n14). In New Haven Colony, slander suits averaged about three per year between 1639 and 1665; Cornelia Hughes Dayton, *Women Before the Bar: Gender, Law, and Society in Connecticut, 1639–1789* (Chapel Hill: University of North Carolina Press, 1995), 288–92. And in Maryland, Mary Beth Norton counted 145 cases of slander in the first half century of the colony's legal history; "Gender and Defamation in Seventeenth-Century Maryland," *William and Mary Quarterly*, 3d ser., 44 (January 1987): 3–39.

[145] *Records of Colony of Massachusetts*, 2:178; *Archives of Maryland*, 1:286, 343, 54:173 ("one hundred oathes.") When the Kent County court was informed that William Price and Jane Salter "have bene accustomed to take the name of God in vaine," they were fined 10 pounds of tobacco for "everie Oath" (five in all), with one half going to the "informer." *Archives of Maryland*, 54:51.

[146] *Records of Colony and Plantation of New Haven from 1638 to 1649*, May 4, 1647, 308.

concluded in 1659, though they refrained from condemning Smith to death in the hopes that he "hath spoken p[ro]phainly" rather than "blasphemously."[147] In other cases, it was clear to the magistrates (as it often was in England) that "blasphemous language" was nothing more than the slip of a drunken tongue. When Thomas Thornhill of Barbados was accused of the crime, the judge concluded that "the whole company was so far gone in drink that none could remember what was said," and dismissed the charges.[148]

When blasphemy was a capital crime, as it was in Massachusetts, it was a matter of life and death to get it right. A jury had a hard time deciding whether to convict Benjamin Sawser, a soldier, for blasphemy in July 1654. While the evidence was clear that Sawser, "beinge in drinke," had "spoken profainely & Ignorantly Blasfemus words in say[ing] Jehova is the Devel & knew noe god but his sworde and that should save him," the grand jury, trial jury, and Court of Assistants all diverged on the crucial question of whether these words warranted the death penalty. The grand jury indicted Sawser for blasphemy, but the trial jury ("the jury of life and death") acquitted him "on point of ignorance"; in their review of the verdict, the higher court "did finde the prisoner guilty of speaking that which we apprehended amounteth in substance to what the lawe expresseth so farr as to make the offence capital." Poor Sawser languished "in chains" in prison while the courts hashed out his fate but managed to escape before the issue could be resolved.[149] Even the stern magistrates of New Haven, who rarely showed leniency in matters of religion, agreed that George King should be whipped rather than mutilated for swearing "by God": "The Govern'r told him that when the son of an Egiptian blaspheamed the name of God it was not borne. It's the piercing through the name of God in passion, which is a high provokation of God . . . & by a mans words he may loose his life. It was hoped it was only a rash & sinful oath, some have bin boared through the tongue, others have bin in the stocks & their tongues in a cloven stick. But hopeing it was not dispitfully don, the centance of the court was, that he should be whipped."[150]

Ministers came in for their fair share of abuse, especially in the southern colonies where the established Church of England struggled to maintain its foothold among the desperate young men who arrived by the boatloads as

[147] Ibid., 292.
[148] Lt. Governor Stede to Lords of Trade and Plantations, March 19, 1687, CO 31/4, pp. 24–28.
[149] *Records of Colony of Massachusetts*, 3:35–37.
[150] *Records of Colony and Plantation of New Haven from 1638 to 1649*, 293.

indentured servants in the seventeenth century. One poor parson in Virginia
weathered a barrage of insults in the 1620s from his parishioners: "stoned priest
and piurde man," "blockheaded parsone," "base baudie fellow," "foole, dunce,
base fellow."[151] The Protestant ministers of St. Mary's County, Maryland, complained that they "doe daily suffer" from the abusive speeches of one William
Lewis, "who saith that our Ministers are the Ministers of the divell; and that our
books are made by the instruments of the divell." In his defense Lewis charged
the ministers with preaching anti-popery, "vizt that the Pope was Antichrist,
and the Jesuits, the Antixian [Antichristian] ministers." Because "these his offensive speeches & other his unseasonable disputations in point of religion
tended to the disturbance of the publique peace & quiet of the colony," the
court fined Lewis five hundred pounds of tobacco and ordered him to remain
in the custody of the sheriff until he could post bond for good behavior.[152] Disputes between ministers and their congregations tended to be, not surprisingly,
more doctrinal in New England where the theological literacy of the laity was
renowned. In Connecticut, George Hubbard took issue with the predestinarian
preaching of Mr. Stow, who "did expresse, that those that were not in visible
Covnant are dogs & among dogs and in the kingdom of Sathan, & at Sathans
command." Another disaffected parishioner corroborated that Stow "was a
pestilent person, a plague to the place and that what hee preached was not
worth hearing"; an unsympathetic court ordered both men to "bee publickly
reproved by the Magistrate at the next lecture."[153] At the height of the free grace
controversy in Massachusetts in the 1630s, the laity were so inflamed against
the "faithful Ministers," Thomas Weld wrote, that "you might have seen half a
dozen Pistols discharged at the face of the Preacher (I meane) so many objections made by the opinionists in the open Assembly against our doctrine."
Weld was speaking metaphorically, but his choice of metaphor was apt.[154]

As was the case in England, the sacraments proved to be a fraught zone of
encounter between ministers and dissenting brethren. There is even evidence
that the tradition of mock sacraments made its way across the Atlantic,

[151] *Minutes of the Council and General Court of Virginia, 1622–1632, 1670–1676, With Notes
and Excerpts from Original Council and General Court Records Into 1683, Now Lost*, ed. H. R.
McIlwaine (Richmond, 1924), 88–89.

[152] *Archives of Maryland*, May 1638, 4:35–39.

[153] *Records of the Particular Court of Connecticut, 1639–1663* (Hartford: Connecticut Historical Society, 1928), 182.

[154] Thomas Weld, preface to *A Short Story*, in *The Antinomian Controversy, 1636–1638: A
Documentary History*, 2nd ed., ed. David D. Hall (Durham, N.C.: Duke University Press,
1990), 209–10.

though here we are relying on the highly prejudicial accounts of outraged Anglican ministers, several of whom reported that Atkinson Williamson christened a bear while intoxicated in South Carolina in 1683.[155] The *New-England Courant* printed a story in 1725 about a group of young people who "made a Disturbance" during the sacrament in the Norwich meetinghouse, "one of them having a Chair ty'd behind him," for which they were ordered "to be whipt ten Lashes, and one Fifteen."[156]

In a handful of cases, enough detail (testamentary or contextual) survives that we can draw out the discursive threads I've been emphasizing in this chapter between malediction and somatic disorders of the tongue, digestive tract, and sexual organs. Perhaps the first recorded blasphemer in English America was a victim of Virginia's infamous "starving time." George Percy's narrative chillingly reveals the connection between eating and speaking, for Hugh Pryse was driven to curse God out of extreme hunger. "One thinge hapned wch was very remarkable wherein god shewed his juste Judgment for one Hugh Pryse being pinched wth extrem famin In A furious distracted moode did come openly into the markett place Blaspheaminge exclameinge and cryeinge owtt thatt there was noe god. Alledgeinge that if there were A god he wolde nott suffer his creatures whom he had made and framed to indure these miseries," Percy wrote. Like other early modern sinners, Pryse suffered a fitting demise: "itt appeared the same day that the Almighty was displeased wth him for goeinge thatt afternoone wth A Butcher A corpulentt fatt man into the woods to seke for some Reliefe both of them weare slaine by the Salvages. And after beinge fownde gods Indignacyon was showed upon Pryses Corpes wch was Rente in pieces wth wolves or other wylde Beasts And his Bowles Torne outt of his boddy being A Leane spare man." (The "fatt Butcher," who had not blasphemed, was untouched.)[157] Disembowelment was a particularly apt fate for a blasphemer, whose sacrilegious words (as we have seen) were often believed to originate deep in the stomach.

Another graphic case of disembowelment occurred in the neighboring

---

[155] The Atkinson affair was an embarrassment for the Society for the Propagation of the Gospel in Foreign Parts (SPG) missionaries who struggled to earn the respect of the Carolina Presbyterians. Mr. Stevens to Secretary, Goose Creek, S.C., February 3, 1707/8, and Mr. Smith to Mr. Robt Stevens, January 16, 1707/8, Society for the Propagation of the Gospel in Foreign Parts, Letter Books, Series "A," 1702–1737, vol. 4.

[156] *New-England Courant*, July 31–August 7, 1725.

[157] Mark Nicholls, "George Percy's 'Trewe Relacyon': A Primary Source for the Jamestown Settlement," *Virginia Magazine of History and Biography* 113 (2005): 212–75 (quotation on 251).

colony of Maryland in the 1640s. According to the resident Jesuit missionary, a "scoffer" who was offended by the annual ritual of firing off the cannons on July 31 to honor St. Ignatius (the "patron saint" of Lord Baltimore's colony) mocked the Catholics and their saint. "Away to the wicked cross with you, papists!" he roared. "I have a cannon too, and I will give him a salute more suitable and appropriate to so miserable a saint." To the "insolent laughter" of his companions, he then let out a loud fart. Soon he was "complaining of an unusual pain in his bowels," and by the end of the day the blasphemer was in agony, crying out, "I am burning up! I am burning up! There is a fire in my belly! There is a fire in my bowels!" The next day, "his bowels began to be voided, peacemeal"—some pieces were "a foot, some a foot and a half, some two feet long"—and by August 3 the man was dead. For months afterward, the residents of St. Mary's City were treated to the spectacle of the intestines of the dead man, "blackened as if crisped up by fire," hanging on fence posts as a grisly warning to would-be blasphemers.[158]

A cluster of cases linked blasphemy to serious, indeed capital, crimes of sexual misconduct in ways that illuminate the entangled etiology of verbal and sexual disorder in the early modern understanding of sin. The first comes from the ultra-Puritan commonwealth of New Haven, which was plagued by an outbreak of bestiality accusations in the 1640s and 1650s that have long fascinated historians.[159] George Spencer was a one-eyed servant who found himself accused of committing bestiality with a sow when a piglet with "butt one eye in the middle of the face, and thatt large and open, like some blemished eye of a man" was born in 1642. The theory of correspondences led his neighbors to identify Spencer as the probable father of the deformed "monster": "The aforementioned George Spencer so suspected hath butt one eye for use, the other hath (as itt is called) a pearle in itt, is whitish & deformed, and his deformed eye being beheld and compared together with the eye of the monster, seamed to be as like as the eye in the glass to the eye in the face." As the court records make clear, though, there were ample grounds for suspicion beyond his unfortunate facial disfigurement. Spencer had a reputation as "a prophane, lying, scoffing and lewd speritt," a man of "atheistial carryag": he was a proud and insolent servant, a man who "scoff[ed] att the ordinances,

---

[158] Andrew White, S.J., *Relatio Itineris in Marylandiam. Declaratio Coloniae Domini Baronis de Baltimore, Excerpta ex Diversis Litteris Missionariorum . . . Narrative of a Voyage to Maryland [with] Excerpts from Different Letters of Missionaries* (Baltimore, 1874), 95–97.

[159] The classic study remains John M. Murrin, "'Things Fearful to Name': Bestiality in Colonial America," *Pennsylvania History* 65 (1998): 8–43.

wayes, and people of God," one time mocking the Sabbath by "calling itt the Ladyes day" instead of "the Lords day." There were dark hints of unnamed "acts of filthyness" with "Indians or English" and unspecified "wicked and bitter speeches" directed against his social superiors. Spencer's polymorphic sexual desires and his verbal incontinence were of a piece, symptoms of a disordered spirit—perhaps, even, of a diabolical influence—and together they doomed him. He was duly executed on April 8 after being forced to watch the defiled sow slaughtered before his eyes.[160]

The next two cases come from a very different jurisdiction, Catholic Maryland, but present a similar narrative of perverted sexual and verbal impulses. William Mitchell and Jacob Lumbrozo were, like George Spencer, men of dubious sexual reputation who had long tangled with the law over their immoral behavior. Mitchell was a serial adulterer, a brutal and violent wife beater, an abortionist, and a man of scandalous religious beliefs. The list of particular charges brought against him in 1652 included, first, that "he hath not only professed himself to be an Atheist, but hath also endeavoured to draw others to believe there is noe God, making a Common practice by blasphemous expressions and otherwise to mock and deride God's Ordinances and all Religion." Second, he "hath Comitted Adultery with one Susan Warren." Third, he "hath Murtherously endeavouerd to destroy or Murther the Child by him begotten in the Womb of the said Susan Warren," and, finally, "he hath Since his late wife's death lived in fornication with his now pretended wife Joane." His heterodox views could be considered vaguely freethinking; amid a "Company of Gentlemen" he "wondered the world had been Soe many hundred Years deluded with a Man and a Pigeon" (i.e., Christ and the Holy Spirit) and on another occasion ridiculed his lover's Christian faith, saying, "Ah thou may'st well be called a woman that will believe any thing that is told you, Such a thing as God believe it not thou art meerly led away with what your Parents hath told You . . . thou art a fool." In the view of the court (which convicted him on all counts but let him off with the shockingly light fine of five thousand pounds of tobacco), his blasphemous opinions were at the root of his wickedness: they "open[ed] a way to all wicked lustfull licentious and prophane Courses."[161]

[160] *Records of Colony of New Haven*, 64–73.

[161] *Archives of Maryland*, 10:173–86. Mitchell's lover, Susan Warren, displayed her own sacrilegious wit; when some nosy neighbors confronted her about her pregnancy, she replied, "if She were with Child it was inspired by the holy Ghost, and not by man." For these and other "prophane and blasphemous expressions," Warren received the much stiffer sentence of thirty-nine lashes. *Archives of Maryland*, 10:149, 184.

The "Jew doctor" Jacob Lumbrozo had a similarly checkered career in colonial Maryland in the 1650s and 1660s as a libertine and blasphemer, accused of rape by several different women and of attempting to force an abortion upon one of them. As in the case of Captain Mitchell, his heterodox views opened up an investigation into his sexual habits that revealed a disturbing pattern of coercion and intimidation. Lumbrozo was charged with blasphemy in 1658 after a conversation with his neighbor John Fossett turned to theological matters. Fossett deposed that he and Lumbrozo, "falling into discourse concerning Our B[lesse]d Saviour Christ his Resurrection," exchanged sharp words over the question of Christ's divinity. Fossett's avowal that Christ "was more then man, as did appeare by his Resurrection," prompted Lumbrozo to reply "That his Disciples stole him away" after his death. Pressed to explain the miracles performed by Christ, Lumbrozo answered "That such works might be done by Negromancy, or sorcery, or words to that purport. And this Depon't replyed to the sd Lumbrozo, that hee supposed, tht the sd Lumbrozo answer tooke Christ to be a Negromancer. To wch the sd Lumbrozo answered nothing byt laughed." Another neighbor, Josias Cole, testified that "the Jew Doctor, knowne by the name of Jacob Lumbrozo," when asked "what hee was that was Crucifyed att Jerusalem," answered, "hee was a Man. Then the sd Cole asked him how hee did doe all his miracles? And the sd Lumbrozo answered hee did them by the Art of Magick." Lumbrozo escaped the death penalty by a twist of fate when Richard Cromwell proclaimed a general amnesty for all colonial prisoners in 1658, but meanwhile his sexual indiscretions with two maidservants came to light. Marjorie Goold and her husband, John, testified that the doctor had used "force" to make Marjorie "his whore," and Elizabeth Gold told the court that he had tried to abort their child.[162] Only his hasty marriage with Gold avoided further prosecution, and Lumbrozo lived out the remainder of his days in Maryland as a successful (though highly litigious) planter and merchant.

The Lumbrozo case is unique in that it pitted Christian against Jew, but it highlights the important role that blasphemy charges played in sectarian conflicts in the English colonies. The Anabaptist movement was strong in the colonies, where there were signs of an active Baptist congregation as early as the 1630s. In Essex County, William Winter was presented for saying "that

[162] *Archives of Maryland*, 4:203–4.

they who stay while a child is baptised worship the Devil, etc."[163] One case that generated quite a bit of press both in the colonies and abroad was that of Obadiah Holmes, who was charged with heresy and blasphemy in 1650. The sentence of the court was relatively mild—Holmes was ordered to pay a fine of £30 or to be whipped. His obstinacy turned a routine trial into a spectacle: Holmes refused to pay the fine and demanded the right to address the people who had gathered to watch his flogging, "seeing I am to seal what I hold with my blood, I am ready to defend it by the Word." As the clothes were stripped from his back and he was lashed thirty times with a three-corded whip, he taunted the magistrates: "You have struck me as with roses." (Infuriated, the minister John Wilson "cursed me, saying, *The curse of God or Jesus go with thee.*")[164] John Rogers, a Baptist resident of New Haven, was "accused of blasphemy" and ordered to "sitt on the gallows with a halter about my neck, and from thence to return to prison, and there to continue till I paid £5 for reproaching the Ministers." Rogers's ordeal was not over after the mock hanging; he complained that he was "cruelly scourged," whipped a second time when he refused to ask for mercy, and returned to prison "where I was chained to the sill, without bed or covering, and neither meat nor drink offer'd me in the space of three days, where I lay six weeks in this perishing manner." He would spend the next three years in prison.[165]

At least the Baptists disputed their fellow Protestants on recognizably Christian grounds. Other colonists went much further, disregarding Christianity and even revealed religion altogether. William King "uttered & declared i.e. that he was the Eternal son of God & yt he was holy & pure as God himself," for which he was "severly whipt with Twenty Stripes."[166] In a rare case of cross-cultural prosecution, Pawquash, a Quillipiock Indian, was brought up on charges in New Haven in 1646 for having "blasphemously sa[id] that Jesus Christ was mattamoy & naught & his bones rotten, & spake of an Indian in Manitoieses plantation assended into heaven." The court

---

[163] February 1645/6, *Essex County Quarterly Courts*, 1:92.

[164] Quoted in Isaac Backus, *A History of New England with Particular Reference to the Denomination of Christians Called Baptists* (New York: Arno Press, 1969; reprint of 2nd ed., 1871), 189, 192.

[165] Petition of John Rogers to Governor and Company of Connecticut, enclosed in Letter from Charles Congreve to Mr. Popple, December 4, 1704, CO 5/1262, nos. 92, 92i.

[166] *Records of Colony of Massachusetts*, 1:253–54. Carla Gardina Pestana discusses the King case in "The Social World of Salem: William King's 1681 Blasphemy Trial," *American Quarterly* 41 (June 1989): 308–27.

sentenced him to be "seaverly whipt for thus scorning at our worshipping God & blaspheame the name of our Lord Jesus, & informed him that if he should doe soe hereafter or now, it had bin against the light he now has, it would hazard his life."[167]

The battle between Quakers and Puritans that had been waged so spectacularly in Civil War England was renewed in the colonies, as waves of Quaker missionaries arrived in the 1650s and 1660s, bringing their lurid brand of sacred theater with them. Alexander Colman was "whipt with 15 stripes on ye naked body well laid on" for "endeavoring to make disturbance of the people in time of publick worship on the last Lords day in the 3d meeting house in Boston by Going in wth only a dirty frock of canvice all bloody & no other cloaths." A handful of Friends were dismembered or mutilated during the high-water mark of Puritan repression in Massachusetts in the 1650s. Humphrey Norton was "severely whipt and burnt in the hand with the Letter H for spreading his Heretical Opinions," while John Copeland, Christopher Holder, and John Rouse were sentenced to "have your right ears cutt off by the Hangman."[168] Even the restoration of Charles II in 1660 did not stop the violence. The infamous 1658 law under which four Quakers (Marmaduke Stephenson, Mary Dyer, William Robinson, and William Leddra) were executed was superseded by the "Cart and Whip Act" of 1661, which ordered all "vagabond Quakers" to be "stripped naked from the middle upwards and be tied to a cart's tail and whipped" from town to town until they were driven out of the jurisdiction. Repeat offenders were to be branded on the left shoulder with the letter R and again whipped out of the colony.[169]

Under these provisions some of the more disturbing persecutions of the colonial era occurred. According to one chronicler, the Quakers "suffered more than one Hundred and Sixty Whippings, most of them very cruelly laid on" in a seven year period, with one woman, "Aunt Coleman, being whipt almost to Death." The instrument of choice was the "three-stringed whip" with knots on the end, which turned ten stripes into thirty. Elizabeth Hooten,

---

[167] *Records of Colony and Plantation of New Haven from 1638 to 1649*, 262. John Cotton had argued that those Indians who recognized English sovereignty were bound by the Ten Commandments: "It hath been an Article of Covenant between such Indians as have submitted to our Government, that they shall submit to the ten Commandments, which they thought reasonable." *Bloudy Tenet Washed*, 148.

[168] Francis Howgill, *The Popish Inquisition Newly Erected in New-England, whereby Their Church is manifested to be a Daughter of Mysterie Babylon, which did drink the blood of the Saints, who bears the express Image of her Mother* (London, 1659), 13, 26–28.

[169] *Records of Colony of Massachusetts*, vol. 4, part 2, p. 2.

an elderly Quaker minister whose sufferings had already received extensive sympathetic coverage in England, received ten lashes on her bare back in at least fourteen different locales during the mid-1660s. Her ordeal was explicitly compared to the ritual torture and forced march of Indian captives by Quaker chroniclers, as if to underscore the wolvish nature of their Puritan persecutors: "Her Skin and Flesh being thus torn and beaten with the aforesaid Extremities, they put her on Horse back and carried her a-weary Journey many Miles into the Wilderness, and towards Night left her there, where many Wolves and Bears, and wild Beasts used sometimes to set upon living Persons."[170]

As was the case in England, Quakers were especially vulnerable to accusations of blasphemy; and in fact the vast majority of the blasphemy cases in colonial records involved Quakers.[171] Joseph Gatchell was ordered to stand in the pillory "& to have his tounge drawne forth out of his mouth & peirct through with a hott Iron" for his avowal of the Quaker principle of universal salvation at the home of his kinsman Jeremiah Gatchell. When challenged by his cousin, who asserted that "whosoever Repents & believes shall be saved," Gatchell "Answered if it be so, he [Christ] was an Imperfect savior & a foole." Solomon Eccles was ordered by the governor of Barbados to "stand in the pillory in the Open Market on St. Michaels town one day from 12 till one of the clock at noon with these Words, For Blasphemy over his head & on his back and breast in Capitall Letter" in 1681.[172] Once they got going, Quakers were difficult to shut up. John Burton of Salem stormed the court "in an uncivil manner" and reproached the magistrates "by saying they were robbers and destroyers of the widows and fatherless, that their priests divined for money and their worship was not the worship of God, interrupting and affronting the court, and upon being commanded silence, he commanded them silence and continued speaking until the court was fain to

[170] Joseph Bolles, *An addition to the book, entituled, The spirit of the martyrs revived. It being a short account of some remarkable persecutions in New-England; especially of four faithful martyrs of our Lord and Saviour Jesus Christ, who suffered death at Boston* (New London, 1758), 18–19.

[171] Jane Kamensky has argued that the decade-long effort in New England to suppress the Quakers was "at bottom a struggle over the cultural meanings of speech." Speech was central to the Quakers' own sense of themselves as a distinctive community and the most fraught site of their encounters with religious rivals. Kamensky, *Governing the Tongue*, 118; Bauman, *Let Your Words Be Few.*

[172] *Records of Colony of New Haven*, 242–47; Abstract of the Sentences given by his Excellency Sir Richard Dutton . . . Governor of Barbados, August 16–27, 1681, CO 1/47, no. 49.

commit him to the stocks."[173] Quakers didn't just blaspheme—they *cursed*, in the medieval sense of malediction rather than profanity. From the gallows where he awaited death by hanging, Marmaduke Stephenson cried out that the magistrates "shall be cursed for evermore."[174] Much of the dramaturgy around the punishment of Quakers revolved around efforts—usually ineffectual—to silence them, by muzzling them with fists, gloves, and other implements (in one case, a key "tyed cross" the mouth), and beating drums loudly to drown out their words as they were marched to jail or the scaffold.[175]

When the constables came to the home of Richard Crabb and his wife on May 31, 1658, "to demand the Quakers books," they were met with a volley of venom from Goody Crabb. "The vengeance of God hangs over your heads at Stamford for takeing away o[ur] land without commission & wronging of them," she spit, "& then she fell a railing o the ministers & said they were priests & preached for hire & called them Baalls preists, & she would not heare them, & said we was shedders of bloud, ye bloud of the s[ain]ts of God." Her husband stood idly by and "did not so much as rebuke her," the court noted in disgust. Goody Crabb continued her tirade for "almost a houre together," pausing only to call "for a drink to refresh her, wch . . . she did to strengthen her to goe on in those wicked speeches." Goody Crabb's outburst—and the court's contempt for her husband's acquiescence—alerts us to the gendered dimensions of speech, and malediction, in early modern Anglo-America. Cotton Mather, echoing other jeremiads, had warned the "daughters of Zion" in 1692 to mind their tongues: "Be careful that you don't Speak too soon. . . . And be careful that you don't Speak too much. . . . [For] 'tis the Whore, that is Clamarous, and the Fool, that is Full of words."[176] The Quakers were notorious for, among other things, allowing women to preach in public, and the female missionary—unaccompanied by husband or children, traveling the Atlantic circuits of empire with only her faith to guide her—was a destabilizing figure throughout English America in the seventeenth century.

[173] *Essex County Quarterly Courts*, 2:337.
[174] Marmaduke Stephenson, *A Call from Death to Life, and Out of the Dark Ways and Worships of the World* (London, 1660), 26. On the "holy curses" uttered by Quakers, see Hall, *Worlds of Wonder*, 188–89; and Carla Gardina Pestana, "The Quaker Executions as Myth and History," *Journal of American History* 80 (September 1993): 441–69.
[175] Howgill, *The Popish Inquisition*, 12 (key), 33 (hand and glove); Bolles, *An addition to the book*, 4 (drums beating).
[176] Cotton Mather, *Ornaments for the Daughters of Zion* (Boston, 1692), 49–51.

From the beginning, the campaign to suppress the Quaker "invasion" centered on controlling women's bodies (their tongues as well as their sex).[177] The traditional "scold's bridle" was repurposed for Quaker women. Dorothy Waugh recounted being "violently haled off the Crosse" and ordered to endure three hours with a "steep cap" pinned to her head when she tried to preach in 1656: "I stood their time with my hands bound behind me with the stone weight of iron upon my head and the bit in my mouth to keep me from speaking."[178] When the first female missionaries arrived in Boston in 1656, they were seized and subjected to an invasive bodily search that no male Quaker ever faced. As George Bishop's widely read account of Quaker "sufferings" in New England (written, typically, in the accusatory second person) demanded, "Did ye not *shamelessly* cause Two of the women aforesaid, viz. Mary Fisher and Anne Austin, to be stript *stark* naked, and so to be *search'd* and *mis-used*, as is a shame to Modesty to name? and with such Barbarousness, as One of them, a Married Woman and a Mother of Five Children, suffered not the like in the bearing of any of them into the World?" Such cowardly manhandling of innocent women called into question the "Manhood" as well as the "Civility" of the colony's magistrates who "entertained" these Friends from abroad "not as Men and Women of the same Generation as you, and Creation, but as *Beasts of Prey*." Recalling our discussion in the first chapter of the sacramental overtones of the colonial mistreatment of religious dissenters, Quakers likened their persecutors to "*Men drunk indeed with the Blood of the Innocent*" or "wrestlers with flesh & blood, blood-suckers." But in this case it was often female blood that was consumed.[179]

---

[177] Phyllis Mack, *Visionary Women: Ecstatic Prophecy in Seventeenth-Century England* (Berkeley: University of California Press, 1995).

[178] *The Lambs Defence Against Lyes* (London, 1656), 29–30. On the use of bridles to punish women's speech, see Lynda E. Boose, "Scolding Brides and Bridling Scolds: Taming the Woman's Unruly Member," *Shakespeare Quarterly* 42 (Summer 1991): 179–213; and David Underdown, "The Taming of the Scold: The Enforcement of Patriarchal Authority in Early Modern England," in *Order and Disorder in Early Modern England*, ed. Anthony Fletcher and John Stevenson (New York: Cambridge University Press, 1985), 116–36.

[179] Bishop, *New England Judged*, 12–13, 25; Howgill, *The Popish Inquisition* ("blood-suckers," 51). Austin narrated her ordeal to Humphrey Norton, *New England's Bloody Ensigne* (London, 1659), 3. Bishop's account is a masterpiece of the Quaker martyrological genre in terms of its fascination with violence against the body and the piling on of examples with no attempt to create a hierarchy of suffering; as Bishop promised in the preface to the Second Part, his goal was to "promiscuously manage the sufferings as they were promiscuously inflicted." All suffering—from the mundane to the spectacular—was of a piece in Quaker narratives. Bishop, *New England Judged: The Second Part* (London, 1667), 4.

The association of Quakers with the world of disorderly female bodies and tongues is a recurrent motif in controversial literature, a motif that would only grow as the sectarian threat morphed into the more deadly sin of witchcraft—where women's bodies were once again scrutinized, abused, and demonized.[180] The witch, like the female Quaker, was a blasphemous figure whose verbal aggression was the outward manifestation of her pact with Satan, the original blasphemer. "The *tongue* is a *witch*," George Webbe had proclaimed in 1619.[181] The witch in effect ventriloquized the devil—reviling God and mocking his church. Those who were believed to be possessed by the devil were quite literally his mouthpieces; as Jane Kamensky notes, to early moderns the ventriloquist was known as "one that has an evil spirit speaking in his belly." And so those "horrid and nefandous Blasphemies" that issued from the mouths of demoniacs were literally "belched forth" from hell itself.[182] As does the blasphemer, the witch inverts the sacramental order by cursing instead of blessing, turning pious rituals (communion, baptism, prayer, the sermon) into obscenities.[183] Witches were the preeminent maledictors, for "*what they said came true.*" Elizabeth Goodman threatened Allen Ball's pigs when he refused to lend her some buttermilk, and the pigs died. Goody Batchelor predicted that some of her neighbor's cows "would dye" and some "would live," and "as she sayde so it came to pass."[184] This was potent word magic, and in their pursuit of witches colonial magistrates were policing the very boundaries of godly and profane speech. (Witchcraft accusations were much rarer in the southern colonies, but the

[180] The connections between heresy, blasphemy, and witchcraft in early modern Anglo-America are well established; see, especially, Kamensky, *Governing the Tongue*. In the case of the Quakers, the association was more than rhetorical, as Christine Leigh Heyrman argued in "Specters of Subversion, Societies of Friends: Dissent and the Devil in Provincial Essex County, Massachusetts," in *Saints & Revolutionaries: Essays in Early American History*, ed. David D. Hall, John Murrin, and Thad Tate (New York, W. W. Norton, 1984), 38–74. The classic treatments of witchcraft as a gendered crime are Carol Karlsen, *The Devil in the Shape of a Woman: Witchcraft in Colonial New England* (New York: W. W. Norton, 1987), in the American context; and Lyndal Roper, *Oedipus and the Devil: Witchcraft, Sexuality, and Religion in Early Modern Europe* (London: Routledge, 1994), in the European context.
[181] George Webbe, *The Arraignment of an Unruly Tongue* (London, 1619), 22.
[182] Kamensky, *Governing the Tongue*, 168, 271n115.
[183] We saw this in Chapter 1, where the devil's "Red Bread and Wine" was consumed at the witches' sabbath, along with other acts of ritual inversion. Joshua Scottow, "A Narrative of the Planting of the Massachusetts Colony" (1699), in *Collections of the Massachusetts Historical Society* 34 (1858): 279–330 (quotation on 309).
[184] Kamensky, *Governing the Tongue*, 154 ("*what they said came true*"), 160 (Goodman) and 161 (Batchelor).

association of women with diabolical cursing can be found throughout the colonial records. A neighbor testified that he heard Dorothy Holt of Maryland "cry for many Curses to God against her husband, that he might rott limb from limbe.")[185]

Blasphemy charges could serve blatantly political as well as sectarian and conversionary ends. John Coode, the former Anglican priest turned rebel, was accused of blasphemy in the 1690s after he fled Maryland seeking refuge across the border in Virginia. Depositions filed in 1696 claimed that Coode, "though holding priest's orders in the Church of England, said amongst other things that religion was but policy, and that all religion was to be found in Tully's Offices." For these and other inflammatory statements, the "deformed, club-footed" Coode, with a "face resembling that of a baboon," was outlawed for "horrid impious blasphemy and contriving rebellion" by Governor Nicholson.[186] As we have seen, there was a natural logic between the coupling of blasphemy and rebellion, and the threat of political disorder lay behind many of the blasphemy cases heard in colonial courts, most obviously in the case of the Quakers but in less overt ways in other cases as well. A dispute over a stolen cow between two Maryland farmers escalated into a heated exchange in 1658; when Gregory Murill "Swore by (gods) blood," Thomas Ringold retorted that Murill "was not Fitt to live in a Commonwealth."[187] The best example comes from Pennsylvania, where an unseemly doctrinal spat in the 1690s among Quakers about the "two bodies" of Christ spilled out into the political arena, resulting in the imprisonment of George Keith and several of his followers on charges of behaving "offensivlie" toward the colony's leadership. Keith was accused of "being Crazie, turbulent, a decryer of magistracie, and a notorious evill Instrument in Church and State," and he in turn accused his opponents of blasphemy and defamation. It was a sorry affair all around, with insults flying back and forth across the Atlantic (in one pamphlet, Keith called his adversaries "*fools, ignorant heathens, infidels, silly souls, lyars, hereticks, rotten ranters, muggletonians*"; they lobbed back the epithets "*Brat of Babylon, Accuser of the Brethren, Apostate, Pope, Father Confessor,*

[185] *Archives of Maryland*, 10:110–11. Holt was ordered to receive "50 lashes," a penalty that would qualify as torture under the customary threshold of thirty-nine lashes as the legal limit for corporal punishment.
[186] Minutes of Council of Maryland, September 21, 1696, CO 5/741, pp. 148–59; Copy of Proclamation, Enclosed in Governor Nicholson to Council of Trade and Plantations, James City, Virginia, February 27, 1699, CO 5/1309, no. 75iv.
[187] *Archives of Maryland*, 54:164.

Lyar, Devil, Muggletonian"), leaving the entire Quaker colony besmirched.[188] This was a political feud, not a religious one, though the language of religious insult provided the primary weapons.

To at least some of their contemporaries in England, the severity of colonial laws bespoke a bloodlust unbecoming a Christian people. Certain cases generated unfavorable press abroad—the four Quaker executions, most notably, but also less notorious incidents such as that of Philip Ratliffe, the servant who was whipped, lost his ears, and banished for "uttering malicious and scandalous speeches against the government and the church of Salem" in 1631. The harshness of the penalty evoked concern within Puritan circles in London; Edward Howes wrote to John Winthrop Jr. that "I have heard diverse complaints against the severitie of your Governement especially mr. Indicott's . . . about cuttinge off the Lunatick mans eares." There are "a thousand eyes watching over you, to pick a hole in your Coats," he warned.[189] And whenever Parliament wanted to censure or rebuke the Massachusetts Bay for political insolence, they raised the Quaker executions as proof of the colony's hypocrisy and tyrannical leanings. "They have put many Quakers to death, of other Provinces (for which also they are Petitioned against) first they banished them as Quakers upon Payne of death, and then executed them for returning, they have beate some to Jelly, and been other ways exceeding cruell to others," the Commissioners of New England wrote in 1664, yet they "constantly pray for their persecuted Brethren in England."[190]

---

[188] *Minutes of the Provincial Court of Pennsylvania*, vol. 1 (Philadelphia, 1852), 378; *True Copy of three Judgments given forth by a party of men, called Quakers at Philadelphia, against George Keith and his friends* (Philadelphia, 1692), 14–15. As Jon Butler argued, the Keithians promoted "an extraordinarily muscular" version of Quakerism that emphasized the human as well as the divine nature of Christ. Butler, "In Pennsylvania's Spiritual Abyss: The Rise and Fall of the Later Keithians, 1693–1703," *Pennsylvania Magazine of History and Biography* 101 (April 1977): 151–70 (quotation on 156). See also his "'Gospel Order Improved': The Keithian Schism and the Exercise of Quaker Ministerial Authority in Pennsylvania," *William and Mary Quarterly*, 3rd ser., 31 (July 1974): 431–52. The most recent treatment of the Keithian schism is Andrew R. Murphy, "Persecuting Quakers? Liberty and Toleration in Early Pennsylvania," in *The First Prejudice: Religious Tolerance and Intolerance in Early America*, ed. Chris Beneke and Christopher S. Grenda (Philadelphia: University of Pennsylvania Press, 2011), 143–65.

[189] Edward Howes to John Winthrop Jr., in *Winthrop Papers*, vol. 3, *1631–1637* (Boston: Massachusetts Historical Society, 1943), 3:76.

[190] State of the Colony of Massachusetts, From the Commissioners of New England, 1665, ff. 433, Egerton Mss. 2395: 1627–1699, British Library. Parliamentary agents repeatedly interrupted their reports on the colony's internal affairs with lengthy discursions about the persecution of dissenters; see, for example, Papers on the state and government of New England, circa 1660–64, 1675, ff. 396, 397, 414, 522, in ibid.

In this long narrative of religious persecution, it would be easy to miss the fact that not a single colonist was executed for the crime of heresy or blasphemy in seventeenth-century English America. (Although at least thirteen people were banished for religious heterodoxy in Massachusetts, a punishment that—as in the infamous case of Anne Hutchinson—could certainly have lethal consequences in a frontier environment. As Roger Williams said, "banishing is a kind of death," akin to "put[ting] an innocent man into a bear's skin, and so caus[ing] him as a wild beast to be baited to death").[191] Judicial death in the New World was reserved for those convicted of sedition, not for religious nonconformists. The four Quaker "martyrs" hanged on Boston Commons between 1659 and 1661 are the exceptions that prove the rule: all were banished repeatedly and put to death only after they defiantly returned to Boston to preach in what many at the time considered an act of sacred suicide. The official cause for which they were executed was sedition, not heresy. Even that "Grand Heresiarch," Samuel Gorton (whose travails I recounted in the first chapter), avoided execution, though by only the slimmest of margins in the General Court.

The glaring gap between mandated and the actual penalties for heresy and malediction—between the "bloudy laws" that so outraged crown officials and the paltry record of enforcement—demands our attention. On the one hand, this was nothing new: historians have long recognized that early modern English law operated *ad terrorem*, by threatening far more than it actually did. Capital crimes almost never exacted the ultimate penalty, and this became even more pronounced as the number of capital crimes ballooned in the eighteenth century. The reasons propounded by scholars range from the reluctance of English juries to sentence defendants (who, after all, were often their neighbors) to death to the theological tension between the dictates of the Old Testament and the New Testament (vengeance versus mercy).[192] On the other hand, the codification of law in the New World—a unique feature of colonial jurisprudence—meant that the underlying tensions of English law that surfaced on an individual basis were now exposed to public view as never

---

[191] Quoted in Backus, *History of New England*, 211–12. Williams's nemesis, John Cotton, scoffed at the notion that banishment was a form of "persecution": in such an open and "fruitfull" country as New England, "Banishment . . . is not counted so much a confinement, as an enlargement, where a man doth not so much loose civill comforts, as change them." Cotton, *A Reply to Mr. Williams his Examination; And Answer of the Letters sent to him by John Cotton* (London, 1647), 8.

[192] Cynthia Herrup, "Law and Morality in Seventeenth-Century England," *Past & Present* 106 (February 1985): 102–23.

before.[193] Everyone knew in colonial Massachusetts and Maryland that the law demanded death for blasphemers. These laws were not dictated from on high by colonial governors or crown officials but were the product of legislative action—of deliberation, debate, and decision by freeholders in their respective colonies. We can question the degree to which the General Court or the Maryland Assembly fully represented the views and wishes of the settler population, but the fact remains that these laws were enacted by and on behalf of the citizens of these polities. The power to put malefactors to death was singled out by Increase Mather and the other New England agents sent to London in 1688 to protest the dissolution of their charters (a grievance rendered moot almost as soon as he arrived by "the happy Revolution") as essential to a godly commonwealth. Ironically, as Mather noted in his account of the protracted negotiations, the old charters had not in point of fact included "Power in *Capital Cases*"—a defect he hoped to remedy.[194] The embrace of Mosaic law by colonial assemblies from Puritan New England to Anglican Virginia and Catholic Maryland is yet another indication that the spirit of the Old Testament governed men's hearts and wills in their New World sanctuaries.

This chapter has argued that the English brought to the New World a heightened sensitivity toward malediction—"bad speaking"—born of the intense sectarian battles of the 1630s, 1640s, and 1650s, decades that saw the passage of the first new blasphemy acts in England since the Reformation and an overheated pamphlet war over the dangers of sacrilegious speech. In their eagerness to avoid the disorders that an unregulated speech market had produced at home, the first generation of colonial leaders passed law codes that made blasphemy a capital crime and vigorously pursued profane swearers. The fact that they preferred to stigmatize rather than execute evil speakers can be interpreted as evidence of magisterial impotence or faintheartedness; but the result was the creation of a class of malefactors who bore the permanent

---

[193] On the codification movement, see Mark D. Cahn, "Punishment, Discretion, and the Codification of Prescribed Penalties in Colonial Massachusetts," *American Journal of Legal History* 33 (April 1989): 107–36; and Barbara Shapiro, "Law Reform in Seventeenth-Century England," *American Journal of Legal History* 19 (October 1975): 280–12. On the relationship between Puritan jurisprudence in Old and New England, see Richard J. Ross, "The Career of Puritan Jurisprudence," *Law and History Review* 26 (Summer 2008): 227–58; George L. Haskins, *Law and Authority in Early Massachusetts: A Study in Tradition and Design* (New York: Macmillan, 1960); and G. B. Worden, "Law Reform in England and New England, 1620 to 1660," *William and Mary Quarterly*, 3rd ser., 35 (October 1978): 668–90.

[194] Increase Mather, *Brief Account*, 14. Mather pointed out that under the old charter, Massachusetts was a corporation, not a province, and corporations in English law do not have the power of life and death.

marks of their heterodoxy on their very persons. John Cotton had warned his fellow New Englanders of this danger in the 1640s. Against heretics and blasphemers, magistrates should "maketh use . . . not of Stocks and Whipps (for these doe not remove, but exasperate the malady): but of Death, or Banishment, that may cut him off from opportunity of spreading the leaven, and Gangrene of his pernicious wayes."[195] Those who lost ears or lips, or who were branded in the hand or forehead, became living monuments to the power of the Word. In the next chapter, we turn to another type of "living monument"— the icon—and the intense fear and loathing it inspired among Anglo-American Protestants, Calvinists in particular.

[195] Cotton, *Bloudy Tenet Washed*, 95.

CHAPTER 4

Iconoclasm

No one who sees the iconoclasts raging thus against wood
and stone should doubt that there is a spirit hidden in them
which is death-dealing, not life-giving, and which at the first
opportunity will also kill men.

—Martin Luther, 1525

Immense crowds of gods have issued from the human mind.

—John Calvin, Institutes of Religion, I:5

On a cold winter night in February 1714, some "wicked and Sacrilegious" persons broke into Trinity Church in New York, the temporal and spiritual home of the Church of England in the colonies, and left the sanctuary in shambles. Having "broke into ye North Window of the Steeple," the vandals "broke down the window of the Vestry room did cut or tare off the Sleve of one of the Surplices that was in the said Room, and did Rent and Tare another to pieces." Not content with breaking windows and ripping up priestly garments, they proceeded to carry the surplice "with several common prayer books and Psalm books" into the churchyard and, spreading their loot on the ground, "left their Ordure on the Sacred Vestments as the greatest outrage and most Villanous indignity they could offer to the Church of England Her Holy Priesthood and in defiance of God and all Religion."[1]

---

[1] Charles Vesey's Petition, 1714, vol. 9, no. 6, New York Papers, p. 191, Society for the Propagation of the Gospel in Foreign Parts, Letter Books, Series "A," 1702–1737 (hereafter SPG Records). The desecration of Trinity Church was reported in the *Boston News-Letter*, March 22–29, 1714, and picked up by the press in London; "A Proclamation," *Daily Courant*, May 22, 1714.

Such acts of scripted blasphemy were, as we have seen, part of a common culture of religious insult in the early modern Anglo-American world. Scorning or reviling took many forms, from profane swearing to impious gestures like baptizing beasts to printed satires that pushed the boundaries of good doctrine and good taste. But the *object* of desecration in this New York episode sets it apart from the kinds of sacrilege I explored in the previous chapter. The church and its ecclesiastical paraphernalia were part of the material culture of Western Christianity, a culture so deeply woven into the fabric of everyday life that disentangling the material from the numinous became one of the most vexed challenges of the Reformation. Late medieval Christians lived in a material environment saturated with spiritual power: stained glass windows and towering steeples bespoke the majesty and glory of God, paintings and murals brought the stories of the Old and New Testaments to vivid life, roods and crucifixes proclaimed the central mystery of Christ's death and resurrection, scraps of bone and clothing were holy relics endowed with the healing power of the saints. Even the humblest of objects like a crude woodcut of the Virgin Mary or a pile of beads fashioned into a rosary could be a spiritual conduit, a tangible means of connection between a sinning humanity and a redeemer God. This material landscape was erected on a sturdy foundation of theological argument about the epistemological and pedagogical function of images in which the visual was privileged as the primary way of knowing God. The commonplace notion that images were the "books of the illiterate" sanctioned a range of representational practices in which the laity was instructed in the timeless truths of Christianity through the contemplation of mimetic scenes. Seeing was truly believing in the visual culture of the medieval church. Dismantling this culture would be the work of generations of iconoclasts.

The desecration of Trinity Church was but one of many incidents in the Anglo-American colonies in which religious *things*—and by this I mean both images and material objects—were the targets of violence by individual settlers or communities. This chapter begins with a consideration of the theology of religious objects and images in late medieval Europe, then surveys the various iconoclastic outbreaks that accompanied the Reformation on the continent and in England before moving on to examine a series of assaults on the material landscape of early America: churches and other sacred objects such as vestments and devotional aids, mission towns, and, in the ultimate act of transfiguration, Indian bodies. Traditional iconoclasm has always been presumed to be nonexistent during the first century of English colonization, and nothing presented here will dispute the essential (if narrow) truth of that assertion since the traditional targets of European iconoclasts (statuary, altar rails, stained glass, paintings of saints) were conspicuously absent as well.[2] But my goal here is more ambitious than documenting the scale of physical damage to ecclesial things in a colonial environment; I want to examine the nature of iconoclasm itself. As we have seen throughout this book, understanding the roots and forms of religious violence is a heuristic as much as an empirical challenge, since what differentiates one form of violence from another is at bottom a matter of interpretation: When is a war a just war, or a holy war? When is a death at the stake a martyrdom rather than an ordinary execution? How do we tell the difference between the destruction visited by nature and neglect on religious buildings and deliberate vandalism? When is an image an idol? Of all categories of religious violence, iconoclasm may be the most heuristically sensitive, since the relationship between signs and things is at the very core of the act. The conceptual vocabulary we'll be working with—idols, icons, images, along with their metadiscourses, iconology, idolatry, iconomachy, iconoclasm—is itself a tangle of mimetic terms whose relationship to the physical world was always a matter of dispute. The form of religious violence I'm exploring here exists at the intersection of ontological categories (words, things, ideas, animate and inanimate bodies), making it a particularly elusive beast to track. It is not a coincidence that I've reserved it for the final chapter.

The "Quick" and the "Dead": The Fate of Images in Western Christianity

Religious images were ubiquitous in medieval Christendom. But so were critiques of image-worship as pagan and idolatrous. The history of image-making and image-theory in the medieval church is a dialectical one, in which affirmations of the power of images to instruct, memorialize, and

---

[2] For two exceptions to this general neglect of iconoclasm in the English colonies, see Nicholas M. Beasley, "Wars of Religion in the Circum-Caribbean: English Iconoclasm in Spanish America, 1570–1702," in *Saints and Their Cults in the Atlantic World*, ed. Margaret Cormack (Columbia: University of South Carolina Press, 2007), 150–73; and Laura Chmielewski, *The Spice of Popery: Converging Christianities on an Early American Frontier* (Notre Dame, Ind.: University of Notre Dame Press, 2012), 233–39.

inspire were always accompanied by fears about the power of the selfsame images to distort, distract, and damn. In biblical parlance, godly images were always in danger of becoming *idols*. The God of the Old Testament reserved his harshest punishments for idolaters—those who would "serve gods, the work of men's hands, wood and stone, which neither see, nor hear, nor eat, nor smell" (Deut. 4:28). Again and again, God's people spurn him for false gods of their own devising, and as their creations become more elaborate, the range of punishments inflicted upon them becomes more primitive. There is an almost kinetic energy in the idolatry depicted in the Bible, with each successive act of idol-making provoking a new cycle of retribution and remorse.[3] An idol is by nature a shape-shifter, an object that begins as one thing and is perverted into another by an act of willful disobedience: an inoffensive piece of wood or stone (or, in time, of canvas, glass, fabric, bone, even of imagination and fantasy) transformed into a god by man's arrogance and ambition. By its very nature, then, an idol is always in the process of becoming, never inert or stable. This ontological slipperiness was what made the idol such a universally feared object in the Judeo-Christian tradition.

The move from idol to icon in Christian orthodoxy had momentous consequences for the history of art, rescuing entire categories of the plastic arts from the taint of paganism, but it did little to restore ontological integrity to the category of "the visual." We can think of the distinction between an idol and an icon as residing in the direction of the viewer's gaze: the idol absorbs the gaze of the worshiper while the icon redirects it toward some transcendent figure who is the appropriate object of veneration. This is the language of modern visual theory, however, and medieval Christians had their own way of understanding the difference. For them, idols were "dead images" whereas icons were "quick images"—vivacious figures that did not merely symbolize but in some crucial sense *were* the living men and women they represented. The idol is simultaneously a material thing and no thing: it exists only for itself and is to be worshiped in itself. The icon, on the other hand, is a sign whose value lies in its relationship to something much greater than itself. Scholars of late antiquity, when the pagan and the Christian worlds coexisted and battled with one another for several centuries before

---

[3] What James Simpson calls "the kinesis of iconoclasm" is really the flip side of the kinesis of idology itself; as idols (or icons) proliferate, so do attempts to destroy them. Simpson, *Under the Hammer: Iconoclasm in the Anglo-American Tradition* (New York: Oxford University Press, The Clarendon Lectures, 2010), 13.

the conversion of Constantine, see this contest as in part a competition between modes of viewing: in the classical mode, statues of emperors and war
heroes were material emblems of human strength and wisdom, whereas in
the early Christian visual regime the images of holy men and women became infused with numinous power. Images came to life, in other words, in
the incarnational culture of Christianity, capable not merely of representing
human virtues but of channeling the life and power of their subjects.[4] (And,
conversely, bodies could become images. A fifth-century account of the
death of St. Daniel the Stylite demonstrates the interchangeability of body
and icon in the cult of saints: when "the people demanded that the holy man
be shown to them before his burial," the archbishop ordered the wood plank
on which the body lay to be "stood upright—the body had been fixed to it so
that it could not fall—and thus, like an icon, the holy man was displayed to
all on every side.")[5] The supreme example of this kind of animate thing is, of
course, the Eucharist, and from the central fact of Christ's incarnation and
his "real presence" in the communion wafer flowed an entire theology of
image-making that broke down the ontological barriers between the material and the spiritual world in transformative and deeply subversive ways. In
the words of James Francis, the icon and the sacrament worked in analogous
ways in the early church—as a "living sign that both symbolizes and effects
what it symbolizes: water and grace, bread and the body of Christ, oil and
the Holy Spirit."[6]

Over the centuries, the liveliness of images became the theological anchor of a range of liturgical and cultic practices in Western Christianity: the
mass, veneration of the saints, pilgrimage, relics and shrines, saints' legends
and other hagiographic texts, sacramental feasts, funeral monuments. The
pedagogical function of images as *libri pauperum*, or "books of the poor," had
been famously articulated by Pope Gregory I in the sixth century and reaf-

---

[4] Sarah Stanbury, "The Vivacity of Images: St. Katherine, Knighton's Lollards, and the
Breaking of Idols," in *Images, Idolatry, and Iconoclasm in Late Medieval England: Textuality
and the Visual Image*, ed. Jeremy Dimmick, James Simpson, and Nicolette Zeeman (Oxford:
Oxford University Press, 2002), 131–50; Jaś Elsner, *Art and the Roman Viewer: The Transformation of Art from the Pagan World to Christianity* (Cambridge: Cambridge University Press,
1995); James A. Francis, "Living Icons: Tracing a Motif in Verbal and Visual Representation
from the Second to the Fourth Centuries C.E.," *American Journal of Philology* 24 (2003): 575–
600; Rachel Neis, "Eyeing Idols: Rabbinic Viewing Practices in Late Antiquity," *Jewish Quarterly Review* 102 (Fall 2012): 533–60.

[5] Quoted in Francis, "Living Icons," 591.

[6] Ibid., 593.

firmed by every church synod and council thereafter.[7] "It is one thing to worship a picture," Gregory wrote to Bishop Serenus, "it is another by means of pictures to learn thoroughly the story that should be venerated. For what writing makes present to those reading, the same picturing makes present to the uneducated." For "the common people" especially, "picturing is the equivalent of reading."[8] Just as icons could "quicken" the lives of the saints they depicted, so too could religious images "quicken" the imagination and memory of the faithful by conjuring up vivid mental pictures of biblical history or sacramental rituals. The root of the word "imagination" is, after all, *imagio*, or image. Gazing upon an image of Christ on the cross or upon the consecrated host as it was elevated by the priest was to be reminded of the painful fact of Christ's suffering and death. Because the cross had been drenched with Christ's blood, Thomas Aquinas argued that it merited a higher degree of veneration than other holy images. (A Lollard would later joke that by the same logic Christians should worship the lips of Judas, which had, after all, kissed Jesus's face.)[9] By the late fifteenth century, the Augustinian Gottschalk Hollen would even claim that people were led to God *more* effectively "through a picture than through a sermon."[10] But more than this, kissing the crucifix or eating the communion host allowed laymen and women to participate vicariously in Christ's Passion—to suffer and bleed, at some visceral or affective level, as he did. The tint of red wine on the lips of the communicant, a fourth-century catechist wrote, was nothing less than "the blood of the truth smeared on the mouths of the faithful."[11]

By the later Middle Ages, the religious landscape of Christian Europe had

[7] Gregory's comments were in response to the Iconoclastic Controversy of the Eastern Church in the eighth and ninth centuries, when the spiritual value of images was under unprecedented attack. The iconomachy of the Eastern Church does not seem to have made much headway in the West, at least until the fourteenth and fifteenth centuries. See Kathleen Kamerick, *Popular Piety and Art in the Late Middle Ages: Image Worship and Idolatry in England, 1350–1500* (New York: Palgrave, 2002); and Carlos M. N. Eire, *War Against the Idols: The Reformation of Worship from Erasmus to Calvin* (New York: Cambridge University Press, 1986). On the role of images in medieval mnemonics, see Mary Carruthers, *The Book of Memory: A Study of Memory in Medieval Culture*, 2nd ed. (New York: Cambridge University Press, 2008; orig. pub. 1990).

[8] Quoted in Carruthers, *The Book of Memory*, 275. The full text of Gregory's letter can be found in Celia M. Chazelle, "Pictures, Books, and the Illiterate: Pope Gregory I's letters to Serenus of Marseilles," *Word and Image* 6 (1990): 138–53.

[9] Kamerick, *Popular Piety*, 26–27.

[10] Eire, *War Against the Idols*, 20.

[11] Georgia Frank, " 'Taste and See': The Eucharist and the Eyes of Faith in the Fourth Century," *Church History* 70 (December 2001): 619–43 (quotation on 632).

become littered with holy images, even to the point of saturation. The magnificent cathedrals of Chartres, Reims, and Lincoln were but the crowning glory of an enormous treasure house of sacred art created from the eleventh to the sixteenth century. In Zurich alone, the commissioning of ecclesiastical works of art increased a hundredfold between 1500 and 1518.[12] By the fifteenth century, Margaret Aston observes, "it was the sheer number of images that worried contemporaries. Belief was being swamped by over-production." An anti-Lollard treatise in England warned that images should not "be multiplied so wijde [widely]" that "at ech chirche, at ech chapel, at ech stretis eende, or at ech heggis [hedge] in a cuntre, be sett such an ymage."[13] Every hamlet seemed to have its own market cross and local saint before which the faithful performed their daily devotions. Crosses were so thick on the ground, a London preacher complained, that passersby could hardly avoid despoiling them: when "there were one cross or few more, men did reverence to them and pissed not there. But when there was in every corner a cross set, then men of necessity were compelled to piss upon the crosse."[14]

The vivid acts of imagining inspired by the medieval visual regime clearly carried dangers as well as pleasures. The ignorant or weak-minded could too easily confuse spiritual imagining with actual metamorphosis, to conclude that they had become deified by their brush with the incarnate God. The periodic rise of false prophets, mystics, and visionaries was a problem for the church, an inescapable feature of the rich numinous landscape of medieval Christianity. But of more immediate concern was the proliferation of saints' cults with their increasingly elaborate, even baroque, celebrations of the sensual and the material over the contemplative. St. Bernard of Clairvaux (d. 1153) chastised the love of gilded saints' images that people mistakenly believed to be "the more holy the more highly colored the image is." In his view, the church had become "radiant in its walls and destitute in its poor. It dresses its stones in gold and it abandons its children naked."[15] The social critique of iconology—that money better spent on feeding and clothing God's people

---

[12] Eire, *War Against the Idols*, 13. On the "image explosion" of the late Middle Ages, see Michael Camille, *The Gothic Idea: Ideology and Image-Making in Medieval Art* (New York: Cambridge University Press, 1989).

[13] Margaret Aston, *England's Iconoclasts*, vol. 1, *Laws Against Images* (Oxford: Clarendon Press, 1988), 25–26; Reginald Pecock, *The Repressor of Over Much Blaming of the Clergy* (c. 1445), ed. Churchill Babington (London, 1860), 1:183–84.

[14] Thomas Arthur, quoted in Christopher Haigh, *English Reformations: Religion, Politics, and Society Under the Tudors* (New York: Oxford University Press, 1993), 62.

[15] Quoted in Kamerick, *Popular Piety*, 21.

was being wasted on sacred art—was a recurrent theme of medieval discourses on the dangers of images and would be resurrected by the Lollards in the fourteenth century.

Late medieval humanists like Erasmus criticized the promiscuous and selfish use of material images in Christian piety, but they reserved their sharpest ire for grosser artifacts such as relics. Meditating on the torn and bleeding body of Christ in the Eucharist was one thing; worshiping the bloody remains of a holy saint was, to many, a perversion of the doctrine of images. Statuary, painting, stained glass, all had an artistic value that redeemed them as devotional objects—they constituted "a kind of silent poetry," in Erasmus's words, that could evoke pious emotions among the laity. But relics—those bits of rag, bone, hair, flesh, "or whatever other kinds of filth human bodies have"—were quite another thing altogether. The whiff of disgust for the coarser material detritus of late medieval piety emanating from the pens of humanists would become a powerful current among Reformers, but they broke with the medieval critics by including sacred art as well as specious relics (as likely to be the bones of dogs and asses as of saints, in Martin Bucer's words) in their critique of religious images.[16]

Complaints about the proliferation of relics began to be widely aired in the centuries before the Reformation as sanctified scraps miraculously appeared in towns and parishes throughout the continent. If all the so-called pieces of the cross masquerading as relics were gathered together in one place, skeptics quipped, they would make a whole forest. How many toes can a Saint Jerome or a Saint Katherine have, others wondered? Medieval historians have described a kind of corpse fetish in which the remains of holy men and women were disinterred, minutely dismembered, and distributed: the body of Thomas Aquinas was decapitated and boiled by the monks of Fossanova, in whose monastery he had died, while the corpse of St. Elizabeth of Hungary was mobbed by a crowd of worshipers who "cut or tore strips of the linen enveloping her face; they cut off the hair, the nails, even the nipples."[17] This "relic-mania" did not afflict the poor and credulous alone; relics—and the shrines built to house them—were big business, generating substantial wealth for local economies as well as for the church. They were also theologically subversive. By offering a quick-and-easy route to salvation (just gazing

[16] Eire, *War Against the Idols*, 43, 50.

[17] Johann Huizinga, *The Waning of the Middle Ages: A Study of the Forms of Life, Thought and Art in France and the Netherlands in the XIVth and XVth Centuries* (London: E. Arnold & Co., 1927), 150; Eire, *War Against the Idols*, 16.

upon a relic could earn a pilgrim years of indulgence), relics and shrines under-
cut the need for true repentance and atonement. A calculating Christian like
Cardinal Albrecht of Brandenburg could acquire an amazingly precise 39,245,120
years of indulgence through his tireless pursuit of material Christianity.[18]

Thirty-nine million years is an absurd number. And there is an unmistakable element of the absurd in the late medieval frenzy for ever-more tangible
signs of God's immanence in the world (or so the Reformers would charge,
and many modern scholars would agree). The seemingly insatiable thirst for
wonder-working saints led to some notable "pious frauds"—statues that wept
tears of blood, crucifixes on which the limbs of Christ flexed in agony, shrines
that levitated and moved from one place to another when pilgrims did not
show sufficient respect. Reginald Pecock's nervous defense of images in the
1440s conceded more than he intended; even if some foolish men believe that
"the ymage dooth miraclis, or spekith at sumtyme, or heerith alwey, or
swetith [sweats] at sum tyme," he wrote, wise people "oonli laughe at suche
folies . . . of which no moral harme cometh." In order to defend the miraculous, however, Pecock was forced to admit that on occasion "it is not incon-
venient that God make thilk ymage of stoon or of tre [image of stone or
wood] forto swete and that the ymage be mooved fro oon place unto an othir
place."[19] Images had become *too* alive, in other words. Not only did they
somehow channel the human essence of their saintly prototypes, they had
begun to act like human beings themselves—walking, talking, sweating. Reformers would delight in unmasking these frauds. John Hoker wrote scorn-
fully in the 1530s that "there was lately discovered a wooden God of the
Kentish folk, a hanging Christ who might have vied with Proteus himself. For
he was able, most cunningly, to nod with his head, to scowl with his eyes, to
wag his beared, to curve his body, to reject and to receive the prayers of pilgrims." The fake god "rolled its eyes, foamed at the mouth, and poured forth
tears down its cheeks."[20] Some saw the devil's hand rather than human chica-
nery in the unnatural vivacity of images. Jacobus de Voragine's popular
Golden Legend, an English version of which appeared in 1483, told stories of
saints casting out demons from idols, and there were several attempted exor-
cisms of religious images in the medieval period.[21]

By the fourteenth century, then, there was a robust culture of image-

[18] Eire, *War Against the Idols*, 15.
[19] Pecock, *Repressor*, 1:156, 186–87
[20] Quoted in Aston, *England's Iconoclasts*, 235–36.
[21] Kamerick, *Popular Piety*, 17.

bashing as well as image-worship in western Christianity. There was not, however, as yet any organized *movement* against images such as had erupted in Byzantium during the Iconoclastic Controversy of the eighth and ninth centuries. This changed in the century before the Reformation. One contributing factor to the growing suspicion of religious images was surely the increasing availability of print; with more and more devotional texts and doctrinal primers coming off the presses in the fifteenth century, the church no longer needed to rely exclusively on images to convey spiritual truths. The "books of the laity" were increasingly just that—books, rather than (or in addition to) pictures.[22] But if growing literacy rates and technological innovations in the printing process made iconography increasingly obsolete, the excesses of the late medieval cult of saints played a much larger role in turning iconography into iconomachy. The gross materiality of religious icons provoked a backlash that would reduce sacred art to rubble in the next two centuries across large swaths of Protestant Europe. And once again, the Lollards charted a path the Reformers would follow.

John Wyclif, the founder of Lollardy, was no iconoclast. "It is evident," he asserted, "that images may be made both well and ill."[23] But he did believe that the abuse of religious images was widespread in the late fourteenth century; "we who call ourselves Christians sin more often in idolatry than do barbarians," he lamented in his treatise *De Eucharista*.[24] The Oxford don was most exercised by the crude anthropomorphism of iconic depictions of God as a bearded old man and by the popular view of relics as possessing magical powers. But he continued to affirm the positive value of good religious images, especially that of the unadorned crucifix. His followers, however, turned his suspicion of images into a full-blown iconomachy that occasionally turned violent. At best, Lollards viewed images as "blynde stockys" and "ded stonys," suited for nothing more than fuel to keep a body warm. At worst, they were tools of the devil designed to trick and seduce men into the sin of idolatry—"the bikynning, cause, and ende of all ivel."[25] Margery Baxter, a defendant in a series of heresy trials conducted against Lollards in

---

[22] On the impact of new print technologies and literacy rates, see Michael O'Connell, *The Idolatrous Eye: Iconoclasm and Theater in Early-Modern England* (New York: Oxford University Press, 2000).

[23] Margaret Aston, *Lollards and Reformers: Images and Literacy in Late Medieval Religion* (London: Hambledon Press, 1984), 137.

[24] W. R. Jones, "Lollards and Images: The Defense of Religious Art in Later Medieval England," *Journal of the History of Ideas* 34 (January–March 1973): 27–50 (quotation on 30).

[25] Ibid., 33.

Norwich between 1428 and 1431, told the judges that "the devils who fell from heaven with Lucifer entered the images in churches, and have continued to dwell in them, so that people who adored them were committing idolatry."[26]

The social injustice of image-worship was a consistent refrain of Lollard preaching. As later humanist critics would do, the Lollards accused pilgrims of squandering their pennies and sympathy on "dead images that neither thirsteth nor hungereth nor feeleth any coldness neither suffereth disesase, for they may not feel nor see nor hear nor speak nor look."[27] Over and over again, Lollard rhetoric set "dead images" of wood and stone against "quick images" of the deserving poor and argued that "ech Cristen man is a perfiter and a fuller and a spedier ymage of Crist than is eny stok or stoon grauen."[28] By this logic, Margaret Aston points out, breaking up or destroying sacred art could be viewed as "an act of charity" rather than of iconomachy. "These images of themselves may do neither good nor evil to men's souls," a Lollard wrote, "but they might warm a man's body in cold, if they were set upon a fire." When William Smith and Richard Waytestathe found themselves short of fuel to cook their meal, they reportedly took an ax to an old wooden statue of St. Catherine and made a bonfire of her remains. Burning the icon was simultaneously a social good and a means of testing the saint's power by the approved biblical method of fire. Lollards proved particularly fond of fire as a clarifying agent that would reveal the true nature of "dead" images: Elizabeth Sampson, cited for heresy in 1509, mocked the image of Our Lady of Willesden for having "a burnt arse elf and a burnt arse stock, and if she might have helped men and women which go to her on pilgrimage, she would not have suffered her tail to have been burnt." The record of actual Lollard iconoclasm is spotty—a reference to "burnt images in Loddon," an isolated case of a parish clerk who cut off and burned the head of an image of the Virgin in Northamptonshire, a nocturnal raid in St. Albans that discovered some service-books in which the

[26] *Heresy Trials in the Diocese of Norwich, 1428–31*, ed. Norman P. Tanner, Camden Fourth Series, vol. 20 (London: Royal Historical Society, 1977), 13. Tanner considered Baxter to be on "the lunatic fringe" of Lollardy, though her heterodox views on images were commonplace within the Norwich Lollard community. As Tanner notes, some defendants believed the sign of the cross was the sign of Antichrist, others "that crucifixes were no holier than the gallows upon which thieves were hanged" (20).

[27] Aston, *Lollards and Reformers*, 155.

[28] As reported by Pecock, *Repressor*, 1:219. An anonymous preacher described the poor as "quicke ymagis of god." Jones, "Lollards and Images," 35.

names of saints had been defaced.[29] But however rare, these instances were well-enough known to inspire an organized countermovement, a series of apologetic treatises that laid out the argument for religious images in the late fourteenth and early fifteenth centuries for a new generation of English Christians. This quite public argument about the nature of images in the fourteenth and early fifteenth centuries reveals, in James Simpson's words, the late medieval era's "profound indecision about whether images are alive." Throughout this entire period, he argues, images are "practicing a kind of *ars moriendi*, learning to die, well before the first iconoclastic law of 1538."[30]

These initial stirrings of discontent against "dead," fraudulent, and greedy religious images became a full-blown assault on *all* images during the Reformation. How the debate moved from an institutional critique of the abuse of images to a radical rejection of the entire visual regime of medieval Christianity is one of the central stories of the Reformation. The revisionist historian Eamon Duffy calls iconoclasm the "central sacrament of the Reformation," a claim suggesting deep chains of meaning linking the outward expression of rage against the material face of medieval Christianity in orchestrated acts of violence to the theological, liturgical, and psychological currents that underwrote such repugnance of *things*.[31] Where this repugnance came from and how it was channeled in new and troubling directions in the English colonies is the subject I want to explore in the remainder of this chapter.

"Religion Naked, Bare, and Unclad": The Reformation of Images

As historians of the Reformation have argued so persuasively, the attack on images was part and parcel of a larger campaign to replace the incarnational

---

[29] Aston, *Lollards and Reformers*, 167–77. Lollardy posed a formidable challenge to orthodox views because it was so well-grounded in the traditional arguments of the church in defense of images, as (for example) when preachers labeled "dead" images "lewed men's books to learn them how they should worship saints in heaven after whom these dead images are shaped" (ibid., 152).

[30] Simpson, *Under the Hammer*, 60. And the question is still, on some level, unresolved; Margaret Aston notes that as late as 1985, the "moving" statue at Ballinspittle, County Cork, in Ireland, was defaced by a group who accused worshipers of adoring "a lump of stone." Aston, *England's Iconoclasts*, 3.

[31] Eamon Duffy, *The Stripping of the Altars: Traditional Religion in England, c. 1400– c. 1580* (New Haven, Conn.: Yale University Press, 1992), 480.

structure of medieval Christianity, with its emphasis on the physical presence of God in the world via the sacrament of communion and the miracles wrought by saints, with a representational culture anchored in the Word.[32] Text-based practices such as reading scripture and hearing sermons replaced the "superstitious" ceremonies and rituals of the mass and the cult of saints, with far-reaching aesthetic consequences: the theology of *sola scriptura* was translated into an aesthetic of the plain: whitewashed meetinghouses instead of baroque churches, hard wooden benches instead of richly furnished pews with embroidered seat cushions and tapestries, simple block-print books instead of rosary beads and stained glass windows, vernacular sermons on practical subjects instead of Latinate treatises on arcane doctrinal controversies. This was an epistemological as well as ecclesiological transformation of epic proportions. As Simpson puts it, "a whole world of once numinous objects" had become "inert, oppressive things."[33] A dense semiotic universe rich with visual, aural, and tactile clues all pointing to the manifold presence of the divine in the world was reduced to a stark landscape of naked souls trembling before a remote and inaccessible deity. God was to be heard, not seen or felt or engaged in the physical world after 1517.

This is, to be sure, a one-sided description of the changes wrought by the Reformation in the fabric of medieval piety. To focus solely on the visual and material impoverishment of post-Reformation Europe is to ignore or slight the tremendous intellectual and psychological richness of a word-centered regime that produced such literary wonders as John Milton's epic *Paradise Lost* and Shakespeare's *Merchant of Venice*. Nor does it take into account the extraordinary invigoration of the inner life, the legendary soul struggles of ordinary men and women like Bunyan's Pilgrim and the London artisan Nehemiah Wallington whose spiritual agonies and triumphs, recorded faithfully in journals and diaries, helped birth a new literary genre, the modern novel.[34] Moreover, the severe visual anorexia of Reformation culture did not last long beyond its formative generation: by the seventeenth and certainly the eighteenth centuries, the material life of Protestant communities had recovered

---

[32] O'Connell, *The Idolatrous Eye*; Julia Spraggon, *Puritan Iconoclasm During the English Civil War* (Woodbridge: Boydell Press, 2003); Lee Palmer Wandel, *Voracious Idols and Violent Hands: Iconoclasm in Reformation Zurich, Strasbourg, and Basel* (New York: Cambridge University Press, 1995); Phyllis Mack Crew, *Calvinist Preaching and Iconoclasm in the Netherlands, 1544–1569* (New York: Cambridge University Press, 1978).

[33] Simpson, *Burning to Read*, 21.

[34] Paul Seaver, *Wallington's World: A Puritan Artisan in Seventeenth-Century London* (Stanford, Calif.: Stanford University Press, 1985).

much of the depth and texture it had lost in the zeal of early Reform (witness the elaborate illustrations of foundational texts such as John Foxe's *Acts and Monuments*). Nonetheless, the notion of the Reformation as a powerful negative force, in which a visually rich material world was destroyed in the name of a severe and uncompromising commitment to the unadorned Word, is not fundamentally wrong.

Everywhere the Reformers seized power in early modern Europe, especially in the Calvinist countries of France, England, and the Netherlands, the destruction of images went hand in hand with theological innovations. Great outbreaks of iconoclastic fervor occurred in the Swiss canton of Basel in 1529, in France in 1560–61, and in the Netherlands during the "Wonder Year" of 1566–67. In Zwingli's Zurich, the spontaneous outbreak of iconoclastic fervor in 1523 that stripped St. Peter's Church of its paintings and statues led to systematic destruction; by 1524 the city's churches had been cleared of all sacred art by organized bands of workmen (Figure 11). Five years later, the scene in Basel was more disorderly as unruly crowds swept through the city, dismantling and defacing the churches and tossing all the images they had looted onto a public bonfire (fittingly, on Ash Wednesday). "Away with them to the

Figure 11. Life-like statues of saints being consigned to the flames in Zurich during an iconoclastic outbreak. "Une scène d'iconoclasme à Zurich en 1524," Heinrich Bullinger, *Reformationschronik* (1564).

fire; that is where the wood belongs" was the iconoclast's cry.[35] England alone
experienced three waves of iconoclasm before the great "deluge" of the 1640s,
during the reigns of Henry VIII, Edward VI, and Elizabeth I (Figure 12).[36]
The first iconoclastic legislation in Europe was passed in England in 1538, and
for the next thirty years, the kingdom entered into an unprecedented experiment to juridically reshape the material face of Christianity. Nowhere else in
Europe was the campaign against images so enshrined in law, and nowhere
else were the iconoclasts so successful in destroying a considerable portion of
the sacred patrimony of medieval artists and builders.

The history of the legislative offensive against images reveals an ever-
widening mandate, as first only "abused" images were targeted for removal
and destruction. Henry VIII, always an ambivalent reformer, was a reluctant
iconophobe, and his 1538 legislative act applied only to religious images
"abused with pilgrimages or offerings." Popular sentiment, however, was
ahead of the king. Spontaneous outbreaks of cross-burning had occurred in
the 1520s and 1530s, and three iconoclasts who had destroyed the rood at Do-
vercourt in Essex were hanged for the offense. By the time Henry broke with
Rome, popular anger at false and deceitful images ran deep and threatened to
get out of hand. Thus the cautious policy of the initial 1538 injunctions. By
1547, Henry's far more zealous archbishop Thomas Cramner had come to believe that "in almost every place is contention for images, whether they have
been abused or not," and he therefore ordered "all the images remaining in
any church or chapel . . . be removed and taken away."[37]

Under Henry's precociously pious son, Edward VI (nicknamed "Josiah"
after the Old Testament boy king for his relentless pursuit of biblical reform),
all images—whether abused or not, whether in cathedrals, chapels, or even
private homes—were marked for destruction. Injunction 28 of the 1547 law
was breathtaking in its ruthless vision of a religious landscape swept clean of
all images: "they shall take away, *utterly extinct and destroy* all shrines, coverings of shrines, all tables, candlesticks trindles or rolls of wax, pictures, paintings, and all other monument of feigned miracles, pilgrimages, idolatry, and
superstition: *so that there remain no memory of the same in walls, glass-*

[35] Ludwig Hatzer, *A judgement of God our spouse as to how one should hold oneself towards all idols and images* (c. 1523), quoted in Aston, *England's Iconoclasts*, 37.
[36] Clifford Davidson, "'The Devil's Guts': Allegations of Superstition and Fraud in Religious Drama and Art During the Reformation," in *Iconoclasm vs. Art and Drama*, ed. Clifford
Davidson and Ann Eljenholm Nichols (Kalamazoo: Medieval Institute Publications, Western
Michigan University, 1989), 92–144 (quotation on 103).
[37] Quoted in Simpson, *Under the Hammer*, 61.

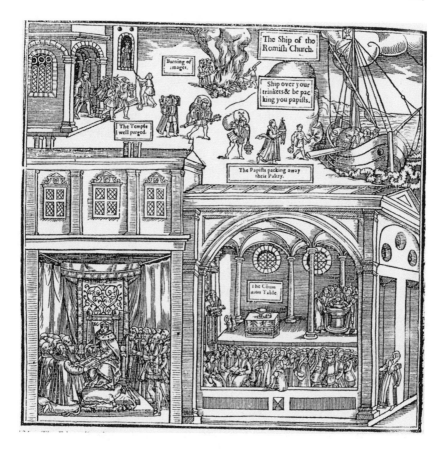

Figure 12. Depiction of popular iconoclasm during the reign of Edward VI, from the ninth book of John Foxe's *Acts and Monuments* (1570). In the upper portion, iconoclasts are looting a church while "papists" flee England with their "paltry."

windows, or elsewhere within their churches or houses. And they shall exhort all their *parishioners to do the like within their several houses.*"[38] There was to be no place of refuge for icons in Edwardian England, not even in the private recesses of the home or the spiritual memory of the church.

We have wrenching firsthand accounts of the anguish this demolishing of the churches inflicted on local ministers and their flock. "Lord, what work was here," one pastor wrote in anger, "what clattering of Glasses, what beating

---

[38] Aston, *England's Iconoclasts*, 256 (emphasis added).

down of Walls, what tearing up of Monuments, what pulling down of Seates, what wresting out of Irons and Brass from the Windows and Graves! . . . what toting and piping upon the destroyed Organ pipes, and what a hideous triumph of the Market day before all the Countrey, when in a kind of Sacrilegious and profane procession, all the Organ pipes, Vestments, both Copes and Surplices, together with the Leaden Crose, which had been newly sawne down from over the Green Yard Pulpit, and the Service books and singing books that could be had, were carried to the fire in the publick Market place."[39] And when the images came down, texts went up. The episcopal injunctions in 1565 for the dioceses of Coventry and Lichfield ordered that the Ten Commandments be placed directly where that most hated object of idolatry—the elevated host—had been: "See that you set up the table of the commandements in the place where the Sacrament did hang." John Stow records that as images were being pulled down all over London in 1547, "texts of scripture were written upon the walls of those churches against images etc."[40]

Edward's untimely death a mere six years into his reign spelled an abrupt end to this first phase of legislated iconoclasm, and Mary moved swiftly to restore as much of the iconography of the English church as she could. When she made her triumphal return to London in 1553, images of saints and the Virgin that had been squirreled away to evade the prying eyes of the king's commissioners were hauled out and put on display in the town's windows. But the task of reclamation was simply too difficult; altar stones that had been repurposed to build roads might be rescued, but the thousands of paintings, roods, statues, inscriptions, and vestments that had been consigned to the flames were simply gone. Moreover, the restored altars, crosses, and crucifixes now carried a polemical rather than a spiritual message; they were a defiant rejoinder to the Reformers' belief that images were by their very nature idolatrous. "Who could now doubt that the faiths of word and image were not allies, but opponents?" asks Margaret Aston.[41]

[39] Joseph Hall, *The Shaking of the Olive-Tree: The Remaining Works of that Incomparable Prelate, Joseph Hall . . . Together with His Hard Measure* (London, 1660), 62.

[40] Quoted in Aston, *England's Iconoclasts*, 367; John Stow, *Annales, or, A Generall Chronicle of England* (London, 1631–32), 595. Texts did not simply substitute for images, however, in this first phase of official iconoclasm; they were often the targets of violence themselves. Books were defaced, torn up, and burned alongside religious images by Edwardian iconoclasts, thus complicating a straightforward story of the triumph of the word over the image. For a discussion of how biblioclasm and iconoclasm were related, see Brian Cummings, "Iconoclasm and Bibliophobia in the English Reformation, 1521–1558," in *Images, Idolatry, and Iconoclasm in Late Medieval England*, 185–206.

[41] Aston, *England's Iconoclasts*, 294.

Elizabeth sent mixed signals in the first years of her reign. One of her first acts was to issue new injunctions in 1559 that retained Edward's sweeping iconoclastic Injunction 28, yet her own chapel continued to display a cross ("that little silver cross, of ill-omened origin") in the traditional central position. She shifted the emphasis back to the destruction of "abused" images only, yet looked the other way when Londoners made indiscriminate bonfires in August and September 1559 of "roods and of Maries and Johns and other images."[42] John Weever's doleful survey of the iconoclasm committed in the early years of Elizabeth's reign, *Ancient Funerall Monuments* (1631), narrated the destruction: "Under colour of this Commission, and in their too forward zeale, they rooted up and battered downe, Crosses in Churches, and Church-yards, as also in other publike places they defaced and brake down the images of Kings, Princes, and noble estates. . . . They despoiled Churches of their Copes, vestments, Amices, rich hangings, and all other ornaments, . . . leaving Religion naked, bare, and unclad."[43]

What Henry, Edward, and Elizabeth had begun, the Puritan Commonwealth finished with a vengeance. Puritan iconoclasm is the subject of popular lore as well as historical inquiry—"Cromwell the destroyer" is "securely enthroned in the realm of folk and children's lore," writes one English historian. During the Revolution, "King-breaking" was fatefully joined to "thing-breaking."[44] The brutal matter-of-factness of the journal of William Dowsing, who was commissioned by Parliament to enforce its ordinances of 1641 and 1643 "for the utter demolishing, removing, and taking away of all Monuments of Superstition and Idolatry," is an eloquent testament to the efficiency of the iconoclastic campaign that had so denuded England's ecclesiastical landscape by the 1640s. December 26, 1643: "We beat down about 110 Superstitious pic-

[42] Ibid., 307, 302. As Aston notes, though Elizabeth was forced to back down and order the removal of all roods in churches, she continued to defy radical reformers by defiantly displaying a cross in her own chapel for years. Twice, in 1562 and 1567, some audacious reformer actually managed to destroy the royal cross. Bishop Parkhurst of Norwich wrote gleefully to Henry Bullinger that "The crucifix and candlesticks in the queen's chapel are broken in pieces, and, as some one has brought word, reduced to ashes. A good riddance to such a cross as that!" He reported sadly eight months later that the cross and candlesticks were back, "to the great grief of the godly." William Fuller was still complaining bitterly in 1586 about "that foul idol, the cross," standing proudly on "the altar of abomination" in the royal chapel (313–14).

[43] John Weever, *Ancient Funerall Monuments within the United Monarchies of Great Britaine, Ireland, and the Ilands Adjacent with the dissolved Monastaries therein contained* (London, 1631), 50.

[44] Aston, *England's Iconoclasts*, 62–63.

tures, besides cherubims and ingravings." January 5, 1643/44: "We beate downe 3 crucifixes, and 80 superstitious pictures, and brake the rayles, and gave order to deface 2 grave-stones with Pray for our souls." One month later: "we brake down 841 superstitious pictures." All recorded without comment. An astonishing 95 percent of the religious images still extant in the 250 parish churches Dowsing "visited" were destroyed at his command.[45]

As had been the case a century earlier, the people undertook their own crusade against hated images. Disaffected Christians pulled down communion rails, dismantled altars, burned crucifixes, stripped pictures of saints from church walls and subjected them to mock executions, mobbed clerics and tore the surplices off their backs, jeered relics whose supernatural powers could not save them from the fire. They turned sacred objects into profanities—the cross-stone at Tukesbury in Gloucestershire was made into "an Hog-trough."[46] This vein of popular iconoclasm exhibited a spirit of vengeance against images that can be startling. Images were not just destroyed. They were *degraded*, tortured, and subjected to the same punishments inflicted on heretics and traitors. Saints' images were hung on trees and whipped before being tossed in the flames; others were nailed to posts in a form of mock crucifixion; a cache of "wooden gods" was confiscated and tied up "by the helles" as felons were and "dr[awn] up & down throw the towne."[47] Even the figure of Christ himself was not spared. The royalist newsbook *Mercurius Rusticus* (Figure 13) reported an incident in which Cromwell's soldiers entered a church and "began a fight with God himself." Observing the image of Jesus embroidered on a tapestry, "one said, 'here is Christ,' and swore that he would stab him; another said, 'here is Christ,' and swore that he would rip

[45] *The Journal of William Dowsing: Iconoclasm in East Anglia During the English Civil War*, ed. Trevor Cooper (Woodbridge: Boydell Press, 2001), 165, 210, 234. Table 1.2 (p. 25) totals the destruction committed under Dowsing.

[46] Robert Chestlin, *Persecutio Undecima, or, The Churches Eleventh Persecution. Being a Brief of the Fanatick Persecution of the Protestant Clergy of the Church of England: More particularly within the City of London* (London, 1681; orig. pub. 1648), 33.

[47] John Walker, "'Abolishing Superstition with Sedition'? The Politics of Popular Iconoclasm in England, 1640–1642," *Past & Present* 183 (May 2004): 79–123 (quotations on 82, 86, 87). See also Sergiusz Michalski, *Reformation and the Visual Arts: The Protestant Image Question in Western and Eastern Europe* (London: Routledge, 1993), 75–98; Margaret Aston, "Puritans and Iconoclasm, 1560–1660," in *The Culture of English Puritanism, 1560–1700*, ed. C. Durston and J. Eales (Basingstoke: Macmillan, 1996), 110–21; Lindley, "London and Popular Freedom in the 1640s"; and David Cressy, "Different Kinds of Speaking: Symbolic Violence and Secular Iconoclasm in Early Modern England," in *Protestant Identities: Religion, Society, and Self-Fashioning in Post-Reformation England*, ed. Muriel C. McClendon, Joseph P. Ward, and Michael MacDonald (Stanford, Calif.: Stanford University Press, 1999), 19–42.

Figure 13. Scenes of plunder from the title page of the royalist newsbook,
Mercurius Rusticus (London, 1647).

up his bowels: which they accordingly did." They then proceeded to fire "forty shot at the least" at another statue of Christ, "triumphing much, when they did hit it in the head or face, as if they were resolved to crucify him again in his figure."[48] More simply, a "Fanatick . . . broke the Neck of the Babe in the lap of the blessed Virgin."[49]

The anthropomorphized cross was a favorite target of iconoclasts. A spate of seriocomic pamphlets lamenting the fate of "Jasper Crosse," who protested "my violent undoing" at the hands of an angry mob in the first year of the English Civil War, hit the London streets in the 1640s (Figure 14). "I Jasper Crosse, scituated in Cheap-side, London . . . was assaulted and battered in the Kings highway, by many violent and insolent minded people, or rather ill-affected Brethren; and whether they were in their height of zeale, or else overcome with passion, or new wine lately come from New-England, I cannot be yet resolved." A second, more serious assault followed in 1643, in which the Cross lost first his nose, then his legs and arms to the mob before finally succumbing to the flames. "I draw no sword, nor do I wear long hair," he cried in self-defense. "They will divide my coat, my flesh, my bones. . . . You will have flesh for flesh."[50] We can find similar cases of iconoclasts treating images as if they were people in other Calvinist countries: Protestants in the Netherlands "hung images of saints from the gibbets erected to execute iconoclasts." Statutes of saints were not merely destroyed, "they were tortured," according to Phyllis Mack Crew, "the eyes and faces of the portraits were mutilated or the heads cut off, as at an execution."[51] And an ocean away, on the Caribbean island of Santa Domingo, Cromwell's invasionary forces "pelted" one image of the Virgin Mary "to death with oranges" and "de-

<hr/>

[48] Aston, *England's Iconoclasts*, 73; *Mercurius Rusticus*, 2, 119–20.

[49] Chestlin, *Persecutio Undecima*, 33.

[50] *The Dolefull Lamentation of Cheap-Side Crosse, or, Old England Sick of the Staggers* (London, 1641); *The Downfall of Dagon, or, The taking downe of Cheap-side Crosse this second of May, 1643* (London, 1642); *A Vindication of Cheapside Crosse against the Roundheads* (London, 1643). See also *The Remarkable Funeral of Cheapside Crosse in London* (London, 1642); Richard Overton, *Articles of High Treason Exhibited against Cheap-side Crosse: With the Last Will and Testament of the Said Crosse* (London, 1642); and Samuel Loveday, *An Answer to the Lamentation of Cheap-side Crosse. Together with the Reasons why so many doe desire the downfall of it, and all such Popish Reliques* (London, 1643). For two analyses of this episode, see David Cressy, "The Downfall of Cheapside Cross: Vandalism, Ridicule, and Iconoclasm," in his *Travesties and Transgressions in Tudor and Stuart England: Tales of Discord and Dissension* (New York: Oxford University Press, 2000), 234–50; and Joel Budd, "Rethinking Iconoclasm in Early Modern England: The Case of Cheapside Cross," *Journal of Early Modern History* 4 (2000): 379–404.

[51] Mack Crew, *Calvinist Preaching and Iconoclasm*, 12, 25–26.

Figure 14. *Dialogue Between the Crosse in Cheape, and Charing Cross* (London, 1641).

forme[d]" another by "flinging of orringes" at the "richlie clad" statue as she perched on the head of an English soldier.[52]

These episodes point to a crucial fact about English iconoclasm: the implicit, sometimes explicit, connection between breaking images and killing people. (In one case, the connection was literal: Friar Forrest's execution in 1538 was, Alexandra Walsham notes, "quite literally an act of iconoclasm, with fuel for the pyre over which he was suspended in chains being supplied by the great wooden idol of Dderfe Gardarn.")[53] This was, at least in part, a rhetorical move, designed to draw a pointed contrast between the traditionalists' love of images and their callous treatment of sectarians. The anonymous author of the pamphlet *The Case for all Crucifixes, Printed in the Climactericall Yeer of Crosses and Cross-men* (1643) compared the destruction of idols to the mutilation of Burton, Bastwick, and Prynne in the Laudian regime: "Six years agoe or thereabouts, three Images were defiled all at once, which could breathe, and smell, and heare. . . . Those three were Pilloried, defaced, stigmatized, in plaine English, markt for Rogues, because they were faithfull and kept close to the Law of their God." Quoting from Judges 8:18, the pamphlet demanded, "*What manner of Images were they, which yee saw (or heard were) so abused?*" The answer: "*living Images* . . . spoyled and left wounded."[54] The playful reversal of the standard trope of medieval iconography (now it was the persecuted dissenters who were the "quick" images against which were arrayed the "dead" idols of the Church of England) made for good press, but it also fundamentally destabilized the referential logic of image discourse. Which images were alive and which were dead? Or, to put it another way, which ones deserved to live and which ones deserved to die? We will see the consequences of this discursive dilemma when we turn to the subject of iconoclasm in the New World.

This abbreviated narrative of violence against icons gives a false impression that all Protestants hated images and wanted to destroy them. There was, in fact, considerable disagreement among Reformers over the legitimacy and role of sacred images. Martin Luther and his more zealous colleague Andreas van Karlstadt fell out in the 1520s over the latter's enthusiasm for image-

---

[52] Quoted in Beasley, "Wars of Religion in the Circum-Caribbean," 164–65.

[53] Alexandra Walsham, *Charitable Hatred: Tolerance and Intolerance in England, 1500–1700* (Manchester: University of Manchester Press, 2006), 77, 177.

[54] *The Case for all Crucifixes, images, &c. made with hands, and for religious use, in the case of Cheapside-Crosse, is discussed whether their militia, the setting of them in a posture of defence, be according to law, Printed in the Climactericall Yeer of Crosses and Cross-men* (London, 1643), 11, 14.

breaking. Karlstadt's 1522 sermon "On the Abolition of Images" defended the popular attacks on churches and religious art that had broken out throughout the city of Wittenberg. "I say to you that God has forbidden images with no less diligence than killing, stealing, adultery, and the like," he preached. Once the laity gained access to the scripture itself rather than the pablum of the *libri pauperum*, they would discover that images are "deaf and dumb" and the "rubbish mart" of medieval Christianity will collapse.[55] Luther had no patience for inflammatory sermons that whipped up iconophobia among Wittenberg's masses, fearing (correctly) that it would lead to bloodshed and dishonor for the Protestant cause. "No one who sees the iconoclasts raging thus against wood and stone should doubt that there is a spirit hidden in them which is death-dealing, not life-giving, and which at the first opportunity will also kill men," he warned in 1525.[56]

Significantly, it was Karlstadt's hard-line stance against images that would lead him, in defiance of Luther, to reject as well the notion of the "real presence" of God in the Eucharist. For there was no "idol" more despised among the radical Reformers than the Eucharist itself—that "idol of the altar," the papist "god of bread." John Knott argued in 1562 that the mass was no less idolatrous than the pagan worship of wood and stone, except that "the poor God of bread is the most miserable of all other idols."[57] The attack on the Eucharist as an idol signaled an important shift in the polemics of iconomachy within the Reformed community: for the communion host was both a material object (bread and body) *and* a sacramental ritual. Over the course of three generations of theological disputation (both among themselves and with their Catholic adversaries), Reformers moved the discourse of iconomachy from a discussion of material things to the realm of symbolic gestures and, ultimately, to the inner recesses of the human mind. The charge of idolatry "rapidly extend[ed], rhizome-like, everywhere, across the entire range of cultic practice and into the psyche," writes James Simpson of the Reformation era. Even the most laudable of thoughts and desires can, if bib-

---

[55] Eire, *War Against the Idols*, 58–60.

[56] Aston, *England's Iconoclasts*, 6.

[57] Ibid., 7–8. There was, Aston argues, "a near relationship between the doctrine of transubstantiation . . . and the theory of images, in which the worship given to the image returned to its prototype. Believing in real contact with saints through their images was analogous to believing in the real presence of Christ in the bread of the Eucharist." As a concrete example of this aversion to the Eucharist as an idol, the Puritan agent William Dowsing reported in his journal that, among other material artifacts, he "brake the popish inscription, *My flesh is meat indeed and my blood is drink indeed.*" *Journal of William Dowsing*, 244.

lically unsanctioned, be idolatrous; "all good intents and good zeals which
are without God's word . . . are nothing else than plain idolatry and worshipping of false gods," declared William Tyndale in 1528.[58] Calvin was the intellectual force behind this steady widening of the definition of the icon to
include nonmaterial, abstract things as well as "idols of wood and stone." The
only "proper" images Calvin allowed in the reformed church were "those living symbols which the Lord has consecrated by his own word: I mean Baptism and the Lord's Supper, with the other ceremonies." So irresistible was the
"powerful infatuation" of men for idols, he warned, that false gods were as
likely to be creations of the heart and mind as of the hands—ambition, lust,
pride, all could lead men to honor themselves above God. The human mind
is a "labyrinth" of profane desires and ideas, such that "every man has had his
own god. . . . Like water gushing forth from a large and copius spring, immense crowds of gods have issued from the human mind," he concluded.[59]

Following Calvin's lead, Anglo-American Puritans conflated the despised
physical objects of "popish" worship (altars, roods, crucifixes) with the rituals
and gestures that had grown up around these objects in medieval ecclesiol-
ogy (kneeling, making the sign of the cross, bowing before the altar), many of
which the Laudian regime had reintroduced only recently to the Church of
England.[60] This was as much a semiotic as an ecclesiastical argument. John
Cotton's treatise on the second commandment argued that "when material,
cut, or carved Images are prohibited, there all representations, material, ae-
rial, real, imaginary, proper, and tropical, are condemned; . . . It matters not
whether the Image be a thing truly existent, formed of any visible matter,
Brass, Wood, or Stone; or whether it have no other being but in the mind of
men."[61] Cotton was Calvin's closest intellectual heir in New England (he condemned "*Lutherans* and Papists" alike for their love of images), and where he
went, other ministers followed. Samuel Mather, in a sermon he delivered in

[58] Simpson, *Under the Hammer*, 64; William Tyndale, *The Obedience of a Christian Man*,
ed. David Daniell (London: Penguin, 2000; orig. pub. 1528), 179.
[59] John Calvin, *The Institutes of Christian Religion*, trans. Henry Beveridge (Edinburgh,
1845), I:xi, 135; I:v, 77.
[60] Kenneth Fincham, "The Restoration of the Altars in the 1630s," *Historical Journal* 44
(2001): 919–40; Peter Lake, "The Laudian Style: Order, Uniformity and the Pursuit of Holiness in the 1630s," in *The Early Stuart Church, 1603–1642*, ed. Kenneth Fincham (Houndmills:
Macmillan, 1993).
[61] John Cotton, *Some Treasure Fetched out of Rubbish, or, Three short but seasonable Treatises (found in an heap of scattered Papers) which Providence hath reserved for their service who
desire to be instructed, from the Word of God concerning the Imposition and Use of Significant
Ceremonies in the Worship of God* (London, 1650), 23.

Cambridge, Massachusetts, in 1672, laid out the logic of Puritan iconoclasm for his colonial auditors. Mather argued for an expansive definition of the sin of idolatry: "Although none but the grosses kind of Idolatry, viz. *graven Images*, are expressly mentioned, yet, *under this one Instance is comprehended all the other sins of the same kinde, all other Inventions of men are included and comprehended under this* [emphasis in original]." The long list of Anglican "idols" he recommended for demolition included (in descending order of venality) the sign of the cross in baptism, kneeling at the Lord's Supper, bowing to the altar, and bowing to the name of Jesus, along with the more conventional targets of surplices, organs, and the Book of Common Prayer. When once a true Christian ventured down the path of idolatry, the road to hell was swift and certain. Like "bodily uncleanness," the lure of idolatry is "insatiable," Mather warned. "If you do but wear a Surplice for peace sake, why not as well admit the sign of the Cross in Baptism, or bow to an Altar, and in a little time you will find that the same Reason is as strong for bowing to an Image, to a Crucifix, and why not as well say Mass too, for the peace of the Church, and then at last swallow down everything, Submit to the Pope, worship the Beast, and so be damned and go to Hell."[62]

This capacious understanding of idolatry seemed to sanction a range of iconoclastic gestures among the Puritan faithful. Ann Kibbey suggests that what distinguished popular Puritan iconoclasm from more traditional iconomachy was "their extension of iconoclastic motives to nonviolent symbolic acts" such as refusing to kneel at the Lord's Supper.[63] A group of lay Presbyterians in New York told the resident Anglican minister that among the other "Idolatrous" ceremonies of the Church of England, "the Sign of the Cross is the Mark of the Beast and the Sign of the Devil."[64] One disgusted churchman complained in the 1640s that the sectarians were "peevishly perverse against the laudable and Christian order of our Church. When we stand up reverently, they unmannerly sit on their Bums. When we kneele, either they sit or loll on their elbows. When we are bareheaded, they have their

---

[62] Samuel Mather, *A Testimony from the Scripture Against Idolatry & Superstition, in Two Sermons* (Cambridge, 1672), 7, 26, 35. The official homilies of the Church of England made much the same point, declaring that "the seeking out of images is the beginning of whoredom." Quoted in Patrick Collinson, *From Iconoclasm to Iconophobia: The Cultural Impact of the Second English Revolution*, Stenton Lecture 1985 (Reading: University of Reading Press, 1986), 25.

[63] Ann Kibbey, *The Interpretation of Material Shapes in Puritanism: A Study of Rhetoric, Prejudice, and Violence* (New York: Cambridge University Press, 1986), 43.

[64] George Juirson to Secretary, August 4, 1708, SPG Records, vol. 3, no. 168, p. 467.

Bonnets, and hats on their zealous Noodles."[65] A group of Parliamentary vol-
unteers disrupted a church service in Norwich by marching up to the altar
where they "turned their backs upon it in great derision lifting of their bumbs
and holding downe ther heads against it in a derideing manner." These ceremonial skirmishes often focused on the iconic status of the body itself, con-
stituting (in John Walker's phrase) a literal "revolt of the lower body": one
man was prosecuted in the church courts for "turning his backside to the
holy table," while a woman was presented for "very irreverently sitt[ing] on
her Arse" rather than kneeling to pray.[66]

Once iconomachy was unhinged from the material world, it was free to
roam. England's iconoclasts set their sights on a steadily moving target from
the fourteenth to the seventeenth century: first church architecture and religious art, then crucifixes and clerical vestments, then symbolic gestures like
kneeling and kissing the cross, and finally their own idolatrous thoughts and
feelings. In the process of transplanting this iconoclastic regime to the New
World, however, images once again assumed material form. From the stone
idols of Mexico and Peru to the flesh-and-blood Indians of English America,
the assault on images was fought on new terrain and against new targets.

"Flesh for Flesh": The Logic of
Iconoclasm in the New World

The long shadow cast by the Roman church and its sacramental culture over
the dreams and nightmares of Reformers, Puritans in particular, was felt as
far away as the colonial seaports in the seventeenth and early eighteenth centuries, despite the absence of anything remotely resembling Europe's chapels
and cathedrals in these provincial outposts. But the first iconoclasts in the
New World were not Reformed Protestants but Spanish inquisitors, who undertook several campaigns of extirpation against native idolatry in New
Spain in the sixteenth and seventeenth centuries, and French missionaries
who waged their own private war against the "idols" of New France. That
history is beyond the scope of this book but, like the Spanish and French

---

[65] Richard Carter, *The Schismatick Stigmatized: Wherein All Make-Bates are Branded,
whether they are Eves-dropping-newes-carriers, Murmurers, Complainers, Railers, Reproach-
ers, Revilers, Repining Reformers, Fault-finders, Quarrel-pickers, and Corner-creepers, with all
the rabble of Brain-sicks, who are enemies to Old England's Peace* (London, 1641), 3.

[66] Walker, "'Abolishing Superstition with Sedition'?" 100, 101.

colonial literature on cannibalism, serves as an important discursive backdrop to the story of Protestant iconoclasm in English America.

With striking consistency, the battle against "idols" in New Spain was
waged using the same rhetorical arsenal developed by radical iconomachs in
Europe. The irony is supreme: at the exact same time Catholic churches and
sacred art were under attack by iconoclasts in Protestant countries, the religious orders in Mexico and Peru were breaking the idols and destroying the
temples of those they sought to convert. The sacrificial practices of American
Indian peoples certainly provided new fodder for religious controversialists
in Europe (as we saw in the first chapter), and the widespread presence of
wooden and stone figures in Indian religious practice seemed to prove, once
again, that paganism was alive and well in the New World.[67]

The extirpation campaigns in colonial Peru, for example, focused on the
huacas, or natural stone forms that were believed to be the material incarnation of powerful beings ("god-men") who had once lived upon the earth.
Shrines built up around these *huacas* and became sites of pilgrimage for people who brought gifts (animal or even human blood, meat jerky, and cakes of
crushed maize) as offerings to the gods. In the eyes of Catholic missionaries,
the *huacas* were "ugly stones," "dead gods" (*dioses muertos*), rather than the
one "living God" (*Dios vivo*): "Tell me brother, how can you put your hope in
a rock as if it were the true God; do you not see that this stone does not have
the wisdom to know what you ask? Do you not see that it has not the will to
love you ... no eyes to see you, no ears to hear, nor mouth to console you?
And if it could talk it would say: 'Indian, you are mad, you are blind to place
your hope in me. I do not have any power; I cannot give you anything you ask
of me. Do you not see that I am a stone, and that the birds and skunks soil
me? If I am a stone, as you see that I am, how can I be God?' "[68] These dead
gods were only fit for the fire. Extirpation campaigns usually ended with a
public *auto-da-fé* in which all the *huacas, malquis*, and other religious idols

---

[67] As Frank Manuel has argued, the discovery of the New World resurrected paganism
from a dead academic subject to a "living flesh-and-blood reality." Manuel, *The Eighteenth
Century Confronts the Gods* (Cambridge, Mass.: Harvard University Press, 1959), 18–19. See
also Sabine MacCormack, "Limits of Understanding: Perceptions of Greco-Roman and Am-
erindian Paganism in Early Modern Europe," in *America in European Consciousness,
1493–1750*, ed. Karen O. Kupperman (Chapel Hill: University of North Carolina Press, 1995),
79–129.

[68] Hernando de Avendaño, *Sermons* (1649), quoted in Kenneth Mills, *Idolatry and Its
Enemies: Colonial Andean Religion and Extirpation, 1640–1750* (Princeton, N.J.: Princeton
University Press, 1997), 200–201.

uncovered by the *visitadores* during their investigation were burned in a large bonfire before the assembled village. Even the mummified bodies of holy men and women ("sorcerers") were consigned to the flames, to the horror of Indian onlookers who saw their own deceased parents or relatives go up in flames. One *curaca* was forced to "set fire to his father, to his mother, and to his ancestors" in his town's *auto-da-fé*. Francisco de Avila boasted that he had destroyed eight hundred *idolos fijos* (fixed shrines such as rocks) and twenty thousand smaller idols in the decade of the 1610s as the "Visitor General of Idolatry"; a few years later his successor, Avendaño, claimed he had sent one thousand indigenous priests to jail and incinerated thousands more idols.[69] The consequences could be devastating for local spiritual economies. Catalina Guacayllano, a local priestess, prayed before a burnt *huaca* to restore water and food to her community: "Burned father, parched father, you who guard the irrigation canal, who guard the water and guard the fields, give me water, give me fields, give me food. Ever since you have been burned, since you have been scorched, we are dying of hunger, we have no food."[70]

In the long run, the idols endured. The extirpation campaign seems to have done little to efface the material religion of the Andean people; ecclesiastical visitors who returned to the scene of the public bonfires decades later found that for every idol that was destroyed, ten more had been created in its place. Some idols survived by being hidden in the statues of Catholic saints, a creative act of self-preservation that fostered the syncretic religious culture emerging in New Spain. And, to the utter consternation of the missionaries, the charred remains of former idols were sometimes resurrected as new gods by the Andeans. Francisca Cocahquillay continued to offer sacrifices to Raupoma and Choqueruntu, two round stones that had been destroyed by the extirpators and replaced with a wooden cross. "Flower of fire, tongue of fire, remnant of fire and leavings of fire, eat this, drink this, Burned Lord, so that there may be good food, so that there may be good water," she prayed.[71] The

[69] Iris Gareis, "Repression and Cultural Change: The 'Extirpation of Idolatry' in Colonial Peru," in *Spiritual Encounters: Interactions Between Christianity and Native Religions in Colonial America*, ed. Nicholas Griffiths and Fernando Cervantes (Lincoln: University of Nebraska Press, 1999), 230–54 (quotations on 237, 248n27). Nicholas Griffiths points out that although the extirpation campaign was not officially the work of the Spanish Inquisition, which had been forbidden to extend its jurisdiction over American Indians, it functioned as a parallel system of religious repression. Griffiths, *The Cross and the Serpent: Religious Repression and Resurgence in Colonial Peru* (Norman: University of Oklahoma Press, 1996), 30–38.
[70] Sabine MacCormack, *Religion in the Andes: Vision and Imagination in Early Colonial Peru* (Princeton, N.J.: Princeton University Press, 1991), 408.
[71] Griffiths, *Cross and the Serpent*, 196–98; MacCormack, *Religion in the Andes*, 407–8.

inquisitors' flames had destroyed only the outer material form of the god, not its spiritual power.

There was nothing resembling such an organized campaign of extirpation in New France, but the Jesuit missionaries who labored in heroic isolation among the Algonquian and Iroquois nations fought their own rearguard action against native idolatry. At the Mission of St. Francis Xavier in the upper Midwest, the local missionary complained that the Indians "apostrophize[d]" the chapel itself, "and speak to it, as to a living Thing. When they pass by here, they Throw some tobacco all around the church, which is a Kind of Worship that they pay to their divinities." Another group of missionaries found "a sort of Idol" at the fall of the De Pere rapids to whom the "Savages of that region" offered sacrifices—"either of tobacco, or arrows, or painted objects." The idol was "a rock shaped by nature in the form of a human bust, in which one seems to distinguish, from a distance, the head, shoulders, breast, and more especially, the face, which passers-by are wont to Paint with their finest colors." The missionaries promptly tossed it in the river.[72] Rather than try to destroy all "the little Idols" they found in Indian communities, however, the Jesuits preferred to fight images with images: they showered their neophyte converts with pictures of saints, baby Jesuses, adorned crucifixes, and even relics that they relocated from French shrines to New World reliquaries. Echoing Gregory I, Francis Le Jeune explained that "sacred pictures are half the instruction that one is able to give the Savages."[73] The Ursulines rejoiced when Claude Martin sent them "a particle of the True Cross encased in a crystal, heremetically sealed," and, to the delight of the entire town of Quebec, the complete bodies of Sts. Flavian and Felicité arrived in 1666.[74] Indians, the Jesuits believed, loved religious images with a naïve, even primitive ardor. One neophyte had "quite a special devotion for the images of the saints," which he would frequently fondle and kiss. "When he came to the Crucifix, he kissed it three times. 'Here,' he said, 'is the

---

[72] *The Jesuit Relations*, ed. Reuben G. Thwaites (Cleveland, 1899), 61:151, 55:191.

[73] Margaret J. Leahey, "Iconic Discourse: The Language of Images in Seventeenth-Century New France," in *The Language Encounter in the Americas, 1492–1800: A Collection of Essays*, ed. Edward G. Gray and Norman Fiering (New York: Berghahn Books, 2000), 104.

[74] Julia Boss, "Writing a Relic: The Uses of Hagiography in New France," in *Colonial Saints: Discovering the Holy in the Americas*, ed. Allan Greer and Jodi Bilinkoff (New York: Routledge, 2003), 211–33 (quotation on 214). There is even evidence of the same corpse fetish for relics in New France; Boss notes that before the murdered remains of the Jesuits Brébeuf and Lalemant were sent from Huronia to Quebec City, "the servants of the French missionaries had rendered the corpses further, boiling away remaining flesh and dividing the dried bones into separate silk bags," which they subsequently distributed (225).

likeness of him whom I love above all.'" An eager crowd of Indian congregants mobbed a priest who was "carrying the little statue of the divine infant" in its cradle, wrapped in "a fine linen cloth," in order to "get a nearer view of the holy Child." Their love of sacred images persisted even in the face of pressure from rival English and Dutch missionaries to abandon such "papist" idols: "I will say nothing of the estimation in which This new Church holds all tokens of our holy religion. Crosses and medals are their most precious jewels; they treasure them so dearly that they carry them round their Necks, even into the conventicles of New Holland, where the heretics have never succeeded in snatching away a single bead from their Rosaries."[75]

In colonial Anglo-America, the first idols marked for destruction were also of Indian origin. Burial sites were especially vulnerable, as the most visible material token of indigenous spirituality. During the Anglo-Powhatan war of 1609–14, the Virginians "Tooke down the Corpes of their deade kings from of their Toambes," and in Plymouth Colony in the 1630s the settlers "defaced the monument of the ded at Pasonayessit (by taking away the herse Cloath which was two great Beares skinnes sowed together at full length, and propped up over the grave of Chuatawbacks mother)."[76] But much of the Indians' material religious world was invisible to English eyes—sacred rocks, trees, or other natural features of the landscape, or everyday implements such as bowls and pipes. These objects went up in flames along with Indian bodies in the wars I discussed in earlier chapters but were rarely singled out for special desecration.

English objects were another matter. Under the wide-ranging mandate authorized by Puritan views of icons, even so modest a remnant of Romish culture as the red cross of St. George embroidered in the royal ensign—this "badge of the Whore of Babelon," in Captain John Endicott's fighting words—demanded action.[77] In 1634, the zealous residents of Salem, Massachusetts, ripped out the cross in one of the first recorded acts of iconoclasm in the English colonies. The magistrates, including Governor John Winthrop, were not amused and acted swiftly to censure the unrepentant Endicott for fear that the act "would be taken as an act of rebellion, or of like high nature, in

[75] *Jesuit Relations*, 2:31–32, 61:115, 211.

[76] Mark Nicholls, "George Percy's 'Trewe Relacyon': A Primary Source for the Jamestown Settlement," *The Virginia Magazine of History and Biography* 113 (2005): 212–275 (quotation on 245); Thomas Morton, *New English Canaan Or, New Canaan. Containing an Abstract of New England* (Amsterdam, 1637), 106.

[77] Papers on the state and government of New England, 1675, ff. 396, 397, 414, 522, in Egerton Mss. 2395: 1627–1699, British Library, London.

defacing the king's colors; though the truth were," Winthrop was compelled to acknowledge, "it was done upon this opinion, that the red cross was given to the king of England by the pope, as an ensign of victory, and so a superstitious thing, and a relique of antichrist." In full sympathy with the thought behind the act ("we were fully persuaded that the cross in the ensign was idolatrous"), the General Court nonetheless acted to safeguard the Puritan commonwealth's political autonomy by ordering the ensign repaired.[78] When archaic relics of popish superstitions cropped up far from the prying eyes of the colony's Parliamentary masters, the magistrates exercised no such restraint: the infamous maypole erected by Thomas Morton on his Plymouth plantation in 1623 was "cut down," by none other than the iconoclast John Endicott, and Morton's house burned by order of the General Court. (The "smoak" that arose from the ashes "appeared to be the very Sacrifice of Kain," Morton would later write, another example of the sacrificial mode of speaking in English colonial texts.) On a much less grand but probably more effective scale, Puritan ministers doctored the "horn books" sent over to help teach the Indians to read and write by "blott[ing] out all the crosses in them, for feare least the people of the land should become Idolaters."[79] Nature itself sometimes lent a hand, as when John Winthrop Jr. discovered in 1640 that among the many valuable books in his extraordinary library, only a copy of "the common prayer" (which was bound with his "Greek testament") was "eaten with mice, every leaf of it." The godly book was untouched.[80]

Crosses and maypoles, especially those that could be easily removed, were one thing; brick-and-mortar churches quite another. For much of the first half century of their existence, the English colonies were spared the need to confront in any tangible way the presence of competing versions of Christianity in the form of chapels, meetinghouses, or churches. (The southern colonies present something of an exception to this generalization, which I'll explore shortly.) But the Restoration of the Stuart monarchy in 1660, and

[78] Winthrop's Journal, "History of New England," 1630–1649, 2 vols., ed. James Kendall Hosmer (New York, 1908), 1:137, 151, 182. For a good discussion of this episode in the context of Puritan views on symbols, see Francis Bremer, "Endecott and the Red Cross: Puritan Iconoclasm in the New World," Journal of American Studies 24 (April 1990): 5–22.
[79] William Bradford tells the story of Thomas Morton and his "idle or idol maypole"; Of Plymouth Plantation, 1620–1647, ed. Samuel Eliot Morrison (New York, 1952), 206. See also Morton, New English Canaan, 164, 153; Winthrop's Journal, 1:53. Thomas Morton's account of this episode narrates the attack on the maypole as an anti-Anglican plot, of a piece with the Puritans' detestation of other Anglican relics like "the sacred booke of common prayer." New English Canaan, 138.
[80] Winthrop's Journal, 2:18.

especially the political and religious compromises of the Parliamentary settlement known as the Glorious Revolution in 1688, permanently altered the
ecclesiastical landscape of English North America. When the king's agent Edward Randolph arrived in Boston in 1686 with his Anglican clergyman in
tow, Massachusetts's Puritans were alarmed. "For the first time in New England's history," writes Kenneth Silverman, "a minister had worn a surplice
and had publicly read the liturgy from the Book of Common Prayer." More
outrages were to follow. On Good Friday, the Puritans were forced to allow
the Anglicans to use their meetinghouse for their own services, an uneasy
arrangement that continued until King's Church opened three years later.[81]
The era of Puritan hegemony was over.

In the eyes of "hot" Protestants such as the Mathers, the elegant brick
buildings that churchmen in Boston began to erect in the aftermath of the
Restoration were nothing less than an abomination in the eyes of God and a
direct challenge to their holy commonwealth. And they seized the first opportunity to make their hatred known. The ouster of the Catholic James II
and the bringing in of the Protestant monarchs William and Mary of Orange
in 1688 ignited a mini-wave of iconoclastic fervor in the New England colonies. The call to arms came in a sermon by the inimitable Cotton Mather
against the use of the Book of Common Prayer, which Edward Randolph
believed "persuaded the people that we were idolatrous and therefore not fit
to be entrusted longer with the Government."[82] When the residents of Boston
rose up against their royal governor, they attacked the Anglican church as
well: "The Church itself had great difficulty to withstand their fury, receiving
the marks of their indignation and scorn, by having their Windows broke to
pieces, and the Doors and Walls daubed and defiled with dung, and other
filth, in the rudest and basest manner imaginable."[83] The Quaker Thomas

[81] Kenneth Silverman, *The Life and Times of Cotton Mather* (New York: Harper and Row,
1984), 62–63. The Book of Common Prayer had, in fact, been used (briefly) in Plymouth
Colony in the late 1620s by two malcontents who set up a rival meeting before being told by
Governor Endicott "*That* New-England *was no place for such as they*" and shipped home.
Morton, *New Englands Memoriall*, 76–77.

[82] Edward Randolph to the Bishop of London, "From the common gaol in Algiers," October 25, 1689; Records of the Colonial Office, National Archives, Kew Gardens, London
(hereafter CO), 5/855, no. 42.

[83] C. D., *New England's Faction Discovered, or, A Brief and True Account of their Persecution of the Church of England* (London, 1690), 259. While Mather dismissed the charge, arguing that "All the mischief done is the breaking of a few Quarels of glass by idle Boys," the
historian Charles Andrews concludes that the charge of desecration "had a basis in fact." Andrews, ed., *Narratives of the Insurrections, 1675–1690* (New York: C. Scribner's Sons, 1915), 259.

Maule corroborated this account, accusing his fellow Bostonians of "break-ing the Church Windows, tearing the service Book, making Crosses of Mans Dung on the Doors, and filling the Key-holes with the same."[84] The Anglican minister Samuel Myles begged the king to intervene. "We are in a deplorable condition. . . . Young Mr. Mather informs the people that the reason for our calamities is permitting the little chapel for the Church of England among us. It is insufferable for it to stand, according to him, though it is battered and shattered most lamentably already."[85] Puritan New England was not the only region to experience iconoclastic outbreaks during the Glorious Revolution. The royalist faction in New York fought fire with fire in their battle against the Protestant party headed by Jacob Leisler, who reported the "miraculous deliverance from a fire which had been kindled in three different places in the turret of the church and in the fort. Six thousand pounds of powder were under the same roof with the fire, and the offender is suspected to be a papist who has been there before. Thus the city and people were saved from this hellish design." In New York, anyone who questioned the rebels' seizure of power was "Popishly affected."[86] And in Maryland, where the Jesuits' "good brick Chapell" had graced (or scarred, depending on one's perspective) the landscape of St. Mary's City since the 1660s, complaints about this popish abomination featured prominently in the revolt of the Protestant Association against the Catholic governor. Although the rebels did not attack the build-ing directly, they succeeded in destroying it as a functional meeting place for Maryland's Catholics by persuading the sheriff to lock the "Popish Chapel" and bar all worshipers.[87] In all three colonies, the campaign to oust the exist-ing administration was waged in explicitly religious terms, as a continuation

[84] Thomas Maule, *New-England Persecutors Mauled with their own Weapons: Giving some account of the bloody laws made at Boston against the Kings subjects that dissented from their way of worship* (New York, 1697), 51.

[85] Abstract of a Letter from Samuel Myles, Minister at Boston, December 12, 1690, CO 5/855, no. 127.

[86] Jacob Leisler to William and Mary, New York, August 20, 1689, CO 5/1081, no. 50; Owen Stanwood, *The Empire Reformed: English America in the Age of the Glorious Revolution* (Philadelphia: University of Pennsylvania Press, 2011), 131 ("Popishly affected"). David William Voorhees explores the anti-Catholic roots of Leisler's rebellion in "The 'fervent Zeale' of Jacob Leisler," *William and Mary Quarterly*, 3rd ser., 51 (July 1994): 447–72.

[87] *Archives of Maryland, Proceedings and Acts of the General Assembly September 5, 1704—April 1, 1706, Vol. 26*, ed. William Hand Browne (Baltimore, 1906), 45–46. On the "Glo-rious Revolution" in Maryland, see Lois Green Carr and David William Jordan, *Maryland's Revolution of Government, 1689–1692* (Ithaca, N.Y.: Cornell University Press, 1974); and John D. Krugler, *English and Catholic: The Lords Baltimore in the Seventeenth Century* (Baltimore: Johns Hopkins University Press, 2004), chapter 9.

of the long holy war against Catholic superstition and tyranny that militant Protestants had been engaged in for a century and a half.

And in fact, war with Catholic France swiftly followed the installation of William and Mary on the English throne, and fears of Anglican inroads in the Puritan commonwealth became quickly swallowed up in more widespread fears of a revitalized papacy operating just beyond the borders of New England. The military conflict between New England and New France in the 1690s had its iconoclastic moments as well. In Maine, the English militia under Thomas Westbrook targeted the mission church in Penobscot for destruction as part of a coordinated effort to remove the Jesuit missions that had operated for decades along the northern border of New England.[88] When the combined forces of British, colonial, and Indian troops attacked the Canadian settlement at Port Royal in 1690, the Catholic chapel was burned along with the houses of royal officials and the town's warehouse. The official report of the expedition made it clear that the destruction of the church was not simply collateral damage but a premeditated act of violence modeled on the iconoclasm campaigns of 1641–43: "We cut down the Cross, rifled the Church, Pull'd down the high Altar, breaking their Images."[89] Governor Bradstreet boasted to his fellow rebel governor, Jacob Leisler of New York, that the fort was demolished and "their Crosses & Images broken down." The booty that the commander of the expedition, Sir William Phipps, brought with him upon his return to Boston included, according to Owen Stanwood, a "variety of Catholic baubles, including surplices, communion wafers, and priestly vestments."[90]

It is not difficult to imagine the reactions of ordinary Bostonians to these "baubles" of popery circulating in their midst. Fears of a vast Catholic conspiracy to subvert Protestantism in Europe and the New World had been part and parcel of imperial expansion from the very beginning and had received fresh support from the supposed "Popish Plot" of 1678 in England and the revocation of the Edict of Nantes by the French king in 1685. In the closing decades of the seventeenth century, settlers from Maryland to New Hampshire rose up against royal governors and a resurgent Anglican establishment while following closely the alarming news from the continent, which

---

[88] Laura Chmielewski, *The Spice of Popery: Converging Christianities on an Early American Frontier* (Notre Dame, Ind.: University of Notre Dame Press, 2012), 202.

[89] *A Journal of the Proceedings in the Late Expedition to Port-Royal* (Boston, 1690), 6. The firing of the church at Port Royal is also described in the letter of Lieutenant Governor Usher to the Council of Trade and Plantations, June 28, 1708, CO 5/864, no. 225, Enclosure 3.

[90] Stanwood, *Empire Reformed*, 158–59.

included a brutal Catholic offensive against the Huguenot minority in France as well as more immediate threats at home from the crypto-Catholic Stuarts. Puritans fully anticipated that their New World utopia would not be spared the ravages of renewed Catholic persecution. "The cup is going round the world," Cotton Mather warned in a 1686 sermon. "'Tis come into America."[91] Anti-Catholic polemics poured from the presses of New England with titles such as *A Sermon Wherein is shewed that the Church of God is sometimes a Subject of Great Persecution* (Increase Mather, 1681) and *The Church of Rome Evidently Proved Heretic* (Peter Berault, 1685). Crosses once again despoiled the landscape of New England, though in visionary rather than material form: Thomas Cobbet interpreted the "perfect crosse through the moone" that appeared in the skies over Ipswich, Massachusetts, on Christmas Day in 1682 as a portent of "a vigorous prosecution and spreading of popery, east, west, north & south."[92]

More ominous than these apparitions of popish power was the presence on the borders of British North America of a new kind of Catholic enemy: the Indian tribes allied with New France and New Spain who assaulted frontier communities with special vigor in the half century of nearly continuous imperial warfare that stretched from 1690 to 1763 with a brief hiatus in the 1720s and 1730s. There is tantalizing evidence of traces of iconoclastic violence in the literature on Indian war. The one clear instance is the burning of Indian Bibles during King Philip's War, which Edward Gray suggests was motivated by the same spirit that led Spanish conquistadores to destroy Aztec pictographic texts during the conquest of Mexico, as tokens of idolatry. Book burning was a common form of early modern iconoclasm, as books were often the only ecclesiastical objects at hand in the New World. From the English corsairs who threw Spanish devotional books "on the floor and trampled on them and tore them up" in 1576 to the public burning of Quaker tracts by Puritan authorities in New England in the 1650s, religious texts were defaced and destroyed across the Americas.[93] By the conclusion of the war in 1676, almost no copies of John Eliot's famed Indian Library survived, as Eliot himself admitted to a Dutch missionary. "In the late In-

---

[91] Quoted in ibid., 38.

[92] Thomas Cobbet to Increase Mather, February 19, 1683, *Collections of the Massachusetts Historical Society*, 4th ser., 8 (1868): 296–97.

[93] Beasley, "Wars of Religion in the Circum-Caribbean," 157. David Cressy has noted the surge in flamboyant spectacles of book-burning in England in the 1620s and 1630s; "Symbolic Violence and Secular Iconoclasm in Early Modern England," in *Protestant Identities*, 19–43.

dian war all the Bibles and Testaments were carried away and, burnt or de-
stroyed," he lamented.[94] Indian warriors targeted English Bibles as well as
Algonquian ones, in one notable incident by ripping open the corpse of an
Englishman who had tried to shield himself with his Bible "and put[ting] his
Bible in his belly" in a macabre echo of Reformation-era violence.[95] The ma-
jority were in all likelihood, however, destroyed by furious Puritan militia-
men, for whom book burning had been something of a specialty during the
English Civil War.

Indian Bibles aside, the material damage inflicted in the Indian wars was
largely limited to English houses, gardens, and livestock. But if we're willing
to look beyond the concrete to the symbolical, we can detect intriguing evidence of a more penetrating iconoclastic impulse at work in the representation of maimed bodies (Indian and English) that punctuated Puritan
narratives of war and captivity. In an important sense, Indians constituted
"living images" whose destruction was sanctioned by the same reasoning that
demanded the stripping of altars and smashing of idols in Reformation Europe.[96] The notion of "living images" powerfully captures the fluidity of Puritan understandings of idolatry and its remedy, iconoclasm, as encompassing,
in different places and different times, physical things, symbolic gestures, and
flesh-and-blood human beings.

When we turn our attention to Puritans in the New World, and in particular to the context of Indian warfare and captivity, the same logic we saw at
work in the dismantling of "Jasper Crosse"—"flesh for flesh"—is present, but
with a perverse twist. The dismembered Cheapside Cross, torn limb from
limb, has its referential counterpart in the dismembered corpses that Indian

[94] Edward G. Gray, *New World Babel: Languages and Nations in Early America* (Princeton, N.J.: Princeton University Press, 1999), 80.

[95] N. S. [Nathaniel Saltonstall], *A New and Further Narrative of the State of New-England*,
6–7. Natalie Zemon Davis describes similar incidents occurring in the French wars of religion in "The Rites of Violence: Religious Riot in Sixteenth-Century France," *Past & Present* 59
(May 1973): 51–91.

[96] My analysis builds on the insight of Ann Kibbey that violence against Antinomians,
Indians, and witches constituted a form of iconoclasm in Puritan thought; *Interpretation of
Material Shapes* (1986). Kibbey's focus is on the formal rhetorical homologies linking various
figura in the sermons of John Cotton, whereas my analysis moves beyond formal semiotics to
encompass the broader cultural milieu in which Old World acts of iconoclasm and New
World Indian warfare took place. I have also been influenced by Margaret Aston's argument
about iconoclasm as "a process of scapegoating": "images were surrogates or dummies on
which were vented some of the anger felt towards inaccessible human agents. Rage against
the living might be discharged on images of the dead. To some extent all iconoclasm was a
process of scapegoating." Aston, *England's Iconoclasts*, 73–74.

and English raiding parties alike left in their wake as gruesome reminders of their power to desecrate as well as defeat their enemies. Torture, beheadings, and hacking and hewing of living bodies were forms of violence that colonial Americans were all too familiar with from their harrowing encounters with hostile native Americans, in which the posthumous desecration of corpses and the scalping of the near-dead figured prominently as the most distinctive hallmarks of Indian warfare. During King Philip's War in 1675, two English prisoners were "taken by the Indians, who ripped them up from the bottom of the belly to the throat, and cleft them down the back throughout, and afterwards hung them up by the neck on a tree by the River side, that the English might see them as they passed by." Over time, English soldiers proved to be as if not more adept than Indians at using corpse dismemberment as a tactic of terror. When the English troops finally cornered Metacom, the leader of the bloodiest Indian war in American history, they dragged his body—"a doleful, great, naked, dirty beast"—out of the swamp, and had him beheaded and quartered. The body parts were distributed among the soldiers as war trophies. Benjamin Church insisted that this was done in deliberate retaliation of the Indians' own customs of bodily desecration: "for as much as he had caused many an English man's body to lie unburied and rot above ground, not one of his bones should be buried." The widespread practice of providing bounties for Indian scalps produced a steady stream of Indian body parts (hair, sometimes with the head still attached) into New England's towns and villages for public display.[97]

The notion that native Americans functioned on some level as icons to be smashed as well as military and political foes to be vanquished is, I would argue, one particularly good example of what Robert St. George has called the "poetics of implication." "In seventeenth-century New England," St. George writes, "if not among today's practicing historians, word and thing were inextricably linked, referentially interdependent, constantly implicated in each other's ways of making meaning."[98] The rhetorical parallels between

[97] Increase Mather, *A Relation of the Troubles which have Hapned in New-England by Reason of the Indians there* (Boston, 1677), 46. For a discussion of Anglo-Indian treatment of corpses in war, see Andrew Lipman, "'A meanes to knit them together': The Exchange of Body Parts in the Pequot War," *William and Mary Quarterly*, 3rd ser., 65 (January 2008): 3–28; Erik Seeman, "'Not One of his Bones Should be Buried': Corpses and Cross-Cultural Religious Violence" (paper presented at "Religion and Violence in Early America," April 2008, New Haven, Conn.).

[98] Robert Blair St. George, *Conversing by Signs: Poetics of Implication in Colonial New England Culture* (Chapel Hill: University of North Carolina Press, 1998), 3.

descriptions of broken images in European iconoclastic literature and broken
bodies in New World depictions of Indian war resembles the referential strategy St. George identifies as "symbolic diffusion," or the entanglement of the
material world with the charisma that resides in sacred icons. The discursive
parallels between descriptions of broken images in European iconoclastic literature and broken bodies in New World depictions of Indian war, however,
masks a fundamental reorientation of symbolic logic: whereas European
iconoclasts attacked objects *as if* they were people, New England Puritans
attacked people *as if* they were objects. Moreover, hanging an icon on a gibbet to mimic the persecution of actual people or dismantling the statue of the
body of Christ was not an act meant to grant equivalence but rather constituted a rejoinder, a counterargument to Catholic idolatry: *You treat images as
if they were Gods; we will destroy images to show you that they are NOT Gods.*
It is more difficult to decipher the logic behind New World bodily desecrations that seem, in both form and purpose, to imitate some of the character-
istic traits of Old World iconoclasm. Yet what had been an act of parody in
one context had become an act of near-genocide in another context, with
devastating consequences for Indians and English alike.

For the English knew they had violated important cultural boundaries in
their treatment of native American bodies, including the boundary between
legitimate cultural politics and outright savagery. As good Puritans, they
looked to the scenes of Indian war for providential meaning. What message
did God intend by allowing his American children to be slaughtered like
sheep? "Now since the INDIANS have been made by our God, The *Rod of His
Anger*, 'tis proper for us to *Enquire*, whether we have not in some Instances,
too far Imitated the *evil manners* of the *Indians*?"[99] The suggestion that English Puritans have become "*Indianized*" in the New World brings the iconoclastic metaphor full circle. For as good Calvinists, the Puritans knew that the
lure of idolatry was a snare that could entrap the most faithful Christians.
The jeremiads that poured from New England presses in the late seventeenth
century, accusing the settlers of everything from Sabbath-breaking to wearing periwigs, drove home the central message that the very success of the
Puritan "errand into the wilderness" had bred new idols: wealth, security,
fashionable dress, pride, complacency, sanctimony. In their comfortable
homes and prosperous villages, New Englanders worshiped false gods of
their own, no better than the savages who so tormented them. Their most

[99] Cotton Mather, *Observable Things*, 211.

bitter enemy, the Quakers whom they persecuted ruthlessly until ordered to desist by Charles II in 1661, told them so. "Such a Generation of *Blood-thirsty* men, Ravening after the Prey, after *Blood*, the *Blood* of the *Innocent*, who have been Ancient in your Cruelty, and have long been filling up your measure, who as soon as you had escaped the hands of those you feared in England, & gotten large Farmes about you, you sat down at Rest, and then soon began to exercise Dominion, & became Lords over the Faith of others," accused George Bishop. "Ye bloody *Butchers*! Ye Monsters of *Men*!"[100] Much as they wished to close their ears, New Englanders knew in their hearts that they had become idolaters too.

So far, I have been telling a largely Puritan story about the mutability of images and the referential imperative that drove New Englanders to declare iconoclastic war against enemies both visible and invisible, including idols of their own making. What happens to the story if we widen our investigation beyond the well-tilled soil of New England and turn to the middle and southern colonies, where Anglicans ruled with a lighter touch and religious conflict was largely confined to verbal skirmishes? Here, too, we find churches attacked, anti-Catholic rhetoric deployed to justify sectarian violence, and Indians who functioned as stand-ins for more traditional enemies of church and state. Here, too, the crucible of imperial warfare served as the catalytic force converting Old World animosities into New World atrocities. The long and bloody border war between South Carolina and New Spain's northernmost territory, in particular, provided numerous occasions for the expression of colonial iconoclasm in ways that parallel in intriguing ways the history of religious violence in New England.

The colonial South had one thing New England did not: actual Catholics who were neither foreign nor Indian. To be sure, there were English Catholics who ventured into Massachusetts during the seventeenth century, but they didn't stay long, for obvious reasons. And they certainly did not leave behind any tangible reminders of their religion, such as chapels or crucifixes, for Puritans to attack. Anglicans, not Catholics, were—as we have seen—the primary targets of Puritan iconoclasm in New England. Further south, however, there was a sizable English Catholic population in Maryland, founded by Lord Baltimore in part as a refuge for his persecuted coreligionists, and a smaller but stable community of Catholics in South Carolina. Catholic

---

[100] George Bishop, *New England Judged, Not by Man's, but the Spirit of the Lord: And the Summe sealed up of New-England's Persecutions* (London, 1661), 119, 171.

worship was discrete and rarely visible, however, in deference to the dominant English prejudice against the "Whore of Rome" that held sway even in Maryland. Baltimore cautioned his first governor in 1633 to "cause all Acts of Romane Catholique Religion to be done as privately as may be, and . . . [to] instruct all the Romane Catholiques to be silent upon all occasions of discourse concerning matters of Religion."[101] The spotty historical record of religious encounters in the seventeenth century suggests these instructions were largely followed, though the rosy picture of religious harmony painted by early promoters—here, extolled George Alsop in 1666, there are no "Inquisitions, Martyrdom, [or] Banishments"—is an exaggeration.[102] As we have seen, Maryland's Catholics and Protestants came to blows in 1645 during Ingle's Rebellion, in 1655 at the Battle of the Severn, and again in 1689 when the former Anabaptist preacher John Coode roused the Protestant citizens of the colony against their Catholic proprietors. The Catholic church at St. Mary's was defaced in February 1670 by Robert Pennywell, who "brook the glasse windows at the Chappell" and was ordered to receive twenty lashes "in publique view" for his crime.[103]

More typical, however, were symbolic acts of violence such as that attributed in a Jesuit relation to an apostate who, to express his newfound Protestant zeal, "was accustomed to smoke [his old prayer beads] in his pipe with tobacco, after they had been ground to powder, often boasting that he had eaten up his 'Ave Marias.'"[104] (A more playful form of iconoclasm, perhaps.) Some of our best evidence for this kind of episodic, extralegal sparring over sacred spoils comes from the field reports of the Society for the Propagation of the Gospel in Foreign Parts (SPG), the missionary arm of the Church of England that sent licensed preachers into every colony to combat dissenters and convert the infidels. As was the case in New England, Anglicans were convenient targets for much confessional anger that might otherwise have been directed at Catholics in the British colonies. Anglicans and

[101] *Narratives of Early Maryland, 1633–1684*, ed. Clayton Colman Hall (New York, 1925), 16.

[102] Ibid., 349.

[103] *Archives of Maryland, Proceedings of the Provincial Court, 1666–1670*, Vol. 57, ed. J. Hall Pleasants (Baltimore, 1940), 610–611.

[104] *Relatio Itineris in Marylandiam, Declaratio Coloniae Domini Baronis de Baltimore, Exerpta ex Diversis Litteris Missionariorum . . . Narrative of a Voyage to Maryland [with] Extracts from Different Letters of Missionaries* (Baltimore, 1874), 79. The apostate met a fitting end when he died after being bitten by "a huge fish"; the missionary noted with satisfaction that "he, who a little while before boasted that he had eaten up his 'Ave Maria beads,' should see his own flesh devoured, even while he was yet living."

Presbyterians engaged in an unseemly tug-of-war over the pew cushions in a meetinghouse in Jamaica, Long Island, in 1707. "We had a shameful disturbance, Hauling and Tugging of Seats; shoving one the other off, carrying them out and returning again for more," wrote a disgusted John Bartow to the Society.[105] His neighbor Thomas Haliday complained that, in his parish, the dissenters "most contemptuously carried away all the Goods of the Church and at the same time told me to be gone that I was a knave and a villain."[106] When Jacob Rice arrived at his Newfoundland outpost in the fall of 1711, he was appalled to discover the sorry state of the church. "You may remember Srs that I told you how ye Church in this Country had been defaced by the Enemy," he wrote. Things now were "in a much worse condition than I then represented it, for the Seats, Pulpits, and Communion Table were all destroyed, the wainscot tore down, the floors ript up, the windows broke to pieces, and ye Church made a common field for Cows and Sheep."[107] Inclement weather and human poverty certainly took their toll on the chapels that were springing up everywhere south of Connecticut in the first half of the eighteenth century, even as the "sacramental renaissance" that historians of Anglicanism have identified was in full swing in the colonies.[108] The pace of reform was slow and uneven—while one rector could boast of the "handsome Pulpit, Reading Desk, Clerks Pew, Communion Table & a Chan. Rail'd in, all made of cedar" that his church sported in 1714, another South Carolinian complained the following year that "We are sadly incommoded in our Church, having no Common Prayer Books or Bible, but such as are miserably Spoiled and warn out."[109] As late as the 1760s, southern churches were still in a state of disarray, with some "well ornamented" with "rich Pulpit Cloths and Coverings for the Altar" (St. Philips) and a "Steeple 196 feet high" (St. Michaels), while others had fallen "to decay" (St. James) or were "consum'ed by fire (St. Andrews)."[110]

---

[105] SPG Records, vol. 3, no. 184, December 1, 1707, p. 529.

[106] SPG Records, vol. 9, no. 13, April 20, 1714, p. 116.

[107] SPG Records, vol. 6, no. 153, November 6, 1711.

[108] On the "Anglican Renaissance" in the South, see Thomas J. Little, "The Origins of Southern Evangelicalism: Revivalism in South Carolina, 1700–1740," *Church History* 75 (December 2006): 768–808.

[109] Robert Maule to Secretary, January 23, 1714, SPG Records, vol. 10, no. 9, p. 79; Gideon Johnston to Secretary, December 19, 1715, SPG Records, vol. 11, p. 105.

[110] Charles Woodmason, "A Report on Religion in the South" (1765), in *The Carolina Backcountry on the Eve of the Revolution: The Journal and Other Writings of Charles Woodmason, Anglican Itinerant*, ed. Richard J. Hooker (Chapel Hill: University of North Carolina Press, 1953), 70–81.

Turning the sanctuary into a sty was one way to demonstrate disgust for a rival religion, and the missionaries had no doubts that this was deliberate vandalism, not mere neglect. John Urmston, a bilious sort in the best of times, blasted the rude Scots-Irish Presbyterians who made his tenure a living hell in the swamps of North Carolina. "This is a Nest of the most Notorious Profligates upon the Earth," he swore. "All the Hoggs and Cattle flee thither [the church] for Shade in Summer and Warmth in Winter, the first dig Holes and Bury themselves these with the rest make it a loathsome place with their Dung and Nastiness which is the Peoples regard to Churches."[111] The most pointed attack by dissenters ("a pack of vile, leveling common wealth Presbyterians in whom the Republican Spirit of 41 yet dwells") on an Anglican chapel was recorded by Charles Woodmason: "At the Congaree Chapel, they enter'd and partly tore down the Pulpit," and on the following Sunday "after the Communion was ended, they got into the Church and left their Excrements on the Communion Table."[112] The theme of filth is a recurring one in these reports of chapel desecrations: recall the crosses formed of dung left on the walls of King's Church in Boston in 1689 and the fouling of the priests' vestments in the 1714 attack on Trinity Church in Boston with which I began this chapter. Excrement is, of course, a universal motif in the anthropological literature on pollution, but it may have had even greater symbolic weight in a colonial environment where the line between civilization and nature was blurred to begin with and where animals and humans lived in alarmingly close proximity to one another.[113]

Filthy churches, damaged pews and altars, with the stink of swine and other, human, pests befouling the sanctuary: such was a common sight in the American backcountry, if these Anglican gentlemen-preachers are to be believed. (These backcountry Presbyterians were only imitating the example of English corsairs who defiled Catholic sacred spaces throughout their depredations in Spanish America, in one notable case throwing "filth and offal of cattle they slaughtered in the churches" into graves they had broken open.)[114]

---

[111] SPG Records, vol. 7, no. 2, July 7, 1711.

[112] *Journal of Charles Woodmason*, 46n40.

[113] The classic work on the theme of pollution in anthropology is Mary Douglas, *Purity and Danger: An Analysis of the Concepts of Pollution and Taboo* (New York: Praeger, 1966). Natalie Zemon Davis identifies pollution as the unifying motif in Catholic and Protestant accounts of desecration during France's wars of religion in "The Rites of Violence."

[114] Beasley, "Wars of Religion in the Circum-Caribbean," 162. Beasley notes the porous line between vandalism and iconoclasm, arguing (as I have) for an expansive definition of sacrilege that encompasses both degradation and desecration.

Yet for all the damage inflicted, either deliberately or by the ravages of nature, on southern chapels, no sight was more evocative of iconoclastic rage than the charred remains of mission churches that successive waves of imperial and Indian warfare had left behind as monuments of intolerance in the early eighteenth century. In the early years of Queen Anne's War, a combined force of 50 colonials and nearly 1,500 Apalachicola Indians under the command of the choleric James Moore attacked mission towns "with fire and sword" over a two-hundred-mile-wide swath of territory in the no-man's-land between English Carolina and Spanish Florida.[115] Moore's report of the expedition highlighted the destruction of churches and homes, and the enslavement of thousands of Indian men, women, and children. In the town of Ayaville, his troops assaulted the fort by "breaking the church door, which made a part of the fort, with axes." After two hours of fierce fighting, "we thought fit to attempt the burning of the church, which we did."[116] It was a scenario that would be repeated in town after town. By August 1704, Jon Sensbach reports, "more than one thousand Apalachee and Timucuan Catholics had been killed or enslaved," a figure vastly exceeding any casualty figures for religious conflicts elsewhere in the colonies. Sensbach makes a strong case that the Apalachee raids should be considered a species of holy war, in which the destruction of churches and religious objects such as Bibles and crucifixes figured prominently.[117] And indeed, the surviving documents make clear the lengths to which the Spanish went to safeguard their religious art from the marauders. The Spanish governor in Ayaville noted with satisfaction that although the church had been destroyed, the "images [were] with some risk saved." On July 13, 1704, orders were issued that all the "statues, ornaments, and other objects of the Divine Cult" should be "withdrawn to this presidio." The deputy of the Apalachee mission, Manuel Solana, wrote to Governor

---

[115] David Ramsay, *History of South Carolina from its First Settlement in 1670 to the Year 1808* (New York, 1858; orig. pub. 1798), 87. See also Steven J. Oatis, *A Colonial Complex: South Carolina's Frontiers in the Era of the Yamasee War, 1680–1730* (Lincoln: University of Nebraska Press, 2004), 50–51.

[116] *An Account of what the Army Did, under the Command of Col. [James] Moore, in His Expedition last Winter, Against the Spaniards and Spanish Indians. In a Letter, from the said Col. Moore to the Governor of Carolina, The Boston News, May 1, 1704* (New York, 1836), 574–75.

[117] Jon Sensbach, "Religion and the Early South in an Age of Atlantic Empire," *Journal of Southern History* 73 (August 2007): 631–43; see also his "Seventeen Stations of the Cross: Reassessing the Destruction of the Florida Missions" (paper presented at "Religion and Violence in Early America," April 2008, New Haven, Conn.).

Zúñiga that he had told his men to "transport the images and ornaments so that they may not be burnt here."[118]

Even more compelling than the evidence that religious objects were being targeted by the "pagan" forces of Moore and his Indian allies, the testimony gathered by the Spanish crown in the aftermath of the war highlights the close connection between the burning of bodies and the destruction of icons. At Ayubale, after the resident priest promised martyrdom to all who would "fight against the pagans that came to disturb the law of God and destroy the Christian provinces," Moore's men set fire to the mud-walled church, killing the warriors within and taking prisoner those who fled the flames. The friar was found the next day, "beneath a fragment of mud wall and burned wattle. Half of his body was burned to ashes, and the beads of his rosary which he had at his neck, as well as the body, were charred. A crucifix which he always carried with him was almost entirely melted, and the body of the Father had been so burned that when they went to carry it off it fell to powder."[119] In the ultimate fusion of martyrological and iconoclastic tropes, several accounts describe the ritual torture and death of captives while tied to a cross. Two men were "sacrificed" by being tied to "a cross of fagots rich in rosin." A soldier was "found burned at the foot of a cross." After first cutting out Balthazar Francisco's tongue, eyes, and ears, his tormenters "slashed him all over, stuck burning splinters in the wounds, and set fire to him while he was tied at the foot of a cross." In a final gruesome scene, horrified Spanish troops found "as many as seventeen burned, most of them upon the Crosses of Calvary and of the *Via Crucis* which was around the plaza of Patale."[120] The spectacle of Catholics (Indian and Spanish) burning on a cross at the hands of Protestants makes a mockery of the notion that iconoclasts destroyed things only, not people.

When the formidable Yamasee nation struck the Carolina settlement in 1715, in one of the bloodiest wars on record in the colonial era, they applied the lessons they had learned from the English attacks on Spanish missions, burning and desecrating churches in remote parishes from Santee to Stono. In the parish church of William Bull, Creek warriors were intent on "break-

---

[118] Governor Zúñiga to the King, September 30, 1702, in *Here They Once Stood: The Tragic End of the Apalachee Missions*, ed. Mark F. Boyd, Hale G. Smith, and John W. Griffin (Gainesville: University of Florida Press, 1951), 37; Council of War, July 13, 1704, in ibid., 57; Deputy of Apalachee, Manuel Solana, to Governor Zúñiga, July 8, 1704, in ibid., 55.

[119] *Extracts from the auto of an inquiry into the deaths of the Fathers in Apalachee*, June 1705, in *Here They Once Stood*, 74, 78.

[120] Declaration of Bartholomé Ruiz de Cuenca before the Governor of New Vera Cruz, 1705, in *Here They Once Stood*, 71; *Extracts from an inquiry*, 76, 81, 82.

ing a few of ye windows & tearing off ye lining from one of ye best pews,"
while the spectacle of churches in flames reminded one chronicler of a "Spanish *auto de fe*."[121] (Fittingly, this "barbarous & cruel war broke out in Passion
Week.")[122] The comparison is apt. Like so many of the southeastern tribes, the
Yamasee were at one time mission Indians, converted en masse by the Spanish with whom they forged a close political alliance. That alliance had been
sorely tested in the decades leading up to 1715, as Spanish depredations drove
many converts away from the church.[123] Yet even in their newly settled villages, far from the Spanish missionaries who had proved such untrustworthy
friends, the Yamasee included within their ranks a large proportion of Catholic converts who regarded their English neighbors as heretics. David Ramsay recorded the speech of an Indian warrior who told him that "the English
were all wicked heretics, and would go to hell, and that the Yamasee would
also follow them if they suffered them to live in their country." And indeed
the Spanish welcomed the defeated Yamasee back into their fort at St. Augustine after the English drove them out of Carolina with "ringing of bells, bonfires, and other demonstrations of joy."[124] Clearly the epic wars of religion
between Catholic and Protestant that had reduced so many towns in Europe
to ashes were not yet over. The New World had its own "passion play" to
stage, this time with an Indian cast.[125]

How far did English colonials in the South reflect on their own culpabil-
ity in these holy wars? Did they, like their Puritan counterparts to the North,
engage in the kind of intense soul-searching that such horrific violence elic-
ited in the jeremiads of Cotton Mather and company? We might expect the
"swamp warriors" of the southern backcountry, long depicted in colonial historiography as utterly devoid of religious or even humanitarian sensibility,
inured to brutishness by their intimate experience with African slavery and

[121] Dr. Hewit, *An Historical Account of the Rise and Progress of the Colonies of South Caro-
lina and Georgia* (London, 1779), in *Historical Collections of South Carolina: Embracing Many
Rare and Valuable Pamphlets and Other Documents*, ed. B. R. Carroll, 2 vols. (New York,
1836), 1:197. The desecration of Bull's church is described in William L. Ramsey, *The Yamasee
War: A Study of Culture, Economy, and Conflict in the Colonial South* (Lincoln: University of
Nebraska Press, 2008), 122.

[122] Nathaniel Osborne to Secretary, May 28, 1715, SPG Records, vol. 10, no. 99.

[123] Oatis, *Colonial Complex*, 95.

[124] Ramsay, *History of South Carolina*, 89–90 ("wicked heretics"); Joseph Boone and Richard Beresford, Agents for the Commons House of Assembly in South Carolina, to the Council of Trade and Plantations, December 5, 1716, Enclosure i, Committee of the Assembly of
Carolina, CO 5/1265, nos. 44, 44i–v ("ringing of bells").

[125] Oatis, *Colonial Complex*, 1.

Indian warfare, to pass lightly over the religious symbolism of burnt chapels and tortured Indian bodies. And to some extent our skepticism would be warranted. While the occasional SPG missionary like the sensitive Francis Le Jau agonized over the providential meaning of the Yamasee War, "this Terrible Judgment,"[126] most were more concerned with rebuilding their parsonages and dunning the Society for back pay. Here, as in Boston, there were Quakers to call them to account: the former governor of the colony, John Archdale, prophesied in 1707 that the English in Carolina would "suffer a sort of Transmigration of the Wolfish and Brutish Nature to enter our Spirits, to make our selves a Prey to our Enemies" for their many sins against the Indians and the Spanish, including the "Plunder of their Churches or Places of Worship."[127] Indians called Christians who displayed such brutishness "mad Wolves, and no more men."[128] The relative indifference of most white Protestants to the carnage inflicted by them or in their name on New World Catholics, Spanish and native, makes it difficult to assign clear iconoclastic motives to their actions. Yet when we consider the Old World background of these settlers, many of whom knew firsthand the brutality of religious persecution (Huguenot refugees, Scots-Irish Presbyterians, Anabaptist and Quaker exiles), and the inflamed religious rhetoric surrounding the early eighteenth-century wars between Protestant England and its Catholic rivals, a good circumstantial case can be made that the Carolina settlers knew, and approved, the iconoclastic message their actions conveyed.

Jump ahead sixty years in time. The American colonies stand on the brink of war with their imperial masters, and John Adams is taking a break from his labors as a delegate to the First Continental Congress to explore the religious back alleys of Philadelphia. Wandering into St. Mary's Catholic Church during Sunday mass, he writes to his wife, Abigail, in October 1774 of the "awfull" scene he is witness to:

> This Afternoon's Entertainment was to me most awfull and affecting. The poor Wretches, fingering their Beads, chanting Latin, not a Word

---

[126] Le Jau to Secretary, May 10, 1715, SPG Records, vol. 10, no. 114.

[127] John Archdale, *A New Description of that Fertile and Pleasant Province of Carolina: with a Brief Account of its Discovery, Settling, and the Government Thereof to this Time* (London, 1707), 306.

[128] John Lawson, *A New Voyage to Carolina: Containing the Exact Description and Natural History of that Country: Together with the Present State thereof. And a Journal of a Thousand Miles, Travel'd thro' several Nations of Indians* (London, 1709), 200–201.

of which they understood. . . . Their holy Water—their Crossing themselves perpetually—their Bowing to the Name of Jesus, wherever they hear it—their Bowings and Kneelings, and Genuflections before the Altar. The Dress of their Priest was rich with Lace—his Pulpit was Velvet and Gold. The Altar Piece was very rich—little Images and Crucifixes about—Wax Candles lighted up. . . . Here is every Thing which can lay hold of the Eye, Ear, and Imagination. Every Thing which can charm and bewitch the simple and Ignorant. I wonder how Luther ever broke the spell.[129]

Performing a kind of verbal iconoclasm for his wife, Adams offers a striking summary of the ceremonies and objects that so enraged Protestants in Europe and the New World during the Reformation era. His description tells us just how far the ecclesiastical landscape of the British colonies had come from its visually and materially impoverished beginnings, and just how far the colonists themselves had come in their ability to observe such "baubles of popery" without resorting to violence to eradicate them. Nicknamed the "Last Puritan" by his contemporaries, Adams is a good barometer of changing attitudes toward religious things in late colonial North America. Historians speak confidently of the inexorable march toward legal and de facto toleration of religious difference in the Anglo-American world over the course of the eighteenth century, and the primitive urge to smash altars is usually considered one of the casualties of a modern legal regime—along with the desire to hang sharp-tongued old women as witches.

The story of John Adams's tour of St. Mary's is certainly compatible with this progressive narrative, but it also tells us more. It tells us that the material face of Catholicism still had the power to shock, to overwhelm sober Protestant sensibilities with its vibrant color, texture, and richness; that the old argument between images and words as reliable conduits of divine truths was alive and well in late colonial Philadelphia; that enlightened Protestants were still fearful of the bewitching effects of Latin on the "ignorant and simple"; that the cause of Reformation—to "break the spell" of the medieval church— was not yet completely won. Adams took up his pen rather than "fire and sword" to do battle with these cunning idols, and this, too, tells us that an important shift in tactics had occurred between the 1714 vandalism of Trinity

---

[129] Joseph Casino, "Anti-Popery in Colonial Pennsylvania," *Pennsylvania Magazine of History and Biography* 105 (1981): 279–309 (quotation on 283n8).

Church and the 1774 rhetorical demolition of a Catholic mass. The old ways
did not die easily, however, and in fact the Revolutionary War saw an upsurge
in iconoclastic violence that rivaled the destruction of Anglican symbols
during the Glorious Revolution a century before. A mob in Hebron, Connecticut, tarred and feathered several Anglicans in September 1774 and, in
the words of the horrified local minister, proceeded to destroy St. Peter's
"Windows and rent my Cloaths, even my Gown, etc. Crying out down with
the Church, the Rags of Popery etc." As the empire came to an end, Americans "engaged in an orgy of iconoclastic violence in the streets," writes Brendan McConville, "attacking churches, ripping down tavern signs, beheading
royal statues, searching for any imperial symbol to destroy."[130] John Adams was
not the "last Puritan" after all, it seems.

What, in the end, are we to make of this long journey from the burning of
Algonquian Bibles in 1675 to the burning of Anglican chapels in the Revolutionary War? However we slice the evidence, it is still incontrovertible that
iconoclastic violence in the British American colonies never reached the levels of destruction seen in England, France, Germany, and the Netherlands
during the religious wars of the sixteenth and seventeenth centuries. There
were simply too few religious objects to attack, even if the will to destroy was
there. Merely counting the number of churches vandalized and Bibles burned
and crucifixes ground to powder would yield a rather paltry sum. Their very
rarity, however, made these isolated acts of violence exceptionally stark. Considered against the total number of Anglican and Catholic churches in existence in the British colonies, the dozen or so attacks that we can document
amount to a substantial ratio. This is especially true in the American South,
where perhaps 30 percent of Anglican parishes reported some form of vandalism or acts of desecration in the fifty years between the first arrival of
Anglican missionaries in the 1680s and the outbreak of the Great Awakening
in the 1740s. That's a pretty impressive figure.

The one area in which we have seen violence on a mass scale, the killing
of Indians and the burning of mission towns, had unmistakable iconoclastic
echoes, I have argued, and not only in Puritan New England. Here, religious
and racial enmities were so interwoven as to be analytically inseparable. The
most we can say—and it is saying a lot—is that the rage expressed in the desecration of Indian bodies and mission chapels derived in part from a deep

[130] Brendan McConville, *The King's Three Faces: The Rise and Fall of Royal America, 1688–
1776* (Chapel Hill: University of North Carolina Press, 2006), 296, 306.

well of spiritual anxieties and animosities whose source lay in the bloody European past as much as in the unsettled American present. If we add these thousands of native deaths to our list of the victims of settler iconoclasm, the historical record would suggest that English America experienced its own "deluge" of iconoclasm during the formative years of empire-building despite the material barrenness of its ecclesiastical landscape and the institutional weakness of its orthodox establishments.

Conclusion

> We start as we turn from this picture of Christian love to the
> dark enthusiast close beside him. . . . At his back is slung an axe,
> wherewith he goes to hew down the carved altars and
> idolatrous images in the Popish churches; and over his head he
> rears a banner which, as the wind unfolds it, displays the motto
> given by Whitefield, CHRISTO DUCE, in letters red as blood.
> —Nathaniel Hawthorne, "Sir William Pepperell," 1832

By the time Nathaniel Hawthorne was creating the image of the persecuting
Puritan that has become so deeply imprinted on the national imaginary, English colonists had become American citizens. In Hawthorne's literary world,
the "dark enthusiast"—the fanatical Puritan who hacked apart idols and raised
the bloody banner against his fellow Christian—was a figure against whose
barbarisms modern Christians (and modern Americans) could chart their
progress. Historians of early American religion have wrestled with the legacy
of Hawthorne's crabbed view of Puritanism for a long time now, and I count
myself among the legion of scholars who have strived to dislodge his distor-
tions in our classrooms and books. There was nothing inherently violent or
persecutory about the Puritan self or its American mission. Puritans, like
Protestants everywhere in early modern Europe, believed in the coercive
power of the state to enforce religious conformity, but they balanced this commitment to legal orthodoxy with compassion for the frailties of men and
women and an unswerving belief in the power of God's grace to overcome the
sins of humanity (at least, the remnant of humanity God had chosen to save).[1]

---

[1] See David D. Hall, *Worlds of Wonder, Days of Judgment: Popular Religious Experience in
Early New England* (Cambridge, Mass.: Harvard University Press, 1989); Charles Lloyd Cohen,
God's Caress: The Psychology of Puritan Religious Experience (New York: Oxford University
Press, 1986); and Charles Hambrick-Stowe, *The Practice of Piety: Puritan Devotional Disciplines in Seventeenth-Century New England* (Chapel Hill: University of North Carolina Press,
1982), for three particularly influential examples of the revisionist effort to reclaim the Puritans' compassion and expansive view of God's grace from the damning legacy of Hawthorne.

Where, then, is this compassion, this generosity, in the narrative of religious violence I have just laid out? For every dissenter who was whipped or imprisoned by the colonial religious establishment for heresy or blasphemy, there were hundreds who worshiped quietly in the privacy of their own home or the homes of neighbors. For every dissenting chapel that was desecrated or vandalized in the colonial backcountry, several more continued to serve their congregations unmolested by the authorities or by angry crowds. For every sermon stoking the fire of religious prejudice and exhorting congregants to expel nonconformists in their midst, there were many more sermons on the comforts of sanctification and the pleasures of a godly life lived in the bosom of family and friends. Even in the one arena where the rhetoric of religious violence seems to loom largest—the Indian wars of the seventeenth century—disease and dislocation killed far more native peoples than did holy warriors.

So, yes, there was peaceful coexistence among rival religious communities, joy in the hearts and households of the faithful, and a surprising amount of toleration for religious difference in seventeenth-century English America (along with a fair share of indifference to all matters religious, even in New England). And the tragedy of the decimation of native peoples is not just a story about religious violence—it is as much a story of greed, prejudice, and politics (imperial and native). But these are not the stories I am telling here. My aim has been to put under the microscope several virulent strains of Protestant rhetoric in order to test the proposition that certain discursive paradigms that took shape in the cauldron of Reformation Europe were reinvigorated in the unsettled conditions of English America. The four paradigms I've chosen—blood sacrifice, holy war, malediction, and iconoclasm—are, to be sure, neither inclusive nor sharply distinguishable from other related phenomena of sacred violence, but they seem to me to be the ones that resonate most clearly in the colonial literature. Anchoring each paradigm is a complex history reaching back to the waning years of the medieval era when Christendom was experiencing the first tremors of dissent and discontent that would become an earthquake in the sixteenth century, forever shattering the unity and hegemony of the Church.

Each paradigm rested on a rethinking of the relationship of the past to the present. The Reformation was an effort to rewrite history, or perhaps more accurately, to rethink history itself as a sacred discipline. Successive generations of reformers sought to recapture the primitive spirit of Christianity from a millennium and a half of churchly corruption. At the same time they reached back to the Old Testament as typology—a literal prefiguring of events in the New Testament and (in the most extreme view) in the current age. These twin projects of historical rediscovery meant that reformers were unusually sensitive to the echoes of the past in their own religious practices and beliefs even as they dismantled centuries of ecclesiastical tradition within Latin Christendom. What some scholars have identified as a melancholy strain in Protestant devotionalism—a tendency to dwell on past sins and despair of redemption—may be the psychological effect of the reformers' conflicted relationship to the past.[2] The past, as William Faulkner once said, "is never dead. It's not even past." This was especially true for Protestants in the century following the break with Rome. Every effort to obliterate the past—the smashing of altars, the repudiation of key Catholic tenets such as transubstantiation and purgatory, the burning of heretical bodies and texts—left material and ideological traces that were reconfigured into a new reality.

This book has traced these entanglements with the past in four arenas of discourse. The concept of blood sacrifice was, on the surface, definitively repudiated by reformers as an anachronistic holdover from the pagan past, one sign (among many) that the medieval church had never fulfilled Christ's promise to end the sacrificial economy altogether by his own death. The argument that the eucharistic host consisted of Christ's very body and blood was, to Calvin and Zwingli especially, a pagan barbarism masquerading as Christian doctrine. Transubstantiation was nothing more than a crude form of blood sacrifice, in Protestant polemics. Yet—in certain places, under certain conditions—Protestants too easily fell into a sacrificial mode when defending themselves and their new practices from enemies both internal and external. In the New World, Indians and sectarians became victims of blood sacrifice in the Old Testament sense—offered up on the altar of God to appease his wrath.

They were also the victims of a new, Protestant version of holy war— another supposedly discredited holdover from the medieval past. Crusades were something that Catholic kings and Muslim potentates did; Protestant rulers were supposed to command the hearts and bodies of their subjects

---

[2] Andrew Hiscock, *Reading Memory in Early Modern Literature* (New York: Cambridge University Press, 2011); John Owen King III, *The Iron of Melancholy: Structures of Spiritual Conversion in America from the Puritan Conscience to Victorian Neurosis* (Middletown, Conn.: Wesleyan University Press, 1983); Paul Seaver, *Wallington's World: A Puritan Artisan in Seventeenth-Century London* (Stanford, Calif.: Stanford University Press, 1985).

through the inculcation of internal virtues and restraints. The Weberian notion of an internal revolution in the minds and souls of Protestant believers is one of the most entrenched shibboleths of Reformation historiography. A corollary to the argument that Protestants controlled the self through the patient exercise of word-centered disciplines is that Protestant rulers controlled their kingdoms not through coercion but by good government.[3] And when they were forced to go to war to defend their kingdoms, they followed the rules of "just war" (defensive and limited) not "holy war" (offensive and total). Yet—again, in certain places and under certain conditions—Protestant polities unleashed the dogs of war (quite literally in the case of English Virginia, where "blood-hounds" and "mastives" were used to "teare" the local Powhatan) with a bloodlust that evoked parallels with the Old Testament wars of extermination.[4] The brutality of Indian war in the New World is not a new story. But certain dimensions of the story may look different when we consider that English settlers came from a society that had been immersed in a debate over the nature and extent of "holy war" since the early seventeenth century and that was veering into civil war—a war which to many partisans looked a lot like a new holy war—at the very moment the first colonies were taking shape in North America. Though it seldom occupied center stage in the literature of war, invocations of the religious imperative to "exterminate" New World Amalekites and other heathen nations worked to keep alive the holy war tradition well past its supposed demise in the era of Grotius.

Another kind of old enemy—the unreformed tongue—was the target of extensive campaigns in England and its colonial outposts to crack down on blasphemy in the wake of the linguistic revolution that was at the heart of the Reformation. Blasphemy was both an ancient and a new crime: a reminder of the "babel of tongues" that had provoked the wrath of Jehovah in the Old Testament and an unintended (and unwanted) byproduct of the renewed logocentrism of Protestant modes of worship. In the evil words of blasphemers reformers heard echoes of pagan languages and mockery of their own godly speech. While it is an exaggeration to say that the Reformation "invented" blasphemy, it certainly made it a priority for Protestant polities in

---

[3] The classic study remains Michael Walzer, *The Revolution of the Saints: A Study in the Origins of Radical Politics* (Cambridge, Mass.: Harvard University Press 1965).

[4] Edward Waterhouse, *A Declaration of the State of the Colony and Affaires in Virginia. With a relation of the barbarous massacre in the time of peace and league, treacherously executed by the native infidels upon the English* (London, 1622), 24.

devising new legal and moral codes to support the devotional revolution of the sixteenth and seventeenth centuries. This juridical effort to tame the unruly tongue went furthest in the English colonies where, uniquely within the Anglophone world, blasphemy was a capital crime in the first offense. A preoccupation with disorderly speech in all its forms, from cursing to slander to outright blasphemy, can be detected in colonial court records up and down the coast of English America. The New World was, to colonial authorities, the new "Babel."

No term was more redolent of Old Testament longings and fears than "idolatry." Of all the terms I've explored in this book, idolatry is the most expansive and heuristically supple. For Protestants, idolatry was the ur-sin, the transgression that encompassed all the other sins the Reformation had sought to eradicate. Atavistic notions of blood sacrifice, of transubstantiated hosts, of crusades, of malediction—all were symptoms, or manifestations, of idolatry: of venerating a human invention (the sacrificial scapegoat, bloodlust, verbal power) over God. Idolatry turned good into evil with a single act, a single thought even. The Protestant war on idols was unremitting, sweeping everything from material objects to physical gestures to words and ideas themselves into its vortex. History itself could be an idol, if it was invoked to legitimate spiritual corruptions in the name of tradition. Some radical pietists, like the Quakers, even flirted with the notion that the Bible was an idol. This relentless push to search out and destroy the "immense crowds of gods" that men had created since the beginning of time (Calvin) came face-to-face in English America with new gods, some of the settlers' own making. With the long history of rhetorically pitting "living" against "dead" images in western Christendom in mind, I've argued that iconoclasm in English America was directed not only against the material remnants of popish superstition (chapels, rosary beads, crucifixes) but against Indian bodies, whose devilish form represented "living" icons analogous to the statues of saints whom iconoclasts in England and Europe had tortured to death.

This image of a world of inert material objects come to life in English America neatly captures the central dynamic of the story I've told here. The persistence of the material in the face of Protestant resistance to the presence of the sacred in the created world is the theme that unites colonial wars against Indians and sectarians, blasphemy prosecutions, and iconoclastic campaigns. We should perhaps not be surprised that the material dimension of religion was more palpably present in the New World than it was in the

Old, since what was "new" about this world was precisely its physical environment: every voyager to the Americas in the age of exploration commented on the startling abundance of new species of flora and fauna on display—enormous flying fish, exotic fruits bursting with seed, four-legged beasts taller than men who ranged over acres of wilderness.[5] Such material abundance repelled as much as it attracted the first colonists, and over time they found ways to name and tame the land and its inhabitants. But the persistent habit of labeling one's enemies "ravening wolves" that we have traced through the discourse of Indian war, sectarianism, malediction, and iconophobia reveals just how raw was the New World and its creatures. So an old aversion to the material confronted a new material reality that was bigger, stranger, more fecund—more potent, in a word.

Here, by way of conclusion, let me trace some of the important ways the material world of English America shifted from the end of the seventeenth to the end of the eighteenth century, thus transforming the shape and meaning of sacred violence in a colonial context. This is by no means a comprehensive overview of the religious landscape of colonial America in its second century of development, a century that saw the emergence of a more fully sacralized environment south of New England, a transatlantic religious revival, the first organized movements against religious bigotry and the enslavement of Africans, waves of new Presbyterian and pietist migrants from the British Isles and the continent, political battles over the future of Anglicanism, and—finally—a revolution.[6] The push-pull between orthodoxy and heterodoxy became ever more strained as new church establishments solidified even as older ones weakened under sectarian pressure and the centrifugal power of religious revival. While generalizations are thus difficult to make regarding the overall trajectory of religious change from the 1690s through the 1770s, we can identify a few trends that are important for understanding the persistence or weakening of sacred violence in the colonies.

One trend is the growing power of enlightened discourses about the evils of religious enthusiasm—including bloodlust. Killing, and dying, in the name of God came to seem uncivilized, acts unworthy of a confident, commercial

---

[5] Susan Scott Parrish, *American Curiosity: Cultures of Natural History in the Colonial British Atlantic World* (Chapel Hill: University of North Carolina Press, 2006).

[6] Jon Butler's *Awash in a Sea of Faith: Christianizing the American People* (Cambridge, Mass.: Harvard University Press, 1990) provides a good overview of some of these trends.

people.[7] We can see this clearly in the waning purchase of holy war ideology. Calling military violence an act of God was largely a rhetorical exercise in the eighteenth century. As tensions rose in the first half of the century among the great imperial nations of England, France, and Spain, the educated public in Britain wrote to the press to express their disdain for the very idea of a modern "religious war." The crusades of old were "wars of superstition, in which knaves planned and fools acted."[8] Today's politicians were no better, complained London's weekly newspapers: religion is "made the Stalking Horse of the World," serving as "a Varnish to all these State intrigues." (Only the Turks were true holy warriors in this day and age, one wrote in begrudging admiration—"they are the Truest Fighters for Religion that I know of in the World.")[9] The chorus of disdain for treating modern imperial wars as crusades resounded throughout the British Isles after 1700.

In North America, imperial wars were always fought with Indian allies or proxies in the eighteenth century, so we might expect the rhetoric of holy war to linger longer in American texts than in English ones given the centrality of Indian diabolism in colonial apologetics. In addition, a series of backcountry rebellions accompanied the imperial wars of the mid-eighteenth century, turning whole communities into armed camps. From Maine to the Carolinas, the frontier was the scene of brutal fighting that recalled the scorched-earth tactics of the seventeenth-century Anglo-Indian wars. Colonists turned again to religion to explain what was happening, but this time they were more likely to condemn than to condone appeals to God to sanction the killing. Benjamin Franklin excoriated the massacre of peaceable Moravian Indians at Lancaster by backcountry settlers in 1764 as religion-baiting, camouflaging racial bigotry under the banner of piety. "The only Crime of these poor Wretches seems to have been that they had a reddish brown skin, and black Hair. . . . But it seems these People think they have a better Justification; nothing less than the *Word of God*. With the Scriptures in their Hands and

---

[7] J. G. A. Pocock, "Enthusiasm: The Antiself of the Enlightenment," *Huntington Library Quarterly* 60 (1998): 7–28; Michael MacDonald, *Mystical Bedlam: Madness, Anxiety, and Healing in Seventeenth-Century England* (New York: Cambridge University Press, 1981). Ethan Shagan describes this as a shift from "moderation" (by which he means not the modern notion of evenhandedness but the early modern ideal of restraining excess through aggressive governance, even to the point of violence) to "politeness"; *The Rule of Moderation: Violence, Religion, and the Politics of Restraint in Early Modern England* (New York: Cambridge University Press, 2011), 330. As Shagan points out, politeness was often still coercive, though the mechanisms of control were different in the eighteenth than in the seventeenth century.

[8] *Whitehall Evening Post*, June 12, 1781.

[9] *Review of the Affairs of France* (London), November 28, 1704.

Mouths, they can set at naught that express Command, *Thou shalt do no Murder*, and justify their Wickedness by the Command given to *Joshua* to destroy the Heathen. Horrid perversion of Scripture and of Religion!" Council member William Logan charged that the "Irish rebels" who had killed the Conestoga Indians "pleaded Scriptures a Duty for Extirpating the Heathen from ye Face of the Earth." Ignorant Scots-Irish Presbyterians had thought they were "vanquish[ing] the *Catananites* . . . in the Name of the Hosts of Israel" when, in reality, they were killing innocent men, women, and children.[10] This, in fact, was precisely what earlier apologists for Indian war did—use scripture to argue for "extirpating" the heathen. But now, a century later, some colonists found such rhetoric appalling.

Yet if we put aside for the moment the palpable distaste of Franklin and his merchant friends for religious enthusiasm, and more particularly for Scots-Irish enthusiasm, and look more closely at the actual arguments made by backcountry rebels, we can see how holy war ideology still resonated at least for some at the margins of empire. The Seven Years War in Pennsylvania offered frontier residents an almost irresistible trifecta of religious enemies: the Catholics of New France, native Americans both heathen and baptized, and wealthy Quakers whose pacifism and political condescension infuriated their Presbyterian neighbors struggling to eke out an existence in the backcountry. Propagandists of war stoked fears of religious violence by imagining the fate of the colony's Protestants should the French prevail: "must we have Persecution? Images Crucifixes &ca. &ca. Alas! Alas!" A fictional French officer crowed, "Fire and Gibbet will be their Portion if they do not fall down and worship the Images we shall set up. . . . We shall sing *Te Deum* and celebrate Mass in those Places which have long been defil'd by the Breath of *Heretics*."[11] (Under such provocations, some "ill-minded persons" in Lancaster burned St. Mary's Catholic Chapel to the ground in 1760.)[12] Even worse, because more subtle, were the Quakers whose famous (or infamous) amity with the colony's Indian peoples had long been a source of frustration for the backcountry. "The *Papist Indians* think they do God Service by killing us as Heretics," thundered the Reverend William Smith. "The *Quakers* think they

[10] Benjamin Franklin, *A Narrative of the Late Massacres in Lancaster County of a Number of Indians* (Philadelphia, 1764), 13; Peter Silver, *Our Savage Neighbors: How Indian War Transformed Early America* (New York: W. W. Norton, 2008), 183 ("Irish rebels"); [Isaac Hunt], *A Looking-Glass, &c., Numb. II* (bound with his *A Looking-Glass for Presbyterians*, 1765), 15.

[11] George Stevenson to Richard Peters, September 17, 1756, quoted in Silver, *Our Savage Neighbors*, 41; "De Roche," *A Letter from Quebeck* (Boston, 1754), 7.

[12] Silver, *Our Savage Neighbors*, 98.

do the same, by looking calmly on, while we are killed by their Hand. Such a RELIGION ought to be rejected, and, if possible, extirpated from the Face of the whole Earth."[13] We have come full circle here from the genocidal impulses of the seventeenth century: now it is religion itself (or a bastardized version of religion) that needs to be "extirpated from the Face of the whole Earth."

If enlightened men were quick to repudiate the idea of killing for God, they were not so eager to deny themselves the satisfactions of dying for God—or, at least, of assuming the role of the martyr when it suited their interests. The image of the martyr underwent a profound shift in the period between the Quaker executions of 1659–61 and the first stirrings of colonial discontent a century later. Martyrdom became more an act of narration than of sacrifice—a way to talk about one's trials than a form of physical suffering. Of course, from the Reformation on, narratives of persecution had been as important as the experience of the lash or stake in shaping the devotional style and religious subjectivity of English Protestants. This was as true in 1550 as it was in 1750. But what did change in the intervening two centuries was a steady migration of the experience of violence from the physical to the textual, from the realm of law, rough justice, and organized campaigns of repression to the realm of pamphlets, broadsides, and newspapers.

We shouldn't overstate this change. More people read about religious violence than experienced it firsthand even in the embattled years of the English Reformation, thanks in no small part to the popularity of Foxe's *Book of Martyrs* (not to mention the vernacular Bible). And there was real religious violence in the eighteenth century: dissenters continued to be imprisoned, chapels desecrated, and "heathen savages" massacred. But in the late seventeenth and eighteenth centuries, magistrates and juries on both sides of the Atlantic were increasingly unwilling to impose corporal punishments on heretics and blasphemers, and spectacles of violence (executions, public whippings, the parading of malefactors through the streets with symbols of shame branded on their bodies or pinned to their clothes) became increasingly rare. By the end of the colonial era, religious dissent had been either decriminalized or tacitly condoned by the lax enforcement of laws which, for the most part, took money rather than blood from the occasional victim. Just as men and women convicted of sexual misconduct rarely faced corporal punishment after 1700, the handful of dissenters or blasphemers who

[13] William Smith, *A Brief View of the Conduct of Pennsylvania, for the year 1755; so far as it affected the general service of the British colonies, particularly the expedition under the late General Braddock. . . . In a second letter to a friend in London* (London, 1756), 61.

appeared in colonial courts in the eighteenth century were usually let off with a small fine and an admonition. (The Baptist revival in the South in the 1760s did produce a spike in the imprisonment of dissenters, but this was a temporary lapse in the overall trend of decriminalization.) Even the Quakers quieted down after the turn of the century, preferring to worship in silence among themselves rather than provoke angry crowds by their theatrics. The disappearance of the belligerent Quaker "witness" from meetinghouses and courtrooms is a particularly visible sign of the more tempered religious climate of eighteenth-century British America.

Yet a quick read in eighteenth-century journals, pamphlets, or newspapers would leave a very different impression. For tales of religious persecution continued to be produced and to sell briskly right up to the political crisis of the late colonial period. In fact, eighteenth-century British America was (to quote Brad Gregory, speaking of a very different era) "awash in martyrological literature."[14] The colonists proved avid consumers of martyr tales—both imported and homegrown.[15] We find "martyrs" everywhere in colonial texts: Indian captives such as Mary Rowlandson who saw their ordeal as a testing of faith; Anglican missionaries who loved to recount the hardships and deprivations they endured in their pursuit of souls in America's wild backcountry; long-suffering colonial magistrates and governors who felt persecuted by the ungrateful and importunate masses they were supposed to be governing. One such story comes from the journal of the Anglican missionary Charles Woodmason as he navigated the "wild woods" of the Carolina backcountry in the 1760s. "I am exactly in the same situation with the Clergy of the primitive Church, in midst of the Heathens, Arians and Hereticks," he complained. Woodmason dwelled obsessively on the "apostolic sufferings" he experienced in his missionary work. But what, exactly, constituted Woodmason's theater of martyrdom? Fatigues, aches and pains, hunger, money problems, loneliness—and, above all, the countless indigni-

[14] Brad S. Gregory, *Salvation at Stake: Christian Martyrdom in Early Modern Europe* (Cambridge, Mass.: Harvard University Press, 1999), 4.

[15] Adrian Chastain Weimer traces what she calls "the folklore of martyrdom" in seventeenth-century New England in *Martyrs' Mirror: Persecution and Holiness in Early New England* (New York: Oxford University Press, 2011).. See also Sarah Covington, *The Trail of Martyrdom: Persecution and Resistance in Sixteenth-Century England* (Notre Dame, Ind.: University of Notre Dame Press, 2003); and Susan Juster, "What's 'Sacred' About Violence in Early America? Killing, and Dying, in the Name of God in the New World," *Common-place: The Interactive Journal of Early American Life* 6.1 (October 2005, available online at http://www.common-place.org/) for two discussions of the Protestant idea of martyrdom.

ties heaped on the civilized Londoner by the rude and vulgar Scots-Irish Presbyterians who laughed at his pretensions of gentility, hooted during his sermons, scribbled unflattering graffiti on the walls of the chapel, unleashed a pack of dogs (fifty-seven in all) in the meetinghouse during service, and made cruel puns on his name. One New Light "to shew his Wit, went quibbling and quirking on my Name. He told the Audience . . . that tho' I was a Wood Mason, He queried if I was a Good Mason—but as Wood was a perishable Matter, and serv'd for Fuel, so that I should Perish Everlastingly and serve for fuel for Hell fire." No fiery stake for the would-be martyr of Carolina, then, just a verbal roasting that injured his pride rather than his body.[16]

We are a long way here from the public burnings and tortures endured by English believers from the Reformation through the upheavals of the seventeenth century. (Though Woodmason reported with typical hyperbole that some sectarians "lately kill'd a Travelling Parson and cut Him into Atoms singing Hymns, making Processions and Prayers, and offering up this inhuman Sacrifice to the Deity, as an acceptable Oblation.")[17] There is something parodic about Woodmason's insistence on his unparalleled sufferings. More discerning eighteenth-century missionaries were aware that their sufferings, while painful, were not quite "apostolic." "It is perhaps as hard to be racked with the gout, or to burn several days in a fever on a sick bed, as you or I may be forced to do, as to be for a few minutes with Shadrach and his companions in a burning furnace, or to feel for a fleeting moment the anguish of bruised flesh and a fractured skull, with the triumphant martyr," a Methodist itinerant wrote defensively in his journal.[18] What was really being "martyred" in these missionary journals was not the individual believer but the very idea of martyrdom itself: the possibility of a heroic death, a noble sacrifice in the name of God. In eighteenth-century British America there was only room for martyr tales, not martyrs. And, as David Hall once said, "to read about the martyrs was not the same thing as becoming one."[19]

But reading about violence could in itself be a kind of experience—a way

[16] *The Carolina Backcountry on the Eve of Revolution: The Journal and Other Writings of Charles Woodmason, Anglican Itinerant*, ed. Richard J. Hooker (Chapel Hill: University of North Carolina Press, 1953), 27, 111.

[17] Ibid., 78.

[18] Elmer T. Clark, ed., *The Journal and Letters of Francis Asbury*, 2 vols. (Nashville, Tenn.: Abingdon Press, 1958), 2:715. The missionary martyr was a stock figure in French narratives of colonial conquest, as Emma Anderson demonstrates in *The Death and Afterlife of the North American Martyrs* (Cambridge, Mass.: Harvard University Press, 2013).

[19] Hall, *Worlds of Wonder*, 130.

to feel the dread, terror, and ecstasy of suffering without risking life or limb.[20] Eighteenth-century pietists excelled in this kind of vicarious experience of sacred violence, as they resurrected the "blood and wounds" theology of late medieval Christianity for a new audience. The graphic depictions of the crucified Christ that so alarmed Calvin and Luther in the 1500s made a comeback in the 1700s, this time in the guise of Moravian painted cards of Christ's bloody "side wound" and passionate hymns to the "dead eyes, bloody foam from your back, sweat-soaked hair, . . . nail-bored feet'" of Jesus the Savior.[21] This was a form of imaginative violence, a mode of worship that resembled the early modern Protestant visualization of the bleeding body of Christ in the Eucharist in place of the Catholic doctrine of the "real presence." Moravian piety was exceptionally lurid in its formative phase—no other pietist sect dwelled so obsessively on the blood of Christ—but its devotional practices represent in exaggerated form a common tendency in eighteenth-century pietism to resurrect the body and blood of Christ in the minds and hearts of believers.[22]

The dissemination of lavishly decorated Moravian cards and hymnals points to another important trend: the emergence of a rich material culture of religion in the eighteenth century. The asceticism of the seventeenth-century New England meetinghouse (spare white walls, no ornamentation,

[20] Peter Silver makes a comparable argument in *Our Savage Neighbors* about the literature of Indian-hating, which colonists produced in large quantities during the eighteenth century, especially during the French and Indian War. Though horrific in tone and graphic in content, much of this literature was written by men and women who had never encountered a real Indian or faced a real tomahawk. What Silver calls "the agreeable horror of Indian-hating" nicely captures the potent mixture of pain and pleasure such narratives produced in their readers.

[21] Craig D. Atwood, *Community of the Cross: Moravian Piety in Colonial Bethlehem* (University Park: Pennsylvania State University Press, 2004), 235. On late medieval versus Reformed views of Christ's body and wounds, see Sarah Beckwith, *Christ's Body: Identity, Culture, and Society in Late Medieval Writing* (New York: Routledge, 1996), and Sarah Covington, *Wounds, Flesh, and Metaphor in Seventeenth-Century England* (New York: Palgrave, 2009).

[22] Patrick Erben, "Book of Suffering, Suffering Book: The Mennonite *Martyrs' Mirror* and the Translation of Martyrdom in Colonial America," in Linda Gregerson and Susan Juster, eds., *Empires of God: Religious Encounters in the Early Modern Atlantic* (Philadelphia: University of Pennsylvania Press, 2011), 191–215; Atwood, *Community of the Cross*; Aaron Fogleman, *Jesus Is Female: Moravians and the Challenge of Radical Religion in Early America* (Philadelphia: University of Pennsylvania Press, 2007). On pietists more generally, see the essays collected in *Pietism in Germany and North America, 1680–1820*, ed. Jonathan Strom, Hartmut Lehmann, and James Van Horn Melton (Farnham: Ashgate, 2009); and F. Ernest Stoeffer, *The Rise of Evangelical Pietism* (Leiden: Brill, 1965).

hard wooden pews) was gradually diluted as more prosperous congregations built more embellished worship spaces in the eighteenth century. By 1712, Boston's fabled First Church had acquired a steeple, and by the 1750s New Haven's brick church on the green sported one too. The first church bells heard in the colonies swung from these steeples, sometimes with unforeseen results: the town officers of Guilford, Connecticut, ordered the town's 120-foot steeple rotated "so as to have the Bell Swing east and West; the better to prevent the rocking of the Meeting House."[23] South of New England, Anglican chapels experienced a building boom in the early 1700s that sacralized the landscape. Handsome brick churches appeared in Virginia and Carolina, complete with triple-decker pulpits, chancel screens, and communion rails; in 1707, the vestry of Christ Church in South Carolina was reported to be "Rayling in the Communion Table." St. John's had "a Chancel Railed in" by 1714, and the minister of St. Helen's Parish was pleased to note that the communion table in his church was "Decently railed in." As early as 1677 the vestry of Petsworth Parish in Virginia paid a local craftsman "for draweing the Cherubin" in their church, and a large painting of "Angels floating on clouds" adorned the Lamb's Creek Church in the 1740s.[24] What the iconoclasts had pulled down in England, colonial congregations put back up as symbols of provincial wealth and pride.

These new monuments to material religion did not go unchallenged, as we saw in Chapter 4, but alongside sporadic outbreaks of iconoclasm we see the emergence of a lively trade in religious objects that transcended confessional differences. Most of the tombstones erected in Anglican graveyards in the South were chiseled by New England artisans.[25] Even in a region as remote from the centers of Atlantic trade as frontier Maine, Catholics and Protestants "engaged in a frontier recycling program of religious material culture,"

[23] Quoted in Jon Butler, *Becoming America: The Revolution Before 1776* (Cambridge, Mass.: Harvard University Press, 2000), 194. Butler surveys the material transformation of the colonial spiritual landscape in his *Awash in a Sea of Faith*, 107–16. See also Richard Bushman, *The Refinement of America: Persons, Houses, Cities* (New York: Knopf, 1992), 173–76; and E. Brooks Holifield on the "sacramental renaissance" in Puritan piety between 1670 and 1730 in *The Covenant Sealed: The Development of Puritan Sacramental Theology in Old and New England, 1570–1720* (New Haven, Conn.: Yale University Press, 1974), 197–224.

[24] Louis P. Nelson, *The Beauty of Holiness: Anglicanism & Architecture in Colonial South Carolina* (Chapel Hill: University of North Carolina Press, 2008), 88, 155; Dell Upton, *Holy Things and Profane: Anglican Parish Churches in Colonial Virginia* (Cambridge, Mass.: MIT Press, 1986), 119.

[25] Diane Williams Combs, *Early Gravestone Art in Georgia and South Carolina* (Athens: University of Georgia Press, 1986).

writes Laura Chmielewski. Anglicans raided Catholic churches for chalices, baptism fonts, and bells and then sold their booty to other Protestants eager to decorate their spartan churches. St. John's Anglican Church in Portsmouth, New Hampshire, housed a marble baptismal font built in Senegal for a Catholic mission church in Canada that had been seized off the Maine coast by a New England privateer in the 1750s. Such "war trophies" turned up in unexpected places, including the very heart of Boston—cherubim dancing around the organ at Christ Church reportedly came from a looted Quebec convent.[26] By the middle decades of the eighteenth century, religious objects were part of a vigorous (if still clandestine in some areas) commerce in European-manufactured goods that historians call the "consumer revolution." Alongside the textiles, furniture, spices, and almanacs that colonial merchants imported for resale could be found communion silver (even in Puritan New England), brass candles, mahogany pulpits, psalters, and hymn books.[27] Many Anglican parishes in the South had their own collections of sacred books; St. James's parish in Goose Creek, South Carolina, boasted an impressive theological library of 233 titles already by the end of the seventeenth century. Few ministers anywhere in the colonies could boast a personal library the size of Thomas Treackle's of Virginia which, in 1697, contained a whopping 333 volumes (including more than one hundred books on biblical exegesis alone—almost as many, Jon Butler notes, as could be found in the library at Yale College).[28]

As churches filled with sacred paraphernalia—material emblems of theological positions—we might expect old confessional debates to resurface. The communion altar was not just a piece of wooden furniture but a statement about the Anglican view of the Eucharist as a transcendent (if not transubstantiated) ritual that needed protection. The placement of the baptismal font at the entrance or in the nave signified the difference between viewing baptism as a rite of incorporation or a rite of sanctification. And certain religious

[26] Laura Chmielewski, *The Spice of Popery: Converging Christianities on an Early American Frontier* (Notre Dame, Ind.: University of Notre Dame Press, 2012), 239, 240–41.
[27] Mark Peterson explores the "material piety" of New England Puritans through their use of objects like silver communion cups in "Puritanism and Refinement in Early New England: Reflections on Communion Silver," *William and Mary Quarterly*, 3rd ser., 58 (April 2001): 307–46. On the consumer revolution, see T. H. Breen, *The Marketplace of Revolution: How Consumer Politics Shaped American Independence* (New York: Oxford University Press, 2004).
[28] Nelson, *The Beauty of Holiness*, 164; Jon Butler, "Thomas Teackle's 333 Books: A Great Library on Virginia's Eastern Shore, 1697," *William and Mary Quarterly*, 3d ser., 49 (July 1992): 449–91.

symbols remained off-limits throughout the colonies; no Protestant steeple displayed a cross until the nineteenth century. But, for the most part, the furnishing of churches and chapels proceeded in the eighteenth century free of the kind of doctrinal wrangling and conflict that had surrounded material religion in the seventeenth. Perhaps the fact that these objects were now bought and sold in an expanded Atlantic market helped defuse the theological tensions implicit in their very form.

From smashing to stealing to selling: this is one way to narrate the fate of religious objects in early America. But here, too, we find traces of older paradigms lurking behind the commodification of religion that seemingly turned dangerous icons into benign consumer goods. "Living images" populated eighteenth-century colonial life, as did the impulse to destroy them—even if the weapon of choice was usually satire rather than a hammer or fist. A few men of God did fulfill their wish for a martyr's death, or a good scourging; tales of preachers being whipped by inflamed crowds during the revivals of the Great Awakening made the rounds in evangelical circles (helped by the appearance of a new genre, the religious magazine). In the 1740s, New England congregations were once again the scene of scripted defiance as itinerant preachers forced their way into pulpits or were driven out of doors by outraged ministers. Something of the tumult and excitement of the Quaker invasion was rekindled by this new wave of evangelical insurgents a century later, and there were even legal attempts to gag some of the more flamboyant itinerants. James Davenport was arrested for disorderly conduct in Connecticut in 1742, though he was ultimately found to be non compos mentis. (He published a retraction two years later claiming that he had been possessed by "demonic spirits.") Radical New Lights recycled the Quakers' repertoire of scripted blasphemy, as when Davenport exhorted a New London crowd to throw their books and fineries into a public bonfire.[29] But for the most part, the violence of the revivals was rhetorical rather than physical. Evangelicals and their opponents both resorted to inflamed language to cajole and condemn—apocalyptic metaphors (floods, earthquakes, fire) abound in the literature of revival.

For all the parallels with the Quaker invasion (and the severe response of

---

[29] The most recent overview of the Great Awakening is Thomas S. Kidd, *Great Awakening: The Roots of Evangelical Christianity in Colonial America* (New Haven, Conn.: Yale University Press, 2007). On the violence of the revivals, see Rhys Isaac, *The Transformation of Virginia, 1740 to 1790* (Chapel Hill: University of North Carolina Press, 1982); and, with reference to Moravians, Fogleman, *Jesus Is Female.*

the civil authorities), the sacred violence of the midcentury revivals were of a different order. The true violence of the evangelical movement was internal: in the hearts and souls of converts, who experienced an annihilation of the self at the moment of conversion that could be deeply traumatic.[30] The evangelical "New Birth" was a radically telescoped version of the older Protestant notion of conversion, which had stressed the need for lengthy preparation and careful testing. Converts in the transatlantic revivals were more likely to be able to pinpoint the exact time and place of their spiritual awakening and to feel the change more deeply in their bodies. The physicality of New Light conversions—the jerking, twitching, and shouting that were the outward manifestations of the Spirit—was one of the more controversial aspects of the revivals, decried by conservatives as fraudulent if not demonic symptoms of "enthusiasm."[31] On the surface it looked a lot like the "quaking" for which Quakers got their name. But whereas seventeenth-century Friends quaked in demonstration of Old Testament typological truths, eighteenth-century evangelicals shook because the spirit of God had invaded their bodies. One kind of somatic piety pointed to the collapsing of sacred and historical time, the other to the annihilation of the old self and the birth of a new one. One, in other words, was prophetic, the other psychosomatic. There is a world of difference between the two: the world of enlightened theories of human nature, of new models of self and society derived from scientific and intellectual discoveries, of new modes of individual subjectivity and the emergence of economic and political systems premised on the self-regulating subject, of new literary modes (the epistolary novel) in which to narrate these new lives.

The "enlightened self," we have learned after a generation of scholarship, was a mixture of benevolence and savagery—capable of rethinking the moral and social bonds that knit humanity together and of devising new ways of subjecting whole populations to repressive disciplinary regimes. The century spanning the demise of Puritanism and the rise of evangelicalism is a century of paradox: corporal punishment began to disappear from the judicial landscape, but the disciplining of slaves reached new heights of terror; blood feuds and shaming rituals were discredited by republican theorists, but pietistic movements restored the language of blood and sacrifice to religious

[30] Philip Greven, *The Protestant Temperament: Patterns of Child-Rearing, Religious Experience, and the Self in Early America* (New York: Knopf, 1977).
[31] On the changing model of conversion in the evangelical revivals, see Susan Juster, *Disorderly Women: Sexual Politics and Evangelicalism in Revolutionary New England* (Ithaca, N.Y.: Cornell University Press, 1994), chapter 2.

practice; the sentimental novel captured the hearts of Anglo-America's middle classes, but quasi-pornographic tales of sadistic cruelty and sexual viola-
tion moved the souls of abolitionists and other middle-class reformers.[32]

The same admixture of liberality and repression characterized the American Revolution, to many at the time (and since) the crowning achievement
of the Enlightenment. We know that sacred violence had a role to play in the
revolutionary crisis, even as historians have disagreed about just where and
how religion factored into the political calculus of rebels and loyalists. At
least some of the violence of war was directed against religious objects such
as churches and statues, as we noted in Chapter 4, and religious figures played
a prominent role in mobilizing and sustaining the passions needed to fight a
protracted war against such formidable odds. We can even find disturbing
reverberations of the sacramental mode of speaking in the propaganda of
war: the British and their Indian allies supposedly sat down to a bloody communion service in December 1775, where they "were invited to FEAST ON A
BOSTONIAN AND DRINK HIS BLOOD."[33] For their part, the rebels certainly believed their cause was just and holy, sanctioned by God himself. But we find
no calls for "loving violence," or targeting of specific religious communities,
or comparisons of the British to Amalekites or other Old Testament pagan
kingdoms. Patriot preachers did speak in prophetic tones about the revolution as a sacred event, the final fulfillment of God's promise to make America
a new Israel. And the fever of war could become bloodlust; there were atrocities committed on both sides, as there are in every war, and some of these
evoked comparisons with Old Testament battles. We should not be surprised
to discover that revolutionary zeal could look a lot like a crusade for some
people, in some circumstances. But most Americans, most of the time, recognized the difference between a just war and a holy war in the 1770s and
knew which one they were fighting.[34]

Thus it is surprising to see a debate break out on the floor of the House of

[32] Thomas Haskell, "Capitalism and the Origins of the Humanitarian Sensibility, Parts 1
and 2," *American Historical Review* 90 (April and June 1985): 339–61, 547–66; Michael Meranze, *Laboratories of Virtue: Punishment, Revolution, and Authority in Philadelphia, 1760–
1835* (Chapel Hill: University of North Carolina Press, 1996); Saidiya V. Hartman, *Scenes of
Subjection: Terror, Slavery, and Self-Making in Nineteenth-Century America* (New York: Oxford University Press, 1997); Karen Halttunen, "Humanitarianism and the Pornography of
Pain in Anglo-American Culture," *American Historical Review* 100 (April 1995): 303–34.

[33] Quoted in Silver, *Our Savage Neighbors*, 235.

[34] Melvin Endy, "Just War, Holy War, and Millennialism in Revolutionary America," *William and Mary Quarterly*, 3d ser., 42 (January 1985): 3–25.

Commons about whether this was indeed a "holy war." The year was 1781, and the war had dragged on already for six long years with no conclusion in sight. Tempers were short, much blood and treasure had been spilled, and the British public was weary of a campaign they found difficult to understand or justify. As one disaffected citizen wrote at the very beginning of the conflict, Britons were "at a loss to fix on an epithet strictly applicable to the present American warfare: it is not a war against our natural enemies, therefore not honorable; it is not a domestic war, because the scene of action is not at home; it is not a holy war, because the certain consequence amounts to the spilling of Christian blood. What shall we call it then?"[35]

In the face of mounting opposition, Charles Fox introduced a bill to withdraw British troops. The rhetoric was heated on both sides. Lord Westcote, whose son had been killed in the naval engagement between the British and French fleets earlier in the year, made an impassioned plea to continue the crusade. "So far from calling the war on our part, a wicked war, originating in injustice," he "was of the opinion, if he might be permitted the expression, that it was a holy war. The motives which gave it birth were generous and noble . . . [and] it continued to be a war, carried on for the sole purpose of natural preservation, against the deep-laid schemes of our ambitious and inveterate enemies to effect our total overthrow."[36] Other MPs were willing to grant the "epithet"—but for wholly different reasons. Yes, Thomas Townshend replied, this was a holy war just like the crusades of old: "Like the holy wars carried on in Palestine, it was conceived in injustice, prosecuted with cruelty, whetted by false zeal, and had ruined and depopulated the country which had engaged in it. It was the effect of bigotry and superstition; it was designed to aggrandize a few at the expence of thousands. Like the holy wars, it drained the country of its best blood and of its chief resources. Like the holy wars, it exhibited a herd of fools and madmen, led on to ruin and death. . . . Like the holy wars . . . it concealed the worst, the most revengeful and diabolical purposes of blood, slaughter, and public and private oppression." Noble fools like Lord Westcote "might put on the cross, and appear at the head of his mad crusaders," but he hoped "the House would come to its senses." Townshend's argument won the day: William Pitt the younger took up the cudgels, agreeing that the American war was "the most accursed, wicked, barbarous, cruel, unnatural, unjust, and diabolical war—conceived

[35] *Morning Chronicle and London Advertiser*, January 28, 1775.
[36] *Morning Post and Daily Advertiser*, June 12, 1781.

in injustice, nurtured and brought forth in folly, its footsteps marked with blood, slaughter, persecution, and devastation."[37]

None other than Ben Franklin himself had prophesied that the American war would come to be debated in these terms. Charles Fox reminded his fellow MPs that although "the application of the word Holy to the present war may have appeared new to every gentleman present, it is not new to me, and I will tell the House why it is not. I was over at Paris, just at the eve of this very war, and Dr. Franklin honored me with his intimacy. I remember one day conversing with him on the subject, and predicting the fatal consequences. He compared the principle of the war, and its probable effects, to the ancient Crusades. He foretold that our best blood and our treasure would be squandered and thrown away to no manner of purpose; that like the Holy War, while we carried ruin and destruction into America, we should impoverish and depopulate Britain." How right was the "great philosopher of 1776," said Fox![38]

In the conventional narrative of American history, Benjamin Franklin stands for an age of skepticism, moderation, and tolerance—all virtues notably absent in the different forms of sacred violence I've traced in this book. Yet there is something patently self-serving about Franklin's invocation of the evils of crusade to condemn British meddling in American affairs. And this reminds us that, in the seventeenth as in the eighteenth century, the rhetoric of religious violence was always political even while it was also theological or scriptural. To invoke God—to recall or reenact his death in the sacraments, to call down his wrath, blaspheme his name, venerate icons or destroy idols— is always an act of power. That power resided uneasily in the material world the colonists encountered, as well as in the doctrines, texts, practices, and images they brought with them to the New World. Franklin himself knew this, despite the efforts he made to convince his readers (and future generations) that he had put revealed religion behind him as a man of the Enlightenment. His first pen name, Silence Dogood, came straight from Cotton Mather, the fearsome hunter of witches and apologist for Indian war.[39] And when Congress asked Franklin to draft a "great seal" for the new United States in 1776, he featured a scene of sacred violence from the Book of Exodus, with God commanding Moses from a pillar of fire to destroy the Egyp-

---

[37] *Parliamentary History of England, from the earliest period to the Year 1803*, ed. William Cobbett (London, 1814), 22:453.

[38] *Whitehall Evening Post*, June 12, 1781.

[39] Cotton Mather, *Bonifacius, or, Essays to Do Good* (Boston, 1710). When Franklin returned to Boston in 1716, one of his first visits was to Mather.

tians. Circling this scene was the motto "Rebellion to Tyrants Is Obedience to God."

The figure of Moses leading his people to freedom would be invoked by other Americans in the eighteenth and nineteenth centuries: enslaved men and women who resurrected Franklin's motto for purposes he never intended. I want to end with one last scene of religious violence that points both backward and forward in time. Among the many disturbing vignettes Frederick Douglass penned in his *Narrative of the Life of a Slave* is the following description of a cruel overseer. "Mr. Severe was rightly named: he was a cruel man. I have seen him whip a woman, causing the blood to run half an hour at the time; and this, too, in the midst of her crying children, pleading for their mother's release. He seemed to take pleasure in manifesting his fiendish barbarity. Added to his cruelty, he was a profane swearer. It was enough to chill the blood and stiffen the hair of an ordinary man to hear him talk. Scarce a sentence escaped him but that was commenced or concluded by some horrid oath. The field was the place to witness his cruelty and profanity. His presence made it both the field of blood and of blasphemy."[40] Here is a nineteenth-century version of the "bloody frenzy" that gripped medieval devotional life and was recast in new forms during the Reformation and carried to English America to animate violence against native peoples. Here, too, is the cruel delight in shedding blood that we saw in the most extreme accounts of colonial Indian war, and the power of profane words to bring unholy desires to life. The slave driver who operated in a "field of blood and of blasphemy" tells us that sacred violence did not end with the Enlightenment, the American Revolution, or the disestablishment of religion. It migrated to new fields—the slave plantation, Indian removal, the evangelical soul. The battlefields of America's great passion play, the Civil War, were the site of a new "baptism of blood," which in the eyes of many historians created the modern nation we live in today.[41] The men and women who left home in the 1600s to settle English America would have expected no less.

---

[40] *Narrative of the Life of Frederick Douglass, An American Slave, Written by Himself,* ed. David W. Blight (New York: Bedford/St. Martin's, 1993), 45.

[41] Harry S. Stout, *Upon the Altar of the Nation: A Moral History of the Civil War* (New York: Viking, 2006). On the essentially sacred nature of American war, see Stout, "Review Essay: Religion, War, and the Meaning of America," *Religion and American Culture: A Journal of Interpretation* 19 (2009): 275–89.

INDEX

Acosta, José de, 39
Act Concerning Religion (Maryland), 102–103, 172–173
Act of Toleration (1689), 126
Adams, John, 238–240
Altars, 17–18, 36–37, 70–71, 102, 216, 233, 234, 239, 244, 255; desecration of, 156, 159, 210–212, 217–218; imagery of, 4, 28; and Reformation, 1, 14, 24–25, 208, 215, 228
Amalekites, 10, 78, 89, 121–122, 125, 245, 258
Ames, William, 30, 90
Anabaptists, 145, 146, 161–163, 180–181, 232, 238. *See also* Baptists
Anglicans, 5, 13, 99, 111, 113–114, 148–149, 163n110, 164, 175–176, 187, 192, 216–217, 223n79, 224–226, 240, 247, 254–255; and law, 163n110, 190; missionaries, 231–234, 240, 251–252; and sacraments, 25n20, 29–30, 73, 177
Anglo-Virginia (also Anglo-Powhatan) Wars, 47, 49–50, 104, 222
Anthropophagy. *See* Cannibalism
Anti-Catholicism, 73, 114–115, 176, 178, 216, 225–227, 231–232, 239, 249
Antinomians. *See* Free grace controversy
Aquinas, Thomas, 81, 197, 199
Archdale, John, 43–44, 238
Armstrong, Karen, 10–11
Aston, Margaret, 198, 202, 208, 209n42, 215n57, 228n96
Augustine, Saint, 79, 92n49
Auto-da-fé, 1, 137, 219–220, 237

Bacon, Francis, 86
Bacon's Rebellion, 64–65, 118
Bainton, Roland, 79–80
Baltimore, Lord. *See* Calvert
Baptism, 14, 19, 24, 32, 38, 59, 101, 156, 158, 217,

255; metaphors of, 39, 261; mockery of, 72, 157–158, 177, 186, 193
Baptists, 57, 148, 181, 251. *See also* Anabaptists
Barnes, Thomas, 89–90
Berkeley, William, 64–65, 76, 113–114
Best, Paul, 150–151
Bible, 7, 100, 123–124, 129, 131, 137–138, 142, 195, 246; Algonquian translation, 227–228, 240; methods of interpretation, 4, 58–59, 118–119, 131, 141–142, 144, 189–190; and Reformation, 8, 127, 140–142, 144, 146, 204, 208, 215, 250; violence against, 227–228, 233, 235, 240; and war, 54–55, 78–79, 97, 105, 125
Biddle, John, 151
Blasphemy, 4, 127–128, 138–139, 146, 155–156, 245–246, 261; and bodies, 132–136, 149, 159, 177–178, 193, 256; in colonial law, 126–127, 165–168, 170–171, 189, 250–251; as crime, 126–128, 137–139, 150–152, 170, 173–178; definitions of, 128–131, 137–138; in England, 139–140, 159–164, 190; in English Civil War, 146–164; in medieval Europe, 127n4, 128–139; and sexual disorder, 178–180, 184–185; and war, 110–111
Blood, 10–11, 15, 25, 26, 34, 131, 133, 144, 159, 197, 200, 243, 261; bloodlust, 12–13, 68–69, 79–80, 92–93, 188, 245, 247–248; as form of sacrifice, 4, 6, 19–20, 23–24, 28–29, 31–32, 60, 62, 100, 244, 246; and New World, 32–33, 36–37, 44, 52, 59, 60–61, 70–71, 74–75, 219; in medieval theology, 23, 25, 52, 74–75, 82, 197, 199, 200, 251, 253; metaphors of, 27–30, 33, 49, 51, 60, 63, 67, 136, 257–258, 260; and war, 40, 47. 49–50, 61–62, 65, 78, 82, 83, 89, 92–93, 97, 120–121
Body of Liberties, Massachusetts, 167–168
Book of Martyrs, 8, 117, 143, 144, 160. *See also* John Foxe